SEEDS
OF
FIRE

石在，火種是不會絕的。

"As long as there shall be stones,
the seeds of fire will not die."

Lu Xun, December 1935
(from the original manuscript)

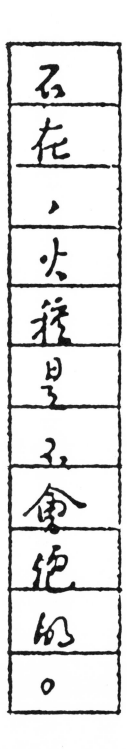

SEEDS
OF
FIRE

*CHINESE VOICES
OF CONSCIENCE*

**Edited by
Geremie Barmé
and
John Minford**

Foreword by
Orville Schell

THE NOONDAY PRESS
Farrar, Straus and Giroux
NEW YORK

Library of Congress Cataloging-in-Publication Data
Seeds of fire.
   Bibliography: p.
   1. Chinese literature—20th century—Translations
into English.   2. English literature—Translations from
Chinese.   I. Barmé, Geremie.   II. Minford, John.
PL2658.E1S44   1988   895.1'8508'08   88-19861

Substantial portions of this book were first published by
   Far Eastern Economic Review Ltd., Hong Kong, 1986

To Lu Xun,
on the fiftieth anniversary of his death,
October 19, 1936.

... the voices of China's conscience and hope, repeatedly gagged and always rising again in endless relay, verify the words of Lu Xun, China's most illustrious rebel: "As long as there shall be stones, the seeds of fire will not die."

—*Simon Leys*, The Burning Forest

Contents

I: WALLS   *1*

Walls that conceal and restrict, protect or suffocate; paths that circle, enter and disappear within them.

II: PROLEDIC: The Chinese Gulag   *63*

Labour camps, prison trains, cadre schools, places of exile.

VII: MISTS   233

A brief introduction to the New Poetry.

VIII: YELLOW EARTH   251

*The controversy surrounding the young director Chen
Kaige's internationally acclaimed film.*

IX: FIRE BEHIND BARS   271

Four of the leading personalities in the Democracy Movement.

X: THE SHADOW'S FAREWELL

The last word is Lu Xun's.

MORE STONES, MORE SEEDS

Introduction

XI: DISSENT

A Chinese scientist speaks out.

XII: BOURGELIB

Political movements with Chinese characteristics.

XIII: PRESSURE POINTS

Voices from the Chinese Velvet Prison.

XIV: BÖD

Tibet under Proledic.

Foreword

by Orville Schell

ON THE NIGHT OF June 3–4, 1989, as soldiers and tanks from the People's Liberation Army stormed into central Peking, killing and wounding thousands of unarmed civilians, China passed over that critical line of demarcation which separates reform from revolution. Evincing a repressive fury more savage than even that of Chiang Kai-shek's Nationalists in their efforts to exterminate the then fledgling Chinese Communist Party, Deng Xiaoping and his cohorts opened fire on China's newest generation of intellectuals and subsequently embarked on a vengeful crackdown of manhunts, summary trials, jailings, and executions. Like an overflexed piece of steel finally giving way under too much strain, China's aging gerontocracy snapped back with brutal force, having been pushed to the very edge of its understanding by the complex mix of forces set loose by its own program of reform. What had previously been only a fissure, albeit a growing one, between the Chinese people and their government suddenly yawned as an unbridgeable chasm. Instead of pondering what tactics the Party and the government might still be able to take to rescue reform in their country, Chinese intellectuals now spoke of the urgent need to get rid of the Party and the government altogether. In the parlance of dynastic China, *tianming*—the mandate of heaven—had passed the Communists by. During imperial times, it was from this mandate that an emperor or ruler was said to derive the moral force necessary to rule effectively. The Chinese believed that the absence of *tianming* would be made manifest by a righteous popular uprising against the dynasty, a uniquely Chinese version of the right of rebellion. Whereas before June the Party leadership had been viewed as a more or less legitimate government (albeit corrupt, autocratic, and inept), after the Tiananmen Square massacre more and more Chinese came to look upon Deng and his lieutenants as an obsolete and bankrupt political faction which had lost both the ability and the right to rule.

Like a single catalytic agent which when added to a compound completely changes its chemistry, the clearing of Tiananmen Square suddenly and radically altered the political climate in China. In a historical instant the students and workers who had been nonviolently demonstrating all across China for democracy and freedom of expression were transformed from peaceful supplicants seeking to redress their grievances into implacable underground foes dedicated to overthrowing the Chinese Communist Party. It is not unlikely that future historians will view the events which took place in Tiananmen Square as the beginning of the end, not only of Deng's government, but also of the whole Communist era.

In the aftermath of the massacre, most informed Chinese found it almost unimaginable that Deng's aging cabal of senile comrades-in-arms from the 1920s and 1930s (and their lusterless factotum, Li Peng) could long prevail. Although they might carry on for some undetermined length of time, just as fingernails on a corpse keep growing even after death, so moribund had the Party and its leadership become that there seemed little hope of real regeneration under its aegis. What was most striking was that, besides those members of the Party's upper echelon and military who went along with Deng after his crackdown, there was almost no active support for him among other sectors of Chinese society. Rarely in recent history has such a broad social spectrum been so alienated from those who purported to rule it. What is more, whereas in most other revolutionary situations—including that which gave rise to the Chinese Communist Party itself—one socioeconomic class (often represented by the government) finds itself pitted against another class in a social revolution, in post-Tiananmen China the Party has increasingly aligned itself against the bulk of what it calls the "broad masses."

Stunned beyond belief by the spectacle of the People's Liberation Army firing indiscriminately on the peaceful demonstrators, the Chinese have fallen into a thrall of compliance before the military might of their government. But few knowledgeable observers believe that they will long stay so immobilized. If nothing else, the seven weeks of demonstrations in Tiananmen Square gave the Chinese an intoxicating suggestion of what real freedom feels like. It was a lesson in "liberation" which few will soon forget. This whiff of freedom of assembly, press, and speech, coupled with an already existing sense of profound alienation from the government, has conspired to rupture in a final and unremedial way that fundamental bond which must exist between a government and its people if leaders are to rule effectively.

Having lost their moral authority and their ability to rule, Deng and his cohorts are left with repression as their only means of retaining political control. Reverting to tactics which had once worked in the past (when people still looked up to the Party with fear as well as with a lingering yearning to believe), China's aging hard-liners have turned to ideological bullying, threats of intimidation, arrests, summary court judgments, long prison sentences, and even executions in hopes of staying the tide against them.

Apart from the senseless disruption and loss of life which the ruthless crushing of this so-called counterrevolutionary rebellion entailed, the other tragedy of the spring of 1989 was that, once more, reform had failed China. Whereas the eighties had been ushered in on a great wave of optimism about the prospects of piecemeal reform, the decade would now close with a deep sense of pessimism, even foreboding, about the future. The Tiananmen massacre has thus left people both angry and deeply depressed: not only are the government and the people openly in a state of seemingly irreconcilable conflict, but there are no longer any grounds for maintaining even a fantasy of peaceful change and development.

As has repeatedly happened during this past century in China, a brief and hopeful flowering of reform has ended in failure—crushed by conservatives in a bloodbath of reaction. In its aftermath, yet another generation of educated Chinese youth is now estranged. Like earlier generations of progressive reformers, they are left with three stark alternatives: political surrender, violent overthrow of their government, or exile. Their great-grandfathers had been forced to flee abroad at the end of the Qing Dynasty when abortive reforms ended with arrests and executions. Their grandfathers and fathers had fled to the West during the years of Nationalist rule when Chiang Kai-shek tried to tar almost all dissent as Communist subversion. And now a Chinese government had once more turned on its best and brightest, creating a new diaspora among those very people whom a modernizing China so desperately needs. Some forty thousand Chinese, moreover, were said to be studying in the United States in 1989; after June 4, virtually none of them has shown any inclination to return home.

And yet, what is most paradoxical about the situation in which these newly exiled Chinese democrats find themselves is that U.S. President George Bush has given them virtually no support, even though their peaceful pro-democracy movement took much of its inspiration from the

American political experience. When Bush visited Peking in February 1989, shortly after his inauguration, he never publicly raised the question of China's democratization or of the government's human-rights violations. When the students began marching in mid-April, he had few words of encouragement for them. After the bloody crackdown in June, Bush continued to stress the overriding "importance" of China's official relationship to the United States, while reserving judgment on Deng's responsibility for the events in Tiananmen Square (although Deng, as paramount leader, was surely an architect of the massacre). Even after the executions had begun, Bush rejected any but the mildest sanctions against China. Coming from the leader of a nation which had spent four decades locked in a costly Cold War against Communism and in defense of the "Free World," Bush's reticence seemed strangely inconsistent. Who could explain to an arrested Chinese demonstrator that the country which had supported Solidarity in Poland (by imposing strict trade sanctions after the declaration of martial law), which had officially encouraged refuseniks and dissidents in their struggle against the Soviet Union's "evil empire," and which had given hundreds of millions of dollars to Contra "freedom fighters" to wage war against the iniquities of Sandinista Marxism in Nicaragua, would now fail to give equal support to China's non-violent, independent, democratic protest against a Marxist–Leninist dictatorship? When it came to application of standards for human rights abroad, it was hard not to conclude that the U.S. government operated on a double standard. As China's dissident astrophysicist Fang Lizhi declared after Bush failed forcefully to protest his exclusion from a Peking presidential banquet at the end of February, "Some say that Bush was too soft . . . I will only say that the West should not operate on a double standard by criticizing human-rights violations in the Soviet Union but not in China."

As *Seeds of Fire* so clearly reveals, those forces of disaffection among Chinese intellectuals which culminated in the extraordinary events in Tiananmen Square were well advanced long before the spring of 1989. Although older Party leaders were always deeply ambivalent about the ways in which Deng's "open door" policy and his bold economic reforms allowed what they viewed as "spiritual pollution," "wholesale Westernization," and "bourgeois liberalization" to flood into China, they were nonetheless hesitant to crack down on free thinkers as they had done in the past. They rightfully feared that overly repressive measures would serve to alienate China's new intellectual and technocratic elite, on whom the country's modernization drive depended. It was this hesitancy and ambivalence among Party leaders which afforded Chinese intellectuals a much-needed respite from the total Party control which had suffocated them for so long. As if awakening from a long, cold winter of hibernation, these intellectuals began timidly to reenter the cosmopolitan world once the post-Mao reforms began in earnest after 1978. At first they seemed groggy and bewildered by what they saw; much of what they said and wrote initially evinced a certain naïveté and clumsiness, which after their long and numbing regimen of Maoist didacticism was hardly surprising. But as they slowly made greater contact both with the outside world and with their own traditional culture, they began to come alive again, and their work soon displayed a new sophistication and boldness. However, they all too quickly began training their literary and political sights not only on the Cultural Revolution's "ten dark years of chaos" (a target officially sanctioned by the Party) but on the Party itself and on Deng's unrelenting authoritarianism as well. While Deng's regime had allowed a strong measure of economic change, it had continued to be wary of significant political change. The tension between these two inseparable aspects of reform kept building, and upon reaching a critical point, it triggered the tectonic political movement of "China's Spring."

Although no one could have foreseen the development of a massive and overt opposition movement before the death of former Communist Party leader Hu Yaobang on April 15, 1989, there were signs long before last spring that growing disaffection among Chinese students and intellectuals was reaching some sort of crescendo. The writings contained in this book, antedating as they do the spring of 1989, are ample and telling testament to the depth of this disaffection. With *Seeds of Fire*, Geremie Barmé and John Minford provided the English-speaking world with its first comprehensive look at a full range of China's long-suppressed dissenting voices. Anyone who had the chance to browse through *Seeds of Fire* before the spring of 1989 was undoubtedly less surprised by what later transpired than were those who did not. By giving voice to those who had dared to speak out against the political system and its leaders, these writings served as a prescient warning of what was to come. It was a prophetic book that foreshadowed the political drama of Tiananmen Square. Now, in the aftermath of last spring's tumultuous events, one might well wonder whether or not these writings are *ex post facto* passé. But nothing could be further from the truth. If anything, they have acquired an even more important if unforeseen relevance. As propaganda bureaus once again endeavor to defoliate the Chinese landscape of all dissenting publications and voices, and as independent Chinese thinkers are driven underground or are forced to flee abroad, *Seeds of Fire* provides us with an invaluable "who's who" of Chinese dissident thinkers. It also provides us with a record of what they would be saying now if they were still able to speak out. These writings, in short, are a reminder not just that China has had brave voices of conscience but that in the aftermath of the Tiananmen massacre they have been forced to fall silent.

San Francisco
July 14, 1989

Introduction

*I didn't know that before the Cultural Revolution there had been
  a May 4th;*
*I didn't know that after the Cultural Revolution there would be
  an April 5th;*
I didn't know that today would come before tomorrow;
I don't know if there will be a tomorrow after today.

> —JI NAN,
> May 22, 1989,
> from a student magazine

ON THE NIGHT of June 3–4, 1989, the Chinese Army began a violent massacre of peaceful student and civilian protesters in Peking. The slaughter, which went on for days and resulted in the death of thousands, marked the beginning of the most bloody and ruthless purge in post-Mao China. This has been a purge with a difference, for in its early stages it enjoyed full media coverage in the West, as it followed some six weeks of protests and saturation satellite transmission. The protests had begun with the death of Hu Yaobang, the former Party General Secretary, on April 15. Hu himself had been a victim of a previous purge launched by Deng Xiaoping in late 1986; his successor, Zhao Ziyang, would be the highest-ranking casualty this time around.

The present purge—one that, quite apart from its cost in terms of human lives and personal suffering, threatens China's economic modernization program as well as its relations with its neighbors and the Western world—is the sixth and most successful campaign Deng Xiaoping has orchestrated against independent thinking, political dissent, and cultural freedom in his ten years in power. The five previous purges are documented in this book, which was first compiled in 1986 and expanded in late 1987. *Seeds of Fire* was edited in the hope of helping non-Chinese readers to hear China's dissident voices, and to understand the political, literary, and artistic debates that have taken place in China since the Cultural Revolution. These debates have been at the center of what

China's leaders perceive as an ideological malaise, which they first hoped
to cure through intellectual campaigns and have now decided to overcome
with brute force.

In *Seeds of Fire* the voices of some of China's more controversial
writers and thinkers speak directly to Western readers on the subject of
their country, its ancient cultural burden, and the complex problems it
faces today. They are concerned voices, and they represent a wide spectrum of ideas—some hopeful, others plainly despairing—but, above all,
they are voices of conscience. Many of those whose works we present in
these pages have paid dearly for their outspokenness.

Honesty and integrity were also the qualities that distinguished
China's greatest twentieth-century writer, Lu Xun, who died on October
19, 1936, fifty years before *Seeds of Fire* was first published. The title of
this work is taken from one of his essays, and the book is still dedicated
to his memory. The year the first edition appeared, 1986, also marked
the tenth anniversary of a popular demonstration which Lu Xun would
have wholeheartedly supported, the first Tiananmen incident—the starting
point of the post-Mao era in China.

On April 5, 1976, Chinese All Souls' Day, crowds gathered in Tiananmen Square in the heart of Peking, ostensibly to pay homage to Zhou
Enlai, who had died in January of that year. In reality, the majority of
the demonstrators sought to protest against the oppressive rule of the
Communist Party and the bloody Cultural Revolution that it had led since
1966. All the might of the state apparatus was unleashed on these "counterrevolutionaries." Many were killed or wounded early that evening for
refusing to leave the square, and many others were arrested and executed.
But after Mao's death in September 1976 and the arrest of the Gang of
Four one month later, the Cultural Revolution came abruptly to an end.
In late 1978 the Communist Party, which was moving rapidly toward de-
Maoification and denunciation of the Cultural Revolution, declared the
demonstration to have been an expression of popular will, and its leaders
were rehabilitated. This dramatic reversal of policy inspired many of the
original protesters to take to the streets once more, and they were joined
by many others who saw this as a rare opportunity to voice openly their
own demands and hopes. Thousands of posters went up on a wall near
Xidan on Chang'an Avenue in central Peking, containing poems and
stories (which were often recited to the crowds before the wall), as well

as political manifestos and pleas for justice from victims of the Cultural Revolution. This "Democracy Wall" soon became the most visible emblem of what was popularly known as the Democracy Movement, though in fact it was more a spontaneous outpouring than a concerted "movement."

The more active participants were young people in their late twenties and early thirties, the ex-Red Guard generation that had grown up under socialism after 1949; Mao had used them to overthrow his opponents, and then had sent them off to oblivion in the countryside. In the winter and spring of 1978–9, not satisfied with the transitory nature of wall posters, they started producing their own unofficial publications, in the form of rough, mimeographed political and literary pamphlets and magazines, which they often distributed from the wall itself. Unlike many of their dissident counterparts in the Soviet Union and Eastern Europe, these reformers (with the notable exception of Wei Jingsheng) still saw democracy as a way for the Marxist state to achieve social harmony and progress, not as a path for the blossoming of the individual. Their freedom of expression, however, was short-lived: Deng Xiaoping, having successfully used the "movement" to prove to his opponents that the Cultural Revolution and its policies had no popular support, threw these young people aside again, just as Mao had used and discarded them more than ten years earlier. In April and May 1979, the Party clamped down on the "Peking Spring," banning most of the unofficial publications and arresting many of the leading pamphleteers (in fact, arrests continued as late as 1985). Posters and gatherings were forbidden, commercial advertisements began to cover the wall, and in the end it was converted into a series of display cases illustrating the latest achievements of socialist modernization.

The Democracy Movement was crushed and the official media turned its leaders into non-persons. The power of the Chinese propaganda machine is matched only by the susceptibility of the Chinese to indoctrination, or "thought-mold," and until this year virtually no one talked openly about the events and personalities of 1978–9. To keep reminding people outside China of the significance of that brief period—a period thrown into relief by recent developments—is an important task and is one of the purposes of this book. But it is equally important to realize that even now, some ten years later, the energies and enthusiasms it released are still active and more potent than ever. For a decade they were simply pushed underground, or channeled into less obviously political areas. The main activists were jailed, but their writer and artist contemporaries (with whom they were always closely associated) continued to experiment and search for new modes of self-expression, in many cases abandoning their demands for political reform in favor of a more individual quest. At least such was the situation until this year, when artists, writers, and student activists alike took to the streets of Peking, petitioned the government, and called for greater freedoms and political reform. But times have changed: this time around, not only have the political leaders of the 1989 Democracy Movement been arrested, but establishment writers and intellectuals who supported them have been rounded up as well.

A fascinating early instance of the link between the political and literary aspects of the new consciousness that developed in the late 1970s occurs in the "Prison Diary" of Liu Qing, the former editor of the "democratic" journal *April Fifth Forum* (see Section IX).[1] In his prison cell Liu was lamenting the tragic fate of the young Yu Luoke,[2] who had been executed several years earlier during the Cultural Revolution and was later hailed in 1978–9 as a martyr and one of the precursors of the Democracy Movement. "He is gone," writes Liu in his diary. "He has been gone for many years now. His grave is deserted. It has no fresh flowers, no green grass grows there. Only a solitary wild goose occasionally gives a sad cry as it passes by in the sky. Truly: 'Honour is the epitaph of the honourable.' " This last sentence, quoted without any explanation, is (as many of his younger readers would have immediately recognized) a line from the poem "The Answer" by Bei Dao (see p. 236), a man who with his friends had launched the unofficial literary journal *Today*.[3]

In China more than anywhere else in the world, literature and politics have always gone hand in hand. Literature has always had a strong didactic function. Statesmen have tended to be litterateurs, and most writers have been socially and politically engaged. Even seemingly esoteric and apolitical poetry often has a hidden political significance. The present is no exception. At a time when disillusionment is so widespread, when the old socialist ethos is little more than a thing of the past and a spiritual vacuum

---

[1] This magazine was revived shortly before the Peking massacre in June 1989.

[2] The elder brother of Yu Luojin. Yu Luojin was later herself to become a controversial writer of autobiographical fiction—see below, pp. 200–8.

[3] See below, p. 236. Another line from the same poem, "I—do—not—believe!," was later widely quoted and attacked (again, there was no need to give the poet's name) by the Party authorities during their infamous campaign against "Spiritual Pollution" in 1983–4. The line was used again by demonstrators in 1989.

has taken its place, many have looked to the writers and artists, not to the discredited Party and its hired hacks, for enlightenment and fresh hope. Bei Dao, the poet just quoted, also writes fiction, and his haunting story "13 Happiness Street" (pp. 2–16) expresses more powerfully than almost any other single work the angst of his generation:

> Fang Cheng was sent to the lunatic asylum.
> When he looked at the people running in circles around the desolate grounds and the outside wall covered with weeds, he finally understood: so now he too was inside the wall.

The poetry of Yang Lian (a contributor to *Today*) returns again and again to the image of the ruins, the "broken sundial buried in the earth," the "aftermath of shattered dreams." The "torch" of revolutionary idealism is out:

> *An infinite wasteland as far as the eye can see.*

And the poet turns instead to his own inner resources:

> *Today I come here*
> *No language but my heart*
> *No road but my heart*

This kind of literature, despite its apolitical mask, has naturally been seen as threatening by the Party. But they grudgingly tolerated it, as they tolerated the more liberal economic experiments, uncertain all the while where it would all lead—until this year.

Prominent in this anthology are the voices of poets such as Bei Dao, Gu Cheng, Jiang He, and Yang Lian (pp. 236–49),[4] who launched their search for a new set of values in the post-Cultural Revolution wasteland, a search that has drawn them far beyond the confines of orthodox Marxism, using language that was for many Chinese readers startlingly modernistic and incomprehensible. Their achievement—which enraged the cultural establishment—indirectly encouraged similar developments in fiction, theater, film, art, philosophy, and aesthetics, and later even traditional opera. As a striking example of this type of parallel development, we have provided a synopsis of one of the most important films of the 1980s ("Yellow Earth"), together with extracts from the heated debate

---

[4] All four poets are now in exile.

held by the critics on its artistic and ideological virtues and defects (pp. 252–69). We have translated extracts from two of the more controversial plays produced during 1985 ("The Detour" and "Urbling Winter," pp. 38–45 and 105–16, respectively) and have used some of the work of younger painters, photographers, and sculptors as a counterpoint to the poetry and prose. In this way, we hope to give the Western reader some insight into the ferment beneath the surface.

At the same time, we have included some of the more enlightened writers of the older generation (people like Yang Jiang, Chen Baichen, Huang Yongyu, and Ba Jin),[5] who have somehow managed to retain their integrity and have refused to turn against the younger generation. Some, like Niu Han (pp. 291–2), as liberal-minded editors, actively supported these new voices, while other older writers who had taken a brave stand subsequently caved in to intense Party pressure (for example, the poet Sun Jingxuan, pp. 121–8). Others again, in their forties, like Liu Xinwu (pp. 19–28) and Dai Houying (pp. 153–60), genuinely strove to sharpen their own ideological independence and to deepen the artistic impact of their work through the study of more modern techniques. Theirs, too, is decidedly a "literature of conscience."

On the other hand, the historian Jin Guantao (pp. 131–3), whose initial studies of the "feudalist" phenomenon bespoke great promise, became more of an organization man dabbling in new ideas, an enlightened apparatchik—apprehensive about the consequences of some of the ideas he had unleashed.

By way of offering some totally independent views of events "within the Wall," we have also included Chinese writers from outside the Mainland. These are Chinese voices too, but ones able to speak in a more liberal context and therefore freer to use humor and satire, and to approach Chinese problems relatively unencumbered by censorship. Especially in recent years, as the Communists call for the swift reunification of Hong Kong and Taiwan with the "motherland," the role of Chinese writers and intellectuals in Hong Kong and Taiwan has become increasingly significant. The Taiwanese essayist Bo Yang (pp. 168–76), for example, offers some particularly ironic reflections on the reunification problem in "The Ugly Chinaman."

[5] See pp. 80–7, 88–101, 193–7, and 381–4, respectively.

If we look back at the history of reform in China over the past century and a half, the Chinese diaspora can be seen to have played a very important role in mediating between China and the outside world—daring to do and say what people "within the Wall" did not dare; introducing foreign ideas and technology to China; interpreting China and its strange ways to the barbarians; and sometimes protecting and sheltering Chinese political outcasts. This role is exemplified by the work of the cultural historian Sun Longji (or Lung-kee Sun, as he himself prefers to write his name). His book *The Deep Structure of Chinese Culture*, published in Hong Kong in 1983, has been read with intense fascination by many readers in Mainland China, and is viewed with correspondingly intense disapproval by the authorities. His ideas, while not systematically presented, are fresh and provocative. They are the product of an inquiring mind that is both Chinese and cosmopolitan, using every intellectual means at its disposal to confront the dilemma of being Chinese in the twentieth century—very much in the spirit of Lu Xun. Sun is not the first to apply analytical methods such as Freudian psychology and psycholinguistics to the workings of traditional and modern Chinese culture,[6] but he absorbs these methodologies in a Chinese manner, and applies them with an insider's eye, illustrating his argument with a wealth of compelling examples. Extracts from his book are scattered throughout his anthology, because they cover such a wide variety of topics.

Two distinguished émigré writers have also found their way into *Seeds of Fire:* the novelist Chen Ruoxi (now living in America, see pp. 46–61), and Bao Ruowang (now resident in Paris, see pp. 70–8). Although both are writing about the past (in Chen's case, the Cultural Revolution; in Bao's, the late 1950s and early 1960s), what they have to say is still very relevant. In this context, it is helpful to recall the words of Simon Leys:

> Some time ago I witnessed this scene at a university seminar in Europe: a number of political scientists were discussing the various political shifts in the history of the People's Republic and were trying to assess the implications of the latest changes brought about by Deng Xiaoping. After they had analyzed at great length and with subtle nuances all the possible and future

[6] See, for example, Lucian W. Pye, *The Spirit of Chinese Politics* (Cambridge, Mass.: MIT Press, 1968); and Richard H. Solomon, *Mao's Revolution and the Chinese Political Culture* (Berkeley: University of California Press, 1971).

implications of Deng's innovations, they finally asked the opinion of a distinguished scholar who had said nothing so far, but who had happened to be the only person there with genuine insight on the subject, since he himself was a Chinese and had just arrived from the People's Republic. With a smile of infinite weariness, he said simply: "Political changes? I haven't noticed any during the last thirty years. Why should we expect any in the future?"[7]

This book is organized thematically, into fourteen sections, including four sections, "More Stones, More Seeds," which deal specifically with the events of 1986–7 (for more detail on these, see pp. 325–6).[8] The first section, entitled "Walls," is really a miniature anthology in its own right. It takes the image of the Great Wall as a starting point, and from there story writer, poet, social psychologist, and dramatist branch out, to confront various "dead ends," culs-de-sac, and traps—cultural, economic, political, and psychological.

The second and ninth sections form a pair, and are (together with the Appendix and Sections XI and XII) the most overtly political parts of the book. The second section deals with "Proledic"—the Dictatorship of the Proletariat, whose organs (the Public and State Security apparatus as well as the army) are in effect the "other China," the Chinese Gulag, the ever-present (but often intangible) tentacles of which reach into every workplace, enfolding the lives of every member of society. Running foul of Proledic is a harrowing business, as is further chronicled in the ninth section, "Fire Behind Bars," devoted to four of the leading Democracy Movement activists, all now serving long prison terms. Over the past two months, the world has seen Proledic in action on its television screens. Now, partially in response to the international outcry resulting from those shocking images, the state apparatus continues its deadly work off-screen: countless arrests are made, confessions extracted from victims, trials and

---

[7] From "Is There Life After Mao?," in Simon Leys, *The Burning Forest: Essays on Chinese Culture and Politics* (New York: A New Republic Book/Henry Holt and Company, 1986).

[8] In order to introduce as many writers and ideas as possible, we have often extracted material, shortened it, or adapted it. Those who wish to consult the originals in their entirety are directed to the list of Chinese sources at the end of the book. And in order to create some sort of context for these works—this is, after all, not the record of some gentlemanly literary debate in the columns of a Sunday newspaper—we have from time to time added bits of the official Party bullyings (known as criticisms) and of the authors' abject rituals of self-flagellation (known as self-criticisms).

executions carried out in secret, dossiers sifted through during interminable political-study sessions, and punishments meted out by Party bosses to their employees for past slurs, ideological errors, and "attitudinal problems." The only truly modern and efficient arm of the Chinese government, fitted out with the high technology readily provided by the developed countries over the past decade, Proledic is now cutting a wide and bloody swath through the whole nation.

The third and fourth sections—"Spectres" and "Humanity!"—can also be grouped together. Here poet, historian, story writer, and theoretician debate some of the broad ideological issues—feudalism, totalitarianism, humanism—that preoccupy many Chinese intellectuals concerned with the continued stagnation and backwardness of their society. Feudalism in the Chinese context means something extremely complex—the poem "A Spectre Prowls Our Land" (pp. 121–8) evokes this paralyzing force very effectively. The story "Lingering Fear" (pp. 137–48) expresses the widespread anxiety about a reversion to the totalitarian excesses of the Cultural Revolution. Humanism is a complex idea in the Chinese context, best understood as a blanket term for anything "humane" that seems to offer a remedy for the malaise, the pervading sense of alienation, the inhumanity. It may be thought of as a series of questions: Can socialism be given a human dimension? Can a spiritual civilization be built on the ruins of a failed social experiment? Are Marxism and humanism compatible?

The fifth section deals with the essayist and the satirist. Significantly, three of the four writers in this section, entitled "Thorns," are from Hong Kong and Taiwan. Their liveliness, the literary acupuncture they practice (again, the legacy of Lu Xun), have much to offer toward revitalizing the energies of the "buried dragon," but, alas, their wit and sharp insights seldom reach the inner sanctum of the Central Committee, and when they do are condemned as the ravings of traitors and spies. In the sixth section, "Clouds: But No Rain" (an allusion to the common Chinese euphemism for sexual intercourse, the "clouds and rain"), we witness the beginnings of an awareness of—and reaction against—Confucian/Marxist sexual repression. It is certainly far too early to talk of sexual liberation in China, for although some taboos have been broken, one of the main targets of the 1989 purge of culture is the flood of sex writing that has appeared over the last few years.

"Mists" and "Yellow Earth," the seventh and eighth sections, are brief introductions to the innovations in poetry, art, and film referred to above.[9] Readers may have a strong sense of *déjà vu* when witnessing the (to Western eyes) old-fashioned modernism of these young artists, but when we remember the depths to which creative art of any sort sank after 1949, these are signs of the survival of aesthetic and spiritual life in China. The film "Yellow Earth" was shown at the 1985 Hong Kong Film Festival, with both director and cinematographer present, and a public discussion was held afterward, during which a member of the audience rose emotionally to his feet and said in halting Cantonese–Mandarin: "For all these years I had despaired for China. Now I see hope!" Four years later, that fragile hope was to be destroyed in a single night.

In the tenth section, the Shade of Lu Xun, irascible, unpredictable, devastatingly honest, which has been brooding over the book, takes a somber farewell. In 1940, four years after his death, when he could no longer protest, Lu Xun was hailed by Mao (who respected and probably feared him) as the "chief commander of China's cultural revolution . . . not only a great man of letters but a great thinker and revolutionary"— an expression that later became almost a slogan. And yet, in precisely the same work, Mao was propounding his own version of Stalinism for Chinese literature and art, which opposed everything Lu Xun had stood for, and which continues to this day to set the limits for freedom of expression. Lu Xun was again used and promoted at the beginning of the Cultural Revolution itself (October 1966, the thirtieth anniversary of his death) for having "dared to declare war on all enemies and to thrust his sharp-edged pen at their very hearts." This despite the fact that Lu Xun had himself written that "good literature always refuses orders from outside— it never cares about the consequences, it springs spontaneously from the heart." He once commented that his own works were too dark, "because I often feel that only 'darkness and emptiness' are 'reality.' I am determined, nonetheless, to launch a war of resistance in despair against them." He summed up the relationship between the writer and the revolution (he was talking of the Soviet experience) in the following words: "During the era of revolution, writers have a dream in which they imagine how beau-

[9] For a wider selection, see the anthology *Trees on the Mountain*, ed. Stephen Soong and John Minford (Hong Kong: Chinese University Press, 1984).

tiful the world will be after the success of the revolution. But when the revolution has succeeded, they find things entirely different from their dream. Hence they have to suffer again. They cry out but will not succeed in their protests. They cannot succeed by going either forward or backward. It is their destiny to witness the inconsistency between ideal and reality."[10]

Such, too, has been the destiny of the writers in *Seeds of Fire*.

This is therefore in essence an "anti-reader" on China, though certainly not an "anti-China" reader. It is a book that has been substantially enlarged since the 1986 Hong Kong edition, and as we write, the cataclysm of June 1989 has, sadly, given these pages a new significance.

In the events that led up to the protests of April-May 1989 and the massacre of June, the name of Wei Jingsheng (pp. 277–89), one of the most outspoken dissidents of the Democracy Movement of 1979, figured prominently. Wei, who criticized Deng Xiaoping for his autocratic ways and called for a "fifth modernization," democracy, was sentenced in October 1979 to fifteen years in jail on trumped-up charges of selling state secrets. It is an open secret that it was Deng Xiaoping himself and not the trial judge who decided the length of Wei's sentence, even as Deng was publicly calling for "rule by law." Fang Lizhi (pp. 328–40), the astrophysicist who declared in 1987 that he was carrying on Wei's work, wrote a letter to Deng Xiaoping in January 1989 calling for the release of Wei and China's other political prisoners. He appealed to Deng to declare an amnesty to mark the bicentennial of the French Revolution and the fortieth anniversary of the People's Republic of China.

Fang's letter led to similar petitions by writers, intellectuals, university professors, and scientists in February and March. Many of the signatories are represented in this book: Bei Dao, Chen Ruoxi, Gu Cheng, Jin Guantao, Li Tuo, Liu Xiaobo, Mang Ke, Niu Han, Wu Zuguang, and Yang Lian. For this they are now dubbed by the government as "instigators of turmoil."

---

[10] See Lin Yü-sheng, "The Morality of Mind and Immorality of Politics: Reflections on Lu Xun, the Intellectual," and Merle Goldman, "The Political Use of Lu Xun in the Cultural Revolution and After," in Leo Ou-fan Lee, ed., *Lu Xun and His Legacy* (Berkeley: University of California Press, 1985).

Deng Xiaoping on the Path to Dictatorship

Many figures in positions of authority become intoxicated with their own personal power, and lose sight altogether of the popular verdict; others are driven by private ambition and seek to set themselves up as dictators—to this end they exploit the gullibility of the people in the most despicable fashion. For example, Deng Xiaoping's speech on March 16 (1979) exploited the people's past confidence in him. He relied on this to get away with attacking the Democracy Movement. He accused the Democracy Movement of all sorts of crimes, tried to hold it responsible for China's economic woes, made it the scapegoat for the failure of his own policies.

Does Deng Xiaoping deserve the confidence of the people? The answer to that question is that no leader deserves unconditional confidence; it is policies that deserve confidence, not individuals. . . . In a democracy, any person in authority must bow to popular opposition.

But Deng does not bow. . . . Is he simply intending to perpetuate the Mao-brand of dictatorial socialism? If so, we can never forgive him, however good his performance may have been in the past. A new Mao-style dictatorship can only further damage the people's livelihood, it can only do them further untold harm. To forgive such a crime is to be its accomplice.

Does Deng want democracy? Certainly not. He will not try to understand the sufferings of the common people, he will not allow them to take back into their own hands the power that has been stolen from them by an ambitious clique. He describes the struggle for democratic rights—a spontaneous movement—as a deliberate act of manipulation, as political trouble-making, a disruption of public order; it must therefore be suppressed. This way of responding to criticism, to aspirations for social progress, these methods he has resorted to, demonstrate the extreme fear with which he views this popular movement.

The people must beware of and take precautions against Deng's degeneration into dictatorship.

From Wei Jingsheng's editorial for the special edition of *Tansuo* (*Exploration*) of March 25, 1979. Wei was arrested four days later.

The figure of Wei Jingsheng cast a long shadow over the events of the first part of 1989. But it was the first Tiananmen incident of April 5, 1976, that many people recalled as the Peking protests, which began in memory of Hu Yaobang, escalated to encompass issues of democracy and freedom and to involve the citizens of the whole city. Thirteen years ago the square had also filled with people who by mourning a recently deceased "hero" (Zhou Enlai) were expressing their opposition to (Mao's) dictatorial rule. Then, too, the demonstrators were brutally crushed, and a reformer (Deng Xiaoping), who had at that time been a symbol of hope for the protesters, was thrown from power. Within six months of that Tiananmen incident, the autocratic Mao died, his extremist cohorts fell from power, and the Cultural Revolution came to an end. This left the way open for Deng to return to power and to launch China on its course of the Open Door and Reform. Now, in one of the supreme ironies of history, many wait for the death of the aged Deng and his senile "gang," in the hope that the massacre and the purge that has followed in its wake will one day be denounced by a more rational and responsive government.

In 1976, the protesters had placed little bottles (*xiaoping*, in Chinese) around the square as a sign of their support for Deng; in 1989, bottles were also present as a symbol—this time smashed or overturned by demonstrators. Tiananmen Square, the scene of the tumultuous developments of the past months, is itself rich in historical allusion and symbolism. In imperial times, decrees were read from the Tiananmen Gate; Yuan Shikai, the autocratic first President of the Republic of China, used it for a grand review of troops when he was inaugurated; and for a time Sun Yat-sen's portrait hung on it. The small square in front of the gate has been used as a rallying point for student demonstrations from 1919 onward. From the rostrum of Tiananmen on October 1, 1949, Mao proclaimed that the Chinese people had finally "stood up," and that the People's Republic was born. Later it was the site of the regime's Nuremburg-like rallies and of the "Maosoleum"—the Fourteenth Imperial Tomb. In 1989, the students and ordinary people of Peking decided that they were to be the masters of ceremonies for once, and the square was subverted to become the arena for a new form of "people's political theater."

It is significant that this site, one so intimately linked with the patriotic and intellectual protests of twentieth-century China, was radically altered after 1949 at the will of its new dynastic rulers. The gate was rebuilt in concrete, the area in front of it expanded into a massive parade ground, and the alignment of the city was turned around: the north-south axis of the traditional capital—its celestial geometry—was broken and replaced by an east-west thoroughfare, Chang'an Avenue. It is this avenue that has borne the weight of numerous government parades, the last one on October 1, 1984, marking the thirty-fifth anniversary of the Communist state and unofficially celebrating Deng Xiaoping's eightieth birthday. This year, the students, marching out of their universities in the city's north-west, entered Tiananmen from Chang'an Avenue, and during the protests, Chang'an was the site of numerous demonstrations. On June 3–4, again it was the east and west arms of the avenue that brought the army into the square; and in the days that followed, it carried the new and massive weight of tanks, armored personnel carriers, and troop convoys. The arena for student demonstrations, for a popular and peaceful revolt against forty years of Communist rule, was thus occupied by the machinery of totalitarian power.

After Hu Yaobang's death, and in particular following the first student hunger strike, which started on May 13, Tiananmen Square became a magnetic field, drawing into itself people from all over the city and from the rest of China. For those heady and unsettling weeks of May, to be in Peking meant being drawn into the square. People would sometimes rise at night, half-fearful, crazed with curiosity, and would be attracted to the vast open space as if sleepwalking. It was filled for a time with hunger-wracked bodies, screeching ambulances, milling crowds, peddlers, piles of garbage, and weary onlookers anxious for yet fearful of government action. As never before, the square was the stage on which the heroism and tragedy of Chinese history was to be played out.

The students understood too little of history to be deterred by its lessons—even recent ones. Their youth and their innocence liberated them momentarily from the dead weight of history. They yearned not to recall the past but rather to be in history, to make history, to live history. It was an infectious and passionate enthusiasm. One of the earliest slogans during the present movement was "We are writing history." When it became obvious that the authorities were too involved with their own machinations to deal with the demonstrators, Peking residents went into the streets *en masse* to write themselves into this new story as well. To be part of the weave of the fabric of history was just as compelling a motive for endless numbers of Chinese as was their desire to express support for the students, or their will to reject the inhumanity of the Party leaders.

Certain writers had at the outset sensed the futility of it all; they were already too familiar with the shapes of darkness and death, too profoundly aware of the deadly formulaic pattern of the past, the crushing burden of destiny. For instance, Yang Lian, writing in 1984, after weathering one of the nastiest of Deng's previous campaigns, wrote:

> *For ever climbing*
> > *for ever falling,*
> *The universe submits*
> > *to its own icon,*
> *Is thrown into dawn's ever tautened noose.*
> *A million cries—*
> > *and silence.*
> *Mankind:*
> > *the cud of history,*
> > *chewed on*
> > *like an old adage,*
> *A corrupt text,*
> *An obscure footnote,*
> *An ancestral comma.*

But even Yang Lian and Gu Cheng (adamantly apolitical, ever more intent on exploring childhood memories and dreams) responded with passionate involvement to the sense of "history in the making," participating from their place of exile in New Zealand, writing petitions and letters of protest, and finally grieving for the tragic denouement in a powerful "Elegy for the Dead," the only work they have ever written together.

The subversion of symbols, cultural, intellectual, or historical, was a central facet of the recent movement; it is also a motif that runs through this book. To a great extent, the wellsprings of this "subversion" are to be found in the deep structure of China's Communist culture. The parades and marches, the rhetoric, the banners and slogans, even the organization of the student and intellectual movements (and its concomitant faction-alism) reflected a hierarchy of symbols and a special, militant language born of the Communist Party's struggle against the KMT and further refined during the Cultural Revolution. Initially, the demonstrations of

1989 were generally naïve and innocent, then they became heroic and awe-inspiring. But throughout we have seen the realization of Mao Zedong's dire prediction of 1966, that after his death people would "use the red flag to oppose the red flag."

The response of the intellectuals has been fascinating. Bo Yang, the Taiwan-based writer and historian, viewed the developments with skepticism from the start, predicting in April that nothing but calamity would result from the student protests. He traveled to China in late 1988 after an absence of forty years to discover a land even more benighted than he had previously imagined. He was able to visit—although not without considerable difficulty—Wang Ruowang and Fang Lizhi, two of the Mainland writers he admires most. He commented afterward: "It is a curious fact that China always treats its finest people in such a shabby fashion." Purged from the Party in 1987, both Wang and Fang have been vilified again in 1989. The Hong Kong editor Lee Yee (pp. 274–6) has actively attacked the Mainland government for its murderous reaction to the peaceful protests and has used his magazine *The Nineties* as a forum for outraged intellectuals. Since June 4, he has joined many prominent figures in censuring the British government for its refusal to offer refuge to Hong Kong passport holders.

As for many of the other artists and writers represented in these pages, there is as yet little news. Some are in exile, some have been arrested, some are still in hiding, others await their fate calmly at home. The Stalinist-style purge continues, and although it may spare some, it will devastate cultural and intellectual life in China for years to come, just as the massacre in the streets of Peking will traumatize the nation well into the next century. Of all the writings in this book, perhaps it is Su Ming's story "Lingering Fear" which seems most disturbingly prophetic today.

The young social scientist Liu Dong, a signatory to the March 1989 call for the release of political prisoners, was most concerned about what role "independent intellectuals" could play in the mêlée leading up to the June massacre. Writing in commemoration of the seventieth anniversary of the May Fourth Movement this year, Liu recalled the tragedy of the eminent scholar and humanist Hu Shi (1891–1962): "He [Hu Shi] was determined to be an independent intellectual in an environment of political decay, when in fact what he really needed was political order. He knew what role he could play in a rational, democratic political situation, but was at a loss as to what to do with himself under an irrational authoritarianism."

After years of keeping out of politics, Hu Shi was finally convinced that people like himself had to make their voices heard. He emphasized, however, that a person must be truly intellectually independent before becoming *engagé*; otherwise, there was too great a risk of falling into the service of some new form of despotism. This has been precisely the sorry fate of the majority of intellectuals in post-1949 China. Now, however, figures such as Liu Dong are in danger not of serving despotism but rather of becoming its victims.

Hu Shi himself said that "the most powerful man is the loneliest." This sentiment is echoed strongly by Liu Xiaobo (pp. 395–7), a highly controversial Mainland critic and writer in his early thirties. Not satisfied merely to play the role of the concerned and superior bystander and commentator like Liu Binyan (pp. 354–9), he cut short his stay in the United States at the end of April 1989 and returned to Peking, joining the protesters, many of whom were his own students. Liu became an adviser to Wuer Kaixi, the student leader now in exile, and participated in the June 2–4 intellectuals' fast, the last desperate protest before the bloodshed.

In 1987, Liu wrote that intellectuals are often ahead of their time; although branded as miscreants, they have more rarefied perceptions and higher aims than the silent majority. But even in the halcyon days of "reform," such inspiringly independent figures were few indeed, and during the demonstrations, speeches and pamphlets produced by the movement indicate that students and intellectuals alike craved above all some form of official recognition, their own place near the helm of the ship of state, a niche in the post-Mao velvet prison. The traditional role of the Chinese scholar-bureaucrat dovetailed neatly with that of the Stalinist "engineer of the human soul," and with the students' desire for a voice in government. The protesters did not want, as Deng Xiaoping has claimed, "to overthrow the Communist Party, topple the socialist system and subvert the People's Republic of China so as to establish a bourgeois republic." Rather, the students, and the majority of their supporters among establishment intellectuals and cadres, wanted to save a Party and government that was being subverted by the nepotism and corruption of its own leaders, to help it to achieve unity and stability in the face of the failure of economic reform. Eager to salvage the Republic, they were caught up in the complex machinations of internal Party factional politics, used as pawns in the struggle, and finally sacrificed.

In the previous Dengist dispensation there seemed to be some hope that intellectuals would come into their own, and members of think tanks, maverick writers, and various radical intellectuals vied for the attention of Hu Yaobang's successor as Party leader, Zhao Ziyang. Yet Zhao's callous use and abuse of these eager and frustrated technocrats had disaffected the Party and state bureaucracy from the early 1980s. During the recent years of economic mismanagement, intellectuals outside Zhao's select group became disenchanted with his incompetence as a reformer, doubtful of his political acumen in acquiescing in the ouster of Hu Yaobang, and scornful of his devaluation of education and his disregard for the increasing impoverishment of the intellectual elite. Given the chance, intellectuals and students would eagerly have been coopted; but the monumental incompetence of the leaders—including Zhao—forced even this pliant stratum of society into rebellion.

The price of revolt has been high. Liu Xiaobo was detained by the police late on the night of June 6 and denounced virulently in the national media as one of the "black hands" behind the student protests. Many other writers and artists in this volume were active in the movements of 1989 and are now threatened by Party fiat.

Over recent months, Liu Binyan, the loyal ex-Party journalist, has finally been forced into the open and has denounced Deng Xiaoping's senile rule, while Wu Zuguang (pp. 368–72), the outspoken playwright, commented approvingly on a terrorist threat to kidnap Deng's son in Washington while he was visiting the United States in April. He said: "It takes a hoodlum to deal with a hoodlum." While Liu is safe to denounce the Chinese government from his base at Harvard, Wu returned to China to live under martial law.

The poet and novelist Bei Dao, now exiled in Europe, marched in the bicycle parade that led the celebrations of the bicentennial of the French Revolution on July 14 in Paris, while the film director Chen Kaige, now based in New York, is planning to express his outrage and protest in a film to be made in America.

The pop singer Cui Jian (pp. 400–2) performed in Tiananmen Square during the students' hunger strike (May 13–19), the lyrics of his songs speaking deeply of the emotions many felt. And the works of the "misty poets" of 1979 reappeared during the demonstrations. Bei Dao's "The Answer" was reprinted in the major student newspaper, and Gu Cheng's famous line "The darkness has given me eyes to find the light" was featured in the marches.

Others signed appeals to the government to engage in an active and frank dialogue with the students; these included the venerated older writers Yang Jiang and Ba Jin. One of these appeals was organized by the playwright Wang Peigong, author of "WM" (see "Urbling Winter") and an ex-army writer, who resigned his Party membership the day martial law was declared on May 20. Wang was reportedly arrested in early July. Liu Xinwu, a writer and editor who has carefully negotiated the treacherous waters of Chinese political culture since the beginning of his career (as a children's writer during the Cultural Revolution), joined other prominent literary figures to demonstrate in favor of the students. His protest was featured on Hong Kong television, and prior to the massacre he concentrated his energies on collecting material on the reaction of average urban residents to the revolt. Wang Meng (p. 408), a fellow writer and Minister of Culture, seems likely to have finally fallen from his political tightrope, and is expected to lose his portfolio for condoning "bourgeois liberalization."

In April, He Xin, a forty-year-old Peking social scientist who has gone from being something of an iconoclast to finding favor with such crusty cultural conservatives as Hu Qiaomu (p. 151), was eager to point out to the Politburo possible solutions to the mounting crisis. On April 27, having witnessed the victory of a massive student march and the reluctance of the army and security organs to deal with it, He Xin offered the leadership some sage advice. His analysis touched on the long-term causes of the protests and suggested that if the authorities did not handle the problem of the students with great care the nation would be fatally destabilized. If a low-key approach and dialogue failed, he wrote, then:

> The crisis will deepen, and the dissatisfaction and disappointment of members of all social strata will increase. . . . The achievements of the last ten years will be snatched away and China will enter an age of political uncertainty marked by constant disturbances of varying scale. This in turn will lead to the failure of the economic reform. Economic crisis will add to class antagonisms and widespread riots. Civil war, a military coup, and pop-

ular uprisings affecting China for decades to come are now far from being unthinkable.

He Xin's warning went unheeded.

When commemorating the seventieth anniversary of the May Fourth Movement of 1919, a patriotic movement which called for democracy, science, and a "new culture," the veteran writer Bing Xin, one of the "living relics" of that period (who had already added her signature to Bei Dao's open letter calling for the release of political prisoners), reminded her readers of the significance of the marble *huabiao* pillars on either side of the Tiananmen Gate. These pillars, she said, are stylized versions of the Boards of Criticism and Protest used by emperors in the mythical Golden Age to allow them to hear the complaints of the people. Again, on June 1, Children's Day, shortly before the massacre, Bing Xin wrote a simple calligraphic inscription for the youth of China: "The students love the nation, I love the students." She also commented to a *Ming Pao* reporter on the student movement, "The students can think for themselves, we can't impose our ideas on them. I'm an old woman, young people have more hope than the old." The movement had had a cathartic effect on the people of China, she said, and the broad-based support for the students had allowed for a new cohesion among the masses. Using pre-1949 Communist rhetoric, Bing Xin said of the worsening crisis in China, "This is the dark night before the dawn."

No one could have predicted how dark the night of June 3–4 would be. Amidst the brutality, the carnage, the trauma, the broken promises, and betrayed ideals lies one victim that will be mourned for years to come: the fitful but strangely burgeoning intellectual and cultural life of the nation.

We recall the spirit of Lu Xun many times in the following pages. We have said much here about protest and the shedding of blood; perhaps it would be appropriate to end this introduction with his words. On March 18, 1926, a group of unarmed citizens and students petitioned the Peking government. Forty died in the ensuing massacre. Lu Xun cried from the depth of his despair:

> If China is not to perish, then, as past history tells us, the future holds a tremendous surprise for the murderers.
> This is not the conclusion of an incident, but a new beginning.
> Lies written in ink can never disguise facts written in blood.

> Blood debts must be repaid in kind. The longer the delay, the greater the interest!

Lu Xun called March 18, 1926, the darkest day since the founding of the Republic in 1911, and the regime he was writing about fell some two years later. His comments are a fitting epitaph to the regime that committed collective suicide on June 3–4, 1989, the darkest day in the history of the People's Republic of China.

We would like to thank our publisher, Steve Wasserman of Hill and Wang, for his timely decision to reprint this book in a paperback edition, Orville Schell for writing the Foreword, Ian Buruma and Derek Davies of the *Far Eastern Economic Review*, Lawrence Macdonald of Agence France Presse, Jane Macartney of United Press International, our friend and teacher Pierre Ryckmans, and in particular Linda Jaivin, who read the manuscript and offered many useful suggestions. We are also deeply grateful to our friends in China, without whose encouragement this enterprise would have been meaningless.

Canberra–Auckland
July 1989

I: WALLS

I have always felt hemmed in on all sides by the Great Wall; that wall of ancient bricks which is constantly being reinforced. The old and the new conspire to confine us all.

When will we stop adding new bricks to the Wall?

The Great Wall of China: a wonder and a curse!

Lu Xun, 1935

There are numerous walls within the Chinese world; the Great Wall itself merely protects the Chinese against Devils from without.

Sun Longji, 1986

13 Happiness Street

Bei Dao

I

A LATE autumn morning. The street was bleak and desolate. A gust of wind rustled the withered yellow leaves on the pavement. The dreary, monotonous cry of an old woman selling ices could be heard in the distance. Fang Cheng pulled his old black woollen coat tightly around himself and kicked a stone on the ground. It wedged itself in the iron grate in the gutter with a clunk. The call from his sister just now had been really too fantastic: young Jun had been flying his kite in this street yesterday afternoon, yes, this same bloody street, when all of a sudden, he had disappeared without a trace; in broad daylight! His sister's sobs, followed by the beep signalling the line was disconnected, had upset him so much that his head was still ringing. Sun, the section head, was sitting opposite him at the time, and had given him an inquisitive glance, so he had put down the receiver and done his utmost to look normal.

Across the road, a row of locust-trees had been sawn down to the roots, the trunks lying across the pavement. A yellow Japanese forklift was parked by the side of the road. Four or five workmen were busy attaching hooks to the sawn-off trees and loading them onto a large truck to the tooting of a whistle.

Fang Cheng approached the old woman selling ices. "Such fine locust-trees, how come . . . . "

"Ices, three cents and five cents." The shrivelled mouth snapped shut.

"Comrade . . . . "

The old woman's strident voice robbed him of the courage to repeat his question. He crossed the road to the truck. A young fellow who looked like the driver was leaning against the front mudguard smoking.

"Excuse me, what's going on here?"

"Don't you have eyes in your head?"

"I mean, what are you sawing the trees down for?"

"Who do you think you are, going round poking your nose into everything? Are you building a house, and you want us to leave you a log for the roof beam? I'll tell you straight, I can't even get one for myself." Flicking away his cigarette butt, the driver turned round and climbed into the cab, slamming the door behind him.

Fang Cheng bit his lip. A middle-aged woman carrying a string bag was walking past. He caught up with her. "Excuse me, where did you get those turnips?"

"At the greengrocer's over the way."

"Oh." He smiled politely and walked with her for a few steps. "How come these trees have been cut down? Such a shame."

"Who knows? I heard that yesterday a kite got caught in the trees, and some young rascal climbed up to get it . . . . " She suddenly fell silent and hurried off nervously.

A long shadow slipped across the ground.

Fang Cheng swung around. A man wearing a leather jacket pulled a green army cap over his eyes, gave him a swift glance and walked past.

It was only then that Fang Cheng noticed the high outside wall exposed behind the stumps of the felled locust-trees. The plaster was so old that it had peeled off in places, showing the large solid bricks underneath. He took a deep breath, inhaling petrol fumes mixed with the sweet scent of locust-wood, and walked back along the wall. Before long he came upon a recess in the wall enclosing a gateway guarded by two stone lions. The red paint on the door had faded and was covered with a layer of dust, as if it hadn't been opened for a long time. On it was a very ordinary plaque with the words "13 Happiness Street", and beneath it a cream-coloured buzzer. Fang Cheng went to press it, but it wouldn't budge. On closer inspection he realized it was moulded from a single piece of plastic and was purely decorative. He stood there bewildered.

As he drew back a few paces, trying to get a clearer view of the whole gate, he bumped into an old man who happened to be passing by.

"Sorry. Excuse me, who lives here?"

He stopped short. The terror that welled up from the depths of the old man's eyes made Fang Cheng's legs go weak. The old man stumbled away, his walking stick beating an urgent and irregular rhythm as he disappeared into the distance.

A young boy walked by, absorbed in whittling a branch from one of the locust-trees with a penknife.

"Hey, where's the neighbourhood committee office, young man?"

"Turn at the lane over there," the boy sniffled, pointing with the branch.

The narrow lane twisted its way through the shoddy makeshift houses. From time to time Fang Cheng had to walk sideways in order to prevent the boards and exposed nails from catching and tearing his overcoat. At the entrance to what looked like a rather spacious court-yard at the far end of the lane two sign boards were hanging side by side: Neighbourhood Committee and Red Medical Station. Both were covered with the muddy fingerprints of children.

He pushed open the door of the room on the north side of the courtyard and stuck his head inside.

"Did you bring the certificate?" asked a girl busy knitting a jumper.

"What certificate?"

"The death certificate!" she said impatiently.

Everything in the room was white: the sheet, the folding screen, the table, the chairs, and also the girl's lab-coat and pallid face. Fang Cheng shivered. "No, no, I've . . . . "

"Listen, if we don't sign it nobody's going to let you hold the funeral service!"

"I'm looking for someone."

"Looking for someone?" She looked up in surprise, lifting her hair back with one of her knitting needles. "Don't you know what's proper?"

"But this is . . . . "

"The Red Medical Station."

Retreating into the yard, Fang Cheng noticed a dense crowd of people in the room to the south. He walked over and knocked on the door.

"Come in," a voice said.

Inside about a dozen people were seated around a long wooden table, all staring at him in silence. The light inside the room was so dim that he couldn't make out their faces, but judging from their heavy bronchial wheezing, most of them were old women.

"Has it been signed?" The question came from a woman at the far end of the table. From her voice she seemed pretty young; she'd be the chairwoman or something.

"No, I . . . . "

"Then they're still alive and breathing," she broke in sharply.

A howl of laughter. One fat old woman laughed so much she started gagging, and someone thumped her on the back.

"I'm a reporter," Fang Cheng explained hastily.

Instantly the room fell deathly silent. They gazed stupidly at each other, as if they were not too sure what he meant.

The chairwoman was the first to break the silence. "Your papers."

Fang Cheng had barely taken out his press card when it was snatched away by the person nearest the door. The card in its red plastic cover was handed round the table for everyone to look at and comment on. As it passed from hand to hand, some of them shook their heads while others spat on their fingers and rubbed it. Finally it reached the chairwoman. Gripping the card, she studied it carefully, then got the old man in glasses beside her to read it aloud. At last she gave a nod.

"Hm. Have you come to take photos?"

A buzz of excited confusion filled the room. Dull eyes flashed, people nudged and tugged at each other, and one old woman who had fallen asleep propped against the table actually woke up. It was as if something that they had been waiting a lifetime for was finally about to happen.

"You can take our picture now, we're in the middle of our political study," the chairwoman said haughtily. "Sit up everyone, and don't look into the camera!"

They all sat up straight, and there was a loud rustle as they picked up the newspapers on the table.

"Hold on, I haven't brought my camera . . . . I'm here on another matter. I'm trying to find out who lives at Number 13 Happiness Street."

"How come you never breathed a word of this earlier?" said the chairwoman, obviously quite put out.

"You didn't give me a chance . . . . "

"All right then, what do you want to know?"

"It's about Number 13 Happiness Street . . . . "

"Someone alive and kicking? That's none of our business. On your way then, and next time don't start gabbling away at us again, these old bones can't take all the excitement."

"Whose business is it?"

"Quiet! Let's get on with our meeting. Now, where were we? Oh yes, this case involving Dumb Chen from over in the Fourth Xiang-yang Courtyard. He'll live on in our hearts forever and all that, but people have started asking why he's still being issued with a face mask every winter . . . . "

"Maybe his corpse is still breathing."

"We'll issue you with a cauldron to lie in when it's your turn to go to heaven, so you won't have to straighten that hunch back of yours . . . . " A strange rasping sound came from the corner.

They started to quarrel, their voices getting louder and louder. Fang Cheng took advantage of the confusion to slip out. When he reached the gate he breathed a long sigh of relief, feeling that he had actually almost died himself.

He took a wrong turn. The buildings inside another compound were being pulled down, and clouds of dust filled the air. A crowd of children pressed around the entrance, peering inside. In the yard the workmen were chanting as they swung a wooden pole against the gable of the house to the east. A structure like a well was under construction in the middle of a stretch of rubble.

"What is this place?" Fang Cheng asked the children.

"The local housing authority," a young girl replied timidly.

Stepping over a pile of lime, Fang Cheng ran into a young fellow carrying a bucket of cement. "I'm a reporter, where is your foreman?"

"Hey, Wang . . . . "

A head popped out from a scaffold. "What is it?"

"The newspapers again."

Wang leapt down nimbly and put down his trowel, wiping his forehead and muscular neck with his sleeve. "Well, you lot are on the ball all right, it's our first go at this particular innovation . . . . "

"Innovation?"

"Sounds as if you're here about cadres doing manual labour again. Your paper's carried that news a good half dozen times already, and the only thing they ever change is my name. If you fellas keep it up it won't be long before I'll have trouble figuring out what I'm called. Take a look at this job. What'd you reckon?"

"What exactly is it?"

"A house, of course. The latest style."

"Actually, it looks like a . . . " he bit back the word "tomb".

"A blockhouse, right? But it doesn't have peep holes in the sides."

"What about windows?"

"They'll all be on the roof." Wang rubbed his hands in glee, flicking off small pellets of mud. "Ideal in case of war, keeps out robbers, protects you against both wind and cold, it's got lots of advantages. It's something we learned from our ancestors."

Our cave-dwelling ancestors, Fang Cheng smiled wryly.

"The thing is that houses like these are cheap, you can build 'em by the dozen with pre-mixed concrete. They're easier to make than chicken coops, and they're more solid than a blockhouse. If this catches on, you and me'll both be famous. For starters I'll get a new house, and sit in an armchair at the bureau office. But don't put any of that in your story. Here, take a look at the blueprints. We're in the middle of a demolition job, so the air's not too clean. Hey, Li, are you taking that shovel's pulse or what? Look lively now and bring a stool over here . . . . "

Fang Cheng felt a bit dizzy. "It's all right, I'll look these over back at the office. By the way, do you happen to know who lives at Number

13 Happiness Street?"

"Dunno, that's not our business."

"Whose is it then? Whose business *is* it to know?"

"Don't blow your top, let me think about it for a second . . . you could try asking around at the bureau, they've got a big map there, it shows everything down to the last detail."

"Good, I'll try them."

"Do us a favour while you're at it, take this blueprint with you and give it to the director. We'll get a pedicab to take you."

"No need, but thanks all the same."

"This time be sure you don't get my name wrong," Wang shouted after him.

Fang Cheng staggered out and stood in the middle of the road, staring at the sky.

II

THE SECRETARY darted out from behind the door, her heels clicking. "Director Ding will be very happy to see you, Comrade Reporter. The other seventeen directors would also like to talk to you, at your convenience of course. Director Ma would like to give you his view on the question of the revolutionary succession; Director Tian wants to give you a run down on his war record; Director Wang would like to discuss the simplification of Chinese characters . . . . "

"Which one of them is the real director of the bureau?"

"Here we make no distinction between the director and assistant directors, we simply list them all in alphabetical order."

"I'm sorry, but I'm a bit pressed for time. I'm here on another matter. Anyway, how do all the directors know I'm here?"

"They were at a board meeting together just now."

"Am I breaking it up?"

"Don't give it another thought. They've been at it for nine days already. They were only too glad to take a break."

The director's office was thick with smoke. A pudgy old man with a healthy-looking complexion standing beside the conference table extended his hand to Fang Cheng with a broad smile. "Welcome, have a seat. Look at all this smoke, it's a form of collective murder . . . . "

"What?"

He waved his arms around in the air in an attempt to disperse the clouds of smoke. "The fact that I'm an optimist has been my salvation, let me tell you. Have you heard of a medicine called 'Anliben'?"

"No."

"It's a miracle drug used overseas for people with heart trouble. Does your paper ever send you abroad?"

"The chances are pretty slim."

"Then could you ask someone to help me get some?"

"I'll see what I can do. Do you have heart trouble?"

The director immediately looked glum. "I'm an old man, getting past it. Who knows, maybe the next time you come it'll be Director Ma sitting in this seat . . . . " He cleared his throat. "But let's get back to the matter in hand. Major political campaigns bring about major changes, and major changes promote further political campaigns. In the current quarter we've completed 158% of our work plan; compared with the same period last year . . . . "

"Excuse me, Director Ding, I haven't come here on a story."

"Oh?"

"I want to make some enquiries about a house. Who lives at Number 13 Happiness Street?"

Beads of sweat appeared on Ding's shiny red face. He pulled out a handkerchief and wiped his face. "You're not trying to trick me with some difficult question, are you? A big city like this, how could I know every house on every street by heart, like a production chart?"

"I heard that you've got a big map here . . . . "

"Yes, yes, I almost forgot." Groping for a small bottle in his pocket, he poured out a few pills and popped them into his mouth. "What do you think of the chicken-blood cure?"

"I haven't tried it."

He pressed a button on his desk and the red curtains on the wall parted slowly. He picked up a pointer, whipped the air with it energetically, and went up to the map. "How about the arm-swinging cure?"

"I'm sure it helps."

"Yes, it's very effective. Happiness Street . . . Number 30 . . . ah, a coal depot."

"I'm after Number 13."

"13 . . . 13 . . . come and see for yourself, my friend."

It was a blank space.

"How come it's not marked?" Fang Cheng asked in surprise.

Director Ding patted him on the shoulder. "Look carefully, there are quite a lot of blank spots on this map. No one knows what these places are."

"No one knows?"

"Nothing to be surprised about. It's just like all the blank spots in our knowledge of medicine."

"Not even the Public Security Bureau people?"

"Why don't you go and see for yourself, we open out onto their back door; it's very handy. What do you think of gadgets like pacemakers, are they reliable?"

"Pacemakers? I don't know much about them." Fang Cheng felt around in his pockets and fished out the blueprint. "This morning I went to the local housing authority and Wang, the foreman, asked me to give this to you. It's the innovation they've been working on."

"That fellow's too active for his own good. He's like a bloody magician, always coming up with some new gimmick. There's still a lot of major business here we haven't had time to get round to yet." Ding frowned, rolled up the blueprint and threw it into a wastepaper basket in the corner. "It's thanks to people like him that there's never a moment's peace and quiet anywhere."

The secretary appeared at the door.

"A message for all directors. The meeting is about to resume."

Fang Cheng showed his press card to the guard standing at the opening in the iron fence which surrounded the Public Security Bureau. "I want to see the director of the bureau."

"Interrogation Room I."

"Uh?"

"Up the stairs, first door on the right."

"I'm a reporter."

The guard looked at him blankly, not bothering to reply.

Fang Cheng went up the stairs, and with the help of the faint light in the corridor found a door with a brass plaque nailed to it: Interrogation Room I. He knocked. No one answered so he pushed the door open and went in. It was sumptuously furnished, with a red carpet on the floor and some leather chairs set around a tea table. It was not in the least like an interrogation room. He heaved a sigh of relief and sat down.

Suddenly three or four policemen came in through a small side door escorting a man in a grey Mao suit. The man was of medium height, and his swarthy face was like an iron mask, cold and stern. A policeman wearing spectacles moved to his side and whispered something in his ear. He nodded.

"This is Director Liu," Spectacles said by way of introduction.

"Please be seated." The director's voice was deep and harsh. He and Spectacles moved to the chairs opposite and sat down. The other policemen stood at either side of them.

"Director Liu, there's something I would like to ask you," said Fang Cheng.

"Just a moment, first I've got a question for you." After a moment's pause, Liu proceeded. "If I gave you five matches to make a square, how would you do it?"

Fang Cheng stared at him in astonishment.

"Now, don't be nervous."

"I'm not nervous." He thought hard, but his mind was a complete blank.

Suddenly, Liu gave a harsh laugh, and turned smugly towards Spectacles. "This is typical of ideological criminals, they always try and find a way to use the extra match. Ordinary criminals are another case altogether . . . . "

"You have a thorough grasp of the psychology of the criminal mind," offered Spectacles obsequiously.

"This is an outrage!" Fang Cheng protested.

"Don't get excited, young man, and don't interrupt me when I'm talking." Liu turned to Spectacles again. "The important thing to note here is that by using psychological tactics you can force the criminal's thinking into a very small space, or shall we say a surface, where he can't possibly conceal himself, and then he's easily overwhelmed. Do you see what I am saying?"

Spectacles nodded. "But . . . but how can you tell he's a criminal? From the look in his eyes?"

"No, no, that's all out-of-date. Ideological criminals can easily disguise their expressions. Listen, everyone you confront is a criminal, and don't you ever forget it."

"Everyone?"

"Yes. That's what class struggle is all about."

"But . . . then . . . that's . . . " Spectacles spluttered.

"All right, you ask too many questions, I have no alternative but to put you down as ideologically suspect." Rudely cutting Spectacles short, Liu turned and looked sternly at Fang Cheng. "State your business, young man."

"I . . . I want to make an enquiry about a house."

"Good, go on."

"Who lives at Number 13 Happiness Street?"

Director Liu froze, but in an instant a barely perceptible smile appeared on his lips. Spectacles, still looking crest-fallen, opened his briefcase and took out some paper, ready to take notes. The two policemen stood next to Fang Cheng. The atmosphere in the room became tense.

"Your name?" Liu asked sharply.

"Fang Cheng."

"Age?"

"What do you take me for? I'm a reporter."

"Hand over your papers."

Fang Cheng drew out his press card and passed it to one of the policemen at his side.

"Examine it and take his fingerprints. Also, find his file and check his ideological status," ordered the director.

"What am I being accused of?"

"Prying into state secrets."

"Is Number 13 Happiness Street a state secret?"

"Whatever no one knows is a secret."

"Including you? You mean, you don't know either?"

"Me? There's a certain continuity to your case, you won't even co-operate during interrogation."

Fang Cheng sighed.

"Next question . . . . "

Towards evening, Fang Cheng was released.

III

THE MUNICIPAL library was empty except for the faint but pervasive odour of mould. Fang Cheng leafed through the catalogue, finally locating the book: *A Study of Grave-Robbing Techniques Through the Ages*. He noted down the call number and rushed upstairs to the reading room.

A middle-aged woman with prominent cheek-bones standing behind the desk looked at the slip and then studied him. "Are you an archaeologist?"

"No, I'm a reporter."

"Are you planning to visit some tombs for a story?" she said half-jokingly.

"I want to uncover some secrets."

"What secrets can you possibly find in this book?"

"A place where life has ended can still contain all kinds of secrets."

"Doesn't anyone know what they are?"

"No, because even the living have become part of the secret."

"What?"

"No one knows anyone; no one understands anyone."

The woman with high cheekbones stared at him. "Good heavens, you must be mad."

"It's not me who's mad, it's heaven."

She turned away and ignored him after that. Nearly an hour later he heard the clickety-clack of the book trolley, and the book landed on the desk, raising a cloud of dust. Putting it under his arm, Fang Cheng went into the reading room and sat down at an empty desk in a corner. He leafed through the book, taking notes from time to time.

A pale square of sunlight moved slowly across the table. Fang Cheng stretched and looked at his watch. It was getting late. Before long he found himself surrounded by other readers. Strange, they were all concealing their faces behind thick books. Looking more carefully, Fang Cheng shuddered. They were all reading the same book: *A Study of Grave-Robbing Techniques Through the Ages*. He broke into a sweat, and stirred uneasily in his seat.

As he slipped out of the library he was aware of a shadowy figure following closely behind. He went into a small lane and then suddenly

turned back. The man didn't have time to conceal himself and they met
head-on: it was the fellow in the leather jacket he had bumped into the
previous morning in Happiness Street. As soon as he emerged from the
lane, Fang Cheng made a dash for a trolley bus at a nearby stop. He
jumped on board, and the doors closed behind him with a squeal.

When he got off the bus he looked around anxiously and only
relaxed when he felt sure he had not been followed. He thrust his hands
into his overcoat pockets and did his best to regain his self-confidence
and courage.

At a crossing a boy ran past flying a kite. The string in his hand
was taut and the kite danced in the air. A high place, of course! Jun had
disappeared while he was flying a kite. It must have been because he
had seen something from a high place. What an idiot I've been, he
thought, why didn't I think of that earlier? How awful, he'd almost let
himself be suffocated like a rat trapped in a hole.

He bought a pair of high-power binoculars at a second-hand store
and set off in the direction of Happiness Street, working his way
towards his target through a maze of lanes and alleyways. Finally he
saw a tall chimney towering alone in a stretch of vacant ground, surrounded on all sides by broken bricks and rubbish.

He made for the boiler-room at the foot of the chimney. A wizen-
ed old man was stoking the boiler as an airblower droned in the background. His tattered sweat-stained work clothes were held together at
the waist and swung back and forth in time with his monotonous movements.

"Can I interrupt you for a minute!" Fang Cheng called out.

The old man slowly straightened himself, turned his long, skinny
body and walked over to the doorway. His face was covered with coal
dust and ashes.

"Who're you looking for?" he asked.

"I wonder if you could tell me where this leads to?"

"Heaven."

"No, what I mean is who's the fire for?"

"How should I know. They pay me, I do the work, that's the way
it is."

"If they pay you, there must be some evidence for it."

"Ah, yes. Now where's my pay slip got to?" he said, patting himself up and down. "Must've used it to roll a cigarette."

"What was written on it?"

"Let me think . . . seems it might have run something like this: 'Burn enough to make a thousand black clouds.' Hah!" The old man grinned, baring his teeth. Against his grimy face his broken and uneven teeth seemed extremely white.

Fang Cheng took off his black woollen overcoat. "Can I trouble you to keep an eye on this for me. I'm going up to take a look."

"You don't want to leave a note for your family?"

"What?"

"You're the twelfth so far. Just yesterday a girl jumped . . . . "

Illustrations from Shanxi wenxue

The old man went back to stoking the boiler. Tongues of flame shot forth.

Fang Cheng gazed up at the chimney, which seemed to lean slightly. He went to the foot of the iron ladder and started climbing. The houses grew smaller and smaller and it got so windy that his clothes flapped around him. When he reached the last rung, he steadied himself. Hooking one arm through the ladder, he turned around and began to survey the scene with his binoculars. Rooftops, date trees, courtyard walls . . . all came clearly into view. Suddenly he stiffened, and the hand holding the binoculars began shaking. He couldn't believe his eyes. Finally he managed to collect his thoughts and refocus the lenses. He searched carefully in every corner, but didn't see even a single blade of grass.

"Oh bloody hell . . . " he muttered to himself.

As his feet touched ground he heard someone calling out sharply behind him, "Don't move. Where do you think you're going now?" Not at all surprised, he brushed the dust off his clothes and turned around. The man in the leather jacket gave him a shove, and they walked towards a jeep parked some distance away.

Twisting his head, Fang Cheng saw the old man stoking the boiler while thick smoke continued to billow out of the tall chimney.

"Black clouds," he said.

IV

FANG CHENG was sent to the lunatic asylum.

When he looked at the people running in circles around the desolate grounds and the outside wall covered with weeds, he finally understood: so now he too was inside the wall.

Bei Dao (real name Zhao Zhenkai) is a young poet and writer of fiction from Peking. He was one of the founding editors of the unofficial magazine Today, *which was published during the period of the Democracy Movement. He is one of the most widely respected new writers—not with the establishment, but with younger readers, especially students.*

A Nihilistic Trend

Solitude, anxiety, depression, pain, despair, cruelty . . . these are not just isolated psychological elements; they are the key-note that runs through the whole story, and a telltale sign of the author's ideological inclination. This gloomy and pessimistic tone is precisely the literary reflection of the nihilistic trend rampant in our society. It arises from weariness with the strain of the prolonged class-struggle, from disillusionment with revolutionary ideals. This trend denies the rationality of the realistic life order. True, the critical attitude of this trend toward the ultraleftist line (and toward the reality of the "evils" created by that line) has its progressive side; but it does not guide people on to the correct Marxist road. Instead, blindly and without restraint, it seeks free development of individual character, and rejects without exception anything which does not accord with or hampers this development. This trend seeks rational humanism, it strives for "true human worth", it calls upon men to confront an absurd reality. It is true that its opposition to the fascist brutality of the Gang of Four, its endeavour to restore sincere relationships between people, are not without their positive side. But to set universal compassion, human nature and humanism against the Marxist world view is without question erroneous. This kind of philosophy is incompatible with our revolutionary-realistic literature, with our ideal of a socialist literature whose guiding ideology is the Marxist world view. Revolutionary realism requires the writer to bring to light social contradictions; at the same time it requires him to suffuse life with a glow of idealistic glory. It forbids him to lead the reader to pessimism and despair.

This is not an isolated literary phenomenon. Its appearance reminds me of the existentialist trend in philosophy and literature following the Second World War. I am not saying that we already have an influential school of existentialist literature in China. But among young people interested in literature there are some who are influenced by the existentialist trend in thought and literature, and who have produced works permeated with this thought . . . .

A common characteristic of these works is that they take as their guiding ideology the philosophy that reality is absurd and man is free; they adopt a nihilistic attitude toward the objective world and stand for the perfection of man's spiritual nature, attempting to substitute universal human nature and humanism for the Marxist world view.

from the critique of Bei Dao's novel *Waves*,
in *Literary Gazette*, April 1981

The Wall

Shu Ting

I have no means to resist the wall,
Only the will.

What am I? And it?
Perhaps it is
My slowly aging skin,
Numb to wind and sleet
Impervious to orchid fragrance.
Or I am just a plantain,
A pretty
Parasite lodged in one of its crevices,
My fortuity determining its necessity.

At night the wall begins to move
Stretching a soft imaginary foot,
Squeezes,
Twists me,
Forces me into a variety of shapes.
Terrified, I flee to the street,
To find the same nightmare
Hanging on every heel,
Each cowering gaze
An ice-cold wall.

Finally I know
What I have to resist first:
My compromise with walls, my
Insecurity with this world.

1982

Shu Ting is a young poet from Xiamen in Fujian Province. She was originally one of the group of poets writing (together with Bei Dao) for the magazine Today, *and her lyrics won her a large following for their very feminine intensity and sensitivity. Some readers see her as having been co-opted over the past five years by the cultural and political establishment.*

Black Walls

Liu Xinwu

Time: About 7:30 one Sunday morning in summer.
Place: A small courtyard in a Peking alley. A few trees growing in the yard; five or six families in residence.

A MAN BY the name of Zhou had a room to himself on the eastern side of the courtyard. He wasn't a day under thirty; was most probably a bachelor, though he used one of those wash basins with a double-happiness design in red on it. Strange that—maybe he was divorced. Then why did he bow his head bashfully whenever he met one of the unmarried lasses in the courtyard, and do his best to avoid them?

Zhou hadn't been living in the courtyard long. He worked in one of those places with an unpronounceable name. None of the other residents could figure out what he did for a living. That didn't really matter; anyway, you could work out his story yourself: a man of his age with eight years in the countryside behind him and over seven years of work experience—it wasn't hard to get a pretty clear idea of the type of money he was making and what other perks he enjoyed. All in all it was fairly standard stuff. He hadn't caused any trouble since he'd been living there, nor was he much of a one for dropping in on neighbours. If you bumped into him in the courtyard you might take the initiative by asking, "Eaten yet?" but he'd be sure to reply "Yes, thanks," without a hint of emotion. Or maybe he'd be the first to speak: "Having a rest then?" "That's right, thought I'd sit out here for a spell." Then he'd walk straight on without attempting to stop for a chat.

There were times you'd have a chance of drawing him out a bit, though. In a courtyard like that everyone uses the communal tap for washing clothes, to get drinking water and to rinse the rice for meals. You were always coming across your neighbours at the tap; he'd be there as well. He couldn't very well avoid being sociable on such occasions. But he was no great conversationalist, and even though he'd answer when spoken to, he never asked any questions in return. You couldn't really say the neighbours had warmed to him; but they had nothing against him, either.

Zhou was working up a storm this particular morning. It started when he moved all his things out into the courtyard. Then he set to work mixing some stuff in a large basin. He must have borrowed a spray-gun the day before—one of those gadgets you pump with your foot. It looked as though he was going to repaint his room.

Nothing strange about that. When one of the neighbours went over to the tap he inquired, "You going to paint your room?" "Just a quick spray," he offered in reply. The other man did his best to be neighbourly. "Need a hand?" "No, thanks, I've got a spray-gun. Have it done in no time." And they went about their business happily.

A cicada hidden up in the foliage of the scholar tree started singing and the song was taken up by its fellows one after the other. Everyone was used to the racket, so no one got annoyed.

About 7:46.

"Pshhh—pshhh—pshhh—"
Now that was an unfamiliar sound. It didn't take much guessing to figure out what it was: Zhou had started painting.

A few of the young people living in the courtyard were going out as it was their day off. They were all dressed up.

One girl who spent her days selling meat had decked herself out in imitation jewelled ear-rings and marched forth in a pair of cream coloured high heels. Her automatic nylon umbrella with a floral pattern in blue burst open the moment she stepped into the street.

The young fellow who worked in a foundry was sporting a jersey he'd got a hold of somewhere with the legend "Indiana University, USA" printed on it. He was wearing a pair of corduroys made for a safari suit—the type of trousers produced for export that had been sold on the domestic market. He put on a pair of tinted sunglasses with extra large lenses before pushing his fashionable small-wheeled bicycle out the gate.

Then there was the girl who was studying business management at a branch college. She was done up in a pale green skirt that she'd made herself—one that didn't bunch up at the waist. She hurried out carrying a large round straw bag.

What happened then was only possible because they had gone out. But then again it's hard to say whether things would have been any different even if they had stayed at home. That's because one youngster did stay in that day. He sold glassware at a local market and it was his day off too. After breakfast he propped himself up on his bed and lost himself in "The Unlighted Lamp". Later, when his mother tried to get him to take part in the morning's drama, he fobbed her off with a scornful laugh and went on reading.

About a quarter past eight.

The atmosphere in the courtyard was growing tense, though it would be more correct to say, "the atmosphere indoors"—and in one door in particular. It was the Zhaos' apartment on the northern side of the yard.

Zhao was a man of fifty-six. He'd chosen early retirement so his daughter could take his place in the factory—to "carry on the revolution" as it was called. He'd found temporary employment elsewhere, but when they upgraded the production line at this new place, he was retrenched. Although old Zhao was at a loose end for the moment, he was figuring on landing himself another job soon.

It was only natural that the neighbours had congregated in his place. They'd all come to tell Zhao that young Zhou was painting his walls with black paint, not white. He was going to paint his room black of all things! Now, don't ask what he'd put in the concoction he was using; looked like ink, and it was as dark as pitch.

Apart from the initial shock caused by this sensational news, Zhao felt a deep sense of satisfaction that they'd come to him first. It was ten years ago that he'd been sent to a local performing arts ensemble as an adjunct to a Mao Zedong Thought Worker's Propaganda Team. How well he remembered the conspiratorial glee of the "political activists" who'd come to him to report on the "latest developments in class struggle" amongst their fellow artists.

His wife, who was known to everyone as Aunty Zhao, was lost in a similar reverie. To think it was only eight years since she'd been in charge of this "socialist courtyard". This morning was like old times; in fact, just like the time the neighbours had come to report they'd found the remains of a "reactionary slogan" pasted up on the base of the wall behind the date tree. Memories of events buried in the dead ashes of the past suddenly flickered to life.

"We're not going to put up with that." Zhao took a firm stand from the start.

"What can he be thinking of?" Aunty Zhao chorused angrily.

8:25, or thereabouts. Meanwhile—

"Pshhh—pshhh—pshhh—"

Zhou worked on, unaware of the mounting furore.

News update: HE'S PAINTING HIS CEILING BLACK!

Zhao invited his guests to sit down—it was as though they were going to have a study meeting. Meetings always leave someone dissatisfied; but this wasn't going to be one of those meetings that bores everyone silly. In fact, it was just the type of meeting that Zhao liked most of all. He took the initiative.

"This calls for immediate action. Let's report him to the police."

Eight or ten years ago this would have been more than enough to set the tone of the proceedings. But things had changed. Weedy Uncle Qian made an objection without a moment's hesitation.

"Listen, I don't think we should be so hasty . . . . After all, he hasn't done anything illegal."

Old Zhao and his wife stared at him in amazement. You're nothing but an old tailor—they thought in unison. Back in the days when we had you pegged as a petty exploiter you wouldn't have dared talk back like that. Now look at you: just because you make a bit of money by taking in work and sit watching your new colour TV, you think you can speak to us like that!

Damned right he did, sitting there bolt upright on his stool saying exactly what he thought of the matter and at length. He was of the opinion that young Zhou was ailing . . . . I mean it's been in all the papers: a person gets all excited over something and before long they start doing odd things. Just last week I saw Zhou airing his quilt outside his place—none of you others probably noticed—a quilt, mind you, with its outer layer made of red satin. Not all that strange, you may say; but wait for it: the underside was bright red as well! You can't tell me that isn't mighty wacky. So I'm saying it's not the police we should be thinking about: what we need is a doctor. Look, there's a retired doctor of Chinese medicine just down the street. Now I'm not sure he's the type of doctor who could cure Zhou of what he's got, but it'd do no harm if we got him to take a look.

There wasn't much of a reaction to Qian's suggestion, for while he was speaking everyone had been gazing out the window. Through the shade of the scholar tree they could see Zhou working away on his walls blissfully unaware of their concern. He appeared to be singing to himself, and he certainly didn't look sick to them.

The man sitting next to the door scratched his balding pate which was meagrely camouflaged by strands of straggly hair. This was teacher Sun and he had a suggestion of his own to make:

"Well, I think we should go and ask him straight out why he's painting his room black, and if he can't explain himself we'll make him stop—no, persuade him to cease and desist. Yes, that's it, we'll talk him out of it and tell him he shouldn't do it any more."

Mrs Li, who was conveniently seated at the back of the room, immediately took him up on the idea:

"You're right. You can act as our spokesman."

The others readily agreed.

It was past 8:36.

When he had spoken out, Sun naturally assumed that one of the Zhaos would be sent to confront Zhou, so this new development took him completely by surprise. He could have kicked himself for having sat next to the door.

Sun had never taught a class in his thirty years at the primary school. He was in administration. Certainly, he'd been given endless exposure to the finer points of pedantic verbal acrobatics, but now that he had been pushed to the front of the class, he was at a loss as to how he should deal with the situation. He sat facing the others tongue-tied.

8:37.

"Pshhh—pshhh—pshhh—" Meanwhile, the painting continued unabated.

The room back on this side of the courtyard was buzzing with a tense and whispered discussion.

Sun was tapping the fingernail of his left thumb mechanically and staring dumbly at the tip of his shoes. He was against confronting Zhou in person. What if he sent him packing? It would be such a loss of face. And how would he explain it to the others? What'd he do if the young brute gave him a browbeating? How would that look? And would he tell the others the truth about it? But that would be tantamount to informing on the man. Should he try and conceal the truth? Yet if he did so, wouldn't he be guilty of deceiving the authorities? On the other hand, there wouldn't be any witnesses, and when they finally got around to reinvestigating the incident nobody would be able to prove anything . . . .

After some moments of soul-searching, which left his brow glistening with large beads of sweat, Sun finally spoke again.

"I still think Old Zhao should be the one to go and ask what he's playing at."

The others immediately followed suit.

"Yes, Zhao, why don't you go and be done with it."

The old worker didn't move a muscle. Finally, when the tenor of public opinion had abandoned casual suggestion in favour of earnest supplication, Zhao jumped to his feet with the words, "Very well, I'll go," after which he stomped out of the room.

He was followed up to the entrance of Zhou's place by the intense gaze of the other residents. They strained themselves in the hope of catching some stray hint of the exchange, but all they could hear was the unbroken staccato of the cicadas.

8:41.

Zhao returned to the room ashen-faced only to report:

"The nerve of the man. Says he'll come over and explain when he's finished. I knew he'd try something like this. Do you think he gives a damn about any of his neighbours?"

His wife added to the drama of the moment by pointing out the window and crying furiously:

"Now look what's happened. Here's the man who checks the water gauge. See, he's gawking at Zhou's place. Before you know it people outside will be talking about this, mark my word; and they won't be saying that one oddball decided to paint his walls black. They'll be saying our courtyard is the one with the black walls. We'll be tarred with the same brush."

Mrs Li was employed in a workshop where they teased cotton padding. She was a fairly reasonable character and she now ventured an explanation of Zhou's actions that she hoped would calm everyone down:

"Maybe he's only using the black paint as a base coat, and he's going to paint over it with white anyway."

8:43.

"Pshhh—pshhh—pshhh—" The spraying continued and from a distance the room already looked like a black hole. Nobody had taken any notice of her; Mrs Li shot a glance at the other side of the courtyard and her heart sank.

What were you supposed to make of the man? Okay, so he was only painting his place black, but everyone in the courtyard was going to have to live with it. He obviously hadn't given the matter a second thought; but he had no right to involve innocent bystanders.

8:45.

Everyone in the room could agree on one thing: Zhou shouldn't have been painting his room black. How could he do this to them: the walls, the ceiling, everything black? No normal person would have done such a thing. But there he was actually doing it. He was odd, weird, possessed . . . . It was insane; no, it was downright reactionary . . . .

Zhao still felt that reporting him to the police was the right thing to do. Only he didn't feel quite the same way about the police as he used to, so he was reluctant to go. Ten years or so ago the police station had been converted into the headquarters of the local "Steering Committee for Smashing the Reactionary Public Security and Legal Apparatus". At the time, there weren't any real police stations to speak of. The police nowadays lacked the blood-lust of the past, and they were no longer willing to take the initiative. All that nonsense they fed you about "working within official guidelines"—as soon as they gave you that spiel you could be sure they wouldn't take any positive action.

In fact, they probably wouldn't do a thing about the black walls. And this is why Zhao hesitated. He still felt an irrepressible urge to make a report, and to do it immediately. It was his responsibility and duty to do so. He wasn't doing this for himself. What could he possibly get out of reporting such a thing?

Aunty Zhao could see her husband was in a quandary and her heart went out to him. How things had changed for them during the past decade. Her old man had fallen on hard times, all because he didn't have a legitimate trade to speak of. He was kept running from pillar to post looking for casual work, taking jobs as a watchman in warehouses, and so on. But none of these jobs lasted very long. It wasn't that he had no trade to call his own in the past, but they kept encouraging him to get involved in political movements. And with all that "moving" back and forth over the last thirty years, he hadn't had the time to acquire a trade. In the present set-up, that meant he had no way of making money. He had been justifiably proud of his political acumen in the past, not that it did him much good now. He was trying to bring his considerable professional talents to bear on the present case, but his eyes, his deeply lined face and his mouth betrayed his many doubts. It was such a pity. Why should he get so worked up about it? It wasn't as though he was going to get anything out of it for himself.

Qian, on the other hand, was more convinced than ever that young Zhou was ill. It was no use getting a doctor of Chinese medicine —Zhou wouldn't let him get close enough to take his pulse. So that was out. They needed a doctor trained in western medicine. But as hospitals never let doctors make home calls any more, they'd have to convince him to go in for a check-up. That might prove difficult.

Mrs Li felt like going back to her place and dragging that no-good boy of hers away from the book he had his head buried in, to get him to think of something. Maybe he could make Zhou stop this silliness. Then they could repaint his place white together. White was such a lovely colour. How could the walls of a house be anything but white?

Teacher Sun was thinking of slipping off home, but he was too scared to move. He had to be careful to show the right attitude in this matter, so that if the incident was investigated in the future he wouldn't come out looking like a person of confused loyalties. By the same token, when it was Zhou's turn to be vindicated for his actions,

Sun didn't want to appear as a man who had taken an active part against him. Ideally he wanted to avoid any form of criticism for any past, present, and future actions. At the moment he felt he'd fulfilled his obligations adequately by his mere presence in Zhao's house, and now it was time to be going. The hard thing was slipping away without causing any raised eyebrows.

8:48.

Zhao had a ten-year-old grandson everyone called Little Button. At first he'd sat through all the fuss with his head lowered over his drawings. After a time he went and sat next to the door leading to the outer room, listening to the discussion intently. To him the room felt cramped and stuffy. He couldn't understand why grown-ups enjoyed being so uncomfortable.

They all started talking again, and just as the discussion was entering a new and heated phase, Little Button walked over to his grandfather, looked up at him and asked:

"Grandad, what are you all talking about?"

"Run along and play. This is grown-ups' talk," Zhao snapped sternly.

But Little Button wasn't deterred.

"I know you're all angry with Uncle Zhou for painting his walls. You don't know him; he's really nice, he's fun to play with. Once he called me into his room and showed me a pile of cardboard pieces. They were as big as the evening paper, and all different colours. He showed them to me one after the other, holding them right up close to my eyes so all I could see was the colour. Then he asked me lots of questions: 'Do you like this one or not? Does it make you feel hot or cold? Wet or dry? Does it smell or not? Does it make you feel like going to sleep or going out to play? What does this one make you think of—or doesn't it make you think of anything? Does this one make you feel scared or not? Does this one make you feel thirsty? Do you want to keep looking at it or not?' He wrote down everything I said in a little book. He's great fun, really. If you don't believe me, just go and see for yourselves."

With this memory still fresh in his mind, Little Button looked up at his grandfather and shouted:

"Grandad, you've been talking for ages now. You must be tired, why don't you let me have a go?"

Everyone in the room suddenly fell silent and looked over at the boy. Zhao waved his hand impatiently.

"All right then, go ahead."

Little Button asked them all:

"Is Uncle Zhou going to come and paint all of our houses when he's finished his?"

8:49.

The question left them all speechless for a moment.

8:50.

"He wouldn't dare," Zhao spluttered.

"Just let him try," chipped in his wife.

Li and Sun cried in unison, "Certainly not!"

Uncle Qian thought for a moment before responding:

"No, his illness isn't that serious. From what I can tell he'll restrict himself to his own house . . . . "

8:51.

Little Button shrugged his shoulders and blinked in amazement. The pupils of his eyes were even darker than Zhou's black walls and they sparkled brilliantly. He laughed innocently and cried:

"There's nothing to worry about then. Uncle Zhou is painting *his* walls, not ours. So why are you all sitting here talking about him?"

8:52.

There was complete silence in the room.

"Pshhh—pshhh—pshhh—" The sound of spraying continued to issue from Zhou's room. Accompanied by the song of the cicadas, it was crisp and clear.

Summer 1982, Peking

Dredging Up Black Walls

According to a reviewer in the April 1983 issue of Literary Gazette, *the authoritative Party journal of literary criticism, Liu Xinwu was going along very nicely producing inoffensive and timely short stories; and no one had forgotten his sterling effort in writing "Class Counsellor". But recently things had gone very wrong indeed. Liu had earlier declared he was going "to plumb the very depths of literary creation". "Unfortunately," the reviewer comments, "all he has dredged up is 'Black Walls'."*

"Let's have a look at what 'Black Walls' is all about," the despondent critic continues. "A certain fellow by the name of Zhou—a man recognized as being a little 'odd'—paints the walls and ceiling of his apartment black without providing the slightest explanation. An egotistical 'indulgence' of this nature can hardly be seen as normal or acceptable; and since there is no elucidation of the significance or use of such a black room (certainly none is offered in the story), we must assume that this behaviour is 'abnormal'. Confronted by this situation the characters in the story react in various ways . . . the problem, however, is that the author . . . regards the 'abnormal' as 'normal', and is critical of the attempted suppression of Zhou's desire to express his quirky individuality . . . .

"Everyone in the courtyard except Zhou and a ten year-old boy . . . is depicted as bogged down in a mire of primitive ignorance and extreme 'leftist' thinking . . . . The author depicts the contradiction [between Zhou and his neighbours] as one that is so intense as to be virtually unreconcilable. In so doing he has revealed that he lacks a firm basis in life, and that he is out of step with the world around him. He has created a fraudulent set of characters and an exaggerated mise-en-scène in order to express ideas that are neither new nor of any profundity . . . . the work is shallow and flat."

On a lighter note, the Western reader may wish to compare Liu's story with Sue Townsend's The Secret Diary of Adrian Mole aged 13¾, *in which the angst-ridden adolescent decides to paint the Noddy wallpaper in his room black, a symbolic exorcism (no doubt) of the maudlin petit-bourgeois aesthetic forced on him by his uncaring and immoral parents . . . .*

The Deep Structure of Chinese Culture

Sun Longji

Sun Longji was educated in Hong Kong, Taiwan and the United States. His book, which grew out of a series of newspaper articles, was first published in Hong Kong in 1983. It has been reprinted many times, and is a widely read and much discussed work. Copies of it are in great demand amongst the Mainland intelligentsia, even though it is officially "unavailable". The short extracts in this and subsequent chapters (the book is referred to hereafter as Deep Structure*) represent only a fraction of this extremely thought-provoking study of the underlying traits of Chinese culture.*

MY CRITIQUE of Chinese culture, as embodied in my book *The Deep Structure of Chinese Culture*, grew out of my disenchantment with the "leftist" patriotic movement among Hong Kong and Taiwan students studying in the States in the 1970s. Comparisons with their contemporary "radical" counterparts among American and Third World students tended to cast them in an unfavourable light in my eyes. In spite of their radical rhetoric, they were closed in upon themselves, small-minded, and occasionally gave in to cowardice (e.g. not wishing to be identified for what they stood for). What disturbed me most was the overt aversion of such groups toward a full-blown genitality on the part of the individual, and toward the concomitant value of privacy, as well as their penchant for "oral indulgence" (e.g. "eating" was not only regarded as the main sensuous gratification for adults, it was often viewed as a form of "political" activity). For me, the anticlimactic turn of events in post-Mao China was the last straw . . . .

From 1980-1981 I had the opportunity to observe life in Mainland China for the very first time while doing field work there. It struck me as not being simply economically backward (which is excusable), but as generally depressing in terms of "individual" values. To declare that Orientals are more "collectivist" than Westerners is not a very profound discovery. My thesis is that this "collectivism" leads to the "disorganization of Self", and to the detriment of any genuine communal spirit. It leads to dependency and indulgence on the part of the individual, to the extent that people come to rely on the "public" to "clean up" their bodily excretions (snivel, phlegm, litter). Paradoxically, "collectivism" tends to "under-socialize" the Chinese people, with the result that a "civil" or even "civilized" state exists only among a small group of "cooked persons" *(shuren)*, while towards the "raw persons" *(shengren)* at large a state of war exists. There are numerous walls within the Chinese world; the Great Wall itself merely protects the Chinese against Devils from without.

Now, an important point in my book is *not* to lay the blame (or, at least, not the entire blame) for all this at the doorstep of the Communists. What "deep structure" implies is something "deeper" than political or even social causation. It is the enmeshing network of the totality of Chinese cultural "facts" that has added up to this state of affairs. In my book, I arrange these "facts" into a salient "structure".

This "deep structure" is not just to be found in Mainland China or Taiwan. It is no less pronounced in Hong Kong and in Overseas Chinese communities. And yet it seems that when given a chance, the Chinese are hard-working and well-organized and ostensibly less "indulgent" than Westerners, as is evident in capitalistic Chinese communities outside of China. This may be so. But it does not vitiate my argument that the Chinese "individual" is organized and motivated by the "other" (if not the "nation" then the "family"). The Chinese "individual" *per se* does not possess the capability to "unfold" his own potentialities fully, to give himself a willed shape. Even in a so called "free" environment like Hong Kong, I find individual development skewed, and more often than not in a "somatized" direction. Such an individual may look after his own interests very well and, within the framework of Chinese social obligations, may even be indulgent towards others, but nonetheless he is unaware of himself as having a "purpose", and in all likelihood regards himself as an instrument of others. I believe the archetypal model for this kind of interdependence to be Chinese generational relationships. They generate a kind of human being who is not fully aware of the fact that he belongs first to himself, and only then to the world at large; he tends to become the private property of the "family" and its surrogates, thus giving rise to a kind of "selfless" selfishness.

My book also turned out to be a personal catharsis. The writing of it helped me to outgrow my own cultural heritage. It helped me to unlearn what had been inculcated in me, and my personal experience became a public statement.

from a letter dated February 10, 1986

The Network of Sodality

IN CHINESE CULTURE, a man is defined in terms of a bilateral relationship. This relationship is a matter of Sodality [a word chosen as a somewhat artificial translation for the Chinese *renqing*, which literally means "human feelings", but has become a shorthand for the entire network of favours and obligations surrounding Chinese relationships]. But a Chinese will only share this Sodality with his acquaintance—the members of his social circle. We may say that from birth, a Chinese person is enclosed by a network of interpersonal relationships which defines and organizes his existence, which controls his Heart-and-Mind. When a Chinese individual is not under the control of the Heart-and-Mind of others, he will become the most selfish of men and bring chaos both to himself and to those around him. And yet when the definition of his Sodality is extended to the entire community, he is capable of being the most unselfish of men.

The delicate Chinese individual needs to be nurtured by his inner circle of acquaintance. A man may be gentle, humble and obedient towards his acquaintance, but once outside this circle, he may become abrupt and uncontrollable. Because of this, a Chinese will only do business with a man "of his circle", and if this relationship has not yet been established, he will endeavour to draw the other party into the circle before starting to do business with him. The relationship is usually established through a third party familiar with both sides. "Dining together" is a good way to "build up a relationship". In the mainland, a letter of introduction from a famous person or government department will make things a great deal smoother. It serves as a key to the "back door", if not the "front door", of an enclosed circle of social relationships. Indeed, Chinese society consists of a number of such social circles, each of which cares only for the interests of its own members. There is a hierarchy of relationship. A Chinese person makes a clear distinction between close friends and distant friends. His Heart-and-Mind will look after his acquaintance in accordance with this hierarchy of familiarity. He gives whatever advantage or privilege he can to men of his circle. His children, of course, are his foremost concern. No Chinese official wants to retire until he has settled his children's future. Impartiality is a concept totally alien to the Chinese. It implies that one has no circle. In a community which emphasizes Sodality on the one hand and the repression of the individual on the other, this network of human relationships satisfies the individual's need for protection and safety. Mutual assistance from men of one's circle is necessary.

Inner and Outer Circles

A CHINESE DISTINGUISHES carefully between the members of his inner and outer circle. Even within the family, he distinguishes relatives on the paternal side from relatives on the maternal side. In everyday life, it is logical for him to favour members of his circle. But if he meets an "outsider" of high social status, or someone with whom he has just established a relationship, he will tend to show great hospitality by first putting down "his own circle". To win the heart of the outsider, he has to show that he favours him at the expense of his close acquaintances. Chinese parents will beat their own children if they get into a fight with a neighbour's children, and they will not bother to find out the cause first. They do this in order to win their neighbour's approval. Similarly, when they invite friends to a meal, they will keep their wife and children out of the way so that the friends can eat comfortably. The more distant the friends, the greater the hospitality shown.

Even in foreign policy, the Chinese usually try to show their hospitality to foreign visitors by first emptying the place of local Chinese. Some restaurants or shops are specially reserved for foreigners. The Chinese have created a hierarchy of visitors: foreigners rank first, Overseas Chinese second, Hong Kong and Macao residents third and local Chinese fourth. Charges for services also vary according to this hierarchy.

But to show hospitality to outsiders does not mean that you extend Sodality to them. Outsiders are outsiders. Outwardly you give them the best treatment, but secretly you are on your guard. The Chinese government is very sensitive about foreigners, and disapproves of close relationships between Chinese and foreigners.

In this game of "inner and outer circle", every Chinese knows his position. He will not be angered if he is put down, because he knows that he is a member of the inner circle; and equally he will not feel flattered if he is treated with great warmth by a complete stranger, because he knows the rules of the game. But foreigners sometimes feel bewildered and unhappy.

Walls of the Womb

THE WHOLE network of social relationships serves as a womb (family, social group, collective, state). And so man, in the sense of man with a strong ego, has never been born in China. As Lu Xun remarked: "True manhood has not yet been created in the Chinese world."

The Chinese self is permanently disorganized. It has to be defined by leaders and collectives. Clinging to the mother's womb is the norm in Chinese culture.

Today in mainland China, the work unit has become the womb for the individual. When a person is allocated to a work unit, he is there virtually for the rest of his life. Each unit can be compared to a small state. They are separated from one another, and there is little or no communication among them. Each work unit encloses the individual like a womb, gives him warmth and protection. It allocates jobs. It provides accommodation, fixes wages, collects membership fees, rations food and other daily necessities, including consumer goods. It issues marriage or divorce permits. It settles family disputes. It distributes the amount of work and organizes education as well as recreational activities. It even decides when married couples can have their only child. It keeps detailed files on each member. The files are confidential and are kept from the individual, but may be used against him at any time.

When they go abroad, Chinese tend to stick together, and have nothing to do with "foreign devils". This is how they preserve their peace of mind. The trouble is, they regard this seeking of the "mother's womb" as a selfless act of collectivism, and look down on others in their struggle for human rights. They regard such behaviour as "bourgeois individualism". Liberation for the third world is a worthy cause, but women's liberation and gay liberation are immoral.

from Deep Structure

Blaming the
brick wall for
Obstructing
the way.

Hua Junwu

The Burden

I often strain to catch voices wafted from afar
Faint snatches, dead leaves, white snow
Drifting down from a remote dreamworld.
Often in the rainbow wandering in after the rain
I seek the shadow of the Great Wall, proud and comforting;
But the roaring wind only tells me new tales of ruin
—Mud and rubble have silted
The canal, my arteries no longer pulse,
My throat no longer sings.

The aged century bares its brow
Shakes its wounded shoulders;
Snow covers the ruins—white and restless
Like surf—moving among the pitchblack trees;
A lost voice transmitted across time.
There is no road
Through this land that death has lent mystery.

The aged century cheats its children
Leaving everywhere riddles
Snow on the stone, to patch the ornamented filth.

I shall weird this ruin with light,
Hear a song
In this wasteland of stones.

Yang Lian

Yang Lian and Jiang He are two young poets whose writings first appeared in *Today*.
See also below, pp. 62, 135, 244-9 and 312.

I am continually rejected by the world
The sun travels westward, I am rejected
The shadow forever lengthens
Like a long road
Winding
    Twists me
Huge dragon
    Ornament
On the ghostly palace wall
    Railing at the sky
I am rejected
Flaunted
The Great Wall stumbles in the mountain ranges
    The canal flows sadly through the plain

Jiang He

Wang Wenlan

The Detour

Tao Jun

COMPERE: The world is presently full of fakes. Fake watches, fake medicines, fake art and fake socialism. The way to identify a fake is to subject it to a series of laboratory tests.

The same type of thing can be done with human beings. People have numerous faults, though it is very hard to tell what is wrong with a person just from looking at him; what is required is a suitable environment in which tests can be conducted.

What we're going to do now is conduct a few such tests. (*Indicating the set on the stage with a wave of the hand*) Before us we have two roads. One is a bright and sunny highway; the other is a muddy track. They both lead to the same destination. Now, I'm going to place a sign in the middle of the highway. (*Takes out sign*) Please note: on the sign we have written the word "Detour". Watch very carefully, for we are about to witness the unfolding of a fierce struggle between the two roads and the two lines right in front of our very eyes. (*exits*)

(*Characters*: Youth, Old Man, Husband, Wife, Father, Daughter, Young Man, Girl, and a number of incidental passers-by.)

The Detour *is one of a series of skits from a revue entitled* Rubik's Cube, *written by a Shanghai university student in 1985. The title of the revue was explained in the programme notes:*

"The fifty-four coloured squares of a Rubik's Cube represent the infinite changes of the world; twisting, turning . . . .

"It is said that there are one hundred million ways to solve the puzzle of the cube, and everyone must look for their own solution; searching, seeking . . . . "

The playwright's use of thinly-veiled parable saved the play from a government ban, and although the official critics strove to ignore it, Rubik's Cube *attracted large audiences in Peking and Shanghai in late 1985 and early 1986.*

(*An intersection.*)

(*The* TRAVELLERS *come on stage one by one, and respond in various ways to the sign that is blocking their path.*)

YOUTH (*glaring at the sign angrily*): Great, that's just great. The road was clear this morning and now, in less time than it takes to down a beer, it's become a "forbidden zone".

OLD MAN: They must be repairing the road up ahead. They're worried that it might be dangerous for pedestrians, so they've been considerate enough to put up this warning.

YOUTH: Now, I know China's a large country and we've got an over-supply of labour. But why are we always so scared of the mischief people will get up to if they're left to their own devices? That's why we start up these huge construction projects all the time, tearing up roads like this to make sure no one remains idle. When the telephone people finally finish filling in the ditches they've dug along the road, before you know it, the gas company comes along and scoops them out again. All this "construction work" creates the impression that we're really making headway with the Four Modernizations. If they're really repairing the road then how come there's no sign of anyone up ahead?

OLD MAN (*reflecting for a moment*): Maybe they're not doing road repairs at all.

YOUTH: Sure looks like a con to me.

(HUSBAND *and* WIFE *enter, inspect the detour sign questioningly.*)

OLD MAN (*mysteriously*): There's trouble up ahead.

HUSBAND: Trouble?

OLD MAN: That's right. Back at the beginning of the Cultural Revolution I heard that an enemy of the people planted a time-bomb under this road. It still hasn't gone off after all these years!

YOUTH: Still going on about class struggle at your age, old man. You sure don't look the type.

OLD MAN (*testily*): Whadda ya' mean, at my age? I was just pulling your leg. I'm only thinking of your safety; my years of experience have taught me a thing or two. You always have to be on guard against the unexpected.

(*The* HUSBAND *and* WIFE *study the sign.*)

WIFE: What a pain! Here they go blocking up a perfectly good road. My feet will get wet if we have to walk through the smelly water on that track.

HUSBAND (*having discovered something*): Hey, look at that: high tension lines. Maybe one of them was blown down by the strong wind
we had a little while ago?

OLD MAN (*as if realising something*): That's it. Someone nearly got
electrocuted this summer.

   (*An eerie sound can be heard. The group takes fright.*)

   (*A* YOUNG MAN *on a bike with a* GIRL *sitting on the back rides
   down an aisle of the theatre and carries the bike onto the stage.
   He starts to ride down the road with the* GIRL.)

OLD MAN (*blocking the way*): Stop, you can't go that way.

YOUNG MAN: What do you think you're playing at? I wasn't spitting or
anything, so what's all the bother? Get out of the way.

OLD MAN (*attempts to grab the* YOUNG MAN *but inadvertently seizes
the* GIRL *who is sitting on the back of the bike*): Come back here.

GIRL: What do you think you're doing? Dirty old man!

OLD MAN: There's danger up ahead.

YOUNG MAN: Been hitting the bottle, have ya? I just came from there.

OLD MAN: Did you then? Take a look at that sign.

YOUNG MAN (*reading out loud*): "D-e-t-o-u-r". Humph, that wasn't
there a minute ago.

   (FATHER *and* DAUGHTER *enter.*)

OLD MAN: Well, maybe some high tension lines were blown down.

FATHER: High tension lines? (*pulls* DAUGHTER *back*)

DAUGHTER: Daddy, what's a high tension line?

FATHER: It's wire used to carry high-voltage electricity. One wire can
carry over 10,000 volts, so it can be extremely dangerous. You can
be burnt to cinders if you touch it. Uncle Li who lives downstairs
from us lost his arm that way.

OLD MAN: We're all agreed on what's happened then?

   (*The group becomes restless, and the eerie sound is heard once
   more.*)

OLD MAN: Careful! Get back!

   (*They all retreat in terror and look anxiously down the road.*)

   (*The sound slowly fades. The* YOUNG MAN *listens to the sound
   and walks out from the group.*)

YOUTH (*vexed*): Take it easy everyone. If there really was something
wrong with the power lines, a truck from the power company would

have been here ages ago.

FATHER: Maybe they got caught in traffic.

YOUTH: Okay, so if it's the power lines, how come they haven't put up a warning sign? They could have used a picture of a streak of lightning or something.

GIRL: Perhaps the person who put the sign up was so frightened by the fallen power lines that he forgot the picture?

YOUTH: I can't figure it out: why are you all so determined to believe that we can't use this road?

OLD MAN: I reckon, young fella, that you're just too damned stubborn. Don't you see the sign over there?

YOUTH: Sign? Huh, just a few years ago everybody believed in [Mao's] Orders of the Day; now you're all being taken in by this sign.

HUSBAND (*interrupting*): Someone should go and see what's really going on. Otherwise we could go on arguing like this until dark. Then we'll still have to take that muddy track.

YOUTH (*excitedly*): That's telling 'em. We need a few brave people who are willing to take risks. What's wrong with the world is that there aren't enough real pioneers.

HUSBAND: Cut the crap. You could have had a look yourself in the time it's taken you to say all that.

(*Having said this he starts walking along the road, but his way is blocked by the* OLD MAN.)

OLD MAN: Get back, you! That's typical, whenever you young people get together you become aggressive. What do you think you're up to? A young fellow who lived next door to us got himself killed after taking a bet.

HUSBAND: Look here, grandad, this isn't the same. I've been suspicious about this sign all along.

OLD MAN: But you still have to believe it. If you do go along there and end up getting hurt, what are you going to do, make out it was an industrial accident? I think we'd better wait. Maybe the truck from the power company will be here in a moment.

YOUTH (*aside*): Waiting around is something the Chinese do best.

HUSBAND: Some Chinese are pretty good at running off at the mouth, too.

(*He walks forward; his wife stands up and fixes him with an icy glare.*)

Lu Xiaochun

WIFE (*in a chilly tone*): Come back this instant!
> (*The courageous* HUSBAND *stops dead in his tracks. He hesitates for a moment but then retreats to his wife's side.*)
> (*The* YOUTH *walks to the front of the stage and launches into a diatribe.*)

YOUTH (*emotionally*): There's a very fashionable "disease" that's been going around lately; everyone's saying that things aren't what they used to be, that the world gets more depraved all the time. They complain that everyone has become selfish. But people never take a good look at themselves. Everyone says they want others to be more selfless like Lei Feng. They're always grumbling that "Lei Feng disappeared"; or that "Uncle Lei Feng went away." But no, that's not it. Lei Feng is still around all right, it's just that now he has a family. (*He starts getting carried away with his own oratory*) This is a terrible thing. But what's really disturbing isn't the danger that's supposed to be lying before us; it's not this sign on the road. It's not this old man who has learnt from life always to be cautious; it's not the wife who's scared for her husband's safety. (*Moves further to the front of the stage*) What truly terrifies me is you people in the audience. [Cut in later performances:] You, you silent observers. Take a good look at yourselves; your expressionless faces, a stoney wall that reflects nothing. Just a few days ago a pregnant woman was raped by a gang of thugs right under the noses of a group of silent bystanders. The members of that gang will be arraigned in court for what they did, but you got off scot-free and have all come back for another show. Today the road may be closed off forever and yet you stand by watching passively. Won't any of you take a stand and say something? Won't anyone make a plea for common-sense and justice?

COMPERE (*applauding emotionally as he rushes out of the audience onto the stage*): Let me congratulate you on your excellent speech. We were all very moved by it. Have you ever taken part in one of those speech competitions held to discuss the theme of China's Revitalization?

YOUTH: And what's that supposed to mean?

COMPERE: Now don't get me wrong. I honestly believe that we need people today who care enough to speak up and shake everyone out of their complacency. But forgive me, I've interrupted your eloquent speech. I've only come to pick up something that I accidently left on the stage. (*Taking the wooden sign*) Excuse me, please go on. Really, I haven't heard such a rousing speech for a long time. You hit the nail right on the head.

(*Taking the sign, prepares to exit. All the others look at him in dumb amazement.*)

OLD MAN: Come back with that! What do you think you're up to then?

COMPERE: I'm the compère of this revue. Oh yes, I forgot to explain that just now we were subjecting you to a sociological experiment. It's over and I'd like to thank you all for your co-operation. (*Turning to the audience*) Ladies and gentlemen, I beg you all to consider the following question: why didn't anyone take a single step along that road after I put this sign there?

(*The pedestrians all gather in a silent group at the far end of the stage.*)

COMPERE: You can all go now. What's stopping you? Didn't I just say that I was the one who put this sign here? The road is clear up ahead. There is nothing wrong; it was all part of an experiment.

OLD MAN: An experiment? That's just the sort of dirty trick they used to play in the Cultural Revolution. That kind of thing's illegal now.
(*The group starts an animated discussion, encircling the* COMPERE *angrily.*)
COMPERE: How can I explain? (*Finding the* YOUNG MAN *who had made a speech*) Now you have the proof to support your hypothesis. I'm very impressed by your extraordinary oratorical abilities, but now I'd like to ask for your help in convincing everybody that they can go. We need the stage for a performance.
YOUTH (*looking at the* COMPERE *questioningly*): They won't listen to me. They've suffered more than enough for blindly following people in the past. They're too calm, collected and rational to take any notice of me.
COMPERE: But only a moment ago you were convinced that this road was safe. So . . . .
YOUTH: Yes, but your appearance has made me doubt myself. Didn't you say you've been conducting an experiment? Who knows, maybe this is just another one of your experiments.
COMPERE: But that means you don't believe in anything.
YOUTH: That's right, including myself.
(*The* COMPERE *is at a loss what to do.*)
WIFE (*coldly*): Why don't *you* take the road, then?
COMPERE: Certainly. Why didn't I think of that myself? Very well, I will. You people . . . .
(*The group parts to make way for him.*)
COMPERE: What's wrong? Why so deadly earnest? You're all acting as though I'm about to get killed. (*He takes a few steps, but something alerts him to a danger and he hesitates*) Maybe something *has* happened up ahead. Though that's unlikely, as I've been watching all along.
OLD MAN: I knew it all along, you're just trying to stir up trouble. Bloody young people! The way you carry on, no wonder people say you were suckled by the Gang of Four. Really! Okay, first you try to walk down the road, then you chicken out. Go on, get out of it.
COMPERE: But sir, this road is safe.
YOUTH: Practice is the sole criterion of truth. So go on: take a walk.
OLD MAN (*shouts at* YOUTH): Don't pressure him.

Lu Xiaochun

YOUTH (*coldly*): Come on, everyone's waiting for you to do something.
  (*The* COMPERE *hesitates for a moment but finally summons up
  enough courage to walk towards the forbidden zone.*)
COMPERE (*having walked a few steps, he slows down and then stops*):
  My legs won't go any further. (*Turns around and looks at the others.
  They all stare at him blankly. He can hear the eerie noise faintly in
  the distance, but it is getting closer.*) Why aren't any of you following me? Come on.
  (*The mysterious sound grows louder and louder. The* COMPERE
  *gets scared and turning suddenly he takes a few dispirited steps
  back.*)
  (*Silence.*)
  (*After a pause the group finally decides to take the detour, and
  starts moving towards the muddy track.*)
  (*A* SMALL GIRL *runs on stage calling out for her father. She
  searches for him, crying "Father, father", and runs right past the
  warning sign down along the broad and sunny road.*)

                                                  from the play Rubik's Cube

The Tunnel

Chen Ruoxi

EARLY IN JULY Nanjing launched a "Good Men, Good Deeds" movement and Master Hong, a retired worker, was selected by his neighbourhood committee as a "Good Man" and given the additional designation
of "model old man." Master Hong had mixed feelings about the honour
that had come his way: he felt much like a man chewing on a raw olive,
finding it refreshing but also somewhat astringent in taste.

The fact was that Master Hong did not feel old.

He was sixty-four and had been retired from the electron tube
factory for three years, but people in the residence continued to
address him as Master Hong or simply as Old Master, out of affection.
He could see in the mirror that his temples had turned white, but his
pepper-and-salt hair was thick and healthy and felt firm to the touch,
and his short beard gave him an appearance of power and virility. His
flesh was firm and his face remarkably free from wrinkles, though
somewhat mottled by age. His eyes, however, were always blood-
shot from long years of working under strong harsh light in the factory
and had a tendency to water when he was under strain. This more than
anything else betrayed his age. Otherwise, he was healthy and strong of
limb, and proud of the fact that he could walk four or five *li* without
stopping to rest.

---

*Chen Ruoxi (Ch'en Jo-hsi) is one of a talented generation of fiction-
writers from Taiwan. She differs from her contemporaries in that she chose
to settle in Mainland China, finally leaving in 1973 after seven years. This
experience provided her with the raw material for many powerful and carefully written stories, including this one, which though set in the Cultural
Revolution, deals with a deep-seated problem that still persists in contemporary China—the destructive influence of political and social pressure
on human relationships.*

Master Hong did not want to retire so early in life and had several times requested permission to keep on working—but to no avail, because this was the stated policy of the government.

In the matter of retirement, there was a great difference between factory and intellectual workers. According to his oldest son, who taught at the university, many old professors requested permission to retire but were not allowed to do so. These included doddering old men who were virtually invalids. But the university authorities would not let them go, saying that the central government wished to "protect" the old intellectuals.

Master Hong could not understand this policy of the government's. With the retirement of the old professors, the young ones would have a chance for advancement. It would also save money for the government since their pension would be only seventy per cent of their regular salary. It didn't make any sense to him to force this kind of "protection" on the intellectuals.

"The general retirement age of sixty for men and fifty-five for women cannot be applied to intellectuals at present," his son explained to him. "If it were, all professors of sixty and over would retire en masse! It would not only be a great blow to culture and learning, it would damage our national prestige. Don't you realize that foreign visitors always ask to see these professors? They serve an important United Front purpose."

Master Hong could not quite follow his son's reasoning but he accepted it on faith. Was he not a professor at the university and a fully accredited member of the Communist Party? How could he be wrong?

He would have liked to work a few more years, not because his income would be reduced by thirty per cent if he retired, but because he wanted to have something to do. But the work force at the factory was fixed and its regulations required prompt retirement when a worker reached the mandatory age except under special circumstances. As a matter of fact, he should have retired in 1968, but because of the disruptions during the Cultural Revolution, he had been kept on for another year in order to train a batch of new workers. So he did not retire until 1969.

Time passed very slowly the first year. He did not know what to do with his hands, so long used to holding an electric welding gun. He would have liked to be helpful around the house, but there was nothing for him to do. After his younger son's marriage, he had moved into his older son's quarters in the university and lived with him and his wife. His daughter-in-law did not work because she had had tuberculosis and was not strong. However, she was a good housekeeper and managed everything well. His grandchildren were already in kindergarten and he got to see them only mornings and evenings. His son and daughter-in-law were very thoughtful of him. He had worked all his life and deserved all the leisure and comforts of his old age. So they treated him like the lord of the manor and would not let him lift a finger.

Thus Master Hong had nothing to do except go out for a stroll on days when the weather was fine. He had never been to school, but during the first few years after his wife's death he had joined a reading class and learned enough characters to enable him to write simple reports on his work and to read the newspaper quite well. But he was not interested in the papers. They were hard on the eyes and their subject matter was dull and of no concern to him. He never took up smoking and rarely touched alcohol. By his example neither of his sons acquired these habits. His older son had thoughtfully provided him with a bottle of grape wine, but it was no fun drinking alone and he did not indulge in it except to take a few sips on cold nights before going to bed. He could do some carpentry and masonry work and used to fix the leaky roof and collapsed wall of his own adobe house. But even that occupation was denied him now because the university quarters were kept in good repair.

Luckily there was an unprecedented amount of activity during those two years, organizing old and young, and housewives, into neighbourhood committees. A committee was set up in the university compound, affiliated with the larger local neighbourhood committee. Master Hong's family was recognized as a distinguished one. Having been a worker all his life, he was considered a man of superior background—that is to say, one "gravely wronged" and therefore an "implacable enemy of the exploiting class". By virtue of the fact that his younger son was an officer in the Liberation Army, his family became at the same time an "army household", to say nothing of the fact that his older son was a member of the Party and the younger one was going through his probationary period as a party member. His family was thus truly "red". Inevitably he was recruited for the residents' committee and was soon afterwards elected to the neighbourhood committee, where he played an important part in the work of fighting class enemies and investigating men of questionable backgrounds. In the purification campaigns of 1968, several old men were ferreted out for investigation and quite a stir was created. When the time came for making a final disposition of the cases, Master Hong was invited to help. Since he had nothing to do with his time, he never missed a meeting and was always eager to do whatever chores he was assigned. He discovered that his words actually carried weight in deciding the political fate of those under investigation; he exulted in his work. He no longer regarded it as a way of passing the time but felt that he was doing something for the Revolution. He became absorbed in the work and put all his heart in it.

It was during this time that he first heard the name of Li Mei.

AT ONE POINT the neighbourhood committee was deliberating whether or not to brand a certain old man as a bad element. The man in question not only had a complex background but kept bad company. At one time he was a good friend of Li Mei's husband, who was said to be a drunkard, and to have cursed the Communist Party and Chairman Mao, and defied authority, during the Great Leap Forward. He even assaulted some Party cadre, for which he was finally sent to prison. To dissociate herself from such a man, Li Mei asked for a divorce. After it was granted she lived with her little daughter and made a living by baby-sitting, cooking and washing for people in the neighbourhood. The old man under investigation had pestered Li Mei with his attentions and it was said that she had driven him away with a carrying pole. Members of the committee all took the position that Li Mei must have encouraged the man in some way. Master Hong was inclined to go along with the others. Li Mei could not have been blameless, since her husband was a counter-revolutionary, though no one could put a finger on just what she had done.

It was not until the winter of 1970, when in response to Mao Zedong's directive, Nanjing like all large cities in China began a mad rush to dig air-raid tunnels, that Master Hong first met Li Mei.

As it was with all past directives "from the highest level", the latest decree galvanized everybody into action—in government organizations, schools, factories, and residential neighbourhoods. The main tunnels were to be deep enough to afford protection against

atomic bombs and wide enough for buses to drive through. They were
supposed to be spacious enough to accommodate shops and hospitals
and the network was to cover the entire city so that within fifteen
minutes of an air raid warning the entire population of the city would
be able to move underground. The city government decreed that each
unit was to be responsible for the section of the tunnel in its locality
and to begin work immediately without preliminary surveys or blueprints.

There were three entrances to the tunnel planned for the residential area where Master Hong lived, one of which was near a locust
tree not far from his apartment. Most of the teachers in the university
had been sent to the northern part of the province for re-education in
a May 7th Cadre School,* so the responsibility for digging tunnels fell
upon their families, and Master Hong was drafted to direct the work.
The older men and women being too frail for any heavy work, the
actual digging was done by the housewives.

Master Hong had lost his wife ten years earlier and since then
had rarely come into contact with members of the opposite sex. Now,
thrown together with a crowd of women, he felt strange and not a
little thrilled when he happened to come into physical contact with
them in the narrow tunnel. Because of his age, the women did not feel
constrained to be reticent. While they laboured, they kept up a stream
of gossip as if he weren't there at all. One of them was quiet, a middle-
aged matron who worked harder than anyone else, wielding her pick
with abandon. Being a worker himself, Master Hong appreciated her
zeal and wondered who she was.

One day she arrived at work before anyone else and he summoned
up enough courage to ask her name.

"My surname is Li; I am called Li Mei." She gave him a modest
smile with the answer.

So she was the divorced woman! Master Hong was surprised but
there was not the slightest trace of distaste in his feeling toward her.

"How come you are working in our section of the tunnel?"

"I do odd jobs for Professor Sun. His wife is in poor health and
can't do heavy work. I am here to take her place."

Li Mei's voice was soft and low and very pleasant to the ear.

*See p. 79.

Master Hong's wife had had a shrill voice, and when excited she always sounded as if she was quarreling. His daughter-in-law's voice was hoarse and always sounded as if she was short of breath. Li Mei was different. She spoke in a low voice as if whispering into his ears and yet every word she spoke came to him like the clear notes of a bell. He could not hear enough of it and regretted that he had not heard it before. For the first time in his life, he became aware that a woman's voice could actually be enchanting.

That night his mind was full of Li Mei as he rested his weary bones in his bed. Her face was already familiar to him. The image now had a name and was endowed with sound; it had become animated, like a motion picture before his eyes.

Li Mei's face reminded him of the goddess Guanyin whose statue he had seen years ago in the country. It was a roundish face, with arched eye-brows, full of infinite sweetness and compassion for the sufferings of mankind. Physical exertion had given her complexion a healthy glow which suffused the wrinkles that had been created by her smiles, and made them seem like added ornaments to her charm. Her eyes were small, as was her nose; but her lips were full and purplish red like ripe mulberries. Such thick lips would have seemed ugly on another woman, but on Li Mei they suggested a "happy destiny". It seemed to him unjust that, with such a physiognomy, she should be fated to virtual widowhood. She wore a padded coat and trousers, so Master Hong could not tell whether she was fat or thin, but he judged from the fullness of her face that she could not be too thin. His late wife was comfortably plump, and he had always liked women that way. It gave one such a soft, warm feeling.

With this thought, Master Hong forgot about his aching bones. He turned over, put his arms around the pillow, buried his face in it and in his heart called out the name Li Mei.

From then on Master Hong took advantage of every opportunity to be near her. She lived in a lane nearby and once he went to her place on the pretext of notifying her of a meeting. To avoid gossip he stood at the door and called to her. Though he did not go in when she opened the door, he had a good look at her house.

It reminded him of his own old home. Like hers, it had been in a dingy lane, a two-room house constructed of wood with plastered earthen walls and tamped earth floor. The difference was that while

his had become very messy after his wife died, Li Mei's was kept neat
and clean. The unpainted table and stools were well scrubbed and
shiny and the dirt floor swept. The only decoration on the wall was a
portrait of Chairman Mao. He saw her daughter too, bent over the table
doing her lessons. She was a little over ten and looked somewhat like
her mother. It was an ordinary enough house, but with Li Mei smiling
and standing in the doorway, it acquired an air of simple dignity. He
was so absorbed in what he saw that he would have forgotten his errand
if Li Mei had not reminded him of it.

IT WAS PROBABLY because of his lack of education that he could not
appreciate the strategic significance of "deep tunnels", Master Hong
had always admitted to himself. If he had his way, he would simply
spread a quilt under the table and curl up under it, instead of crawling
into the tunnel in the event the Soviets dropped their hydrogen bombs.
But he was very grateful indeed that Chairman Mao's sudden inspiration
should have made it possible for him to meet Li Mei. He would speak
to her whenever he could do so without attracting attention and he was
always alert to keep her out of the way of falling earth or a carelessly
swung pick. Li Mei appreciated his thoughtfulness and cast him grateful
glances.

    In the spring of the following year, the tunnels had reached quite
a depth and were to be joined very soon. Electric lights were installed
and because the air was stagnant and the danger of falling earth was
ever present, the workers were divided into two-hour shifts and the
night shift abolished. Once he followed Li Mei into the tunnel and
heard the sound of crumbling earth just as she lifted her pick. He
sprung forward and pulled her back, with the result that they both fell
to the ground. She wasn't hit by the falling earth but she was much
moved by Master Hong's selflessness in risking his own life to save her.
Her eyes were filled with tears as she was helped out of the tunnel.

    A little after this tunnel construction was suddenly stopped in
Nanjing. It happened that a professor of civil engineering was home on
furlough from farm labour and noticed a slight tilt in his building. He
knew that the sinking was due to tunnel work. He reported the risks
involved and the school authorities had no choice but to stop the
digging. This and similar incidents were brought to the attention of the
city government. In the southern part of the city an entire building

actually collapsed. The tunnels should have been propped up with beams or shored up with concrete after they reached a certain depth, but because of shortages of construction materials the higher echelon of the government had done nothing, except exhort the people to promote the revolution by practising economy. The result was collapsed houses and loss of lives. When the city government realized that it was impossible to accomplish Chairman Mao's pipe dream with the resources available, it did what the authorities in Peking had done: it finished a few sections of the tunnel in style, in areas frequented by foreign visitors, and abandoned the rest.

Though Master Hong was pleased that the government had at last abandoned this senseless undertaking, he was also distressed, because it deprived him of the opportunity to be near Li Mei. The days became as monotonous and tiresome as when he first retired. The only time when life had any meaning for him was when he caught glimpses of Li Mei as she went from one family to another to do their washing and cooking. He discovered that his days were made or spoiled by whether or not he managed to catch sight of her. He missed above all her enchanting voice. In his dreams people spoke without sound and he always woke up disappointed for not having heard her speak. He also cursed himself for making a fool of himself over a woman at his age, and a grandfather too. But that did no good. If anything, he seemed to think about her all the more.

Winter came, with its predictable storms and snow; his daughter-in-law took care to keep him indoors as much as possible for fear that he would suffer exposure. Confined to his room and gazing through the window at the overcast sky, he felt all the more restless. When he did venture out to attend meetings of the neighbourhood committee he made it a point to go by way of Li Mei's home, keeping his eyes fixed on her door as he passed the modest little earthen house, as though hoping to catch something. Once it happened that Li Mei was emerging from the house to fetch coal just as he walked by. Their eyes met and lingered momentarily, and he paused to exchange a few words with her before moving on. For the rest of the way his heart leaped with joy and he found himself all but humming a tune.

As the lunar New Year approached and everyone was making preparations for celebrating the festival, Master Hong wanted to buy something to give Li Mei but was afraid to let his daughter-in-law know.

He waited until the day before New Year's Eve when he finally went out of his way after visiting an old fellow worker and knocked on Li Mei's door.

Li Mei's eyes brightened when she saw who it was and asked him in without a word. Master Hong took from the inner pocket of his padded jacket two ten-*yuan* notes and held them out to her rather timidly, saying, "This is for you to buy something for the little girl, for New Year."

Li Mei stepped back and would not take it, her round face reddening in confusion.

Master Hong had never been eloquent. Now he stood there openmouthed and did not know what to say. Then taking Li Mei's hand, he pressed it to his heart and said, "It comes from here."

After staring at him for a moment, Li Mei freed her hand and then with both her hands she lifted his and touched her thick, hot lips against it.

Master Hong slept beautifully that night, fondling the hand which Li Mei had kissed. On New Year's Eve, he reverted to the old custom of giving his grandchildren "good luck money", which had been condemned by the Red Guards. Thus amid the occasional report of fire crackers, he said good-bye to another year. He had not been so happy for a long time and felt more than ten years younger.

Shortly after the Spring Festival, the university sent Master Hong's son to Shenyang on a "learning" mission, and the old man immediately took upon himself the responsibility of the family's morning shopping. He knew that Li Mei shopped for her employers on her way to work, so he waited for her and walked to the market with her.

LI MEI WAS a good listener, and Master Hong gradually unburdened to her all that was on his mind. He talked about his grandchildren, of his younger son in Qinghai, even of his dead wife. He told her how fond he was of her and how he was afraid that she considered him too old for her. Then Li Mei would comfort and encourage him, assuring him that he looked as strong as when he first moved into the university residence. This made him feel more than ever that he was not old after all.

He became more and more fond of Li Mei. She was a woman of

few words, but she had a good heart and always meant what she said. She had had an opportunity to marry again but she loved her daughter dearly and did not want to risk marrying someone who might not be kind to her. So she chose to remain unmarried and earn her living by doing odd jobs.

Master Hong should have been content with the knowledge that Li Mei was well disposed toward him, but man has a way of courting unhappiness. After a while he began to wonder if she was being nice to other men and to recall the things that had been said about her when he first heard her name. Was there anything between her and that old man under investigation? He was troubled by these thoughts and suspicions.

When Li Mei saw that he doubted her, she was distressed and once burst into tears, saying, "Lao Hong, do you want me to tear out my heart and show it to you?"

He was touched and at the same time ashamed of himself for being jealous like a young man.

"Don't cry, Li Mei," he said to her, taking her hand and squeezing it. "It is only that I—I love you so much."

His cheeks grew hot to the ears as he uttered this word, which belongs to the vocabulary of the young. He never imagined that at his age he would be capable of saying such a thing.

Hearing this, Li Mei threw away all restraint, drew close to him and rested her face on his shoulder.

"Lao Hong, if you do not dislike me and are willing to have me, I would like to throw in my lot with you."

Dislike her? Willing to have her? What absurd talk was this? Master Hong almost shouted right there on the street.

"Li Mei-mei," he was so excited that he stuttered. "For a long time, I have wanted to marry you."

This happened that autumn, a few days before his son returned from Shenyang.

But things will get around. His meetings with Li Mei were observed and talked about, and eventually reached the ears of his daughter-in-law. He had no inkling that she knew, for she never said anything to him. But on the evening of his son's return, the young couple whispered to each other all night. He could not make out what they said but concluded that it was only natural for them to have so much to say to each other after many months' separation. He did not realize what had happened until the following day when they began to reproach him none too subtly.

First his son spoke of his mother who had been dead for fourteen years, how capable she had been, what delicious dumplings she had made, how thrifty and industrious she had been, all for the sake of her husband and her children. Then the daughter-in-law took over and brought up the name of Li Mei, recounted and embroidered upon the rumours about her.

"You can't expect very much of a divorced woman," was her rather arbitrary conclusion. "Otherwise she would have remarried long before this. What could she be waiting for?"

"She only asked for a divorce after the man she married became a counter-revolutionary," Master Hong protested.

"Perhaps she was an opportunist," his son chimed in. "She may have divorced him only to show that she was a good revolutionary. Who knows what was actually on her mind?"

"You're quite right," the daughter-in-law agreed. "She is one hundred per cent an opportunist. The reason she has remained un-married so long is because she is waiting for someone with an un-impeachable background that she can lean upon. She is dreaming. No Party member or cadre would ever have a woman like her. She would only be a burden."

The old man never expected such a violent reaction from his son and daughter-in-law. They had anticipated him and virtually vetoed him before he had a chance to speak. He was crushed and spoke no more. He realized that he was no match for his son, who was a high-level intellectual and a member of the Party. He certainly could not resist the combined forces of his son and daughter-in-law.

He objected strongly to the toadyism of the rank and file of the Communist Party—people like his son. It seemed so unjust to him that they should be ever-ready to accommodate themselves to the Party line while showing no sympathy whatever for an unfortunate and helpless woman like Li Mei. Moreover, the New Marriage Laws had been drawn up by the Communist Party. For a time after Liberation, the people were encouraged to break their old bonds and to form new, revolution-ary ties; yet now his son, a Party member, did not want to be con-taminated by a divorced woman. But when he thought more about the matter, he realized that this double standard was typical of the Communists. His son had not invented it and could not be blamed for it. Both Mao Zedong and Liu Shaoqi divorced their wives and remarried. Yet they would not permit the people to allude to this under penalty of being charged with slandering their leaders and engaging in counter-revolutionary activity. They did not set much store by their own marriage and divorce laws.

Not long afterwards he got a letter from his younger son in Qinghai, expressing concern for his welfare and his desire to have his father come and live with him. This son also said something about how gossip is to be feared and how it might adversely affect the brilliant career that his older brother had before him and jeopardize his own chances of full membership in the Party. After reading the letter Master Hong realized he had absolutely no chance, with everyone in the family against him. He wanted to cry out in protest but felt a lump in his throat; he had to swallow his unhappiness, his feeling of having been misused.

That an old man entertaining the idea of becoming a bride-groom again should be subjected to criticism was more or less to be expected. In this respect the New Society was still very tradition-bound; it gave no thought to the loneliness of the old and their needs. For the sake of Li Mei's happiness and his own, he was willing to brave public prejudice, but there was no way for him to cast off the fetters formed by his own flesh and blood. His children were still young when his wife died. For their sake he had remained a widower, because he was afraid that the woman he married might not be a good stepmother to them. Now that they had both achieved a degree of respectability, it was only natural they did not want anyone to interfere and muddy up clear waters. He had sacrificed his own happiness for theirs when he was still in his prime. There didn't seem to be any valid reason why he should not sacrifice himself again for their sake. He sighed.

He could appreciate his daughter-in-law's point of view too. Of his retirement pay of 56 *yuan* a month, he kept only ten for himself and turned over the rest to her. His son earned 54 *yuan* a month. Even with these two incomes, it took careful management to keep their household of five in a modest degree of comfort. If he were to marry again, the greatest blow would fall on the daughter-in-law. It would be much harder for her to make ends meet, and quite impossible to maintain their accustomed standard of living. The violence of her feelings against Li Mei was only a reflection of her panic.

THUS MASTER HONG's idea of remarrying had to be abandoned. His son went out once more to do the shopping, and he was deprived of the opportunity to meet Li Mei. He was in fact ashamed of meeting her. In his chance encounters with her in the university compound, she looked subdued but uncomplaining, as if she understood the position he was in. He wished he could rush up to her, hold her in his arms and have a good cry.

That winter was unusually cold. Master Hong curled up in his room like a frozen snake, numb to all feelings. He lost interest in everything, and barely managed to attend to the work of the neighbourhood committee. He had lost his former zeal. His only diversion was the delight he took in his two grandsons. He lay awake in the middle of the night, and felt a cold loneliness weighing heavily on him. When it snowed he would stand there, hands in his sleeves, and gaze dumbly at the blank whiteness of the world on the other side of the window-pane. His glance would come to rest across the way on the entrance of the abandoned tunnel near the locust tree. Through prolonged neglect, the tunnel had collected rain-water and become a garbage dump; now the snow covered it all, leaving only traces of a tunnel-mouth like some animal trap. The sight of this recalled to his mind the times when he and Li Mei had laboured shoulder to shoulder, digging and shovelling earth. Then he would become all tensed up and restless, and start walking round and round in his room like a man lost in a maze. He wanted to forget Li Mei, but he found that it was impossible.

Another lunar New Year was soon at hand. As usual the people were exhorted to practice thrift and simplicity and celebrate the Spring Festival in a revolutionary way, and as usual every family did everything it could to buy up what was desired. One day in the afternoon Master Hong decided to go downtown and buy some presents for his grandchildren.

Li Mei happened to be on a shopping expedition too, and the two ran into each other in New Street Square. They were so happy to see each other after such a long absence that they grinned at each other and temporarily forgot all their disappointment and heartaches. The department store was crowded. Li Mei led him in and out of the milling throngs, going from counter to counter, making suggestions and selections for him. No long-married couple could have been more thoughtful and understanding of each other than they. Before they parted, he invited her to see the model film "On the Docks" with him on the Feast of Lanterns, agreeing to meet in front of the cinema.

After that they began to meet regularly every two or three weeks at the cinema. Since there were not many motion pictures available, they soon saw them all, each many times over until they could re-create everything with their eyes closed. But there was no place else to go. In the theatre, Master Hong would take Li Mei's hand as soon as the lights were turned out, place it on his knees and caress it. Li Mei's hands were swollen from long immersion in soapy water, and this was the only time they received any tenderness or attention. Sometimes he would hold her hand against his chest so that she could feel his wild heartbeat, symptom of his restored youth. Then they could close their eyes and luxuriate in the feeling of oneness of body and soul, the touch of flesh against flesh.

A change came over Master Hong. He enjoyed his food and slept well and a smile always played around the corners of his mouth. The beard he had neglected all winter now received meticulous attention. This brought a frown to his daughter-in-law's face. He kept more of his pension for his own use. His daughter-in-law was naturally suspicious but pretended that she noticed nothing and said nothing about it to her husband. She preferred to see him happy than to have him mope around, as he had been doing lately, when hardly a word was exchanged between father and son.

He also took a renewed interest in the affairs of the neighbourhood. He read the newspaper, studied Chairman Mao's writings, organized campaigns for "Remembering the Bitterness of the Past", and took the lead in street-cleaning and other public works. It was no wonder then that he should be the first to be honoured when the movement for "Good Men, Good Deeds" was launched that summer, and that the old men and old ladies were called upon to emulate and learn from him. And it was no wonder that he should be dubbed a "model old man", since just then "model operas" were monopolizing the Chinese stage.

There was a heat wave of more than ten days' duration in July. It was so humid that the stone slabs under the eaves were covered with condensation. On the day agreed upon Master Hong was already waiting in front of the cinema, though its doors had not yet opened for the three o'clock show.

Presently Li Mei came, greeting him with a smile the minute she saw him in the distance. She wore a colourful blouse with short sleeves, a black silk skirt and a pair of black plastic sandals. Because of her work, Li Mei had always worn trousers. Master Hong had wanted to see her dressed like the women in the residence, and he had bought her a piece of silk, and was pleased to see her wearing the skirt she had made of the material.

Li Mei felt as shy as a young girl when she came up to him. Her legs had never been exposed to the sun, and they were white and smooth like radishes that had just been washed and taken out of the water. Master Hong stared at them a while and then feasted his eyes on her bare arms, round and smooth like lotus roots. He could hardly take his eyes off her.

"Let's skip the film today," he suddenly said to Li Mei.

"Where can we go?"

That was a problem. Looking around, he saw a hotel opposite the theatre, but without a letter of introduction from the unit where he worked there was no chance of getting a room. He wanted to be alone with Li Mei, but big as Nanjing was, it afforded no trysting place.

He decided that they should go as far away as they could.

"Let us go to the Zhongshan Mausoleum. Today is Monday. It shouldn't be crowded."

Li Mei agreed and they caught the No. 9 bus.

THOUGH THE PLACE was not as crowded as on holidays, visitors were gathered everywhere in groups of two and three, busily engaged in conversation. It was quiet only in comparison with such thoroughfares as New Street Square. Master Hong had no mind for the scenery; all he was interested in was to find a secluded spot where he could be alone with Li Mei. Halfway up the flight of stairs leading to the mausoleum itself, he turned off and led Li Mei through an orchard and into the woods.

After stumbling around for a while without knowing where they were, they came to an ancient pine with exposed roots that could serve for seats.

"Lao Hong, let's rest for a while and catch our breath."

Li Mei solicitously helped him to sit down on one of the roots and then took out a handkerchief and wiped the sweat from his brow.

He had not done any climbing for a long time and was therefore a little out of breath. He soon recovered his breath but Li Mei kept on wiping his neck, her lotus-root-like arm swinging before him. He suddenly seized it, brought it up to his mouth and bit it gently with his teeth, whereupon Li Mei fell into his arms and sat down on his lap.

Master Hong held her tightly and pressed her soft body against his chest as if trying to quiet his beating heart with her weight. Then noticing her white legs, he freed one hand to stroke them.

Just then they heard the sound of laughter.

Li Mei jumped up with a start, her face red as a cockscomb.

The laughter came from a young couple sitting under a tree not far from where they were. They were stealing glances at Li Mei and Master Hong; the young woman was trying to brush back her hair with her hands and blushing with some embarrassment.

Master Hong stood up and taking Li Mei by the hand walked farther on. The sun was quite low now, and the tree and the closely entwined figures of the young lovers cast long shadows.

The wood thinned out and disclosed the entrance of a tunnel. This tunnel was an impressive one. The entrance was plastered with cement and had an iron gate, which was standing open. It was dark and quiet inside. Here at last was a spot where they could be alone. Master Hong took Li Mei's hand and walked into the tunnel with her.

They walked on hand in hand, leaning upon each other. The tunnel echoed their footsteps but they did not hear: they could only hear the voice of their own hearts responding to each other.

At six o'clock sharp a keeper of the park came and locked the gate. It was opened one day a week to air the tunnel and keep it dry. Another week would pass before it was to be opened again.

An Ancient Tale

Jiang He

I was nailed upon the prison wall.
Black Time gathered, like a crowd of crows
From every corner of the world, from every night of History,
To peck all the heroes to death, one after the other, upon this wall.
. . . .
Ancestors and brothers with heavy hands
Laboured silently as they were piled into the wall.
Once again I come here
To revolt against fettered fate
And with violent death to shake down the earth from the wall
To let those who died silently stand up and cry out.

BLACK & WHITE VI, Ma Desheng

II: PROLEDIC
The Chinese Gulag

If I ever write a book, and want to give a true account of daily life under Proledic, then my experience in the labour camp was an absolutely indispensable prerequisite. The truth is that places like that labour camp are absolutely out of bounds. No writer, however eminent, is allowed to enter them, to taste what life is really like inside. And a person who has not entered Proledic can never have a full understanding of our society.

Yu Luojin

Political and intellectual dissent in Communist China has produced an endless list of martyrs. The first victims fell well before the establishment of the People's Republic, as early as the Yan'an period. Later on, the repressions that successively followed the "Hundred Flowers" and the "Cultural Revolution" decimated the intellectual and political élite of the entire country. Besides these illustrious victims, however, we should not forget the immense crowd of humble, anonymous people who were subjected to mass arrests—as happened in the aftermath of the huge anti-Maoist demonstration in Tiananmen Square (April 5, 1976)—or who are suffering individual persecution all over China. They are imprisoned, condemned to hard labour, or even executed merely for having expressed unorthodox opinions; no one takes notice of them, they never make the headlines in our newspapers. It is only by chance encounter that sometimes, here and there, a more than usually attentive visitor comes across their names and records their fate, from ordinary public notices posted in the streets. Moreover, besides these political dissenters, countless religious believers are also branded as criminals and sent to labour camps simply because they choose to remain loyal to their church and to their faith.

The Chinese "Gulag" is a gigantic topic that has been well described by firsthand witnesses . . . . The reading of these accounts is a basic duty for everyone who professes the slightest concern for China. I have commented elsewhere (in *Broken Images*) on the central relevance of the labour camps for any meaningful analysis of the nature of the Maoist regime. Suffice it to say here that whoever wishes to dispose of the human-rights issue in China without first tackling this particular subject is either irresponsible or a fraud.

Simon Leys, The Burning Forest

Murder at Nenjiang Camp

Liu Binyan

"It happened in April, 1969," Chen went on, as though the incident was still clear in his memory. "It was a murder I witnessed during my term of imprisonment at Nenjiang Labour Camp in Heilongjiang Province.

"There were more than a hundred prisoners in the camp, and one day we were out cutting grass under the supervision of Captain Li,

---

PROLEDIC Defined

"Proledic" is an abbreviation for the term "dictatorship of the proletariat". According to the Marxist scheme of things, prior to the realization of the Communist utopia that will result from the extinction of class struggle and the withering of the state, the proletariat must maintain its leading role in society by exercising dictatorship over the bourgeoisie and all exploiting classes. In socialist countries like China, this means in effect that the Communist Party, in the role of the "vanguard of the proletariat", can avail itself of the whole state apparatus to rule. The Ministries of Public and State Security, the police, the network of prisons, labour camps and state farms and even the army can be employed to enforce Proledic. But Proledic exerts an all-pervasive influence even over the lives of law-abiding citizens: constant surveillance is carried out in every work place by Party cells, which keep detailed dossiers on their employees, and elsewhere by the neighbourhood committees that administer many important aspects of the daily lives of urban residents. In fact, so far from Proledic being a "transitional" phenomenon, it has been more and more deeply reinforced by over three decades of Communist indoctrination, so that now everyone in China carries within them the seeds of Proledic.

Proledic was at its most devastating during the Cultural Revolution (1966-76); but the concept and the organs which enforce it are still strong and can be employed with great effectiveness when necessary.

a young city-bred soldier, and three PLA guards. We each had to cut a quota of three hundred catties. Li Zhirong, a prisoner, who had always been very positive in his attitude towards reform, had already cut 415 catties of grass that morning, and he was busy that afternoon cutting more.

"Our group leader, a man called Liu Deyuan, was marking the area with red flags. Usually four flags were set out in a square, but for some reason on this occasion he planted five of them in the form of a somewhat irregular pentagon. Prisoner Li, who had his head down and was busy cutting, walked here . . . . " Chen made a mark above the upper left-hand corner of the "pentagon", which he had drawn for me on a piece of paper.

"One of the guards shouted at Li, to tell him that he had stepped out of the line. Li protested that he had not. Under normal circumstances, he would have been right. The guard did not like his defiant attitude, and ordered him forward. Li obeyed. He was now about five metres outside that day's perimetre. At that moment, another soldier, he may have been a sergeant, who was warming himself at a fire, walked across to see what was going on. The two soldiers murmured among themselves, and the sergeant asked Li: 'What are you in here for?' 'Counter-revolution.' 'What was your occupation in the past?' 'Platoon leader, Division 208, KMT Youth Army.' 'Did you ever kill a man?' 'Yes.'

"Then the sergeant ordered Li to turn around. Li obeyed. The sergeant meanwhile was fumbling in his pocket for bullets, and in his haste dropped one on the ground, which he stooped down to retrieve. Li was a former soldier himself, and the moment he heard the gun being loaded he spun round. The shot struck him right in the midriff, and he fell flat on the ground, whereupon the sergeant promptly fired again into the air. The captain raced to the scene and, after hurriedly conferring with his sergeant, called a general meeting of all the prisoners on the grass-cutting detail and announced: 'Prisoner Li Zhirong crossed the line in spite of a warning shot fired by one of my men. He was caught red-handed and shot dead. You may cease work for today!'

"Li Zhirong, meanwhile, struggled to his knees, despite the pain his wound was causing him, but collapsed again immediately.

"The prisoners were remanded to their cells and a single soldier was left to keep watch over the body. The following day two prisoners from the Truck Unit were sent to the scene to collect the corpse. On their return they secretly told us that the original arrangement of the flags had been tampered with: they had been moved so that the corpse lay more than ten metres outside the perimeter.

"It was murder committed in broad daylight, in the presence of over a hundred prisoners!" concluded Chen. He then read out in one breath the names of fourteen eyewitnesses. It struck me how haunted he must have been by this event, to be able to recall the details of the scene and the names of the eyewitnesses with such precision after all these years. Then another important fact seemed to come into his mind: "The body was still warm when it was collected the following day! That proves that Li did not die immediately after the shooting. There must have been a period of ten hours or more during which his life could have been saved. And all that time there was a soldier standing guard over him!"

from "A Second Kind of Loyalty"

This self-contained episode comes at the very beginning of a recent work by Liu Binyan—a writer who has specialized in documentary reportage (a Soviet-style genre of literature popular in China). Liu has built up over the years a massive collection of files on various darker sides of Chinese society, but, as a faithful Party member*, he pursues the subject of the labour camps no further, and has never ventured into the forbidden territory of Proledic. Indeed no Chinese writer, whether within China or in exile, has ever tried to give a systematic description of the Chinese Gulag. Instead, the most complete documentation to date has been provided by the London-based organisation Amnesty International (see Appendix). In the remainder of this chapter and in Chapters 9 and 14 can be found a sampling of the fragmentary literature on the subject.

* *In January 1987 he was expelled from the Party. See below, chapter 12.*

Dawn in the Great Northern Wilderness

Tang Qi

Dawn, and our train will soon arrive;
The deathly silence of prison cars arrests all noise.
All but the fearful, restless clanking of the wheels . . .
From the windows, glimpsed in the dark night,
Black snowflakes flutter over the wilderness.

On the vast plain the white snow
Is tramped into a muddy trail,
A long chain of footprints,
Still, desolate, cold.

THE GREAT NORTHERN WILDERNESS, Wang Miao

Countless hearts,
Prisons for countless wronged souls.
The suffering is great, very great,
But there are no sighs, no groans.

Theirs is the fate
Of convicts in a primeval forest.
Axes and saws to cut the year-rings of life.
O, the endless ploughing in the fields!
Ploughshare to crush their shining youth.

Blue light of dawn
Pure white snow
Will bear witness for them:
The suffering was great, very great,
But there were no sighs, no groans.

A long chain
Marches into the desolate, deserted snow.

1957-1958

Tang Qi, with Mu Dan (see below, p. 166), was one of the most promising young modernist poets of the 1940s. He wrote very little between 1949 and 1980.

The Great Northern Wilderness is the common term used for the harsh underdeveloped areas of North East China, to which political undesirables were commonly exiled (see below, pp. 454–62).

Three Scenes from a Labour Camp

Bao Ruowang (Jean Pasqualini) and Rudolph Chelminski

> *Bao Ruowang was born in Peking, son of a Corsican father and Chinese mother. He was educated in Tianjin and Shanghai, and was arrested in 1957. He spent seven years in prison and labour camps, and after his release, wrote* Prisoner of Mao *(with Rudolph Chelminski), from which these extracts are taken. This book still remains the best account of life in the camps. Bao is now resident in Paris.*

Food Substitute

BY THE END of November I had picked up the rhythm of existence at Qinghe.* I was a professional prisoner by then, and felt that I knew how to survive any of the physical or spiritual trials the place could throw at me. In the end I did survive, but it was a much closer thing than I thought it would be. If I was able to adapt to the harshness of the climate, the rough working conditions, the intellectual humiliation and even the semi-starvation of drastically reduced rations, there was little I or any of the others could do about the recurrent waves of disease and debilitation which chose to visit us. As Solzhenitsyn wrote of the Soviet camps, many better men than I broke and many stronger ones died. The strange laws of chance always play.

In the thirteen months that remained before me at that prison farm I was plunged into such a series of personal experiences and human encounters that the outside world I rejoined afterward often seems pale and less significant by comparison. My head so swims with images of what I went through myself, or what others told me about, or what I learned of by accident, that if they come out here in a somewhat kaleidoscopic jumble, forgive me: They are the essence of what it is like to be down and out in a Chinese labour camp.

* Labour camp east of Tianjin. See below, p. 460–1.

The signal that truly desperate times were upon us came in early December, when a horse-drawn cart entered the compound and a prisoner detail began unloading the cargo: dark brown sheets of an unknown material, rigid and light, each one measuring about three by five feet. No one had any idea of what they were. Two weeks later we were called into the auditorium to hear the answer. The stuff was paper pulp, and we were going to eat it. Food Substitute, the prison officials called it—*daishipin*. I'll never forget the words. Since there wasn't enough food to go around in China, the search was on for something to replace it and we prisoners had the honour of being the guinea pigs for the various ersatzes the scientific community came up with. The warder describing the new nutritional policy told us that paper pulp was guaranteed harmless and though it contained no nutritive value, it would make our wo'tous* fatter and give us the satisfying impression of bulk. The new flour mix would be no more than thirty per cent powdered paper pulp. It will go through your digestive tracts easily, he said with assurance. We know exactly how you will feel.

Sure enough, our wo'tous the next day were considerably bigger and we had the pleasant sensation of putting more into our stomachs. They tasted like the normal loaves, but were a bit limper in texture. We ate them without complaint. That evening I saw Ma Erh-kang, the prison doctor. A prisoner like the rest of us, he had no particular respect for most of the warders and certainly none for their medical capabilities. He told me he was worried about the ersatz.

"If I were you, Bao, I'd try to eat some fatty things," he advised, but it was an empty thought under the circumstances.

"You're joking, Ma," I said. "Where in hell am I going to get fat?"

He shrugged and looked preoccupied.

"I don't know, but I don't like that stuff. It may not contain anything poisonous, but I wonder what it will do to the digestive tract. Paper absorbs moisture."

For a while it appeared that his fears were groundless. The bigger wo'tous were popular with the prisoners and they seemed digestible. At the start, anyway. There was hardly any jealousy or complaint, in fact, when the Health Preservation Diet was announced a few days

*Steamed corn buns, a staple food in North China.

later. We should have been alarmed by the ominous title, though. Bao Jian Fan, as it was called in Chinese, was established especially for those prisoners who would be holding key jobs during the winter months and who in the past had earned merits by displaying a proper attitude toward labour—and whose strength would be needed for the crucial spring planting. About 30 of the 285 in our brigade won places on the list, and among them were Sun and Soong, the one we used to call "the Stakhanovite" for his tireless enthusiasm for doing right and serving the government. The Health Preservation Diet consisted of millet flour without ersatz and a soup made from whatever vegetables could be found, often laced with horsemeat or some kind of oil. Even that diet disintegrated as the winter went on, though. After a month or so the only difference was that they had a larger portion of vegetables.

On the second day of the diet old Sun was already too embarrassed to eat his food with us in the cell, as he had done the first day. He ended his personal crisis with one dramatic and illegal gesture. When he walked back from the kitchen his painted tin mug was brimming with a soup of horsemeat, vegetables and fat. He paused long enough to make certain that everybody was watching—and then emptied his mug into our communal soup tub.

"Your health needs preserving, too," he growled. "You can report me if you like."

The Stakhanovite was confused. He wasn't used to breaking the rules. No one thought he would report Sun, but he obviously didn't know what to do now.

"Don't think you're so well off, Soong," Sun said sharply. "Next spring they won't expect these people to work so hard, because they've had a bad winter, but guys like you and me are going to be slaving because we've had all that good food. We'll need all the help we can get."

Soong slopped his mug into the tub. I suppose it must have been those two extra portions of fat over the next two weeks that saved our cell from having any paper-pulp deaths. By Christmas day the whole farm was in agony from what was probably one of the most serious cases of mass constipation in medical history. Sounds comical, doesn't it? It wasn't. Just as Doc Ma had predicted, the paper powder absorbed the moisture from our digestive tracts, making it progressively harder to defecate as each day passed. And painful. Men were bent double with craps. Even soapy water enemas did hardly any good, for those few who had the honour of using the single apparatus in the farm's medical inventory. I had to stick my finger up my anus and dig it out, in dry lumps, like sawdust. The prison authorities finally backed off in alarm, gave us straight mush and instructed us to drink lots of water. I never saw it personally, but we heard that many of the older and weaker ones died trying to shit their guts out. I do recall a little scene in the fields, though, when Sun and I walked by one character squatting down by the edge of the road, shaking and sweating with the effort in spite of the cold.

"Look at that," Sun spat out with surprising rancour. "Another one of Mao's benefits for you."

After paper pulp flopped, someone in central planning came up with the bright idea of trying marsh water plankton. Since plankton was said to be almost 100 per cent protein, the idea seemed brilliant —in theory. They skimmed the slimy, green stuff off the swampy ponds around the camp and mixed it in with the mush either straight or dried and powdered, since it tasted too horrible to eat unaccompanied. Again, we all fell sick and some of the weaker ones died. That particular plankton, they discovered after a few autopsies, was practically unassimilable for the human body. End of plankton experiment. At length our daily ersatz became ground corn cobs, mixed in with the wo'tou flour. Afterward it was adopted as the standard food supplement for the country at large. We had been pioneers.

Camp 585

ONE DRIZZLY DAY in August a new warder I had never seen before came to the infirmary to look us over. He was dressed in a white shirt, khaki shorts and sandals, and seemed totally efficient. He took down our names and asked us about our health histories. When he had left, I asked Dr Ma what his visit was all about.

"Nothing good or bad," he replied obliquely. He often spoke in riddles—it's an old Chinese habit. The next morning the new warder was back again. This time he had that bastard Liu with him.

"The government is always concerned with your welfare," Liu said, and I thought to myself: Here it comes. It *had* to be some sort of bad news. "Number Three Farm is a production unit and as such has neither the means nor the time to care for the sick. For this reason the government has decided to transfer you to a place where there is proper medical care. It is called Camp 585, and it is especially designed for the needs of the sick. Now get your things ready. You are leaving immediately."

Those of us who could walk climbed onto a truck and the rest were carried aboard. We rolled over dirt roads through the fields for several hours before drawing up in front of a roughshod hamlet of red brick and whitewashed buildings surrounded by a flat mud embankment into which was stuck a large wooden panel with the numbers 5-8-5. We clambered down and when I caught sight of the old one-armed warder I had known before, Wang, I realized that this must just be a larger version of Northern Precious Village, the dying farm. Wang remembered me perfectly well, and on the strength of our past acquaintance made me group leader of our bunch.

We spent the rest of the afternoon and evening settling in one of the whitewashed cell units, finding out about rations and generally getting acquainted. Very quickly I saw some familiar faces from Northern Precious Village and got filled in on the situation. The old place had been requisitioned, they told me, when the agronomists had found some crops that would grow well in the surrounding soil. Camp 585 was to be the new consolidation point for all the weak, crippled and aged, and not many of them felt there was any chance of getting back out alive. We were 400 in all, and we ate twice a day, mostly the extras from the other production units. That wasn't much in those days. I shuffled around in the mud of the courtyard, watching some desultory foragers over by the kitchen waste heap, depressed and feeling hopeless and abandoned. It really looked like the end of the road.

The same tiresome, pointless routine continued the next morning, still under a fine, grey drizzle. Since we had no jobs and no work norms, the only activity appeared to be waiting to eat. Some time after noon Warder Wang called me to his office.

"You're leaving," he announced without ceremony. "You're going back to Number Three Farm. Get your things."

I was astonished and exhilarated. Suddenly my future seemed more possible. I didn't know it then, but I learned later that it was

Wang himself who declared me undesirable for 585. It was a very conscious and pointed gesture: He meant to save my life. He knew all too well that 585 was nothing but a death farm.

My exceptional bounce back to Number Three Farm didn't work without complication, though. This time I was accepted into the infirmary with only Class C rations—exactly half what the normal workers were getting. Evidently someone in the hierarchy, probably Warder Liu, had decided that I had shown myself to be a malcontent by having refused the government's benevolent offer of medical treatment in Camp 585. It wasn't until I had written a formal letter of protest to the camp director, explaining that I had been retransferred without my consent or prior knowledge, and had always acted in good faith, that Liu relented and allowed me back in the cell on Class B rations.

"Letter of protest" may sound wildly improbable for those who do not understand the Chinese prison system or the mentality of the cadres. As I learned in Prison Number One, everybody, even a prisoner, is encouraged to speak his mind honestly and fully, for the government wants to know what goes on in a man's head. In this manner if the thoughts are erroneous or not in sync with the party line, they can be corrected. No one would have thought of preventing me from sending my letter up the chain of command. The strange, Alice-in-Wonderland world of forms must always be served. My jailers had absolute authority over my body and soul, but they were obliged to hear me out. On my side, though, it imported that I be careful with my ideology. Free speech is encouraged especially if it remains within the accepted channels.

My recovery after I returned from 585 was surprisingly rapid. I don't know whether to ascribe it to the ministrations of Dr Ma, the diet supplements of Sun and Longman, or simply fear of the death farm, but I was soon out in the fields with the others. One of the first big jobs that fell to us was to weed out the rice paddies and loosen the earth around the young shoots—the classical Chinese bent-back, straw-hatted labour that illustrates millions of prints, cigar boxes and coffee tables in the West. It was the timeless image of Asia, and I was happy to be back inside it. The greatest pleasure of working in the paddies (besides serving socialism) was catching the frogs that proliferated there. I never could understand how they could be so numerous when the past few years had been so disastrously lean, but there they were, and none of us questioned our good fortune. They weren't even particularly difficult to stalk—often they would literally jump into our laps. We would skin them on the spot and eat them raw. The system is to start with the mouth, and the head comes off with the spine. Those with greater discipline would save the meat in their mugs with a little water (at that time of year we always carried our mugs with us, stuck down in the folds of our clothes) and then dry it in the sun to make a type of jerky. Salted, they had a delicious, delicate flavour. Sun roasted them on a stick and they tasted like bacon. Later in the summer when there were more wild vegetables, we would make all kinds of stews with them.

Around wheat-threshing time I witnessed a terrible suicide. Just as we were sitting in the shade for our midday meal of soup and wo'tous, a prisoner in a tattered white shirt and blue pants appeared in the field next to us, running with desperate energy toward one of the big wheat-chopping machines set into the ground. Before anyone had a chance to react, or cut off the machine, he had dived down into the blades. I never knew why he did it, but it wasn't rare for prisoners to get out of the camps that way. This one ended up in pieces.

In early September, Sun let me in on something of a secret, or at least an explanation of why the cellmates had taken such good care of me when I was in the infirmary. We were working the paddies then, and it was around 3 p.m. when he ambled over to me.

"Come on, Bao," he said, "don't knock yourself out. It won't get you anywhere. Let's have a smoke."

Why not? There was no warder in sight, and discipline was somewhat more relaxed now that the wheat was safely harvested and the rice seemed to be all right. We settled back against the bank of one of the raised roadways that intersected the paddies, took off our straw hats, drew out our little squares of newspaper and rolled ourselves a couple of vine-leaf smokes. Sun gestured broadly out at the fields.

"Look at that, Bao, isn't that a magnificent sight?"

It was difficult to tell whether or not he was being sarcastic, for in point of fact it *was* a magnificent sight. It was a cinema-scope day with an intensely blue sky pocked with rich, billowy cloud formations. The vast series of paddies before us stretched limitlessly to the horizon with nothing breaking the geometric pattern except the one long row of acacias and poplars over by the main highway. The dikes and pathways that separated them marched along in disciplined order. Everywhere we looked there were men, bareback or in black shirts, bent to their work, impervious to the world about them, each one lost in his personal universe. There were thousands of them.

"Isn't that wonderful?" Sun asked again. "All those people, and none of them will ever make it out, me included. Lifetime contract. You're the only one who's different, Bao. You might get out the Big Door some day. It could happen to a foreigner, but not us. You'll be the only one who can tell about it afterward if you do. That's why we wanted to keep you alive, Bao."

I was touched, but didn't quite feel his optimism. "I don't know if I'll live that long, Sun."

That wasn't theatrical pessimism on my part. Since August 1960, more than three-quarters of our brigade had died or been dispatched to Camp 585. There weren't many of us left.

"Don't you worry," Sun said firmly, "as long as you're here, you'll live. I can promise you that. And if you get transferred to other camps, there'll be other people who think like us. You're precious cargo, old man."

Sun laughed and sloshed back out into the paddy.

Christmas on Strip 23

THE LAST extraordinary experience I had at Qinghe was the Christmas mass of Father Hsia. Our teams had spent most of the month of December in miscellaneous agricultural housekeeping, such as marking boundaries for rice paddies, cleaning out irrigation ditches and cutting brush. The morning was bright and clear that Christmas day, but the temperature was close to zero, and a force five wind was roaring down from the northwest. The eighteen men under me were laying out paddy markers on Field Strip 23, a plot of clean ploughed earth about two miles long and 120 yards wide, in which we were to mark out sixty paddies, set down the stakes and then turn it over to other teams who would set up the system of irrigation ditches. I divided the section into five teams of three each and sent the remaining three to gather scrap wood for a bonfire.

It was around 9.30 when I noticed a solitary figure approaching me across the strip. Even quite far away, I could tell from his gait that it was Hsia. The earflaps of his ragged old cotton hat danced in the wind as he hurried over to me, and his faded khaki army overcoat and black padded pants were splattered with mud. With the exaggerated politeness characteristic of him, Hsia asked me if he could have a break for a few minutes. I had nothing against that, but he knew we had a deadline for the paddy job—couldn't he wait until lunch? Embarrassed and pained, he looked down at his boots, toying absently with the red-and-white markers he still held in his mittens.

"Don't you remember what day it is today, John?" he asked me in English.

Of course. I had been thickheaded.

"Go on, old man," I said, "but be careful."

He smiled gratefully and scurried away across the road and down the embankment to a dry gully where a bonfire was burning, and where he was shielded from the wind and the view of the warders. A quarter of an hour later, I saw a bicycle against the sky in the distance—a warder was on his way. I hustled over to the gully to warn Hsia.

As I looked down the embankment I saw that he was just finishing up the mass, in front of a mound of frozen earth which he had chosen as an altar. He was making the traditional gestures of priests all over the world. But his vestments here were ragged work clothes; the chalice, a chipped enamel mug; the wine, some improvised grapejuice; and the host, a bit of wo'tou he had saved from breakfast. I watched him for a moment and knew quite well it was the truest mass I would ever see. I loped down the embankment, and when the warder passed on his bike he saw only two prisoners warming their hands.

from Chapters 12 & 13 of Prisoner of Mao
(section headings added)

Intellectuals in the Gulag

Cadre schools were established throughout China as reform camps for intellectuals and public servants in accordance with Mao Zedong's "May 7 Directive" of 1966, in which he called for educated urban dwellers to undergo labour reform by living and working with the peasants. In fact, few were given any choice in the matter, and within three or four years over twenty million people, virtually China's entire professional and university-trained population, had been evacuated from the cities to live in such schools. Most were encouraged to take their families with them, as the process of thought reform was initially expected to continue until the older intellectuals had died out altogether. As a rule, however, their period of rustication did not last as long as that of the Urblings.* Although older Chinese writers generally reminisce about their experiences in the schools in a light-hearted and sardonic manner—often as a conditioned reflex to the terrors of the Cultural Revolution—few have forgotten that many people were persecuted and died in the make-shift re-education camps.

*For Urblings, see below, p. 102.

THE EAST, Cheng Xiaoyu

Digging a Well

Yang Jiang

THERE WAS always lots of work to be done in a cadre school. Labour out in the fields consisted mainly of planting beans or wheat. In the hot weather this meant that the day would start in the early hours around three when everyone would set off to work on an empty stomach. Breakfast would be brought out to you at six, then work continued until midday before you headed back for lunch. Following the afternoon rest, you would return to the fields around dusk and work into the night.

At the beginning we stayed in the peasants' houses in the village, but work started on our own accomodation almost at once. As bricks were unavailable we had to make our own mud substitute. Brickmaking was regarded as the most backbreaking work. Looking after the pigsties and tending the pigs ran a close second, since it was the dirtiest and most unrewarding job of all. Most of the older and less robust "students" such as myself were assigned to the vegetable gardens and kitchens, all of the heavy and tiring work falling on the shoulders of the young.

One night there was an evening of performances and skits on the theme of manual labour. Among the sketches was a short play about a member of a certain regiment who risked life and limb to keep the fire in a brick kiln going even though the roof was about to cave in. Someone said it was based on a true story. Another regiment put on a performance that was simply called "Well-digging". The whole regiment crowded on to the stage and moved around in a large circle as though they were pushing a well drill while they chanted a work song in chorus. There was no script and no other action apart from the circling movement and rhythmic chanting. Everyone moved and worked as one, drilling on without stopping until they reached the right depth. "Hey-ho, hey-ho!"—the choral reverberation reminded me of a once-popular film theme song, "The Song of the Volga Boatmen". Listening to the performers, I could almost see the boatmen on the riverbank pulling their boats along, step by step, struggling forward exhausted and leaning all of their weight against the ropes. Although the well-digging piece was a little monotonous it was more realistic and moving than the heroics in the kiln, with its message "to fear neither hardship nor death." At the end of the evening everyone went away full of praise for the well-digging performance; after all, people said, it didn't require any rehearsal: all they had to do was climb on the stage and do it.

Suddenly someone blurted out,

"Just a minute. There must be something ideologically wrong with it . . . . It must be . . . that is, intellectuals are so impressed by it, it must mean . . . . "

Everyone understood the point he was trying to make and laughed knowingly. This was followed by an uncomfortable silence. We quickly changed the subject.

I was assigned to work in the vegetable brigade. One of our major tasks was the digging of our own well, just like those people on stage, and we did it without any machinery.

The district in which our cadre school was located had had a run of good luck—although it was right next to the flood-prone Huai River, the area had not been washed out for a good two years. On the other hand, the ground was bone-dry and hard as rock, and this made growing vegetables quite a chore. The local peasants had a saying: "It's muddy when it rains and like rock when it's clear." A tractor had gone over the ground before we went to work on it, but all the plough had done was turn up great sods of earth as big and as hard as small boulders, so we still had to put a lot of work into just getting the ground ready to plant. Breaking up those sods into workable earth was not only exhausting; it required the patience of a saint. Once we had finally carved out a few patches of earth and dug out water channels, we discovered that there was no water on hand. In a neighbouring vegetable garden there was a motor-pump well that supposedly went to a depth of ten metres. We were constantly going over to get drinking water from them. The water in a hand-dug well of about three metres' depth was always muddy. To obtain drinkable water from it you had to put disinfectant in the bucket, which always made the water taste very peculiar. But the water from the motor-pump well, ten metres down in the earth, was cool and sweet. Drinking that water after sweating in the sun for hours was like sipping nectar.

Our borrowing was not limited to a neighbourly cup or two of drinking water, since we always took the liberty of washing our dirty hands and feet, too. None of this caused any trouble, but when we tried to use the well to water our vegetables there were numerous problems. For one thing, without a pump we couldn't get any water over to our fields. Once we managed to borrow a pump, but the water from their well had barely started its tortuous route through our carefully dug system of channels—wasting most of itself in the dry earth on the way —when night fell and the people we borrowed the pump from came to take it back. The spinach seeds we had planted took a whole month to sprout, and then did so only after a heavy rainfall. In the end we decided that we would have to dig our own well. After selecting a site we all set to work.

The designated ground was as hard as burnished copper. I picked up a shovel and stabbed down with what I thought was enough strength to gouge out a great hole in the ground, but only managed to make a white scratch on the surface, much to the amusement of the younger people around me. But when even their more energetic efforts were not getting them very far they agreed it was a job for pickaxes. Although I wasn't very good with a shovel, I was pretty fast on my feet, so I volunteered to run over to the tool shed. Before long I was jogging back with the picks over my shoulder to find the others still chipping away at the ground. As soon as I appeared a couple of the young men took the picks from me and began loosening the earth with them. The stronger men worked with the picks in turn while the rest of us shovelled the earth out of the way. We kept at it all day and by dusk had managed to scoop out a fair-sized hole, but there still wasn't a hint of moisture at the bottom of it. One of the younger members of the group, Xiao Niu, began grumbling about women being bad luck and how they were unlikely to find water with us around. There were only two women in the vegetable brigade: myself, the oldest woman in the whole company, and Axiang, the youngest, an overseas Chinese girl barely half my age. Xiao Niu's loud comments came as a shock to her and she couldn't make up her mind whether to be angry or amused. Finally, with a grin she told me she was determined to give him a piece of her mind. In all honesty, however, we were both a little worried that if we didn't find water very soon, everyone *would* blame us. Fortunately, the ground became soggy and then water began appearing at about a two-metre depth.

Shovelling out dry earth had been tiring enough, but scooping the heavy mud from the bottom of the well proved to be even more exhausting. Two people stayed down at the bottom of the well and passed the mud up in buckets to be dumped to the side by those standing at the rim. It didn't take long before the ground around the well was muddy, and everyone was slipping around in bare feet. Axiang seemed to be enjoying herself the most and, having taken off her shoes, had jumped into the well to help pass up buckets of mud. I wasn't strong enough to lift even one of the buckets, but joined in the spirit of things by shovelling the mud around the well into a pile in my bare feet.

The distaste one has for mud—with its usual mixture of phlegm, mucus, urine and excrement—vanished once we had taken off our shoes and socks and started walking around in the warm and yielding ooze. It was slippery and wet, but it did not seem at all "dirty". You felt the way you did about a loved one with a contagious disease, holding hands and kissing without concern for becoming ill yourself. The thought suddenly struck me: is this what they mean about "changing your attitude" toward physical labour?

The digging became harder as water collected in the bottom of the well. Though it was not like using a mechanical drill where you have to keep on digging until you reach the proper depth no matter how long it takes, still we could not afford to slacken our efforts. We decided to follow the same routine as the people planting crops, assembling in the vegetable garden every morning before dawn without eating breakfast. As the time for the morning meal approached, Axiang and I would go back to get steamed bread, rice porridge, salted vegetables and boiled water, load it onto a wheelbarrow and cart it back to the well-site. I would push it on the level and downward sloping parts of the dirt path; Axiang would take over on the sharp turns, bumps and inclines. Although it doesn't sound like a very hard job, it took some practice to keep that cart on an even keel and the open tureens of porridge and hot water from spilling. I tried doing Axiang's job and quickly found that it looked much easier than it was. Luckily for me she didn't begrudge having to do the more difficult work and we got on very well together.

At lunchtime, everyone went back to eat at the regimental mess, and after a midday sleep continued working until dusk. We were always the last ones to get back for dinner. I don't remember how long we kept this routine up, but eventually we hit the three-metre mark. A few days before this the water at the bottom of the well was slowing work up so much that we had to ask a couple of strong young men from other units to lend us a hand. They jumped down into the well and set to work immediately in ankle-deep water. Wells are usually dug in the winter when the earth below is warm, but it was the height of summer and the well was damp and chilly. Axiang and I were afraid they would get a bad chill if they stayed down there too long, but they shouted back that they felt fine and kept on digging. We didn't want to seem like a pair of old hens, but we couldn't help going over to the well every so often to see how they were getting along.

The water gradually rose to knee level. After a while the diggers were splashing up to their thighs and then up to their waists. We had calculated that a three-metre depth would be quite sufficient for our purposes, so when they neared the mark I suggested that I go and buy some wine to warm the men who had been working in the water and to celebrate the completion of the well. After all the work we had put into it everyone was very excited. One of the men who had come over to help us dig was in charge of the catering and supply division. He gave me a few pointers on how I could get some wine. I rushed back to the regiment mess hall to recite to the cook what I had been told and got a bottle from him. On it was a threatening label with a skull and crossbones crudely drawn over the word *POISON*, which was followed by three large exclamation marks—obviously scribbled on to keep others from stealing it. Protectively clasping the bottle, which still had about an inch of wine left in the bottom, I hurried off to the supply store at the central headquarters of the school, about one kilometre west of the vegetable garden. I went as quickly as I could as I was worried about making it before closing time and wished I had one of those old flying-horse talismans tied to my feet so that I could go even faster. But when I got to the store and found they were still open, I still had to talk them into selling me wine without an official authorisation form. Luckily, the fact that I had managed to get hold of a wine bottle seemed to be official enough for them and they sold me a catty of rice spirits with no further questions asked. They didn't have anything on sale to go with the wine so I had to settle for some "sweets" that looked more like hard lumps of mud than anything else. Then it was back to the well-site with my precious cargo.

They had finished the digging and everyone was sitting down for a rest. As soon as they saw me, they all grabbed their drinking mugs and hurried over to pour themselves some wine. We managed to finish the whole bottle I had bought, leaving only an inch or so at the bottom to be returned to the mess. The "sweets" also disappeared and our victory banquet drew to a close.

I had only been doing light work cleaning up around the construction site, and I can't say I personally experienced the tremendous physical exhaustion of well-digging, but at the end of every day I would lie awake listening to my companion tossing and turning in the next bed, moaning in her sleep as though struggling to tear herself away from the aches and pains of the day's toil. I listened with a sense of guilt, knowing I was not really sharing the full burden of fatigue with her. During the day as we were working, you even heard the men say, "Ah, I suppose we're not as young as we used to be," admitting that they no longer had the strength and energy of their early twenties. So even the people who were so much younger than me seemed to feel that they couldn't do as much as they would have liked to.

By the time we bought and installed a hand-driven pump, the well was full. We placed a platform over the top of the well with the pump positioned in the centre, so that a long handle was required to turn it. The advantage of this was that you didn't get dizzy pushing the handle since you had to walk in a large circle. The younger men in the brigade took turns at pumping water, doing from a few dozen to a hundred revolutions in one go. The people who sometimes came over to give our brigade a hand with the vegetables were impressed. They had realized that it took some time to get used to long periods of squatting when working in a vegetable patch, but not that turning a hand pump was also an acquired skill.

I was truly part of the team, going out with everyone else before dawn and returning to base camp only after dark. Though you couldn't say what I did was manual labour in the strict sense of the word, just being with everyone else and doing light jobs around the site made me feel part of it all. I gradually developed a sense of group or team spirit, a fellowship in which I was part of the whole. There was a satisfying feeling of belonging. I had never had this feeling when I had worked on short-term community labour projects in the past; with those, once the assigned work or construction job was completed, everyone had gone their separate ways. Intellectual work is even less conducive to a team spirit. Even when you collaborate with other people, you tend to regard your own individual contribution as the most important. If you write an article with someone else, the person in charge of collecting and collating material and the person who actually writes it up very rarely manage to work as one. In the cadre school it was different: the prospect of an indefinite future of working together with little or no hope of ever going back brought about a strong feeling of community, of "us-ness".

I often heard people who had been sent down to the cadre school comment, "Well *they* never get soaked in the rain or sunburnt from working outside." A few simple words would carve a chasm between "them" and "us". Being part of the "us" by no means meant that we thought and acted as one: although we were now all in the same cadre school together, some had come down after being locked up in the "cowshed".* Despite these differences we were all part of the same category because we were all under "them". But you couldn't say that all of the people in charge of us were equally part of "them", since *they* were only the ones who "never got soaked in the rain or sunburnt". I remember one person who really thought of himself as something special, giving orders and lecturing people in liberal fashion. He was a typical one of "them". Then there were others like "that thick-skinned old fart", or "the joker who thinks he's God's gift to mankind"—without a doubt also part of "them". The difference between "us" and "them" really had little to do with political or social class, yet working in a group all the time did give me much insight into the nature of "class feelings".

The poor and lower-middle peasants—the people we were all supposed to regard as our teachers, the people we had in fact been sent to the countryside to learn from and be re-educated by—actually took

*Intellectuals were generally referred to as "cow spirits and snake demons" in the Cultural Revolution, and the temporary prisons for confining them between struggle sessions became known as "cowsheds".

exception to our presence. One morning we arrived at our vegetable garden to discover that a number of rows of sweet potatoes had disappeared during the night. I lost count of the number of times vegetables we had planted were stolen before they had grown to full size. If you said anything, they'd protest loudly: "Look at you, you buy all of the vegetables you eat anyway. You're only planting these for fun!" They also took all of the saplings we had planted and sold them at the local market. When we were harvesting our soya beans they relieved us of the rest of the crop before we had even finished. To add insult to injury, they would shout out in self-defence: "You people eat grain you've bought from the State anyway."

We were never part of their "us", but only another type of "them", or, as they put it, "well-fed, wrist-watch-wearing oddities who like to dress up in old clothes."

from A Cadre School Life: Six Chapters

Yang Jiang is a translator of English, Spanish and French literature, as well as being a playwright. She was "sent down" to the Academy of Social Sciences cadre school in 1970 at the age of sixty with her husband, Qian Zhongshu, one of China's most respected writers and scholars. Her six-chapter account is one of the best-written recollections of cadre school life to be published to date. Yang's genius lies in her ability to write of her experience without indulging in histrionics or making explicit the overwhelming scale of the horror. Understatement is indeed one of the traditional modes of expression valued by Chinese writers, though it is often a virtue born of necessity. Perhaps, however, it is the very lack of sensationalism in Yang's writing that has prevented her book from receiving the attention it deserves both in China and overseas.

"Oracle Bones": Memories of a Cadre School

Chen Baichen

The Conspiracy

I'VE PUT quotation marks around the hallowed words oracle bones in the title because that was the nickname I gave to a very special member of the revolutionary masses. It was a name known only to myself; for obvious reasons I never dared use it in the man's presence, nor even when referring to him behind his back—to do so would have been tantamount to blasphemy. I prefer to use it now in place of his real name, more out of a desire to remain faithful to my memory of its owner, than from any lingering wish to mock him.

Oracle Bones had just been posted to the Writers' Association when I arrived back in Peking under escort in 1966. I didn't know his real name, and promptly forgot it every time I enquired about it. He was said to have studied the ancient oracle bone script. It struck me from the first as rather bizarre that an antiquarian should have been assigned to work in an institution concerned solely with contemporary literature, and as a result I had little trouble remembering him as the oracle bone man. His unprepossessing appearance—he was short, stocky and hunched over—and the fact that he was given to martial posturing in his leather jacket, added to the comic aspect of the fellow. He had no status to speak of in the revolutionary hierarchy; he was just one of those lowly "all purpose men", ready to wield a writing brush or a bludgeon as the occasion demanded—the type people like me had learned to detest.

The name I gave him was initially meant as a term of derision. Later when it became evident that he played no major role in the drama of the times, and that he was not guilty of any real wrong-doing, I didn't feel so offended by him any more. But the name stuck, for no greater reason I suppose than that it added a touch of fun to the proceedings.

Then later, in the spring of 1970, when we were all in the cadre school together, to my great surprise Oracle Bones rose from obscurity to join the ranks of the infamous. His sudden ascent to "stardom" could be traced back to late 1966 and early 1967, when a super-revolutionary organization started plastering big-character posters up all over the city.[1] The posters appeared under suspicious circumstances, especially as they concentrated their attacks on the old cadres. Nothing seemed to come of the campaign and we were all left wondering whether the organization claiming responsibility existed in the first place. It was also very curious that the renowned hack Yao Wenyuan inveighed against this new faction, which he labelled a counter-revolutionary group in a footnote to one of his articles. Though this went by unnoticed at first, some months later that same footnote set off another political storm that was to sweep the country. The faction, though small, was then declared to be particularly evil and a thorough investigation was ordered immediately. The investigation, it was emphasized, should not get "out of hand". In our part of the world Oracle Bones was the first one to be questioned regarding his involvement in the organization. I must admit that at the time I found this most satisfying, and I can recall saying to people that I could tell the man was up to no good just by the look of him, the net of divine justice never failed to catch wrong-doers, and so on.

One reason I gloated over the man's misfortunes was that we were not the target of the attacks; for once we could stand on the sidelines and watch the unfolding debacle without having to fear for our own safety. During this new campaign we were ignored and thus free, quite content to observe the "revolutionary masses" taking it out on their own kind. So I was more than ready to believe that Oracle Bones was a member of this dastardly new organization. That someone like Oracle Bones, a man regarded by everyone as a nobody, was actually a ring-leader of the group was proof of how cunning the deception had been.

. . . . . .

[1] The underground group referred to throughout this chapter is the "May 16 Organization", which was named after the Chinese Communist Party's *Sixteen Point Resolution on the Cultural Revolution* made on May 16, 1966. The size and supposed threat of this bogus group reached mythical proportions and the campaigns aimed at destroying it were actually used to purge the radical advocates and theoreticians of the Cultural Revolution. Naturally, countless innocents were also sacrificed to this end.

Oracle Bones testified that he'd become involved with the organization at someone else's behest. In fact, everyone detained in connection with the group pointed the finger at the same man. The accused, however, stood his ground and firmly denied any connection with or knowledge of the conspiracy. What did it all mean?

Then there were the struggle sessions. Up till then these had always been public events. This time there were no meetings at all. Individuals were simply called upon to account for their involvement with the organization in front of everyone else. These "confessions" were regularly accompanied by much tearful breast-beating. Why this new format, I asked myself? Prior to each round of public self-flagellation the person concerned would suddenly disappear without even their brigade leader being informed of what was going on. This was the only indication of the impending event. Anything up to a week later the person would reappear "having laid down his butcher's knife and become a Buddha".[2] Then an announcement would follow from the leadership to the effect that "no legal action would be taken against So-and-so, who would continue work as before". In some cases the person involved was given an even better position than before. I was mystified as to what it all meant.

There was this one chap, probably one of Dongfang Shuo's ilk,[3] or maybe he came from a line of stand-up comics, whose public *mea culpa* was a classic.

"In the past I was quite certain that I was *not* a member of the counter-revolutionary organization. But now, thanks to a period of ideological re-education by the leadership, I am quite certain that I *have* been a member of the organization all along."

His statement brought a question from the floor:

"Just what do you mean by that?"

He repeated his brilliantly formulated line for our benefit and all attempts at further questioning were greeted with exactly the same

---

[2] A saying based on a story recorded by the Song dynasty monk Pu Ji, about Guang E, a scoundrel who suddenly laid down his butcher's knife one day and became a Buddha on the spot. The expression is popularly used to describe a person who has seen the error of his ways.

[3] Dongfang Shuo (154-93 B.C.), a minister at the time of Emperor Wu of the Han dynasty, was renowned for his quick wit and offhand manner.

frustrating response.

The original plan had been for him to perform before each brigade, but as a result of this exchange the idea was hastily dropped. Nor was he immediately sent back to his original job as had become the practice. Curiouser and curiouser.

The Giant

FOR ME the most baffling case in this parade of the damned was that of a retired soldier known simply as the Giant. He was a stout northerner and just about as tough as they come. One day he appeared before us at a general meeting that was being held in the mess hall. The convener of the meeting announced that the Giant had also been enlisted into the organization and was before us now to make a full confession. But instead, to our great mystification, he did nothing but sob from start to finish in a display I'm sure was quite genuine. He was eventually led away without having said a word.

The Giant and I went back a long way. He was one of the two guards who escorted me to Peking on September 11, 1966. I always refer to this as my arrest although the authorities tried to avoid the issue by making out that I was being "invited" to the capital. The first news I had of my removal was when the people in Nanjing notified me that my presence had been requested at a denunciation of Zhang Tianyi by my former employer, the Chinese Writers' Association. Ostensibly I had been invited to attend, but when I applied for a few days leave, to recover from a debilitating attack of lumbago, I was curtly refused. They told me the date of the struggle meeting had already been fixed, and I had to be there. This smacked of coercion. When I tried to stall them further by saying that my illness made travel difficult, I was told the Writers' Association had sent two people all the way to Nanjing, to escort me to Peking. So it was neither an invitation nor an arrest; it was more like a "command performance".

The Giant was one of the two escorts who turned up at my house. I got them to have a meal with me before setting off for the station. They were there, after all, to invite me to Peking so it was the least I could do in return. They didn't refuse me, much to the relief of my family, and this way it looked less like an arrest. They spoiled the masquerade as we were leaving, though, by sitting on either side of me in the back of the car, in an obvious attempt to prevent my escape.

This was at the height of the Red Guard movement when young people were roaming all over the country, so the trains were jam-packed. Under normal circumstances my senior status would have assured me a berth, but there weren't any to be had. In consideration of the long trip it was decided that we'd cross the Yangtze River and spend half a night at Pukou (this was before the Yangtze Bridge was built), boarding another train at three in the morning after a few hours of sleep. I saw no reason to object. Our room at the hotel had only two beds, one single and one double. I was certain I'd be given the single, but the Giant made me sleep in the double instead. Aware that compliance was the better part of valour I moved over to the double bed, and as I was undressing I noticed one of those ubiquitous quotations on the wall at the head of the bed. It was that passage quoting Sima Qian: some deaths are heavier than Mount Tai, while others are lighter than a feather. I couldn't help chuckling to myself—the Giant took every opportunity to educate me.[4] I fell into a sound sleep the moment my head touched the pillow, and dozed until they woke me some time before three. It seemed that neither of them had slept a wink.

Things at the station were a bit more orderly this time as they had put an extra carriage on the train. My two escorts managed to get me into the station ahead of everyone else and they pushed their way to the head of a queue on the platform much to the annoyance of the people behind us. I heard some of the comments coming from the people in the queue. One said, "So who's the big-shot then? Look, he even has two attendants." Both of my "attendants" were dressed in PLA uniforms and the fact that neither of them was wearing the all but obligatory Red Guard armbands made them really stand out. How could anyone be expected to guess the truth? I was being treated with such deference by my guards that to a casual observer it would have been impossible to guess that they were both playing the part of Chong Gongdao, the kindly escort in the Peking opera *The Lady is Taken to Court*.

[4]The author is, of course, talking about a quotation from Chairman Mao. In a speech made at a memorial service for a revolutionary martyr in 1944, Mao quoted the Han dynasty historian Sima Qian: "Death is the lot of all men; but a person's death can be heavier than Mount Tai, or lighter than a feather."

The considerate treatment I received during that trip to Peking left me with a favourable impression of the Giant.

Then, during the summer of 1968, we were packed off to the No. 1 Nanyuan Commune to help with the harvest. I was primarily sent along for re-education. One of the greatest thinkers in the leadership decided to hold a joint struggle session after work one day to allow everyone a chance to criticize the urban blackguards along with the Five Evil Elements in the commune.[5] And what a motley crowd we were—adherents of the "black line in the arts" lumped together with a former rich peasant charged with incest. We heard that many revolutionaries were against this type of circus, and I presume the Giant was one of them.

Oracle Bones Shakes a Leg

ON THE DAY they laid on quite a spectacle and the assembly was out for blood. Those of us on display at the front were obliged to bend over at a ninety degree angle as a way of expressing our contrition and the "jet plane" was the order of the day.[6] Any sloppiness of posture was rewarded with a rain of punches and kicks from the stewards standing behind us. It was at the height of summer and boiling hot outside in the sun. Pools of sweat dripped from our faces and formed wet patches at our feet as the village cadres were getting into the full swing of things.

Bing Xin, who was standing next to me, sweated away in silence, but I could hear poor old Tianyi behind me panting heavily. Yan Wenjing, who was over on the side, had already caved in and his plea

[5]That is: landlords, rich peasants, counter-revolutionaries, bad elements and Rightists.

[6]A painful position often demanded of people being "struggled": the legs were to be kept straight, the torso was bent forward at a right angle, while the arms were raised up behind the body in the air. Such a pose was said to resemble a jet airplane.

to be allowed to kneel had been granted.[7] My lumbago was killing me and just as I was about to follow Wenjing's example someone tapped me roughly on the back and blared, "Just take a look at yourself. You're a disgrace. Get out of here." I didn't know what to make of this but I did my best bent over as I was at the waist to walk, or rather, hobble "out of there". After walking a short distance the same voice ordered me to straighten up. It suddenly occurred to me that I'd been let off the hook. Turning around I discovered that my saviour was none other than the Giant, and that Zhang Guangnian along with another old man had been included in his clemency. Pointing to a tree in the distance he told us to go and rest under it. The Giant must have realized that the old man with us couldn't take such punishment and that Guangnian was ill. He knew about my lumbago from when he was my escort. What an exquisite pleasure it was to be able to sit down in the shade and light up a cigarette.

How could the Giant be a member of this counter-revolutionary organization? I just couldn't believe it. His pitiful crying seemed to attest to his innocence.

Eventually, when something like 30% of the entire company had confessed to being involved with the organization, a struggle meeting was ordered by the brigade to deal with the man who had been fingered as the ring-leader. Many of the self-confessed conspirators from the other companies had named this man and it seemed obvious that he had been playing a vital role in the whole organization. For this reason the struggle was being carried out on a particularly grand scale and the leadership hoped to use it as an opportunity to "storm the enemy defences".

Instead it turned out to be a disaster. To repeat the hackneyed style of expression favoured by the chairman of the struggle meeting, despite the fact that there was an "iron-clad" case against the accused, he still "put up a last ditch battle" and "stuck doggedly to his counter-revolutionary position", "brazenly refusing to surrender". In other

[7]Bing Xin (b. 1900), a novelist and children's writer who involved herself in "friendship work" with foreign countries after 1949.

Zhang Tianyi (1906-85), a major children's writer and critic.

Yan Wenjing (b. 1915), novelist, children's writer and critic. Yan was the head of the People's Publishing House until 1966.

words he shot holes through the flimsy evidence of the various witnesses.

A typical example was when a witness declared that he had met with the accused on a certain day; the latter immediately discounted the possibility of this by saying that he had been working somewhere else at the time, and since there was only one of him it would have been quite impossible for such a meeting to have taken place. Or another witness would claim they had had a rendezvous on such-and-such a day. The accused would ridicule this by claiming to have been away on official business. A number of times he even went so far as to point at one of his accusers and roar, "You're playing factional politics, and you know as well as I do that this is all a pack of lies," or something to that effect. Naturally everyone thought him to be "swollen with arrogance". The funny thing was that the witnesses for the prosecution were powerless to protect themselves against his remorseless "testimony". Out of sheer desperation the chairman gave a sign to the fellow in charge of slogan chanting to lead a chorus of "Death is the only way out if he doesn't submit!" and "If he doesn't confess he will die 10,000 deaths!" This provided a very clamorous interlude, though the chanting was unenthusiastic and a little spottier than usual. The meeting came to an abrupt end after the slogans.

The spirited display put on by the accused increased my estimation of him considerably. I only regret that the Giant and some of the others were absent; if they had been able to witness this farce they might have staged a revolt.

After that there was a short lull, although rumours spread like wildfire. Deprived of the right to join in the gossip-making, I was still able to piece things together from snatched comments and chance clues. It turned out that the man responsible for the whole witch-hunt was none other than Oracle Bones. In some way or another he had managed to put the finger on a good third of the people in our company. But my sources failed me when it came to explaining why he had acted in such a cruel and vindictive manner. Not surprisingly he resurfaced a much changed man. From then on he kept very much to himself, and limited his conversation to monosyllables. This new Oracle Bones was quite different from the blustering demagogue we had known in the past.

As the summer harvest approached it was decided to put up temporary quarters out in the fields where we'd be working. We dubbed these new barracks where we'd be eating and sleeping for the summer the Imperial Villa or our Summer Residence. As part of the mad rush to get the harvest in I was also assigned to live in the villa, and of all things I was given a bunk opposite Oracle Bones. Now that we were living together I did my best to be neighbourly, but all of my attempts at conversation were greeted with dumb stares. I took the hint and gave up any thought of socializing with him. Nonetheless, whenever he was in the shed I never took my eyes off him. On the surface he was just like everyone else, going out to work and coming back with the rest of us. But after a day in the fields, while everyone would be having a wash or soaking their feet, or perhaps using that time to catch up on a bit of washing, he'd sit down on his bed, lean back on his pillow wearily, cross his legs and jiggle one foot while puffing away at a cigarette. I can't recall seeing him ever take a wash; though he might have sneaked it in before going out to work. Nor did I ever catch him washing his clothes. After a day of work we'd all be filthy, but he'd just take off his shirt, throw it under his bed, and exchange it for another dirty shirt the next morning. And then the following day he'd be back under the bed to fish out the original soiled shirt, which he put on, and so forth in endless rotation. I thought this was definitely a bit off.

I happened to tell all this to one of my few confidants over at company headquarters. He groaned in disbelief and said, "Don't tell me he's still shaking that damned leg of his!" He then proceeded to tell me all.

It seems that in the beginning the company leadership didn't have a clue as to how they should go about uncovering that so-called counter-revolutionary organization. Reliable sources had it that salvation eventually came in the form of an outside official who was an expert political strategist. He advocated carrying out a preliminary reconnaisance by hauling in a number of suspects for "informal chats". Though the exact contents of these exchanges remained secret, I'm sure they concentrated on making oblique references to "the organization" as well as using a few shock tactics, to test the suspect's reactions. In this procedure, one leader would usually ask all the questions while the others sat facing the man under interrogation in stony silence waiting for a slip up or some spontaneous reaction to the questioning.

The first round of interrogations produced no results, though Oracle Bones had acted suspiciously. It seems he shook his leg through the entire session. The board of investigators concluded that this was a nervous reaction due to guilt. Oracle Bones was seized on as the weak link in the chain and they went to work on him. His interrogators, adhering to the principle that "it's fine for the good guys to beat up scum", finally extracted a confession of sorts from Oracle Bones, who hoped thereby to save his skin. But they weren't satisfied — they wanted him to name his superiors. By this point he was in so deep there was no escaping, so he sacrificed a fellow cadre and appointed him ring-leader. In going on to name his fellow conspirators Oracle Bones cast his net wide, proving that there was no lack of candidates for subterfuge. That he was also willing to pinpoint a leader, however, was a major victory and the interrogators congratulated themselves on their ingenuity. Provided at last with a scapegoat, they did their utmost to exaggerate his importance and the heinous nature of his actions, believing that this would invite greater rewards from on high. That's when things started getting out of hand. Eventually, as we have seen above, the whole business backfired, as these things are wont to do. The wild exaggerations turned out to be of little use, since the accused proved far less malleable than Oracle Bones, and the case against him came apart at the seams. Fortunately, our leaders were able to exhibit a high degree of political maturity when it came to dealing with ig-nominious failure, and they weathered the resultant storm with great skill. In the end it turned out that Oracle Bones was the only one who suffered pangs of conscience, and this was his undoing. And that bless-ed leg of his, the source of all his woes and the cause of the whole fiasco, was still shaking.

Having been told this story I couldn't help feeling a little sorry for Oracle Bones, so I kept an eye on him. That is when I discovered his secret. I happened to wake up in the middle of the night, and saw a point of light dancing wildly in the air. It shocked the blazes out of me, I can tell you. When I calmed down a bit I was able to work out that it was Oracle Bones propped up in bed smoking. He was holding the cigarette in his hand like a pen, and was writing furiously in the air. I know he wasn't practising oracle bone script, as the strokes flowed together, but I couldn't tell whether it was normal or cursive hand-writing. Whatever it was, the words were undecipherable. It made me dizzy to watch him so I gave up and went back to sleep, waking again just before dawn to find he was still going strong. The floor at the head of his bed was covered with cigarette butts.

I felt compelled to report these strange goings-on to the brigade and unit leaders, and so on up to the top. I suggested that they look out for him. Oracle Bones repeated his performance two nights in a row. He never seemed to sleep. On the third night his bunk was empty. I felt sorry about what had happened. Where had they taken him?

A month later I learnt he had been placed in an asylum. Word had it that he was doing quite well, and some months later he was rumoured to have recovered. Fearful of the consequences of sending him back into the environment that had caused him such torment, the authorities decided to assign him work in his home town. There was no way of checking the reliability of these rumours. We saw no more of him. After that I often thought of the radical transformation his personality had undergone.

The Revolutionary Physiognomist

AFTER THE Spring Festival of 1972 I found myself at the receiving end of some revolutionary largesse for the first time. I was given twelve days leave to see my family in Nanjing. At home for something to do at night, and more importantly as a way of avoiding talking about my life in the cadre school, I did my best to entertain my wife and children with tales of some of the absurdities of the Cultural Revolution. One night I told them all about Oracle Bones, thinking his story was sure to amuse them. My children, however, proved to be very unreceptive. I told them about the desperate interrogations the company leadership had been forced to carry out in order to get some leads, but they dismissed such antics as being "typically bookish" and not a patch on a local bureau chief whose method of "revolutionary physiognomy" had had such devastating results. They thought our poor Oracle Bones nothing more than a pedantic dupe. Why, they argued, in Nanjing someone like him could have manipulated the situation to considerable personal advantage. My fellow had got himself locked up in the nut-house for his trouble. Though somewhat taken aback, I begged to hear more.

It appeared that a certain government bureau in Nanjing had been given a citation for its outstanding results in the hunt for the same conspiracy. This achievement was due entirely to the miraculous talents of the bureau chief. When the campaign began he claimed he was an adept in a school of Song dynasty physiognomy which enabled him to tell a counter-revolutionary at a glance. This special talent meant he could dispense with the usual lengthy and exhaustive investigations.

On a day appointed by him the bureau offices were closed to the public and all employees were ordered to stop work. None of the cadres were permitted to return home. The chief then seated himself at the entrance to the canteen and studied everyone as they lined up at meal-times. His method was simple but ruthlessly effective. A person in line with head lowered in silent thought was, according to his diagnosis, obviously troubled by a guilty conscience. If someone was singing a passage from a revolutionary model opera he was doubtlessly trying to disguise his fear and therefore equally suspect. On the other hand, anyone spotted reading a paper was flaunting his political orthodoxy; while someone wearing his cap askew had a headful of improper thoughts. Anyone giggling and laughing in line was attempting to conceal his fear and guilt; and a person with his nose in the air was a conspirator in a future counter-revolutionary insurrection. Similarly, the chief could tell that an employee's unkempt dress was a silent protest; while the fastidious dresser was more likely than not a malcontent lying in wait for a change of leadership. It took the director only three days, or nine meals, to detain seventy percent of his employees for questioning. Following several intense interrogation sessions and spurred on by attendant threats and physical persuasion, every one of the suspects confessed. The investigators were able to report an unprecedented seventy-three percent success rate! The three percent over the quota consisted of cadres from other units who had come to the bureau on official business or simply to see friends, and had been arrested the moment the bureau chief caught sight of their "counter-revolutionary" faces.

My children also initiated me into some of the other ways cadres went about turning such campaigns to their own ends. One leading cadre in the city, although quite unconnected with any group, was denounced by someone as being a member of the counter-revolutionary organization. As we all know, "mud sticks", and on seeing no way out for himself he volunteered the information that he was in fact a key figure in the plot, promising to hand over a list of all his contacts in return for an unconditional release. The authorities were elated with this windfall and lavished rich rewards upon him. For his part of the bargain, he went home and wrote up his list that very night. It consisted of the names of everyone he knew, nearly two hundred people in all; though he did see fit to leave out his blood relations. This startling development shook Nanjing. As the cadre was well-connected, very few of the major government bodies and leading organizations in the city escaped. The people thus condemned were expected to confess and betray others in turn. In no time at all the list had over one thousand names on it. And the man who had started the ball rolling was not only spared all punishment but rewarded with a promotion of two grades.

My reaction to these stories was utter disbelief. I told my children I was sure someone had made them all up and I warned them not to be so easily taken in by such hearsay. Though they swore they were telling the truth, I remained unconvinced.

"You can't expect me to believe that the fellow got a promotion by betraying his friends?"

"No, it wasn't quite that simple," they explained. "He told his friends afterwards that he had no choice, and it was the only way he could think of to protect them all. His reasoning was that if everyone was put down as a member of the counter-revolutionary organization, then it was like saying there was no organization at all."

"And he's still a powerful bureaucrat, even now that the whole business has been discredited?"

"You really are thick, dad. Who do you think would speak out against him? After all, there's been no official disclaimer of the campaign, has there? And plenty of people think he did the right thing, fulfilling his duty to the Party by denouncing himself and others while protecting fellow cadres."

"What utter nonsense," I spluttered angrily.

That is all that was said on the subject and I returned to the cadre school still unconvinced. I told the whole story to my friends back at the school. It's not as if I believed it; I did it rather as a way of proving that what had been happening in the school was not all that extraordinary. I also used it to show that compared to what was going on outside, our school was something of a utopia. At least we were spared the ministrations of experts in revolutionary physiognomy; besides, they hadn't given Oracle Bones a two-grade promotion for shaking his leg.

But something still bothered me. Although all the members of the counter-revolutionary organization were eventually permitted to take up their revolutionary work once more, that one uncompromising man —the hero who steadfastly refused to be implicated—remained under a cloud. A friend said that this had been done in an effort to protect the prestige of the leadership. The case was finally resolved in 1973. I don't know the exact method they used to announce his absolution, if indeed they ever did. My feelings about Oracle Bones are very much influenced by what my children had said about him. He really was a pedant. How had he managed to land himself in a nuthouse instead of getting promoted? But such things are relative: at least he survived the general insanity. What about the hapless multitude whom fear of guilt drove to suicide?

Seen in this light our cadre school didn't seem all that bad.

from On Yunmeng Marsh—Memories of the Cultural Revolution

Chen Baichen, who was born in 1908, was already a committed Communist playwright in the 1930s, and after World War II he gained a reputation as one of China's leading stage satirists. After 1949 he continued to write historical plays, though his varied duties as a cultural bureaucrat, including some years as the secretary of the Writer's Association, took up much of his time. His account of the cadre school, On Yunmeng Marsh, *was to an extent inspired by Yang Jiang's book, although he prefers satire to ellipsis as a means of conveying his message.*

Urblings in the Gulag

"Urbling" is an invented word. The Chinese term means literally "educated youth", and is sometimes mistakenly translated as "young intellectuals". It in fact refers to adolescents and school-leavers from urban areas.

In the late 1950s and early 1960s, when the Chinese economy failed to create sufficient job opportunities for them, Urblings were strongly encouraged to go to the countryside supposedly to live and work with their country cousins. In the early years of the Cultural Revolution, this "rustication" of Urblings became state policy, partly as a result of the closure of schools and universities, but more directly as part of the Party's strategy to evacuate the politically restive youth from the cities.

Several factors, such as the young people's own urban background and the reluctance of the peasants to share their less than ample arable land with unco-operative outsiders, made it difficult for these young exiles to acclimatize themselves to their appointed places of re-settlement. Living conditions in the countryside differed little from those of prisoners in labour camps, though for their part Urblings had fallen foul of Proledic for no other reason than that they had been educated in the cities before the Cultural Revolution. Most of the rusticated Urblings managed to return to their home cities after Mao's death in 1976, and it is this group that produced the activists of the Democracy Wall period (1978-9). The Misty poets, fifth-generation film-makers and new artists are almost all Urblings.

*   *   *

Wu Huan is the son of the playwright Wu Zuguang* and the opera singer Xin Fengxia. His parents were both stigmatized as counterrevolutionaries for many years. He was sent to work in the Great Northern Wilderness, and now, as a writer back in his native Peking, he specializes in "Urbling literature", a genre of fiction that has flourished in China recently.

Wang Peigong is the author of WM from which our extract Urbling Winter is taken. Although of an older generation (he is in his forties), Wang has captured the spirit of the Urblings and the coming of age of China's "lost generation".

* *See below, Chapter 12.*

An Urbling Spot

Wu Huan

It's just like a devil's lair. A few oil lamps flicker in the gloom like ghosts' eyes. Here darkness has everything in its sombre embrace. All things in this place, be they living or dead, sentient or not, are enveloped by night. No detail is perceptible, only murky silhouettes; outlines that differ only in that some can move. They are all one in the blackness. There are no windows, and even in the daytime all that the cracks in the walls let in are sharp slivers of brightness, inklings of light. Even these are clouded in blunt mist like the chill steam reflected from a sword, or bundled souls bobbing in the air.

The place is alive with a music all of its own, an indescribable threnody, a concert that no orchestra no matter how magnificent could ever hope to recreate. In this environment crazed screams and shouts have an endearing familiarity; clipped and violent curses become the language of binding friendship. What passes for laughter in this place sounds strangely abnormal, ten times more fearsome than the distant baying of wolves. Here too entertainment is of a different order: frenzied fights and frustrated beatings; wash basins thrown over bedding; rice bowls hurled angrily at the heated walls; a padded shoe chucked on a stove; a fellow playfully taking off his pants and wearing them on his head.

And the smells! Every imaginable stench and odour has found a home in this shack: sweat, bad breath, feet, tobacco, kerosene, decay, sated fleas, foul smells all of them . . . .

A wooden structure, one huge room seventy or eighty metres long stuck deep in the mountains of Xiaoxing'an. Like a massive burrow. They'd dug into the frozen earth with pickaxes and planted the squared wooden posts, fixing them in the ground with melted snow. It froze solid as it was poured around the stakes. Two-inch-thick planks were nailed to the posts as walls, and even then they were unable to keep the harsh winds and snow at bay. No ordinary place this. Put simply, anyone who has ever lived here, even if only for a day, must be counted a hero, one way or another.

In this environment material civilization is absolutely basic: steamed bread, soy beans and salted vegetables. A serving of meat once a month, but more often than not it is beef from diseased cows; or pork from pigs too old and weak to give birth.

As for the life of the spirit: apart from a few books on philosophy that no one could make anything of—nothing.

from "Black Nights · Forest · Dumb Urbling"

CARICATURE OF AN URBLING
—AH CHENG, by Cao Li

Ah Cheng is an artist and writer who has been active since the Demo-cracy Movement. His novel The Chess Master *(1984), in which he portrays the wayfarer-urbling Wang Yisheng, is regarded as the masterpiece of Urbling literature. Ah Cheng's eccentric ventures as artist, entrepreneur and writer epitomise the confused but self-confident quest of the ex-Urbling in the 1980s.*

Urbling Winter

Wang Peigong

Cast:

YUE YANG *(General)*, son of a retired soldier

LI JIANGSHAN *(Pigeon Mountain)*, son of a Capitalist Roader

YU DAHAI *(Pumpkin Head)*, son of a standing member of a Municipal Revolutionary Committee

JIANG YI *(Pushcart)*, son of a worker

BAI XUE *(Princess)*, daughter of an intellectual

PANG YUN *(Nun)*, daughter of an office worker

ZHENG YINGYING *(Droopy)*, daughter of a Rightist and the granddaughter of a capitalist

(*All imitate the sound of a gusty wind by whistling. They are engaged in monotonous and back-breaking physical labour.*)

LI (*exhausted*): Shit. I'm knackered.

JIANG YI: As the head of this family I officially declare that we can knock off for the day.

(*They walk back fighting against a heavy wind.*)

YUE (*kicks something*): God, that hunk of frozen shit I just kicked was hard.

YU: Sure it was. Now you know what they mean when they call someone "stinking and hard".

LI: "Stinking and hard". Isn't that just like us?

JIANG: Lay off, Pigeon Mountain.

BAI: Intellectuals are called "stinking old nines", aren't they? I wonder what that makes us?

LI: Stinking old tens, of course.

YU: You mean smelly old turds, don't you?

ZHENG (*with a shrill shriek*): Stinking turds.

(*All laugh.*)

YUE (*coldly*): It's not enough for us to be shoved around by everyone else, is it? You even get a kick out of laughing at yourselves. (*angrily*) Let's go.

> (*They walk on in silence. Pushing the door open with their shoulders, they go inside and all collapse exhausted.*)

LI (*lying down*): When we first came I didn't think much of this lousy shack . . . but now I reckon it's great.

JIANG: As the poets say, "Even a tumbledown hut is home, and worth ten thousand strings of cash".

YU: Home? This dump? (*singing revolutionary Peking opera*) "Here on the borders far away, a thousand leagues from home . . . . "

YUE: What the fuck have you got to sing about?

> (*The wind howls outside.*)

ZHENG (*shocked*): Look, the door! . . . It's been blown down.

> (*None of the young men move a muscle.*)

YU: Good riddance. It'll save us the trouble of having to open and close it.

BAI: Come on, hurry up and fix it.

LI: Oh, please, Uncle Lei Feng, come to the aid of these helpless Urblings.

JIANG (*to* YUE YANG): Come on, let's fix it, otherwise we'll freeze our arses off tonight.

LI: Pushcart, we're not much better off than your poor old dad was in the bad old days.

YUE: Come on wind, batter us down, give us a real test. Blow us away if you can—

(*singing Peking opera*): "We shall be like that pine tree . . . .

YUE
YU $\Big|$ (*hoarsely*): growing atop Mount Tai."

BAI: Get on with it, you lazy devils, the snow's blowing in here.

YUE: Don't shout at us, Princess. If you don't lower your voice, a bear's going to get you in the night and I won't be there to save you.

(*The other men laugh.*)

ZHENG: Oh dear!

PANG (*to the other girls*): If they don't put the door back up what will we do?

BAI: We won't cook for them.

PANG: That's right.

ZHENG: That'll show them.

YU: Then we'll just have to feed off the north wind. An ideal chance for us to "reflect on past sufferings and count our blessings." (*singing*) "Stars fill the skies . . . .

ALL THE MEN (*singing as they lie in bed*): . . . and the crescent moon shines bright, as the brigade holds another meeting tonight . . . . "

BAI (*anxious*): You cretins! You're no better than a pack of bums.

YUE: Who are you talking to like that?

BAI: To the lot of you, that's who. There are some dorms where girls have been raped because there wasn't a proper door, you know.

(*The boys fall silent.* YUE YANG *jumps to his feet and all the others respond by getting up reluctantly.* BAI XUE *giggles while the other girls go off to prepare the evening meal, their faces glowing red in the light of the stove. The door is put up.*)

BAI: Dinner's ready: hot water and two corn buns each.

(ZHENG *hands out the buns.* LI JIANGSHAN *goes off to one side.*)

ZHENG: What are you doing? Come and have your dinner.

LI: I'm gonna wash my hands.

JIANG: Quite the little gentleman, aren't we? What bullshit.

(LI *washes his hands regardless and wipes them dry.*)

LI: Hey, where's the clothes I just took off?

ZHENG: Stop making such a fuss. Come and have your dinner. (*She shoves a corn bun into his hands.*)

LI (*in a whisper*): Don't wash them, there's a pair of my underpants in that lot.

ZHENG (*unflustered*): What's the big deal. You're such a fuss pot.

(*The others eat in silence.* BAI XUE *puts something into* YUE YANG's *bowl with her chopsticks.*)

LI (*picking it up and tasting it*): So you're playing favourites now, Princess.

(BAI XUE *gives him some with a laugh.*)

YU: What about us?

BAI: What's so special about a little chilli? (*gives* YU DAHAI *some*) And that's the last of it.

JIANG: Give me that bowl. I'll put some water in it and drink it.

BAI: Oh, Pushcart, pour us some water too.

LI: Yeah, come on, water.

JIANG: Get it yourself, it's just over there.

LI: What?

(ZHENG *pours some water for* LI, *who takes it gleefully. They drink the water out of the same bowl.*)

YU (*slightly jealous*): I see you're taking advantage of people again, Pigeon Mountain. You look like you've been drinking bee's piss. Come on, Droopy, don't play favourites; otherwise I won't help you in the fields any more.

JIANG: Here's your workpoint record books (*hands them out*).

YU (*looking at it*): Aw shit, only five points this month again.

JIANG: What's wrong with that. If you got that score at school you would have been on top of the world.

YU (*counting*): One workpoint is worth 1.4 cents, five times one point four . . . . Hey, that works out to a lousy seven cents a day. Did you hear me brothers: SEVEN CENTS!

LI: How much do you reckon you're worth? No one forced you to come along with us to be "re-educated"!

JIANG: That's right Pumpkin Head. I hear your dad's a member of the

Revolutionary Committee in town.

YU (*spitting*): Sand in the food again.

YUE: Pushcart, why are they only giving you five points when you did ten points worth of work? It's damn unfair.

JIANG: I protested, but they told me up at the brigade office that there's a regulation which says that an Urbling only gets half a peasant's workpoints.

LI: Did you hear that? Pack of tortoise arses they are.

YUE (*annoyed*): Bedtime everyone.

(*The men and women go to their respective sides of the shack and lie down.*)

YU: Didn't we just have dinner? How come I feel hungry the moment I lie down?

YUE: Stop talking nonsense.

LI: Are you really hungry, Pumpkin Head?

YU: Didn't he say it was nonsense?

JIANG: I don't think I even felt this hungry during the "three bad years" in the early sixties.

YU: Then they had to starve us in turns to keep class struggle going.

LI: Brilliant analysis.

YUE: Sounds like a load of rubbish to me.

LI (*to* JIANG YI): Hey, I'll teach you a trick. Don't let yourself think about how hungry you are. You've seen that film "Ascending Gan Crag", haven't you? When they ran out of water, they forced themselves to think about sour plum cordial. So what you should do is imagine that you've just had a really filling meal. You're stuffed, your stomach is about to explode, what with all the steamed buns and dumplings you've just had . . . .

JIANG: It's no good. The more I think about food the hungrier I get.

(YU DAHAI *chuckles merrily to himself.*)

LI: Hey Pumpkin Head, that's the same trick your dad uses to fool himself when he makes speeches, isn't it?

YU (*venomously*): Piss fucking well off.

YUE (*angry*): The next one who opens his mouth's gonna get my fist in it.

(*The men fall silent. Silence. Sound of weeping from the women's side.* PANG YUN, *who has been reading by the light of a torch, gives* BAI XUE *a nudge.*)

BAI (*moving over to* ZHENG YINGYING): What's wrong? Come on.

ZHENG (*gripping her belly with her hands*): My . . . my tummy hurts.

BAI: Are you still hungry?

ZHENG: No . . . it's that time of the month again.

BAI: Hurry up and do something then.

ZHENG: But I don't have any toilet paper.

PANG: Use today's newspaper then.

ZHENG (*throws paper aside with a cry*): Hells bells, it's got an editorial, pictures and everything on it.

BAI: Don't worry, that only proves the "timeliness" of the editorial. (*whispering*) I'll let you in on a secret: that's what I do whenever I can't buy toilet paper. Now hurry up.

    (ZHENG *arranges things hurriedly.*)

PANG (*solicitously*): Does it still hurt?

ZHENG: I'm feeling much better now, thanks.

PANG (*wretched*): Gees, you're lucky, you two. I haven't had a period for three months . . . . I must have anemia, and all this swelling . . . . I'm beginning to wonder whether I'm still a woman.

ZHENG: Let me tell you something. I just dreamt about my grand-mother . . . . I'm sure she must be dead. She just kept staring at me with those haunting eyes of hers.

BAI: That's just because you miss her so much.

ZHENG: You don't understand. My father was persecuted when I was still in my mother's womb, and he died soon after that. My mother . . . went away . . . they paraded my grandad through the streets with a big placard hung around his neck which said he was a "reactionary capitalist", and they struggled him to death. They smashed the piano he'd bought me . . . . I was left all alone with Granny. If it's true that she's really . . . . (*on the verge of tears*)

BAI: Come on, hasn't anyone ever told you: it's the opposite of what you dream that comes true. Now go back to sleep.

    (ZHENG YINGYING *falls asleep leaning against* BAI XUE. PANG YUN *goes on reading.*)

BAI: Are you still reading?

PANG: I'm so cold and hungry I can't get to sleep.

BAI: So you're still dreaming of getting to university some day? They'll never let any of us take the entrance exams. They put up their own people for university places, and you know what that means: you have to jump into the sack with them first. (*giggling*) Do you want to give it a test run?

PANG: Why don't you try it yourself, if you're so smart?

BAI: Who, me? (*sighs*) Lot of bloody good that'd do me. What are those shit-head "comrade students" good for anyway? My dad graduated from a famous Chinese university, studied overseas and everything, fluent in four languages, and they still sent him to a cadre school to herd ducks.... Just forget it and go to sleep. "In sleep you will find your true fortune!"

> (*The women's section falls silent.* YU DAHAI *turns restlessly in bed and farts.*)

BAI: Watch it you lot over there.

YU (*purposefully overreacting*): Who dares disturb the Princess' sweet dreams? Come on, whoever it was, own up. You deserve to be hacked into ten thousand pieces! (*laughs unintentionally*) Don't get so worked up over nothing, all we've got in our stomachs is corn slops and dried sweet potatoes. Don't worry, our farts don't even smell.

> (*Someone's stomach rumbles.*)

LI: Shhh! Listen, what's that? The cow spirits and snake demons are calling.[1]

> (*Muffled laughter.*)

YUE (*jumping up*): Who's in favour of me going out and "plucking" a chicken from the coop?

LI: Long live the General!

YU: I'll go with you.

YUE: Best not to. A raid like this is best done single-handed.

YU (*gives* JIANG YI *a shove with his elbow*): You go along as lookout, Pushcart.

JIANG: We should all stay put. The brigade leader's been watching us anyway. He told me that the peasants in one brigade gouged out an Urbling's eyes for stealing their chickens.

LI (*with a shudder*): Oh shit. And I bet they'd really do something like that.

YU (*furious*): Fuck 'em all.

---

[1] Intellectuals and cadres denounced in the Cultural Revolution were called "cow spirits and snake demons".

YUE (*coolly*): What he means is . . . .

JIANG: Yeah, the same old thing: they can get away with anything they want to.

YUE: Did that shifty-eyed brigade leader really tell you that? Right then, I'll go after his chickens then. Give me your knife, Pumpkin Head.

YU (*passing him the knife*): Be careful.

JIANG (*pleading*): Please, General, whatever you do, don't go after his chooks.

LI: And be sure to leave Uncle and Aunty Wang's alone, too. They're pretty good to us. Remember they've even given us sweet potatoes.

YUE: Don't worry, I know exactly what I'm doing. I've got my sights set on illegal gains only. (*rushes out with dagger*)

    (BAI *gets out of bed and goes out to stop him.*)

BAI: General, stealing chickens is beneath you. Just think of it, the General reduced to a common thief.

YUE: Hmph! The outlaws in *Water Margin* filched chickens too.

BAI: Well, stop playing the hero then. Do you want to lose your eyes?

YUE: Sure I'll be finished if they poke them both out, but if they leave me one I can still be a general. (*closes one eye*) See, a regular Potemkin. (*makes to go*)

BAI (*anxiously*): Don't go.

YUE: What do you think you're doing?

BAI: Don't, if the others are hungry they can go themselves.

YUE (*dismisses her with a laugh*): You're a fool if you think I'm doing it just because I'm hungry.

BAI: But why do you have to be the one . . . . Anyway, I don't want you to go.

YUE (*gazing at* BAI XUE *he says slowly*): Once I've made up my mind, nothing can stop me . . . nothing . . . not even you. (*pulls* BAI XUE *towards him and gives her a hard kiss*)

BAI (*stunned she suddenly strikes out at* YUE YANG): You bastard!

YUE: That's right, but you still get your kicks out of a bastard. (*pushing her aside runs out*)

    (BAI *rubs her cheek and watches* YUE *run off.* YUE *deftly steals a chicken.* BAI XUE *waits for his return.* YUE *runs back excitedly with a chicken in hand.*)

YUE (*waving the chicken in front of* BAI): Look!

(*She turns around and goes inside without a word.*)

OTHERS (*shouting*): Hail the triumphant return of the General!

YUE (*giving an energetic imitation of Lin Biao*): Little generals of the Red Guard! This is further living proof that young people can do great things in the countryside. (*throws chicken over to the others*) Take it.

(*They all pounce on it with glee and set about killing and plucking the creature.*)

YUE: Kill that chook!

CHORUS: Kill, kill, kill!

LI: Pluck those feathers!

CHORUS: Pluck, pluck, pluck!

YUE: Wash it clean!

CHORUS: Rub a dub dub.

(*They gather around the fire to cook the fowl.*)

YUE: Who's going to contribute some kindling?

YU: Burn this. (*hands him a sheaf of paper*) It's the printed study materials on the criticism of Lin Biao and Confucius that my father sent me.

ZHENG: You want the stuff attacking Song Jiang in *Water Margin*?

YUE: Yeah, throw it over. Burn it to cinders—now that's what I call a scorching criticism.

JIANG (*grabbing the book* PANG YUN*'s reading*): Hey, burn this too.

PANG: That's Pigeon Mountain's.

YUE (*glances at it*): Ai Siqi's *Popular Philosophy*. Better keep this. What about those papers of yours, Pushcart?

(*All shout merrily while some of them go over to get them.*)

JIANG: No way. There's articles in them by Liang Xiao on the education revolution. We still have to study and discuss them.

LI (*quoting Mao's poetry*): "Enough of your farting!"

JIANG: What was that, you punk?

LI: I'm . . . reciting Chairman Mao's poem. What's wrong with that? Look, the chicken's done.

(*They grab some and start gorging themselves.*)

YU: That's right, I've heard this new movement's aimed at . . . . (*gestures indicating Deng Xiaoping*)

YUE (*shocked*): But didn't Chairman Mao say "talented people are hard to come by"?

BAI: That's right, and the situation has just started improving . . . .

ZHENG: Didn't they publish that poem by the Chairman at the New Year in which it says "Orioles sing and swallows dance everywhere"?

LI: Sure, but don't forget there's also a line about not being allowed to fart!

(They all seem confused. Silence.)

YU *(lets out a long sigh)*: Aw, let them go screwing things up as much as they want. In another seven or eight years it'll be time for a second Cultural Revolution.

LI *(lying down on the ground)*: A second Cultural Revolution . . . .

YUE *(annoyed)*: Stop talking about it. Princess, play something on the guitar for us.

BAI *(languidly)*: I can't, a rat bit through one of the strings.

YUE: Shit. I'll go and steal a cat tomorrow.

LI *(meaningfully)*: A black cat or a white cat?

YU: As long as it catches rats it's a good cat.[2]

JIANG (*nervously*): Watch out what you're saying, will you? Do you want to get us into trouble?

YU: Come off it, we didn't mention any names.

LI: Okay, okay. Give the revolutionary masses a bit of peace and quiet.
(YUE YANG *is staring at the fire when he suddenly launches into a sonorous rendering of "The Song of the Young Pioneers".*)

YUE (*singing*):
> *Are you ready?*
> *Always ready?*
> *We are the Young Pioneers . . . .*

(*The others stop what they are doing, at first listening quietly and then joining in.*)

ALL (*singing*):
> *We will surely be*
> *Masters of the future*
>
> . . . . . .

(*They lose themselves in the song and gradually get louder and louder.*)

ALL (*singing*):
> *Little brothers*
> *Little sisters*
> *Our future knows no bounds*
> *We will surely be*
> *Masters of the future.*

(*PANG YUN suddenly starts crying. ZHENG YINGYING also begins to sob; even the boys become tearful.*)

BAI (*shouting tearfully*): Go on cry, but remember no matter how wonderful your dreams are, they're still nothing more than dreams. No matter how bitter reality may be, it is still reality.

YUE (*with a derisive laugh*): You wanna be a general? Just look at how many old marshals have been overthrown.

PANG: There's no hope for me . . . .

ZHENG: My piano . . . smashed . . . . The last notes were so beautiful . . . .

---

[2]Deng Xiaoping was the author of the famous line: "It doesn't matter whether the cat is black or white; as long as it catches rats, it's a good cat."

LI: Man? But what is man, really?

JIANG: My dad often says that a person is nothing more than three meals a day, sleep and half a glass of rice wine. Sounds pretty good to me, I guess he's right.

YU: That's a load of crap! Then what's the use of being born in the first place?

LI: Man's nothing more than a speck of dust.

ZHENG: A pitiable pebble.

YUE: Look, I say that we're . . . bricks. We can be used to make the Great Wall, or to put up a chicken coop. It all depends on how they want to use us!

YU (*coolly*): But "they" have cast us aside. Hmph. (*tapping his bowl rhythmically*) We're all bricks . . . .

OTHERS (*joining in*): They stick us wherever they want us to fit.

YUE: And if you ponder on your tough life . . . .

OTHERS (*listlessly*): Remember the rigours of the great Long March.

LI: And if they say: does the work make you tired?

OTHERS (*wearily*): Remember the horrors of the bad old days . . . .

    (*They slump in all directions and go to sleep.*)

BAI (*strumming on her guitar. She gradually becomes more involved in the instrument and starts humming "The Dirge of the Urblings"*):

    An oil lamp flickers on the wall
    Through the night so dark and drear.
    The past it seems so distant now;
    Why is the future so unclear?

    (*She too finally dozes off.*)

from the play WM

The four-act play WM *was banned in November 1985 at the beginning of one of the cultural purges that have become an annual ritual in Deng Xiaoping's China. The playwright himself interprets the title of the play in a number of ways. Apart from obviously being an abbreviation of the Chinese word* wo-men *(the pronoun "us", or "we"),* WM *is also a pictograph of two men, one standing upright, and the other on his head. A third layer of significance is that* W *represents the English word "woman", while* M *is an abbreviation of "man".*

Official displeasure with WM *centred on the play's puzzling romanized title and the belief that the characters were not representative of Chinese realities. One critic derided this reasoning, albeit to little effect, in the major theatre journal* Drama:

> *"Not long ago I was privileged to read a classified speech by a Party official on problems facing contemporary culture. It certainly was an eye-opener! He obviously disagreed with the generally-accepted view of developments that have been taking place in the arts since late 1978. I got the impression that he felt he had remained clear-headed over the last years while everyone else was besotted. He deplored the widespread [ideological] confusion that now reigns in China, and let loose a flood of anti-status quo invective which, coming from a leader in this day and age, seems quite extraordinary. Talking about the use of romanization and western pronunciation [in titles of such works as* WM] *he said, 'Here they [playwrights] are importing the very worst things from the West', and so on. He then commented that the characters presented in these works are intended to be representative of the majority of Chinese people, while the progressive and positive elements in society who are the real vanguard of social change and therefore truly representative of social reality, are portrayed as a small minority. And so, he argued, the proper function of literature is being subverted; works of art like this are little more than cheap stimulants—like the red cape a matador waves in the face of a bull .... The most startling thing about this was that a political leader should be able to dismiss a work for purely subjective reasons without having ever seen it." (quoted by Lee Yee in* The Nineties, *December 1985)*

III: SPECTRES

Feudalism casts an inhibiting historical shadow . . . China has not yet freed itself from the control of history. Its only mode of existence is to relive the past.

Jin Guantao, 1983

Another political upheaval has convulsed China. The Gang of Four has been rehabilitated . . . . If you look at the history of China and the weakness of her political institutions, this is not so totally improbable.

Su Ming, 1979

Liu Changshun

The feudal age of the first Great Emperor has gone, never to return. But the "spectre from within the ancient fortress" still prowls our land. The spectre of Party rule (rather than democracy), of rule by the individual (rather than rule of law), of power (rather than right), still stalks the land. The fate of the leaders of the Chinese Democracy Movement, the regime's opposition to liberalization, the staunch upholding of the Four Principles, are all manifestations of this Spectre.

Hong Kong Express,
4th April, 1986

A Spectre Prowls Our Land

Sun Jingxuan

Those who do not remember the past are condemned to relive it.

George Santayana*

Oh my brothers! Have you seen
The spectre prowling our land?

Brothers! Do not call
Our land fair, our skies bright,
While this spectre,
    like a gust of wind,
    like a wisp of smoke,
Prowls unencumbered o'er our land:
Swaggers into peasant's hut,
Struts into herdsman's yurt;
Issues orders, revels in pride,
Like Great Caesar of Ancient Rome,
Grasps the destiny of us all;
And any thing we have is granted by its spectral whim.

Brothers! Have you seen
The spectre prowling our land?

In this century, this Nuclear Age,
To talk of spectres seems absurd
But it's the truth—the terrible and tragic truth!
This spectre,
    like a gust of wind,
    like a wisp of smoke,
Prowls unencumbered o'er our land;
Trails like a shadow,

*These words are placed by William Shirer at the beginning of his classic study of Nazism, *The Rise and Fall of the Third Reich*, the translation of which has been very popular with Chinese readers. They also stand at the entrance to the Dachau concentration camp museum.

Clutches with invisible claws,
Silently sucks blood and marrow,
Dictates every action, controls every thought;
Tramples on dignity,
Destroys the quest for beauty, the yearning for love.
The slightest hint
And you are locked away for years
        in some dark and gloomy prison-cell!
This spectre decrees death,
        posthumous humiliation,
Or tolerates lives of vexatious vegetation.
You are, then, spectral slave and spectral subject,
Without the right to cry out in protest.

Brothers! Have you seen
The spectre prowling our land?

You may not recognize him,
        though he stands before your eyes,
For like a conjurer,
        master of never-ending transformation,
One moment in dragon-robe of gold brocade
He clasps the dragon-headed sceptre,
The next in courtier's gown
He swaggers through the palace halls;
And now—behold—a fresh veneer!
The latest fashion! And yet
No mask, no costume, no disguise
Can hide the coiled dragon
        branded on his naked rump.

Ah China! Ancient and mysterious land!
Ancient as your Great Wall,
        mysterious as your hieroglyphs,
Wooden plough, spinning wheel,
        water mill, rattan basket,
Innumerable tombs, pagodas, temples,
Palaces, sacred objects and ancestral shrines.

These ancient mysteries have spawned
          legends innumerable
Have made you an abode for gods,
          a haunt for ghosts . . . .
And I, son of a northern peasant,
Was born amidst terror,
               raised in piety . . . .
Childhood! Wretched childhood!
The bleak and dreary village, the tumbledown hovel;
Wrapped in tattered cotton padding,
Curled on the ice-cold earthen kang,
I stared blankly at the smoke-black wall
And its icons:
God of
     WAR majesty on tiger-skin throne;
Goddess of
     PITY on lotus-seat afloat the sea;
And OLD LONGEVITY
(Though I was never the least impressed by his benevolence).
On the altar stood the Tablet, inscribed
     HEAVEN
     EARTH
     LIEGE
     PARENTS
     TEACHER
Loftiest representation of divinity (said Mother)
And when she stuck the joss-sticks in the burner (the usual three)
I knelt at a distance,
     not daring even to lift my head and watch.
At night I dreamt,
          smokey haze-filled dreams
                    of Hell and Heaven . . . .
Such was my childhood,
My infant head stuffed with graven images.
I believed these gods to be
     omnipresent, omnipotent:
Even the old locust-tree outside my home
     breathed a divine aura.

A New Brand of Superstition

Today, a lot of our commentators would agree on one point of faith concerning the Gang of Four: namely, that a handful of people in leading roles managed to transform the character of our country overnight. (Whether they were heroes or criminals, though, depends on whom you ask.) As these commentators see it, it was not a certain set of social relations that created the Gang of Four, but rather the Gang of Four who created a certain type of social relations. This is a new brand of superstition, a new religion! People may worship benevolent gods out of love for them, or they may worship evil gods out of fear and loathing. But in either case this shows that people feel baffled and powerless in the face of seemingly supernatural alien forces.

In a society where people are no longer dominated by the products of their own creation, which seem like alien forces—in other words, in a society where people are able to fully control their own destiny—it would be totally impossible for superstition to take root. And conversely, if such a ridiculous superstition as this "Gang of Four worship" is still in vogue among our commentators today, doesn't that very fact prove that the Chinese people don't yet really, fully, control their own destiny?

*   *   *

The dictatorship of the Party degenerated into a dictatorship of individual leaders. The leaders broke loose from control by the Party and the people. They became veritable gods who could decide the fate of the people, sacred idols who lorded it over society, not tolerating the slightest irreverence. It was the new religion fostered by Lin Biao and the Gang of Four that provided the subjective conditions for this to happen.

Wang Xizhe*

*For more information on Wang Xizhe, see below pp. 273-276.

In time of famine, I knelt beneath the blazing sun,
Closed my eyes, clasped my hands, and prayed to the almighty gods.
But for all my piety and supplication
Life continued hard and wretched,
    Mother Earth remained desolate . . . .

Ancient China! A loathsome spectre
Prowls the desolation of your land . . . .

I shall never forget that heady night
When the misty moon shone on the threshing-floor
And we first learned to sing the Internationale.
"No more gods!" we vowed, "No more emperors!"
The song quickened our hearts,
Taught us the worth and strength of man,
Became our cry, our banner.
Barefoot, spear in hand,
    we roamed the plains and mountains of China.
That song gave us strength to bear the hunger,
To fight from the Changbai Mountains in the north,
    the Taihang range in the west,
Down to south of the Yellow and Yangtze rivers.
Knowing that song, that cry, that oath,
We could hold aloft a new sun,
    in hands and arms that still dripped blood.

The decaying palaces, the dark temples
    crumbled, crashed to the ground
And the Red Flag waved in the bright skies of China;
Like children we wept tears of joy,
Forgot the hardships and sorrows of the past.
But how brief were the days of cheer!
Reality came, dragging with it bitter disenchantment:
We had thought ourselves masters of our fate,
That we could now live happy and free on our land,
But now we found ourselves mere "screws"
Driven tight into some machine;
Numbers on a statistical chart,

Pieces on a Go board—black and white.
Flesh and blood and thinking mind we had
But could not wreak feeling, will or thought.
Oh misery! We were abstractions!
Our bounden duty to raise our hands and clap . . . .
Willingly we forgave errors:
After all, a revolution is no stroll down the street.
A cleansing tide is bound to damage
    ships and homes.
Perhaps this childish goodwill
    lies at the root of our misfortune . . . .
But even we are human,
Even we can think,
And in the end we saw:
Our sweat and blood, given for the Great Edifice of Socialism,
    had built a cathedral of fear . . . .

Brothers! While we lay deep in slumber
A spectre prowled our land.

I cannot forget that year of frenzy
When I went back to my village,
    ancient crossing on the Yellow River,
That once cradled the young revolution,
Suckled it
    like some simple-hearted peasant nurse.
After thirty years, I returned:
The old place was sure to have changed, I thought.
Yes, there were great changes—
The old men of my youth were now laid in their graves,
The youngsters were old greybeards;
A loudspeaker high in a tree
Blared hysteria from dawn till dusk.
In every home I entered, gone were the gods—
    door gods,
    wealth gods,
    kitchen gods:
A new icon had taken their place.

The guerilla-leader had aged,
His face was lined with grief.
From dull despondent eyes he apologized:
"After these thirty years,
    I owe you a good drink.
But my vegetable garden has been flooded
    by the Red Sea,
My little plot of onion and garlic washed away!"
That night I lay awake, brooding,
My heart heavy with an immeasurable grief.
What could I say to these country folk
    who had nursed us?
I felt such shame, for the promises
    of thirty years past.
What could I say?
Had we overthrown the Three Great Mountains
    only to build a new Temple?
Had we toppled Wealth and Mercy
    only to hang a new icon in their shrine?

China! Ancient, mysterious China!
Home of gods,
    cradle of myths, hotbed of tyranny;
In your innumerable temples and palaces
In your countless emperors' tombs,

Worshipping the Great Patriarch

Chairman Mao's Quotations *are also Holy Writ. That is why Lin Biao wrote in his inscription on the first page of the* Quotations, *"Do as Chairman Mao tells you." Although Lin Biao could be suspected of trying to "control the Emperor and rule in his name", Mao did in fact expect obedience. He once complained, for example, of Deng Xiaoping's disobedience. The point here is: if a seventy-year-old man has to take orders from an eighty-year old, then by implication the only "grown-up" in the entire country is the Great Patriarch himself.*

from *Deep Structure*

The spectres come, the spectres go,
    inhabit this man's corpse, that man's soul.
Your vast domain breeds feudalism.
They argue that land in peasant's hands
    breeds capitalism:
False! Tyranny is too well entrenched:
No new class can strike root
    in the feudal fortress.
Which of us has even set eyes on capitalism—
Premature infant, strangled in the cradle?
China, like a huge dragon, gobbles all in its path,
Like a huge vat, dyes all the same colour.
Have you not seen the lions of Africa,
    the lions of America,
Fierce kings of the jungle?
When they enter our dragon's lair
    they become mere guard-dogs,
    rings through their pug nostrils,
    standing guard at yamen and palace gate . . .

Ah China! My beloved China!
You need fresh blood, air,
Wind, rain, sun;
You need to change your putrid soil!
Ah China! do not fear
    jeans, long hair,
    Taiwanese love-songs
    Indian love-songs;
Fear the spectre from within the ancient fortress,
Prowling our land.

October 1980
Chengdu

Sun Jingxuan is a poet from Sichuan Province, now in his fifties. He was attacked as a Rightist in 1958, and did not resume writing again until the late 1970s. He was severely reprimanded for this poem (at the same time as Bai Hua was attacked for the film "Unrequited Love"), and subsequently published an abject self-criticism (which greatly disappointed his admirers).

A Seriously Flawed Work:
Sun Jingxuan's Self-criticism

I began writing this poem in the summer of 1979. At that time, my thoughts were thoroughly muddled and knotted like a ball of string and my mind was in a state of chaos, making it very hard for me to write. Last summer, I had a sudden impulse, and without much effort or serious thought I completed the poem and published it without further revision. Little did I know that the consequences of this act would be irreparable. This in itself was a very painful lesson for me. Writers are the engineers of the human soul, and works of literature, whether good or bad, have a strong influence on society. Thus when writing anything, and especially when publishing what they write, writers should be keenly aware of their social responsibility. Publishing unhealthy and harmful works of literature without giving due consideration to their effect on society is, critically speaking, a kind of moral crime.

My original motivation for writing this poem was to criticize and expose the vestiges of feudal thinking in China . . . . But the question is, was the target of my criticism and exposure actually feudalism? Even more important, what was my standpoint—from what point of view did I criticize feudalism? It was in regard to the last question in particular that I committed serious errors.

In exposing and criticizing feudalism, my viewpoint was totally incompatible with the ideology of the proletariat. Although I sought in this poem to oppose feudalism, I was in fact promulgating and advocating bourgeois liberalism and human rights . . . .

At present there is a tendency among many young and middle-aged writers, myself included, to blindly worship the doctrines of Western "existentialism", to take pleasure in discussing such things as the value of man and human rights, and to advocate the liberation of the individual. All of these things have become very fashionable of late. Yet they are nothing more than a heap of outdated rubbish, reconstituted versions of Western humanism that dates back several centuries. There is actually nothing novel about them.

In short, my poem is a seriously flawed work of literature, a "poisonous weed", to borrow the words of Comrade Hu Yaobang. The entire poem is coloured by bourgeois ideology, filled with doubts about socialism and resentment of the Party; it is an out-and-out expression of bourgeois liberalism. The errors in this poem are extremely serious in nature.

As Comrade Hu Yaobang has said, a number of people "lack a correct understanding of their relationship with the masses." I am one of those to whom he is referring. In the last few years, I believed that I stood on a tall tower from which I could survey history and society, and that my vision was both far-reaching and deep. I believed that I was a person with foresight, that I was a spokesman for the people. I had a very high opinion of myself and indulged in arrogance and conceit. I saw myself as a member of a select band of "fanatics" or "geniuses". I favoured violence, and was cocksure enough to think that I could write "explosive" things that would set the world on fire and make a big name for myself. This is an attitude common among the people Hu Yaobang was speaking of. But actually these people are ridiculously childish and immature. By distancing ourselves from life, from struggle and the masses, and sealing ourselves up in the narrow world of the so-called inner self, we have made it impossible for ourselves to feel the pulse of the times or to share a common language with the masses. We are only able to produce idiotic nonsense and self-conscious fantasies, to indulge in self-expression and exaggeration, and to intoxicate ourselves with self-infatuation. This was a hard but necessary lesson for me to learn. Writers must get out of their exclusive ivory towers and act as faithful sons of the people and the Party. He who divorces himself from the people and the Party is like a child separated from its mother, like a plant removed from the soil.

from *Literary Gazette*, May 1982

THE CAT

"I was the first——to give myself a good licking."

Huang Yongyu

Bones of the Buried Dragon

Jin Guantao

Ultrastability of the Feudal System

WHY HAS CHINESE feudalism persisted for more than two thousand years?

This is an endlessly perplexing question, and one which has become all the more pressing at this time of renewed interest in Chinese history and of intense soul-searching, a time when China stands once more at the crossroads of history.

In 1973 our group of young intellectuals began probing into the causes for the perpetuation of Chinese feudalism. Previous studies of Chinese history and society were all based on single-factor analysis. Some were extremely plausible and commendable. But single-factor analysis at best offered a static, partial truth, only exposing a few isolated bones of the buried dragon. History is a living whole. Historical facts are inter-related and interact. The key lies in finding a methodology which can penetrate and illuminate the living wholeness of history, integrating economics, politics and ideology.

We were excited to discover cybernetics, information theory and systems theory. These provided us with an approach that is the antithesis of mechanical isolated-factor analysis, one that asserts the whole to be not simply the arithmetic sum of its parts but an organic entity of its own.

In cybernetics, stability does not mean motionlessness. It means that a system takes on a recurrent form and acquires an adaptation mechanism, while the structure remains in motion. Stability is closely related to the structure's internal resilience and capacity for adjustment. Chinese feudal society has not been motionless or devoid of development, but rather within a recurrent pattern of disruption and restoration, it has failed to grow into a new type of structure qualitatively different from its predecessor.

In cybernetics, stability is understood in terms of mutual adjustment and adaptation among the constituent parts within a system. What the cybernetic approach looks for when a system is destabilized are the resultant internal changes, and the ways in which the destabilizing element is absorbed by the internal adjustment mechanism, and stability is restored.

This method can be fruitfully applied to Chinese historical studies.

In a social system, the relations between the political, economic and cultural sub-systems undergo a constant process of realignment, creating stresses and strains, and eventual crisis to the system as a whole. The response of a larger system to the crisis follows two possible courses:

1) The old structure may be replaced by a new one. The subsystems regain a new and dynamic mutual compatibility within the context of the new structure. In Western Europe, primitive society gave birth to slave society, feudal society and capitalist society in that order;

2) As the old structure is threatened with collapse, the embryonic features of a new structure are wiped out. The structure reverts to the old order. This collapse-correction mechanism constantly eliminates destabilizing factors, thereby maintaining a bland appearance of permanence. In the terminology of cybernetics such a system is called "ultrastable". It is characterized by a cyclic pattern of formidable and lasting stability, punctuated by spasmodic upheavals. The stability and the upheavals in their different ways both contribute to the perpetuation of the old order.

By applying this method of analysis we found Chinese society to be just such an ultrastable system.

Jin Guantao's book Behind the Phenomena of History, *from which these two extracts are taken, created a great stir in Chinese intellectual circles when it was first published in December 1983. It represented, for China, a radical departure from the stereotyped Marxist analysis of history, and introduced (though somewhat superficially) several new concepts, such as cybernetics and information theory. Jin's analysis of the problems of Chinese feudalism, while carefully couched in the past tense, was seen by many of his readers as an examination of the present.*

The Shadow of History

THE CHINESE feudal system is fragile in that its three sub-systems—economic, political and ideological—must be maintained at a specific point of equilibrium; deviation by any sub-system from this point will bring down the whole structure.

Fragility does not necessarily lead to disintegration. No sub-system is allowed to develop too far. This is the coercive control of Chinese feudalism, which functions in two ways:

1) It forms a communications centre for the efficient dispatch and receipt of information and decrees, and a coercive executive body (bureaucracy, household and land registries, etc.);

2) Whenever a sub-system goes astray, it is brought back into line. The bureaucracy is unwavering in upholding the basic tenets of the empire, but tries to be accommodating in regard to minor issues.

The coercive control exercised by the Central Integrality of Chinese feudalism created a prosperous ancient civilization. But it also cast an inhibiting historical shadow over the social structure of that civilization. China is known more for contemplating past glories than for solving present problems or seeking ways into the future. The primary concern in the political, ideological and economic sphere is equilibrium. Self-determination and self-realization are taboo, venturing out into the unknown is fatal. Balance and harmony are maintained at the expense of growth. The ruthless coercion imposed from the centre inhibits the emergence of new life. It safeguards the absolute power of the monarch, the sages, elders and ancestors as well as the perennial traditions and customs. What should have been a living and ever-changing social structure is frozen.

Historical paragons become the ideal justification for coercion and suppression. China has not yet freed itself from the control of history. Its only mode of existence is to relive the past. There is no accepted mechanism within the culture for the Chinese to confront the present without falling back on the inspiration and strength of tradition.

from Behind the Phenomena of History

Wang Zhiping

Pagoda

Yang Lian

Here I have been made to stand, immobile,
For a thousand years
In China's
Ancient capital
Upright like a man
Sturdy shoulders, head held high,
Gazing at the endless golden earth.
I have stood here
Immobile as a mountain
Immobile as a tombstone
Recording the travail of a nation.

Mute
Heart hard as rock
Pondering in solitude
Pitchblack lips parted
In a silent cry to the sun.

Held fast in a cage I have myself forged,
History of millenia heavy on my shoulders,
Leadweight; my spirit
Shrivels in this venomous solitude.
Ah—grey courtyard
Desolate, empty.
Place where swallows perch and soar.

I stand here like a man
A man of immeasurable suffering, dead but obstinately upright.
Let me destroy this nightmare at last,
And realign the shadow of history.

I shall raise the children
High, high, laughing for joy to the sun.

1981

The Deep Structure of Stagnation

Sun Longji

STAGNATION IN China may be explained in terms of the deep structure of Chinese culture. China has been "ultrastable" for thousands of years, and even now it is a country that still seems to be insensitive and slow in responding to the outside world. Throughout the twentieth century and especially since the establishment of the People's Republic, Marxism has provided the dynamic traditionally absent from Chinese culture. Nevertheless, the success of the Communist movement has largely depended on the fact that it developed during a period of transition, at a particular point in the cycle of order and disorder. After the Cultural Revolution, that Marxist-inspired motivation for action would appear to have died away. The Four Modernizations are no longer adequate to mobilize the Hearts-and-Minds of the people. In contrast, "stability and unity" are emphasized.

This tendency towards stagnation is also evident in the personality of every Chinese individual. A Chinese is programmed by his culture to be "Chinese". In other words, in-bred cultural predispositions make the Chinese what they are and prevent them from being full-blown individuals. Dynamic human growth is an alien concept to the Chinese. Growth is seen as just a physical process. Maturity is to know how to play a proper role in bilateral social relationships. Normally physical growth is accompanied by mental development, but the Chinese are held back by their own culture, and they generally exhibit serious tendencies towards oral fixation. In short, the Chinese do not fully experience the various stages of personality development.

from **Deep Structure**

Lingering Fear

Su Ming

THE MAIN EVENTS in this story take place in the year 2000. Another political upheaval has convulsed China. The Gang of Four has been rehabilitated . . . . A bold supposition, perhaps, but if you look at the history of China and the weakness of her political institutions, not so totally improbable.

This is the story of one man, a man who wrote a poster on Democracy Wall, a man who also participated in this great drama of the future. But his fears are shared by many people in China today.

December 1998. The Central People's Radio suddenly interrupts one of its regular programmes. The familiar voice of an experienced announcer is heard, informing the world with great sorrow that the event everyone has been dreading has finally occurred.

Today, in Peking, at 2:30 a.m., a certain comrade, loved by the one and a half billion people of China, and revered by the people of the entire world, passed away after a long illness!

No other announcement since the early 1990s has dealt such a devastating blow to the Chinese people.

The world grieves.

He will live forever in the hearts of the people.

Crowds flock to Tiananmen Square. There is even talk of a mausoleum . . . .

A black veil several hundred metres long shrouds Democracy Wall.

The United States, Yugoslavia, Japan, France, West Germany . . . all mourn his death. The American President sends a personal envoy with a wreath of flowers from all fifty states.

*

During the following year, several more deaths are announced. Many prominent statesmen fall ill and die. A perceptive observer may notice that no medical details are released. Other leading figures die in car accidents, two are killed in airplane crashes. The body of one has still not been recovered.

Few statesmen of the older generation are left. And of the few that have survived, most have now retired.

U.P.I. Peking reports the appearance of a poster on Democracy Wall, entitled "Why?" A mass rally is held, despite the snow, calling on the authorities to explain the deaths and to put an end to the rumours. After the rally, a spontaneous procession marches to the newly built 30-storey Central Government Office.

Reference News carries foreign press reports speculating that the Chinese Communist Party will be holding a top-level meeting.

December 1, 1999. All major Chinese newspapers print a brief but prominent communiqué of the Fifth Plenum. They also announce the formation of a committee to investigate the circumstances surrounding the deaths.

December 5. The preliminary investigation into what is now described as a "counter-revolutionary conspiracy" is complete. Leading figures in important ministries have been implicated.

December 7. More details of the investigation are released, this time involving leading officials in major provinces and cities throughout China.

December 9. There is an important breakthrough in the investigation: the key figure in the clique is a leading member of Party Central, a man with a complicated "international background". This is being interpreted abroad as a reference to the United States. The *New York Times* publishes an article by one of its columnists, entitled "A Great Figure Disappears, and China Slides Back into the Abyss".

December 11. The Plenum announces the reorganization of the Politburo and Party Central.

December 15. It is revealed that members of the "counter-revolutionary conspiracy", even some of its leaders, work in the Ministry of Justice. Party Central therefore orders a new investigation. One of the officials originally in charge is arrested.

In the interests of national security, all the proceedings are kept secret, although several show trials are held. The defendants make full confessions. Some appear extraordinarily listless and dull in court, and the lawyers assigned to them present a very perfunctory defense. The ex-head of the Supreme Court, now one of the defendants, makes the famous remark: "The law is nothing more than toilet paper for politicians to wipe their arses with—once they've finished doing someone over." He is charged with attacking the legal system, and given an even heavier sentence.

December 20. Details of the "conspiracy" are published in full. It is revealed (to the great indignation of the people) that members of the clique were guilty of reviling Chairman Mao and criticizing the Cultural Revolution, an episode in recent history which has now been re-evaluated and must be seen in a positive light.

A series of articles appear in the press, on radio and TV, expressing the need to rally round the new Party Central and smash the forces of reaction. Organizations at all levels of the Party and government hold denunciation meetings.

December 26. Celebrations of the 106th anniversary of the birth of Chairman Mao reach their climax. The *People's Daily* runs the headline: "Our Great Teacher Chairman Mao is the Never-setting, Red, Red Sun in the Hearts of the People of the Entire World."

New Year's Eve. The Year 2000 finally arrives. Mankind has been dreaming of this moment, and the whole world celebrates it, China on a particularly grand scale. But even in this festive season top priority must still be given to the eradication of popular support for the "conspiracy", and to the sweeping reforms which must be introduced. The strong central government, which has been undermined in the past two decades, must be re-established at all costs. This is the only way to avert the insidious danger of national fragmentation.

September. The Party holds its Eighteenth Congress, condemns the incorrect policy that has prevailed for twenty years, and criticizes a certain leader, who headed the Party for two decades until his death and wormed his way into the people's confidence. It also attacks the bourgeois caucus which he headed in the Party.

During the year, hundreds of memorial services, rehabilitating deceased leaders and resettling their cremated remains, are held in the newly built Revolutionary Columbarium at Babaoshan—three storeys above ground, five beneath.

October 1. The fifty-first anniversary of the founding of the

People's Republic is celebrated in grand style. The new leadership of
Party Central mounts the rostrum at Tiananmen to review the parade
of five million. The new leader delivers the following speech:

> *We must be resolute and ruthless in our efforts to extermin-*
> *ate the capitalists within the Party; we must prevent a re-*
> *occurrence of the tragedy that took place twenty-two years ago;*
> *We must carry through the present reforms and re-establish*
> *centralized Party leadership;*
> *We must wipe out the corrupt bourgeois Western influences*
> *that prevail in all spheres of ideology; the proletariat must*
> *occupy all fronts;*
> *We must freeze wages and stress ideological revolution; we*
> *must limit or eliminate altogether bourgeois legal rights, and*
> *destroy the existing polarization of poverty and wealth.*
> *We must get rid of foreign capital; we must impose strict con-*
> *trols on relations with foreign countries and conduct a re-*
> *volutionary diplomatic policy based on self-reliance;*
> *We must strengthen the public security system and enforce*
> *Proledic rigidly, in order to limit the activities of the bour-*
> *geoisie in every sphere.*

Then the parade begins.

The world's most advanced Chinese-made shuttle-type guided
missile, "Thunderbolt III", is seen for the first time by the foreign
press.

A fleet of strategic bombers and jet fighters, the Chinese-made
"Bomb-20" and "Kill-18", roar overhead.

The "Dumpling" weapons system, still an enigma to the outside
world, is displayed in its aluminium saucepan-like shell, and causes an
immediate sensation.

The imported offensive tank, "Panther III", rolls through the
square.

The infantry marches past, the militia . . . .

The young rejoice with pride in their historical destiny.

People over forty-five are stunned by the complete turn-around
that has been effected in the course of a single year.

*

October 2. A poster appears pasted over the colourful bunting on Democracy Wall, entitled "A Voice from Twenty-two Years Ago". The author signs himself: Lingering Fear. It creates quite a stir.

The poster begins with a short foreword:

"Twenty-two years ago, a poster was pasted up on this very spot. It attracted little attention then, though the author narrowly avoided arrest. Today, everything he predicted has, alas, come to pass. This is a copy of that original poster, put up here in the conviction that we must pause for a moment and reflect."

The text of the original poster begins:

"Last month (November 1978) a Japanese delegation posed a crucial question: 'We compliment Vice-Premier Deng on his excellent speech (on Sino-Japanese relations),' they said. 'But how do we know things won't change next year?' Their question was never answered. The Chinese political scene is indeed too changeable. New laws have no permanence. They can be so easily repudiated.

"Our economy and our standard of living improve at a snail's pace. But political convulsions occur with a speed and intensity that astound the world.

"Why is China so susceptible to this kind of upheaval?

"It is because power is so highly centralized. The stability of the whole country ultimately depends on a single person; the fate of nine hundred million people is determined by a very few. Political, economic and judicial power are entirely in the hands of this centralized leadership. The very acts of eating, drinking, defecating, urinating, the emotions of love, hate, grief, happiness—are all at the mercy of these few individuals. The replacement of one of them reorders our entire universe; the death of one of them brings down the whole system . . . .

"Do we have to say that we are born Chinese, and that it is therefore our fate to be like this? Surely we are human beings! We belong to the 1970s!

"Comrade Deng Xiaoping proposes to . . . . "

The rest of the text is torn down within two hours of the poster having been put up. Less than half an hour later, all that remains is the title.

The correspondent for the *Toronto Globe and Mail* manages to take a picture of the whole poster and cable it to his head-office. Six hours later he is declared *persona non grata* and deported. This news is spread by all the poster's readers.

October 3. The Chinese customs impounds all the copies of the *Globe and Mail.* The Canadian Foreign Ministry summons the Chinese ambassador and protests at China's violation of the bilateral agreement on cultural exchange.

All other foreign newspapers can still be seen on the news-stands, with various reports of the contents of the poster. By nine o'clock in the morning they are all sold out.

The night of October 4. A crowd is gathered in front of Democracy Wall. Those who arrive early are able to glimpse the last scraps of the poster's title. But moments later, nothing is left. Another poster is written summarizing the original poster, but when its authors try to put it up, fighting breaks out. At midnight, the first crowd gradually begins to disperse, but then workers coming off night shift gather at the wall, and so on, till the following afternoon. A scene of confused activity, constant noise.

5 p.m., October 5. The author of the poster appears. He is about fifty years old, with a typically Chinese face; well dressed, with an educated manner. What he says is very simple and direct. It is what everyone else is thinking, but doesn't know how to say—without getting into trouble. He impresses the crowd.

He stands on two bricks and begins to read his old poster. In less than ten minutes, his audience has grown to several thousand. The road beneath the Xidan flyover is completely packed.

A man tries to disrupt the gathering, but is shouted down by the crowd. There are too many people and the secret police cannot operate. Someone gives the speaker a loudhailer and he continues.

Meanwhile, in a room a mile or two away, a dozen important persons are sitting comfortably on a sofa, listening to a radio receiver:

" . . . Comrade Deng Xiaoping proposes to decentralize economic decision-making, to improve the judicial system, to let more people participate in management and have a greater share of power. This he correctly defines as progress. But these reforms, which can be implemented in one day, can be destroyed just as quickly. They can be reversed at any time by Central. Since one person implemented them, one person can also abolish them—it may be the same person, or it may be someone completely different.

"The power is total. Nothing can act against it or balance it. Within the nucleus of the system there may be conflicts and groupings, and the struggle among them may become so acute that there has to be a coup d'état to achieve a resolution. But none of this will ever change the nature of the system itself. Indeed, it can only become more ossified . . . .

"Sooner or later everyone dies. The veteran revolutionaries who lead us now will die in their turn. Our historic reforms may be destroyed by a future power struggle. This is the lingering fear . . . . "

It is dark. The only light is from cameras flashing. A number of people get out of two large cars, their arrival causing great confusion in the crowd. Somewhere the police are clearing a way for the cars.

The poster-writer continues:

"What are we to do? The founding-father of proletarian revolution never . . . . "

Suddenly a stone hits him in the face. Blood oozes from the corner of his mouth. Rotten eggs splatter the people standing next to him. The crowd is in an uproar. Several stout-looking men try to squeeze their way to the front, but are pushed back by the confused crowd.

December 6. The poster is circulated in the form of hand-bills in the supermarkets in Wangfujing and Xidan and in Tiananmen Square. The hand-bills are dropped from the 30-storey building of Peking Railway Station. They drift in the sky for ten minutes. Everyone stops work and gazes at them. Even the police stare coldly at these ominous white objects. Most of the hand-bills disappear before they ever reach the ground.

3 p.m. The author of the poster is arrested in his apartment on the 47th floor of Block 54, Green Residential Zone, Xinjiekou.

April Fifth Bulletin, the last surviving unofficial publication, brings out its final issue. It carries the full text of the poster, and a large colour photograph of the author. Afterwards, the entire editorial group disappears. That issue becomes a rarity, changing hands on the black market for RMB¥5.

"What are we to do? The founding father of proletarian revolution never solved this problem. Marx and Engels virtually never saw socialism in practice. Lenin created the first socialist state during a war. The complications of war called for iron discipline and strong leadership, i.e. concentration of power in the hands of a few reliable revolutionaries. The revolutionary leaders preserved their military style even after socialism was established; and thus the state became a military establishment. Stalin further developed the dictatorial character of the system, and exported it to many other countries, including China.

"It is a system that has been proved in war, but in time of peace it is a failure. Except for the few in power, and those who are too scared to speak the truth, everyone acknowledges this. The laws that govern war are different from those of ordinary everyday life. You can't just issue an order, "Lights out!", and expect everyone to go to bed at 9 p.m.!

"Socialist revolution is opposed to capitalism. It is opposed to all forms of exploitation. We have seen only too clearly the disastrous results of the exploitation, competition, and economic depression that exist in the capitalist system—and therefore we have to destroy it. But why can't we also see the even more reactionary and corrupt nature of the totalitarian dictatorship and economic exploitation that exist in feudal society, especially in our country where feudalism is so deeply rooted and capitalism has never fully developed?

"What are we to do? The present policy of decentralization is correct and necessary. It will give our country a great boost. But we should not be satisfied merely to follow in the footsteps of the Soviet Union. The Soviet Union has achieved everything—except democracy. Even if Soviet economic and military might eventually surpass that of the United States, the Soviet state will still be unable to rid itself of its fatal weakness—totalitarianism. And that will one day be its downfall.

"The people's right to monitor their own rulers is emphatically proclaimed by Marxism. When Lenin created the first socialist state, he emphasized the importance of this right. But we are still far from possessing it. One day someone will lead the people to a solution of this problem, and they will be forever grateful to him for giving them the most precious of all gifts—freedom, and democracy . . . . "

December 26. The pressure of public opinion is such that the government is forced to hold a court hearing. Standing in the dock, the poster-writer expounds the ideas contained in the last paragraph of his poster, with undiminished enthusiasm:

"In the past a man could only offer his lord and master suggestions and beg him to glance at them. The master might then, with a quick look and a few words, reject the labour of ten or more years. Or he might, if he liked the look of what he saw, publish it—to glorify himself. The democratic rights I am speaking of are fundamental; they can give people the true power to become masters themselves.

"They include political, economic and legal rights, rights that have been ignored under our 'people's democracy' for too long: the right to hold elections, the right to personal freedom, the right to express one's opinions freely and to communicate them openly to others . . . .

"Our constitution guarantees many freedoms, but not one of them has been put into effect . . . . If the people could really be given these rights, if they really had these freedoms, the advantages to our society would be incalculable. It would have far-reaching effects. Democracy could rejuvenate China.

"Democracy can inspire enthusiasm more effectively than anything else, it can motivate economic and political development. It can rid us of the disgusting rubbish that passes for art and literature, and be instrumental in producing art the people really want.

"These are not the only advantages, of course . . . . But China has never known democracy . . . . "

The poster-writer concludes his apologia with a poem by the Song dynasty poet, Chen Liang:

> I recall the days of old,
>   when we wandered, penniless and singing.
> Now my hair is grey;
>   what more do I desire?
> Life goes on;
>   what need of plans for the future?
> My protest is made;
>   to what more do I aspire?

His audience ponder the words deeply. The world weeps.

✳

The last day of the year 2000. The poster-writer has been sentenced to life imprisonment as a member of a "counter-revolutionary conspiracy". He is the first, and last, member of this "clique" to be sentenced. The foreign press reports yet another power struggle within the Party, adding that the judgement on this "case" may well be reversed. But no one mentions the poster-writer by name. If he belongs to a faction in Central, then no doubt one day his turn will come to be reinstated.

June 2001. An American publisher makes a fat profit out of a book entitled *An Ant Trampled to Death*, by an author who calls himself Lingering Fear. The foreword describes how the manuscript has been smuggled with great difficulty out of the Chinese concentration camp for political dissidents where the author is being held.

September 2001. A prisoner in a labour reform camp to the west of Shijiazhuang falls from a cliff in a quarry. The previous night this prisoner was lying on the plank bed in his cell and trying as usual to memorize five new English words for the following morning. In the end he went dejectedly to bed. At that very moment a stony-faced official took out a file, and drew a red circle round a name—Lingering Fear (pseudonym)—adding the words: "Accident: fell to his death from a cliff."

October 1. National Day celebrations are being broadcast on the radio. A slim middle-aged woman pours a container full of petrol over herself and burns to death in front of Democracy Wall. A girl, who bears a resemblance to the poster-writer, and a boy with big eyes, like the woman who has just burned herself to death, stand there sobbing. They hand pieces of paper to the passers-by, who try to console them. On the papers are poems, written in a childish scrawl:

> For democracy,
>   Our father and our mother died;
> They left us here to live,
>   For democracy.

And four lines by the famous Hungarian poet, Petöfi:

> Life is precious,
> Love beyond price;

> But both, for freedom,
> I would sacrifice.

By the time the police have had their attention drawn to the two children, they have already disappeared. No one will reveal their whereabouts.

That evening at six. Two short poems in the classical style, dating from the late 1970s, are posted on Democracy Wall. According to the people who have copied them, the woman wrote them. The first is in imitation of the Tang poet Chen Zi'ang:

> There is no freedom;
> No democracy.
> In this desolate universe
> All must grieve and weep.

The second is in the style of an old ballad:

> Democracy Wall
> At Xidan;
> The sky like a tent
> Spans the wilderness.
> Wide is the sky,
> Alone is man:
> When will democracy
> Come to our land?

10 p.m. The large crowd is dispersed by an even larger contingent of troops. An urgent "Announcement to the Nation" from Party Central is broadcast. A bulldozer levels the wall, witness to twenty-three years of history.

The same day, a year later. Countless flowers at the site of the wall. One basket, larger than the others, bears the note: Donation for the rebuilding of Democracy Wall. It contains at least RMB¥10,000.

That afternoon. A Red Flag 2000 deluxe sedan pulls up at the roadside. The news that a certain member of the Politburo has sent a wreath spreads quickly.

Later that night. Festival lanterns are lit. Troops surround the Great Hall of the People—that strange hybrid of a building dating from the 1950s, neither Chinese, nor Western. The troops are heavily armed. They look like a regiment from some distant province.

Rumour has it that inside a special session of Party Central is in progress . . . .

adapted from "A Chinese Tragedy in the Year 2000",
Peking Spring, *May 1979*

"Lingering Fear" was itself first posted on Democracy Wall in early 1979. Although other science fiction stories that speculate about the future of Chinese society have been published in official journals, they are generally optimistic projections designed to inspire faith in the modernization policies of the government.

Ironically, the Democracy Wall which Su Ming envisaged as lasting through the Deng Xiaoping interregnum, was closed down on Deng's orders not long after this story appeared on it.

IV: HUMANITY!

A spectre haunts the intellectual world.
Who are you?
I am Man.

Wang Ruoshui, 1983

Socialist Humanism

Wang Ruoshui

A spectre is haunting the Chinese intellectual world—the spectre of humanism.

I wish to come to the defense of humanism in general, and especially of Marxist humanism.

In the present period, when we are constructing socialism and modernizing our country, we need socialist humanism. What are the implications of this humanism for us?

—It means the determined rejection of the "total dictatorship" and cruel struggles of the Cultural Revolution; the abandonment of personality cults which deify one man and degrade the people; the upholding of the equality of all before truth and the law; and the sanctity of personal freedom and dignity.

—It means opposing feudal ranks and concepts of privilege, opposing capitalism, the worship of money, and the treatment of people as commodities or mere instruments; demanding that people should really be seen as people, and that individuals should be judged by what they are in themselves, and not on the basis of class origin, position or wealth.

—It means recognition that man is the goal not only of socialist production but of all work. We must establish and develop mutual respect, mutual loving care, and mutual help embodying socialist spiritual civilization; and we must oppose callous bureaucracy and extreme individualism, both of which cause harm to others.

—It means valuing the human factor in socialist construction; giving full play to the self-motivation and creativity of the working people; valuing education, the nurturing of talent and the all-round development of man . . . .

Is this socialist humanism not already to be found in our practice? Is it not growing around us from day to day? Why treat it as something strange, something alien?

—A spectre haunts the intellectual world . . . .
"Who are you?"
"I am Man."

January 1983

Humanist Poison

Sloganeering about humanism will only encourage all kinds of un-realistic demands for individual well-being and freedom, and create a false impression that once the socialist system is established, all personal demands will be satisfied—for otherwise, the socialist system would be proven "in-humane" . . . . Some of those who preach humanism have set the value of the individual against the development of the cause of socialist construction, and have even alleged that the "human world continues to deteriorate, while the material world (including authority) continues to gather strength."

Hu Qiaomu, January 1984

LE MONDE HUMAIN,
Gao Xingjian

Wang Ruoshui studied philosophy at Peking University in the late 1940s, and worked as an editor in the political theory department of the People's Daily *after 1950. He was one of the first Party theoreticians to denounce Mao's personality cult in 1979. His defense of the concept of "socialist humanism", the affirmation of which he believes can reduce bureaucratic privilege and facilitate the establishment of democracy in China, led him into conflict with Hu Qiaomu, the Party's chief ideologue and one of Mao's ex-secretaries, in 1983. Volleys were exchanged in the form of ponderous ideological articles in both Mainland and Hong Kong publications, and Wang was summarily dismissed from his senior editorial position in the* People's Daily *and "encouraged" to retire. Still, the controversy continues to smoulder today. Many people, officials and civilians alike, see Hu Qiaomu, who is already in his seventies, as a threatened species, one of the last bastions of Maoist "leftism". This is perhaps overly optimistic, as in fact Hu and his like-minded followers may be more perceptively seen as part of a deep-rooted Chinese tradition that is unlikely to disappear with their passing.*

MANDARIN CANCER,
Fang Cheng

The Vagabond: He Jingfu

Dai Houying

At the centre of the humanism debate was the novel Humanity!, *written by the Shanghai woman writer Dai Houying. One of the principal characters in the book is He Jingfu, a writer and thinker, and a champion of humanism. In this brief extract, he tells of his own life, and the experience that eventually inspired him to write a book on the whole question of humanism.*

IN 1962 the university informed me that I could return from my exile and continue my studies. But I had become accustomed to living in the countryside. I had secretly taken up philosophy, in an attempt to find out how a Marxist should treat some of the basic questions of human life and personal emotions. I no longer wanted to return . . . .

I had never felt more alone. I decided to go away. I left a note for my sister and set out, with no idea of where I was heading. I wandered aimlessly, learning whatever lessons life presented to me. The only books I had with me were *The Dream of the Red Chamber* and *Selected Works of Marx and Engels.*

I became a non-person, completely cut off from the society around me. I had no residence permit, no grain or cotton coupons, no friends or relatives to look after me, not even a postal address. No one cared who I was or what I was doing; no one asked me where I came from or where I was going. People just knew me as Old He—the charcoal burner, the builder, the stone carrier, the blaster, the carter, and even the story-teller. I made enough to keep my rice bowl full, but that was all.

*

One year, I joined a transport team near the Great Wall. I'd just bought myself a horse and cart with my hard-earned cash. It was a lousy horse, but it was cheap.

I love the Great Wall. When I first climbed from the First Pass Under Heaven up to the highest beacon tower, I forgot my vagabond existence completely. Every brick in the Wall seemed to me like an individual. The endless winding Wall was like a mighty army, and I was a new recruit. Almost every stone in the tower had the names of travellers scratched on it. Why do they do that? To make a name for themselves? But I don't think anyone has ever achieved fame in this way. I think they came to enlist, just like me. The stones were our muster roll. But I didn't carve my name on the Wall. I gave it my body instead. Whenever I could, I would climb up onto it. I was prepared to stay there for the rest of my life, and to be buried at its foot when I died.

Our transport team was "black", like each one of its members. Most people know nothing about this of course, but outside conventional society there are all sorts of "black" societies, made up of a mixed bag of people: self-employed labourers, the unemployed, people who have been rejected by society for a variety of reasons; and of course, people whose only interest in life is to make money. We have to form gangs, otherwise we'd never be able to find work or buy grain and cloth coupons on the black market. And every gang must have its chief. I have never been one, and I don't want to be. I've never been able to handle people, no matter how hard I've tried. Until you've been in one of those gangs you can't imagine how weird it all is. There's no greater insecurity than working in one of those deformed miniature societies. Nobody knows anything about anybody else; nobody cares for anybody else. They have joined forces to make money, and that's the only thing that keeps them together. The chiefs are mostly local thugs. They get work contracts to make things legal. The others are all terrorized by them, and let them skim off part of their hard-earned wages. Of course, I too had to pay my contribution to the chief. This particular fellow was a ex-con, that is to say, he'd been released from labour camp. His face was fair and thin, like that of a scholar. But something about the muscles in his face gave him a ferocious look. The flesh on his cheekbones formed big bags under his eyes, making him appear especially terrifying. He looked so greedy and vicious that everybody was afraid of him. I certainly didn't want to rub him up the wrong way.

But one day I discovered, after settling our accounts, that he had taken advantage of the fact that I was a newcomer and paid me eighty *yuan* too little. It wasn't a question of the money, I simply couldn't accept his attitude. I quarrelled with him. He hit me; I hit him back. I had carried many a two-hundred-pound boulder in my day; why should I be afraid of being beaten up by this man? I ended up dislocating his arm.

I was taken to the police station, where they asked for my identity card. I didn't have one. I told them: I am He Jingfu, always have been, always will be. But I have never done anything wrong. You can check it for yourself if you don't believe me! The policeman wasn't a bad sort. He simply lectured me: behave yourself and don't make any more trouble. And they threw me out.

As I drove my cart back to my temporary lodgings, I was on the verge of tears. Identity card! Identity card! I don't have an identity card! Without one, don't I still count as a human being? I whipped the horse violently all the way, driving it to a gallop; I wanted to overturn the cart or to crash into the Wall. If it was to be my death then let it kill me now! What was the point of going on like this? Just then a man drove his cart right in front of mine, but I saw him too late to avoid a collision. My cart wounded his horse, the shaft went right through the beast's shoulder. It took the two of us a lot of effort to pull it out. Blood spurted all over the place, splashing my head and face. I took off my shirt and stuffed it into the wound to stop the bleeding.

After a little while the horse died. The carter grabbed me in case I tried to run away. His horse was state property, and I had no alternative but to hand him my whip. Because my horse was inferior to his, I had to give him my cart as well.

"Well, now I am as naked as the day I was born and as carefree as the wind again," I muttered to myself and lay down on the ground.

The carter was a kind man. Seeing me suddenly bereft of everything I owned, he felt unwilling to abandon me. He took out a small gourd filled with liquor from the inner pocket of his coat and insisted that we have a drink together. He asked me where I had come from and where I was going, and I told him my story. "Don't worry," he kept saying, "every dog has his day. Every dog has his day."

Before he drove my cart away, he offered me the horse's carcass, saying I could make some money out of it. I didn't want it, so he dragged it away. I didn't want to go anywhere. I lay down at the foot of the Wall. How grand and quiet it was! If I died here nobody would ever find me. The Great Wall would gradually absorb my corpse. And yet—to die or not to die, that was the question. I lay there, staring motionlessly at the stars in the sky and began like Hamlet to ponder my fate . . . .

I was just thirty years old, the age by which a man should have made something of his life. But what had I achieved? For myself? My family? My career? Nothing. I had nothing. Not even an identity card. No one needed me. Did life for me consist only of food, drink, clothing, and shelter? Did I really have no choice but to measure the value of my life by the demands of that labour contractor, who fed off my sweat and blood? No!

I jumped to my feet and ran along the Wall up to the highest beacon tower. I took out a pocket-knife and by the light of the stars carved the three characters of my name into the stone: HE JING FU. Now I had enlisted myself into that army. This stone was my identity card, it certified that He Jingfu has Chinese blood, that he is a descendant of the Yellow Emperor. I sat down and leant against the tower. I took a look. One more look over the landscape of China. What a spectacle! Inside the Wall, all was green and luxuriant, while outside it lay a stretch of rolling yellow earth. Yet it was the yellow earth that evoked my tender affection more than anything else in the world. I could feel all the beauty and power buried beneath the earth, lying undiscovered. It enticed men to sacrifice their lives, it fired the imagination.

A shooting star sped across the sky from east to west, and fell. But the sky remained as spacious and serene as before. The stars still winked contentedly, and the "silver river" of the Milky Way still glimmered dispassionately at the separated lovers, the Cowherd and the Weaving Girl, standing poised on its banks. To them it was as if nothing had happened. In this boundless universe, who notices a small shooting star? To the rest of the world my death would amount to little more than the fading of a falling star in the night. It would pass by soundless, unnoticed. And yet I am a human being, a man of flesh and blood.

I thought of my grandmother, who had often told me stories

Tiananmen Square, April 4, 1976   **Peter Griffiths**

Democracy Wall, April 1979   **UPI**

LIU XINWU   Mi Qiu   DAI HOUYING   Jaivin/Asiaweek

SUN LONGJI   YANG LIAN

BEI DAO   GU CHENG

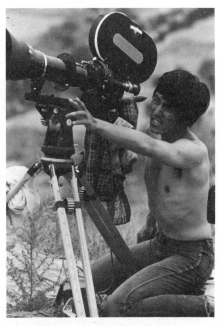

CHEN KAIGE   ZHANG YIMOU

MANG KE at one of the last Today *poetry readings, September 1979.* AP

WANG XIZHE

WEI JINGSHENG at his trial, October 1979. Xinhua

about the Milky Way and the stars.

"Every one of us has a drop of dew above his head, and we all have our own fate," Granny often said to me pointing at the stars in the sky. She said that people were just like the stars, each with its own position in the firmament, each with its own right to exist. The stars still hang in the sky without needing any support or sustenance; and men live on in the world without help or assistance. The stars shine in the sky, the dew glitters on the earth. This was the earliest philosophy I was taught.

Had my own drop of dew really dried up?

No! It had not! It enabled me to see my dead parents, my distant sister, all those whom I loved . . . .

My horse was gone, and so was my cart. But I still had my hands. Why need I be afraid, just because I had no identity card? The value of my existence did not depend on some bureaucratic document.

I sat up all night in front of the tower. Early next morning I came down. I was not going back to the transport team. I needed to find a new job. I went down along the Great Wall, inquiring at every village along the way to see if I could do any odd jobs for them.

It was all in vain. When I had spent all my money, I had to tear myself away from my beloved Great Wall and made my way south, to the banks of the Huai River.

from the novel Humanity!

The Rebirth of My Humanity

TWENTY YEARS ago I graduated from the East China Normal University in Shanghai ahead of my class, to begin a career in the tumultuous and disaster-ridden world of the Chinese arts. Blind faith and ignorance emboldened me, gave me a sense of confidence and power. I thought I had grasped the basic principles of Marxism and Leninism; I believed I had a correct understanding of society and of my fellow man. I stood up at the lectern in the university and declaimed a speech that had been painstakingly composed in accordance with the wishes of the leadership. In it I denounced my teacher's lectures on humanism. "I love my teacher," I announced to the world. "But I love the truth even more!" I felt intoxicated by the waves of enthusiastic applause that greeted these words; I felt proud to have become a "fighter" for the cause.

Now, twenty years later, I am writing novels. And in my novels I try to propagate the very things I so energetically decried in the past. I want to give voice to the concept of humanity in my writing, even though this is just the thing that I tried so hard to suppress and reform in myself. This is the great irony of my life.

A philosopher could sum up the change I have experienced in one simple statement: I have completed the circle of negating the negation. I am no philosopher, however, merely an average individual possessed of quite unremarkable faculties. In all of this I see the workings of fate. For I have witnessed the fate of China, her people, my loved ones, my own individual destiny. It is a fate full of blood and tears, and its meaning resounds with pain. But in it I see traced the tortuous path travelled by a whole generation of intellectuals. And such a weary and treacherous journey it has been!

When I was young, I was warm-hearted and simple-minded. All I ever thought of was the love I felt for the Party and for New China. I knew that I must study hard and serve the people. I was absolutely sincere in my devotion to the Party and socialism. This was because Liberation had provided me with the chance of a university education, a privilege that no one in my family had been able to enjoy. I was the first woman in my family to have an education, and to my young and ardent heart socialism and communism were a world of wonder and excitement. I honestly believed that our cause was just, that our future was bright and that the way ahead was clear and smooth. I didn't have a care in the world, I was completely unselfconscious, entirely without fear. My heart brimmed over with warmth and love.

In 1957 the concept of "class struggle" was encoded in my brain. In 1966 a new programme was added to it: that of "line struggle".

I did my best to see everything in terms of these two "struggles". I was as involved in the front-line assault during the "big criticism" campaigns of the early Cultural Revolution: I was a "rebel soldier" under the command of the Red General. At one time I quite piously believed that everything in the world was a question of class struggle.

We had to keep class struggle in mind every waking moment.

But despite all this I was still a human being. I had not been completely numbed. I too felt the tribulations of life. I could see the bloody wounds on people's bodies, the tears on their faces. I too felt pangs of conscience, I was mindful of the cries that issued from the depths of my soul. And often I would ask in my heart of hearts: Isn't our struggle too extreme? Haven't we wronged innocent people? Was it really necessary to carry out class and line struggle every minute of every day throughout the breadth and width of China?

As the movement to repudiate the Gang of Four continued I came to realize many things I had not known or could not have imagined in my wildest dreams. I was shocked to the very core of my being when it finally dawned on me that the God I had enshrined in my mind was tumbling, and that the pillars of my faith were about to collapse. Nothing made sense any more. I would often sit in a dazed stupor, burst into tears for no reason or start shouting hysterically. How I wished I could take hold of the God I had worshipped for so long, and all those other dieties I believed in, and give them a good shake. I wanted to ask them: Is all of this true? Why did you tell us such a different story? Did you deceive us on purpose or was it really a "process of recognition" for you too? For a time I wandered lost in the night of my soul.

Then I began to reflect, looking deep into myself as I bandaged my bleeding wounds. I read through the diary of my life page by page, straining to make out the footprints that trailed off into the lost distance of my own past.

Eventually, I came to see that I had been playing the role of a tragic dupe in what was a mammoth farce. I was a simpleton who believed herself to be the freest creature on earth, when in fact I had been robbed of the right to think. The cangue that weighed heavy on my soul had always seemed to me a beautiful garland of flowers. I had lived out half my life without having come to any understanding of myself.

I wrestled free of that role and went in search of myself. So I too was mere flesh and blood; I too could love and hate like other people; I too was possessed of all the feelings and passions of man, and I too could think for myself. I knew I had a right to believe in myself and to have a sense of my own worth, that I shouldn't allow myself to be manipulated or made into some "submissive tool".

Gradually a word written in blazing capitals shone before my eyes. That word was HUMANITY: The words to a much-maligned and long-forgotten song welled up in my throat: Humanity, Human Feelings, Humanism.

It was as though I had woken from a dream. Even though the cold sweat of night was still damp on my flesh and my mind was still groggy, nonetheless, I was finally awake. I wanted to tell the world that I was now a conscious human being. So I started to write . . . . The theme of all my works is Man. I write of the caked blood, the welling tears, the twisted souls and the agonized cries. I write of the spark of light that shines in the abyss of darkness. I cry out at the top of my voice: "You may return, oh soul; here is your home!" And I record with joy the rebirth of my humanity.

from the postscript to the novel Humanity!
August 1980, Canton

An Incorrect Interpretation of Life

The author of Humanity! *has failed to interpret life accurately, and is unable to draw correct conclusions based on an overall world-view. It is quite clear from this novel that she has ignored the main political trends in China since the Gang of Four. She misleads her readers with vacuous humanistic sermonizing, as if humanism were the ideal cure-all for the ills of the age.*

Obviously the author of Humanity! *has tried to create in the character He Jingfu a humanistic saviour alienated from the mainstream of political life. She wishes to offer us one possible model for the future. But in doing this, she has omitted many elements which are essential for a complete and accurate picture of reality. The main forces of resistance during the Cultural Revolution—those cadres and common people who fought persistently against the erroneous line—are left out of the picture: instead the foreground is occupied by this image of an idealized humanist. We can learn from this that if writers are unable to interpret life correctly, they will also be unable to describe it accurately, and thus will fail to embody its essential reality in their works.*

Literary Gazette, May 1982

Deng Pufang:
Humanism for the Handicapped

HUMANISM, so decried and laboriously explained from the socialist viewpoint only a few months ago, has been rehabilitated with even greater insistence by Deng Pufang, Deng Xiaoping's handicapped son. [He was reportedly thrown by Red Guards from the third or fourth floor of a building at Qinghua University during the Cultural Revolution—for refusing to disclose his father's whereabouts.] The speech he made at the general meeting of the Chinese Foundation for the Help of the Physically Handicapped was published in the *People's Daily*. Without any theoretical quibbling, Deng Pufang stated quite simply that, to date, the capitalist countries have done more and better than China for the physically disabled, because they have a greater respect for man. This is a serious assertion, he added, since a political regime and social system is most often judged on its social welfare record. If socialism and communism do nothing for the unfortunate, they will be discredited. This, he argued, raises the question to the highest political level, by questioning the very legitimacy of the regime. During his Hong Kong visit, Deng Pufang described the progress his country had already made: free medical care, mutual aid funds and so on. Yet the problem remains essentially one of attitude to human distress . . . and, on this score, he felt bound to admit that he sometimes felt ashamed of Chinese society.

Deng Pufang then went on to describe, indignantly, the attitude of Chinese children and adults who make fun of the disabled and throw stones at what they consider to be worthless creatures. It is impossible to put this sort of behaviour down to bourgeois or capitalist habits, he said, for people in capitalist societies are more humane. He then laid the blame for the evil on China's feudal past. Perhaps he is idealizing the situation of the handicapped in the capitalist world, but this is hardly the point. Moreover, he never draws the distinction between what he calls capitalist humanism and socialist humanism. Many a social worker in any country will recognize his own goals in the aims of the Chinese foundation: "Our work is one of humanism, that is to say we wish to raise the material and spiritual level of the people, so that every man may feel useful, especially the physically handicapped who are particularly unfortunate." Deng Pufang then appealed to the patriotism of his compatriots saying, "What others do among their own, can we not do among ourselves?" Intermingled with respect for the person is a national pride which cannot be described as particularly socialist. What is more, a patriotic call in no way eradicates the inalienable value of the individual.

This value is even better expressed by Deng Pufang when he comes to the qualities required of the members of the Foundation. The fact that a socialist conscience figures at the top of the list is more a matter of form than an introduction to other qualities. Indeed, when he goes into detail, he develops three points which to him are essential. The first is a spirit of sacrifice. Nuns, who live according to an idealistic philosophy, are capable of giving their lives for their beliefs. Why then should communists, firm believers in historical materialism, not do likewise? Life is man's most precious gift and, in the twilight of his days, happiness is the conviction that he has worked to make men's lives better. The second is intelligent commitment. Fine words and grand gestures are meaningless unless backed by practical, logical solutions to the problems facing the disabled. The last is that the collective interests of the Foundation should come before the member's personal interests. Here he quotes the Salvation Army, whose members he met in Hong Kong, as an example to follow. The final sentence of Deng Pufang's speech stresses the depth of his understanding of the problems he is dealing with, when he says that each member of the Foundation "should include handicapped people among his friends, that he might give them practical help and receive spiritual energy in return".

China News Analysis, *no. 1278 (1985)*

The Long March to Man

Sun Longji

The Chinese Concept of Man

IN EXISTENTIALISM, a man "exists" by virtue of retreating from all his social roles and searching his own soul. If he fails to go through this process, he cannot become a man in the philosophical sense.

By contrast, a Chinese fulfills himself within the network of interpersonal relationships. A Chinese is the totality of his social roles. Strip him of his relationships, and there is nothing left. He is not an independent unit. His existence has to be defined by his acquaintance.

This concept of man is best exemplified by the primary Confucian concept of *ren*. *Ren* may roughly be translated as humane. The Chinese written character is made up of two components, "man" and "two", and denotes essentially a bilateral relationship. Only in the presence of another person can our "humanity" be displayed. The relationship may be between emperor and official, father and son, husband and wife, between younger and older brother, or between friends. This Chinese concept of man forms the basic substratum, the deep structure, of Chinese culture and has remained unchanged up to the present day (though extended to the domain of the collective).

When man can only be defined through his relationship with others, a "loner" without social connections is unacceptable. Only when he has a family to define his existence, can he be accepted as an adult being. In the same sense, a man not yet defined by any social relationship is regarded as an "immoral being". In Chinese, the words "single" and "alone" have the connotation of "immoral" and "pathetic". Perhaps in traditional China there was only one man allowed to stand above all these social relationships: the emperor. He was responsible to nobody, and required nobody to define him. In short, he was the only man allowed to be an individual.

Children, not Men

CHINESE PARENTS seldom encourage the development of their children's personality. By contrast, Westerners foster their children's independence. They encourage them to sleep on their own and to leave home when they are grown up. Western children have equal status with their parents. There is no obligation on their part to show filial piety.

In China, the older generation is only concerned for the physical well-being of the young. When a child's concept of self is not yet well developed, that child needs his elders to look after him, to give him food, to put him to bed early, and to take general care of his health. But to treat adults in this manner is to fix them at a particular stage of development. Chinese adults, so it seems, still need others to remind them what to wear. They refrain from smoking or drinking, not as the result of a conscious moral choice of their own, but because they want to prove to their parents that they are still good children.

In a society where the purpose of life is to produce offspring and perpetuate the species, health is not a matter for individual choice but rather a social or moral problem. A Chinese person is responsible both for the procreation of the next generation and for the nourishment of the older generation. He is therefore never an independent unit. Upbringing is not only an investment, it is a way of controlling the personal development of the younger generation, so that they will resemble the old. Among Overseas Chinese, the older generation find it more difficult to control the young. But in the mainland, through the confessional "exchange of Hearts-and-Minds", the government has total control, just as a father controls his son.

Identity

CHINA TALKS about respect for "people" in the abstract—that is, the collective—more than almost any other country in the world. Government, newspapers, banks, publishing houses: they all belong to The People. But every actual person is a mere object of surveillance. His work unit is watching over him. Apart from the pressure exerted by the "masses" of his work unit, there is also the unit head "defining" him—this definition may take the form of care and concern, or it may be expressed as an admonition; it may decree what he should do, what kind of friends he should have, and occasionally whom he should marry. In other words, it decides what kind of a person he should be. It determines his identity.

The Chinese Outsider

OF COURSE, there are some examples of individuals who crave passionately for a more meaningful existence. But they have to express their inner feelings furtively, out of sight of society. If they admit their beliefs openly, they will simply be seen as "negative examples" by the community. So these people continue to be oppressed.

There have been Chinese rebels, people who have broken through the "computer program" of Confucianism. But this breakthrough most often leads to an emotional identification with the collective; it very seldom brings an awareness of individual self.

There are Chinese who have a spiritual awareness. But this is most often directed towards intellectual and cultural affairs. In other fields there is an invisible restraint, and a concomitant impotence. In fact these Chinese outsiders often become mere bookworms, feeble and etiolated scholars—shabby and useless specimens of humanity.

Conventional Chinese culture leaves little room at all for self-realization.

To be a man, one must create oneself—one must make a work of art out of oneself—out of one's body, one's appearance, one's mind, intellect, passion, and will.

Man can be something higher. Man must transcend man.

from Deep Structure

Song of Wisdom

Mu Dan

I have reached illusion's end
In this grove of falling leaves,
Each leaf a signal of past joy,
Drifting sere within my heart.

Some were loves of youthful days—
Blazing meteors in a distant sky,
Extinguished, vanished without a trace,
Or dropped before me, stiff and cold as ice.

Some were boisterous friendships,
Fullblown blossoms, innocent of coming fall.
Society dammed the pulsing blood,
Life cast molten passion in reality's shell.

There too the spell of high ideals,
That drew me through many a twisting mile of thorn.
It is no pain to suffer for ideals;
But O, to watch them change into objects of scorn!

Now nothing remains but regret and remorse—
Daily punishment for past pride.
When the glory of the sky stands condemned,
In this wasteland, what colour can survive?

There is one tree that stands alone intact,
It thrives, I know, on suffering's lifeblood.
Its greenshade mocks me ruthlessly!
O wisdom tree! I curse your every growing bud.

1976

Mu Dan, who died prematurely in 1977, was one of the leading modernist poets of the late 1940s. After 1949 he devoted most of his energy to translating English and Russian poetry. But this did not save him from being attacked in 1958 as a bourgeois individualist and humanistic writer. "Song of Wisdom" is one of a group of late poems published posthumously in his native city of Tianjin.

V: THORNS

To be a satirist is dangerous.

Lu Xun, March 2, 1933

The Ugly Chinaman

Bo Yang

FOR MANY YEARS I've contemplated writing a book called *The Ugly Chinaman*. When *The Ugly American* was published in the United States the U.S. State Department chose it as a guide for policy making. But when the Japanese ambassador to Argentina published his *The Ugly Japanese*, he was swiftly removed from his post. This is a good example of the difference between the Orient and the Occident. In China, however, things would be one step worse. If I wrote a book called *The Ugly Chinaman*, before long you'd be bringing me my meals in jail; that's the reason why I haven't written it yet, though I've been looking for an opportunity to talk about the subject in public for a long time.

How Hard it is to be Chinese*

ON THE CHINESE mainland, the Anti-Rightist campaign was followed by the Cultural Revolution, an earthshaking disaster without precedent in the history of human civilization. In addition to the terrible loss of human lives, the Cultural Revolution caused incalculable damage by destroying humanitarian values and defiling the nobility of the human spirit, without which there remains very little to separate man from beast. Those "Ten Years of Devastation" turned many people into animals. How can a nation whose morality has degenerated to this level ever regain its self-respect? . . . .

Everyone's talking about the Hong Kong question nowadays. When a piece of a country's territory is snatched away by another country, it is always cause for shame. And when that territory is

*Section headings added by the editors of *Pai-shing*.

> *Bo Yang is the pseudonym of Guo Yidong, a controversial Taiwan writer, who was born in Kaifeng, Henan in 1920. Guo moved to Taiwan in the late 1940s, and using the penname Bo Yang, he began writing essays dealing mainly with Taiwan's social problems and the Chinese national character. His penetrating exposés of corruption and special privileges soon won him a reputation as a leading social critic in both Taiwan and among Chinese communities overseas. The influence of Lu Xun is evident in Bo Yang's acerbic style; and, like Lu Xun, it was inevitable that he should incur the displeasure of the KMT authorities. In 1967, he was arrested and jailed for ten years on charges of "defaming the leadership" and "complicity with the Communists".*
>
> *The Ugly Chinaman (from which the following extracts are taken) was a speech Bo Yang delivered at Iowa University on 24 September, 1984; subsequently published in the Hong Kong* Pai-shing Semi-Monthly, *it set off a small-scale "battle of the pens" among the magazine's readers. A translation of one of the more negative letters* Pai-shing *received in reply to Bo Yang is appended to the following abridged translation of the speech. The Ugly Chinaman was published in book form along with a selection of Bo Yang's essays and readers' letters in Taiwan, where it has already gone through numerous reprints. It would be unthinkable for Bo Yang's speech to be published openly in China.**

finally returned to its rightful owner—like a child returning to its mother's embrace—the event becomes a cause for celebration on both sides. You must be familiar with France's ceding of Alsace-Lorraine to Germany. The original loss of the two states was extremely painful, and the reunification a cause for great rejoicing. In the case of Hong Kong, however, no sooner was the news out that the territory would be returned to the motherland than people panicked. How do you explain this? In Taiwan, a number of young people—both native Taiwanese and mainlanders—support the idea of an independent Taiwan. This is the so-called Taiwan Independence Movement. I recall some thirty years ago when Taiwan was restored to China by Japan, we were all overjoyed; it was as if a lost child had found its way back to the arms of its mother. Thirty years later, what is it that has brought about this change of heart, this child's desire to leave home and try to make it on its own again? Chinese people share the same blood, the same physical appearance, the same ancestry and culture, the same written and

---

* But see below, Chapter 12.

spoken languages; only geographical differences divide them. How, then, has the present situation come about?

Even among the Chinese in the United States you will find the absurd situation wherein leftists, rightists, moderates, independents, left-leaning moderates, moderate-leaning leftists, right-leaning moderates, and moderate-leaning rightists can't seem to find a common

"If you never walk you'll never fall over."

Hua Junwu

language and are constantly at each other's throats. What does this imply about the Chinese people? What does this imply about China itself? No other nation on earth has such a long history or such a well-preserved cultural tradition, a tradition which has in the past given rise to an extremely advanced civilization. Neither the Greeks nor the Egyptians of today bear any relationship to their ancient forebears, while the Chinese people of today are the direct descendants of the ancient Chinese. How is it possible for such a great people to have degenerated to such a state of ugliness? Not only have we been bullied around by foreigners; even worse, for centuries we've been bullied around by our own kind—from tyrannical emperors to despotic officials and ruthless mobs . . . .

Chinese People are the Same Everywhere

DURING MY INCARCERATION I spent a lot of time contemplating my fate. What crimes had I committed? What laws had I broken? I continued pondering these questions after I was released and began to wonder whether mine was an abnormal or special case. On this trip to Iowa, where I have been able to meet writers from the Chinese mainland, I have discovered that God has predestined people like me for jail, whether the jail be in Taiwan or on the Chinese mainland. These mainland writers told me: "Someone like you would never have made it as far as the Red Guards or the Cultural Revolution. You'd have been lucky to survive the Anti-Rightist Movement." Why must a Chinese person with the courage to speak an iota of truth suffer this sort of fate? I've asked a number of people from the mainland why they ended up in prison. The answer was invariably, "I spoke the truth." And that's the way it is. But why does speaking the truth lead to such unfortunate consequences? My answer is that this is not a problem of any particular individual but rather of Chinese culture as a whole. A few days ago I had a discussion with the Party secretary of the [mainland] Writer's Association. He literally made me speechless with anger. I used to think I could hold my own in an argument; but this guy knocked the wind clean out of my sails. I don't blame him though; in the same way, I don't blame the agents who handled my case in Taipei. If you were in that environment and conversant with its ways and means, you would very likely act as they do, because you would believe that what you were doing was right. I would do the same, though I'd probably be even more obnoxious than that Party secretary. I often hear people say: "Your future is in your own hands." Having lived the better part of my life, I don't believe that any more. Actually, I should say about one half is in your hands, while the other half rests in the hands of others.

The Scourge of Infighting

ONE OF the qualities for which the Chinese people are notorious is a propensity for quarreling among themselves . . . . They squabble among themselves no matter where they are. Their bodies seem to lack those cells which enable most human beings to co-operate. When Westerners criticize the Chinese for this weakness, I say to them: "Do you know why this is so? It's because God knows that there are a billion of us, and if we ever managed to get it together, you'd never be able to handle us. God has been merciful to you by making it impossible for us Chinese to join forces." But even as I say this, I am wracked by a terrible sense of anguish . . . .

The Inability to Admit Error

CHINESE PEOPLE'S inability to co-operate and their predilection for bickering among themselves are deep-rooted, harmful traits. These behaviour patterns do not stem from any inherent weakness in the moral fibre of the Chinese people, but rather from a "neurotic virus" which infects Chinese culture, making it impossible for us not to act in certain ways in given situations. We may be entirely aware of the fact that we quarrel among ourselves, yet it is beyond our control to stop it. "If the pot breaks, no one can have anything to eat; but if the sky falls, there'll always be someone tall enough to prevent it from falling on me." This tendency towards internecine struggle is associated with a terrible reluctance to admit mistakes . . . .

Chinese people find it hard to admit their mistakes, and produce myriad reasons to cover up for them. There's an old adage: "Contemplate errors behind closed doors." Whose errors? The guy next door's, of course! When I was teaching I had my students keep a weekly diary in which they were supposed to record their own behaviour for the week. The entries frequently read like this: "Today XXX deceived me. I've been good to him in so many ways. It must be because I'm too honest and simple." But XXX's diary revealed that he also believed himself to be too simple and honest. If everyone thinks himself simple and honest, who does that leave to be dishonest? Chinese don't admit their mistakes because somewhere along the line they have lost the ability to do so. We may not admit our mistakes, but they still exist, and denying them won't make them disappear. Chinese people expend a great deal of effort in covering up their mistakes, and in so doing make additional ones. Thus it is often said that Chinese are addicted to bragging, boasting, lying, equivocating and malicious slandering. For years people have been going on about the supreme greatness of the Han Chinese people, and boasting endlessly that Chinese traditional culture should be promulgated throughout the world. But the reason why such dreams will never be realized is because they're pure braggadocio. I need not cite any further examples of boasting and lying, but Chinese verbal brutality deserves special mention. Even in the

Achievements   *Shortcomings*   *Mistakes*

Wang Jingfeng

confines of the bedroom where Western couples address each other as "honey" and "darling", Chinese people prefer such endearments as "you deserve to be cut into a thousand pieces." And in matters of politics and money, or in power struggles of any kind, the viciousness can be out of all proportion. This raises the additional question: What makes Chinese people so cruel and base?

Many Westerners have said to me, "It's hard getting to know Chinese people: you never know what's really on their minds." My reply is: "You think you have problems? When Chinese people speak

with other Chinese, it's nearly impossible to know what's going on."
One way of communicating in these situations is to observe people's
slightest movements and changes of expression, and to cultivate the
habit of beating around the bush. You ask someone, "Have you eaten
yet?" and the answer is "Yes." But this person is actually ravenously
hungry. You can hear his stomach growling . . . .

Stuck in the Mud of Bragging and Boasting

NARROWMINDEDNESS AND a lack of altruism can produce an unbalanced personality which constantly wavers between two extremes:
a chronic feeling of inferiority, and extreme arrogance. In his inferiority, a Chinese person is a slave; in his arrogance, he is a tyrant.
Rarely does he or she have a healthy sense of self-respect. In the inferiority mode, everyone else is better than he is, and the closer he gets
to people with influence, the wider his smile becomes. Similarly, in the
arrogant mode, no other human being on earth is worth the time of
day. The result of these extremes is a strange animal with a split personality.

A Nation of Inflation

WHAT MAKES the Chinese people so prone to self-inflation? Consider
the saying: A small vessel is easily filled. Because of the Chinese
people's inveterate narrowmindedness and arrogance, even the slightest
success is overwhelming. It is all right if a few people behave in this
manner, but if it's the entire population or a majority—particularly in
China—it spells national disaster. Since it seems as if the Chinese
people have never had a healthy sense of self-respect, it is immensely
difficult for them to treat others as equals: if you aren't my master,
then you're my slave. People who think this way can only be narrow-
minded in their attitude towards the world and reluctant to admit
their mistakes.

Only the Chinese Can Change Themselves

WITH SO MANY loathsome qualities, only the Chinese people can reform themselves. Foreigners have a duty to help us, not in the realm
of economics, but through culture. The Chinese ship of state is so large
and overcrowded that if it sinks many non-Chinese will be drowned as
well.

One last point: China is seriously overpopulated. China's more
than one billion mouths can easily devour the Himalayas. This should
remind us that China's difficulties are complex and call for awareness
on the part of each and every Chinese person. Each one of us must
become a discriminating judge and use our powers to examine and
appraise ourselves, our friends and our country's leaders. This, I believe,
is the only way out for the Chinese people.

Developing a Personal Sense of Judgement

IN THE LAST 4,000 years, China has produced only one great thinker:
Confucius. In the two and one half millennia since his death, China's
literati did little more than add footnotes to the theories propounded
by Confucius and his disciples, rarely contributing any independent
opinions, simply because the traditional culture did not permit it. The
minds of the literati were stuck on the bottom of an intellectually
stagnant pond, the soy-sauce vat of Chinese culture. As the contents of
this vat began to putrefy, the resultant stench was absorbed by the
Chinese people. Since the numerous problems in this bottomless vat
could not be solved by individuals exercising their own intelligence,
the literati had to make do with following others' ways of thinking.
If one were to place a fresh peach in a soy-sauce vat full of putrescent
brine, it would eventually turn into a dry turd. China has its own
particular way of transforming foreign things and ideas which enter
within its borders. You say you've got democracy; well we have democracy, too. But the Chinese form of *democracy* is: You're the *demos*
(people), but I've got the *kratos* (power). You've got a legal system;
we've got one too. You've got freedom; so have we. Whatever you have,
we have too. You've got pedestrian crossings painted on the street;
we have too, but ours are there to make it easier for cars to run pedes-

trians over.

The only way to improve the situation of the Ugly Chinaman is for each of us to cultivate our own personal taste and judgement. If we're poor actors, we can at least enjoy going to plays. Those who don't understand what's happening on stage can enjoy the music, lights, costumes and scenery, while those who do understand can appreciate drama as an art form. The ability to make such distinctions is a great achievement in itself . . . . I have my freedom and rights, whether the government gives them to me or not. If we had the capacity to make proper judgements, we would demand elections and be rigorous in our selection of candidates. But without this capacity, we'll never be able to distinguish a beautiful woman from a pock-marked hag.

from The Ugly Chinaman

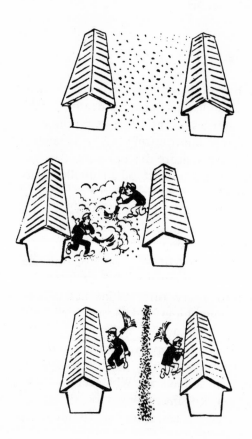

Wu Zengsong

One Ugly Chinaman

Wang Yiling

I am a Chinese and I readily acknowledge that I have numerous faults and imperfections, but I certainly am not an "Ugly Chinaman", nor can I countenance an accusation that decries all Chinese as "ugly". I am not sure whether Bo Yang still thinks of himself as Chinese or not, but if so then he is quite free to say he is ugly. But that doesn't give him the right to lump everyone else in with him.

I am in total disagreement with the basic tenor and argument of "The Ugly Chinaman", although this is not to say there is no merit in the speech whatsoever. A few of the things Bo Yang says are correct, for example his statement that "the Chinese are indeed one of the most intelligent nationalities in the world . . . . "

This speech raises one important question: what is actually so ugly about the Chinese? Bo Yang certainly doesn't avoid this issue, he rambles on at great length and cites many examples in his attempt to prove that the Chinese are "filthy, disorderly, noisy and quarrelsome". I am sure that Bo Yang isn't the kind of person to like slandering others, but even if what he says is true, just what does it prove? What race or country on earth is completely noise-free or unmarred by disputes? Aren't American hippies dirty? Isn't the New York subway system chaotic? Are politics in the US, Europe and Japan free from vociferous debates and shameful infighting? Is there, in fact, anywhere in the world where people don't fight with each other? According to Bo Yang's logic, we should be speaking of Ugly Humanity, not just the Ugly Chinaman.

<p style="text-align:center">*   *   **

Why should an outstanding writer . . . who has consistently claimed that he loves his people and his country use scraps of unconnected and specious "evidence" to slander his compatriots? The truth of the matter is that Bo Yang has a distorted view of traditional Chinese culture, and that his faulty perceptions have led him astray. Perhaps he himself has fallen into the very "soy-sauce vat" that he so delights in vilifying? Its poisonous virus has obviously befuddled his thinking and paralysed his nerves.

The world of Chinese culture is vast and profound. Within it one may find numerous examples of benevolent government and tyranny, humanity,

Good advice is
too unpleasant to
listen to.

Hua Junwu

justice and virtue. There are thieves and whores, honesty and probity, as well as the "wind, flowers, snow and moon" of the effete literati. All of these things have been refined to perfection; it is a world that has something for everyone. There are cesspits and germs aplenty in Chinese culture, besides the "soy-sauce vats" and viruses. When a person uses the filth he dredges up to attempt to prove that the whole of Chinese culture is a pestilent cesspit he unwittingly reveals himself to be a smelly turd beyond redemption, while in no way detracting from the glories of China.

. . . It depends entirely on what you are looking for in the corpus of Chinese culture. Our culture can be used to cure and heal, or it can be used to kill; it can even become an instrument of suicide. It is easy for anyone bent on talking of extremes to find the world of traditional Chinese culture bursting at the seams with "soy-sauce vats" and viruses . . . .

Bo Yang never tires of talking about his nine years and x number of days in prison. He acts as though it has given him some sort of special dispensation to carry on as he does . . . .

To sum up what I've been saying: the Chinese are not necessarily ugly; but there is no lack of contemptible wretches among them.

from *Pai-shing Semi-Monthly*, January 1985,
reprinted in the book *The Ugly Chinaman*

The Absurdities of Master Hah

Hah Gong

Hah Gong is one of Hong Kong's leading satirists. His name, which can variously be rendered as Master Hah, Uncle Hah or the Duke of Laughter—Hah in Chinese is both a surname and the sound of laughter—is a household word among Chinese readers in Hong Kong, although his writings are little known among the local non-Chinese population. But he is not unknown in China. In a report on his first interrogation in Peking after being arrested on a train in Xinjiang in 1980 on alleged spying charges, the Hong Kong journalist Fang Dan stated that among many other questions, he was asked to tell what he knew about Hah Gong.

Hah Gong is the pen name of Xu Zibin, a native of Fujian who emigrated to Hong Kong in 1951, where for several years he supported himself as an artist, art dealer and carver of stone seals. He did not enter the world of journalism until 1976 when he joined the staff of the influential newspaper Ming Pao.

In 1979, his popular column entitled "The Absurdities of Master Hah" began to appear in the newspaper, and although Hah Gong's voice has been silenced on several occasions for various reasons, his column seems to have achieved the status of a local institution, a rare distinction for a writer working in the shadow of the 1997 takeover by China.

Xu Zibin is a gad-fly among Hong Kong China-watchers. His mordant humour is clearly of the blunderbuss school, with only the occasional subtle joust. As one might expect, Xu is a sworn enemy of stultified bureaucracies, Party hacks, special privileges and the other familiar facets of the darker side of contemporary China. It is no surprise then that humourless Chinese cadres and apparatchiki, whether they be in Hong Kong or China, find "The Absurdities of Master Hah" so hard to stomach.

Shoot The Lawyers

THE NEWS that a Chinese court had sentenced a lawyer to prison for "conspiring with the accused" was the source of great dismay among several influential/reactionary/bourgeois lawyers in Hong Kong.

Objectively speaking there is no reason to disagree with the court's decision. The laws of our honourable Motherland, after all, have absolutely nothing in common with those of the foreign devils (N.B., certain other barbarian customs, such as wearing lounge suits, and eating with knives and forks, do not fall within the range of this discussion). In matters judicial, we prefer the progressive Chinese approach, to "hand down a verdict before the trial". Actually, once the authorities have satisfied themselves that the "facts are clear and the evidence ironclad" and that a crime has "given rise to great popular indignation and has had a highly negative effect on society", then the accused can be sentenced to fifteen years in jail and deprived of his

Zunzi

political rights for a further three years, just like that. Wasn't this the fate of Wang Xizhe, Wei Jingsheng, and all the others? They did not fall foul of the Gang of Four, they were not sentenced as a result of the policies of Chairman Mao's dotage: they were victims of the brilliant and correct policies of the Four Modernizations. Did anyone speak out in protest? Not only were there no dissenting voices, the verdicts were accepted without a peep. If a bourgeois lawyer or Queen's Counsel were bold enough to stand up and defend such thoroughly counter-revolutionary and unpardonably wicked criminals as Wang Xizhe and Wei Jingsheng, he would surely be found guilty of "conspiring with the accused", and quite justifiably be sent to jail. I read recently that a lawyer in China was expelled from the courtroom for "aiding and abetting the accused's attempts to avoid incrimination". This time, the incident incurred the censure of both the influential/bourgeois/ reactionary lawyers in Hong Kong and a number of local essay-writing literati, all of whom are hopelessly ignorant of our honourable Mother-land's unique system of "universal law".

Have you ever heard anything more ridiculous? Who needs lawyers anyway? Lawyers are mere lackeys working to protect the interests of the ruling class. We don't even need law. Our exalted Motherland has thrived for five thousand years without a single lawyer ever setting foot in a courtroom. Take for example the story "Judge Bao Cuts Chen Shimei in Two at the Waist". Did Chen Shimei hire a lawyer to defend him in court? All Judge Bao had to do was bring down the gavel, take out his tiger-head scimitar, and Chen Shimei's head rolled off to a new address. Naturally our influential/bourgeois/reactionary lawyers will claim that the good Judge Bao didn't understand the real principles of jurisprudence, and that this is merely a moral tale and not a legal pre-cedent. They will ask what right Judge Bao had to chop Chen Shimei in half so arbitrarily? Do you see how wonderfully subtle our tradition-al system of law is? Even "illicit sexual relations" can get you thrown in the clink for fifteen years. In order to protect the rule of law in our honourable nation, lawyers should not just be sent to jail and expelled from the courtroom; I suggest that all lawyers and indeed anyone possessed of a basic understanding of bourgeois law should be executed forthwith. This having been done, in the future all a judge need do is tap his gavel once and say, "Bring in the accused and give him sixty strokes of the bamboo rod." Beat the shit out of them, and they'll deliver their confessions on a golden platter. Other possible methods that can be used to induce confessions are the chaining of the accused to a pole or the application of heated steel rods .... With time-honoured methods like these, who needs lawyers?

November, 1985

The Ideology of Poverty

TAOIST MONKS and even the Taoist patriarch Lü Dongbin would often refer to themselves as "poor wayfarers".

The Way generally refers to religious faith, while poverty of course has more to do with a person's actual living conditions. Throughout Chinese history, ascetic monks have indeed willingly "accepted poverty" in order to "find joy in the Way".

Things are pretty much that way for devout socialists. In the Soviet Union, for instance, they've been "believing in" socialism for six decades, but they still have to queue up to buy eggs, and wait three years for a pair of glasses.

Needless to say, Chairman Mao was also a man who "accepted poverty" to "find joy in the Way". When thirty million people had died in the wake of the Great Leap Forward, the old boy swore off pork for three years. Mao was no Moslem, so three years of pork deprivation must have been a great trial for him. Later the old boy cooked up the slogan, "Poverty is glorious", and totally discarded all the Great-Leap-Forward balderdash about "Doing in one day what had taken the West 20 years", and "Overtaking Britain and the U.S. in two decades". At that time all good Chinese socialists, like the Commander of the Canton Military Region, Huang Yongsheng—who was later denounced as a Lin Biaoist—tore a couple of holes in their new military uniforms and put patches on them, to demonstrate their sincere "acceptance of poverty" to "find joy in the Way".

I read an "absurdity" recently—not one of my own, by the way —entitled "Poverty Isn't Socialism". My reflex reaction was: If socialism *isn't* the ideology of poverty, what *is*?

We might cite a few statistics at this point. Japan was crippled by the Second World War; today the per capita output in Japan is

Zunzi

US$10,080. In colonial Hong Kong, the figure is US$5,340; in Taiwan, an island still in the hands of the "reactionary KMT", US$2,505; and in socialist China, US$310.

Look at these figures, and ask yourself: if socialism isn't the ideology of poverty, what is?

That "absurdity" had a promissory note attached to it: by the year 2000, China's per capita gross national product would exceed US$800. How much is that? Out with your calculators: if the US dollar is devalued on the international currency market by ten percent per annum, US$800 will be worth US$148.23 by the year 2000, representing a more than fifty-percent discount on US$310. So it looks like China is warming up for a Great Leap Backward . . . .

August, 1984

Bury Capitalism Alive

WE MUST bury capitalism alive.

That's right, just as Comrade Stalin taught us: in order to be proper communist fighters, we must have lofty ambitions and firm determination, and bury capitalism once and for all.

All right then, out with the shovels.

For a start, let's bury West Germany.

West Germany did you say?

That's right, we're going to bury four thousand tons of nuclear waste from West German nuclear power plants.

Don't forget to collect the fee first: six billion US dollars.

Is that all? Only a million and a half bucks a ton?

You don't think six billion is a lot of money? Listen, we've been studying Marxism, Leninism and Mao Zedong Thought for the past thirty-four years; we've been pasting slogans on the walls for the past thirty-four years; and we've been shouting political slogans for the past thirty-four years; but when did any of that shouting ever earn us six billion bucks?

Okay, forget it. Let's just collect the money and start digging the pit.

Oh! I never knew how beautiful the Gobi Desert could be. An endless panorama, stretching as far as the eye can see. China is such a beautiful country, don't you think?

Cut the bullshit and start digging.

The more I dig, the more I worry, what if . . . .

What if what?

What if this nuclear waste starts leaking out of the ground and pollutes the air? What will become of our beautiful country?

We don't give a damn about air pollution. What we're worried about is spiritual pollution.

But I've heard that if the air is polluted by radiation, millions of lives will be endangered.

Only the bourgeoisie are afraid of dying. What do we members of the proletariat have to fear? Listen, you're bound to die sooner or later.

Zunzi

Chairman Mao taught us: Death can be weightier than Mount Tai, or lighter than a feather. To be able to sacrifice your life for the revolution is a privilege.

I'm not afraid of dying myself. It's the lives of my billion compatriots I'm worried about.

Bullshit! If half the population of China kicks the bucket, that'll still leave five hundred million. If half of them die, that'll still leave two hundred and fifty million.

We've got such a huge population, we can afford to get rid of as many people as we like. But Senator Brook doesn't seem to think so.

Don't pay any attention to that counter-revolutionary humanitarian baloney. Just keep digging.

Maybe we should let our billion fellow countrymen know what we're doing before we start.

No, no, you don't understand. This is a state secret. Anything involving nuclear power is top secret in China. The people have no right to know anything about it.

February, 1984

Fish Scales

TODAY I NOTICED that my side-kick the Pink Panther was busy copying out a strange list called The Five Cautions, The Four Beauties and The Three Zeals.

I asked him what he thought he was doing, and he told me that although his memory is still reasonably sound, he often gets mixed up about some of the number-slogans they're so fond of in China. So he decided to put them all down in writing for future reference.

I gave this a bit of thought and realized it makes a lot of sense.

I remember writing about The Five Cautions, The Four Beauties and The Three Zeals in the past, and saying that they weren't much different from the sort of thing you frequently see on menus in Chinese restaurants: Whole Chicken Cooked Three Ways, or a Four-Dish Set Meal. But despite my above-average IQ, my memory does sometimes fail me, and when friends question me I sometimes stumble over certain phrases, such as First Poor and Second Ignorant, The Three Supports and Two Militaries, The Four Cardinal Principles, The Five Red Elements, and The Seven Black Elements.

Zunzi

Lately these number-slogans seem to have multiplied at an astounding rate. The co-existence of socialism and capitalism in China (i.e. post-1997) is to be called One Country, Two Systems. When local currency, Foreign Exchange Certificates, Hong Kong dollars (or US dollars), and a fourth currency called "Special Economic Zone currency" circulate in the same country, this will be called One Country, Four Systems of Currency. When the same seat on an airplane is sold at three different prices depending on whether the passengers are foreigners and Overseas Chinese, "compatriots" from Hong Kong and Macao, or citizens of China, this is called One Ticket, Three Prices. In hotels, restaurants and shops in Canton and Shenzhen, when you pay with Hong Kong dollars it's one price, and if you pay in local currency, you're charged forty percent more than what the price would be according to the official exchange rate; this is called One Item, Two Prices. Then the Customs rules state that "compatriots" from Hong Kong and Macao may bring two bottles of liquor and two cartons of cigarettes into China duty free; Overseas Chinese four bottles and three cartons; Taiwan "compatriots" six bottles and four cartons . . . . As you can plainly see, these birdbrained homegrown "new economic policies" come in a blinding variety of shapes and colours, and if you don't keep a careful copy of them like the Pink Panther, you'll never get 'em straight.

After copying the entire list of Cautions, Beauties and Zeals, the Pink Panther recited them once over to himself to make sure he hadn't left anything out. Next on his list was the slogan One Corpse, Two Prices, but before he could go on, I queried it. I knew of the Chinese idiom "One Corpse, Two Lives", which refers to the death of a pregnant woman by suicide, murder or in an accident. But I told him I'd never heard of the saying One Corpse, Two Prices. The Pink Panther just started laughing out loud and told me how hopelessly out-dated I was: One Corpse, Two Prices is a revolutionary development within the hallowed tradition of adulation of things foreign.

Following a recent tragic accident at Jiangmen near Canton in which a passenger ship sank in the middle of the river, an *ad hoc* Shipwreck Victims Loss Settlement Committee announced that they would pay RMB¥3,500 to the next of kin of each Chinese ticket-holder who died in the accident, and RMB¥7,000 to the families of each deceased ticket-holder from Hong Kong. Isn't this a perfect example of One Corpse, Two Prices? Upon consideration, this too seemed to make a lot of sense. Salted fish, a favourite condiment in Cantonese cuisine, can be prepared from fish of all sizes; but, let's not forget that those large silvery-white fish fetch a much higher price when salted than piddling little sprats. This in itself may have nothing to do with the adulation of things foreign. But, as in the case of One Corpse, Two Prices it is a peculiarly Chinese way of doing business—and as such should of course be encouraged and instituted far and wide.

April, 1985

Maosoleum

Yau Ma Tei

A dark and stormy night. Inside the Chairman's Maosoleum all is gloomy and chill. Two soldiers stand motionless like outsized dolls flanking the sides of the crystal sarcophagus, which contains the embalmed remains of the great leader and teacher.

A flash of lightning lights up the coffin for an instant, and an eerie blue haze seems to emanate from its sides. A deafening clap of thunder starts the place shaking and the eyes of the corpse pop open. A stiff hand creeps up the side of the bier and pushes open the lid. While the storm continues to rage outside, the Chairman sits bolt upright . . . .

The guards are taken completely by surprise and step back from the coffin in terror.

CHAIRMAN: "Zhang, where's my Little Zhang?"

"Present and accounted for!" *The* FIRST GUARD *snaps to attention with a shout.*

CHAIRMAN: "And who are *you* supposed to be?"

FIRST GUARD:"Permission to report, Chairman. I'm Zhang Weidong, protector of the east. Everyone calls me Little Zhang."

THE SECOND GUARD (*pale with fright nods in agreement*): "I'm Li Xiangyang, he who faces the sun."

CHAIRMAN: "I want Zhang Yufeng, my bedside amanuensis. Where's she got to then? And what about my wife Chairwoman Jiang?" (*feeling in his pocket*) "Bring me my cigarettes."

SECOND GUARD *fumbles in his pocket, takes out a packet of Flying Horse cigarettes and presents them to the corpse with a trembling hand. He lights the cigarette for the* CHAIRMAN.

"Hmph!" *The* CHAIRMAN *takes a deep drag on the cigarette.* "I repeat, where's Chairwoman Jiang? You know, Comrade Jiang Qing. Now I left implicit instructions for the others to help Comrade Jiang

Ma Long

Qing keep the red flag flying. So where is she? And Chunqiao,
Wenyuan and Little Wang . . . ?"
"Mr Chairman, Sir, well, you see, it's like this . . . . " *The* FIRST GUARD
splutters lamely. "They're all, um, they spend all their time in Qin
Cheng . . . . "*
"Oh, do they indeed?" *says the* CHAIRMAN, *wide-eyed.* "I get the
picture. All right then, what about my hand-picked successor Hua
Guofeng?"
FIRST GUARD: "Who? Hua what? Oh, you mean Chairman Hua. I've

*Or Qin Cheng No. 1, China's top political prison. See below, pp. 279-289.

heard he's taking classes over at the Party cadre school." (*laughs nervously*)

CHAIRMAN: "What about my bodyguard Wang Dongxing? I suppose you're both from my personal guard, Unit 8341?"

"Wang, Wang who? . . . never heard of any Wang," *the* SECOND GUARD *stammers.* "We're from Unit 1438. You know, the new one, 1438."

"Heh, heh, heh," *the* CORPSE *chuckles to itself.* "So that's how it is. And I suppose the man in power now is that little what's-his-name, Deng . . . . "

"Yes, yes, Deng Xiaoping." *The* GUARDS *snap to attention as they chime the name in chorus.*

"Bloody fucking hell! What's the world coming to?" *the* CORPSE *spits out a cloud of smoke indignantly.* "He said he'd never go back on his word. I should have known he couldn't be trusted." *Gazing outside he sees his portrait hanging on the Gate of Heavenly Peace.* "But that's me. My picture's still up there."

FIRST GUARD: "Certainly; but, you see, it's the last one in China."

"What did you say?" *Unconvinced, the* CORPSE *points down Chang'an Avenue.* "What about those red neon lights? Don't they spell out 'Long Live Chairman Mao'?"

"I'm sorry, Chairman," *offers the* SECOND GUARD. "That's an advertisement for Seiko watches."

A song can be heard in the distance:

"Flowers may bloom but they must fade one day;
Times of happiness must to grief give way . . . . "

CHAIRMAN: "What's that they're singing. It's a very odd tune, doesn't sound like *The East is Red* to me. Come to think of it, it doesn't sound like the model Peking opera *The Red Lantern* either. Is it from some new revolutionary opera?"

FIRST GUARD: "If it please your Chairmanship, it's the Taiwan pop star Teresa Teng singing 'When Will You Return'."

"What type of rubbish is that?" *The* CORPSE *cries in a fury.* (*quoting emotionally from his own poems*) " 'Long have I harboured a wish to return to Mt. Jinggang,' ah, to make revolution once more. 'How can this be; I want to soar through the sky . . . . ' 'Enough of your silly farting, behold the world is in foment . . . . ' "

With this he angrily throws the butt of his cigarette away and struggles to his feet, standing unsteadily in his crystalline display case. Just as he is about to step out of the coffin the booming sound of a gong is heard. A hatch in the ceiling swings open and a large hammer drops out scoring a direct hit on the Chairman's shiny pate. The corpse keels over backwards into the coffin.

The following day a large notice is hung up outside the Mao-soleum. It simply reads: "Closed for repairs."

from Playhouse

Yau Ma Tei is the pen-name of Xiao Tong, a satirist and Chinese opera aficionado born in Peking in 1929. Xiao moved to Taiwan in 1949 and then to Hong Kong in 1961, where he works as a newspaper columnist. Playhouse *was a regular feature Xiao Tong wrote for the independent Hong Kong current affairs magazine* Pai-shing Semi-Monthly *until 1984. Yau Ma Tei is the name of the Kowloon residential district in which Xiao lives.*

The Bestiary of Huang Yongyu

Huang Yongyu is a major contemporary artist, sometime poet, essayist and humorist. Born in Hunan in the mid-1920s, Huang is generally known only as a painter, but as a raconteur and occasional satirist he is undoubtedly unique among China's older established writers.

The Bestiary is a series of comic aphorisms first written in the 1960s and subsequently listed as one of Huang's major "crimes" in the Cultural Revolution. A number of them were reprinted in Today, *the principle literary journal of the Democracy Movement.*

The Bee
Without my "gun", I'm a goner.

The Clam
Softies like me need a hard shell.

The Dog
Now I don't have a master,
I'll wag my tail at any old stranger.

The Silverfish

*What, me — no theory? You should just see
all the books I've gone through.*

The Flounder

*To keep things simple,
I grew both eyes on one side of my head.*

Lice
So long as we're onto someone,
who cares where we're going?

The Spider
In my superstructure you'll find
the remains of many a careless trespasser.

Bedbugs
Go on, kill me. But it's your blood.

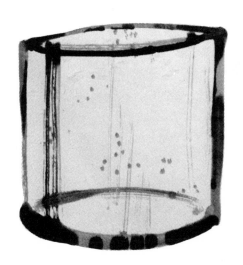

Germs
The fear of what you can't see,
now that's real fear.

VI: CLOUDS
But No Rain

The novel *Golden Lotus* was written as a warning against sexual indulgence. Only people with dirty minds will consider it obscene.

Jiang Ruizao, 1915

This is the real poison, your feudal distrust of other human beings. It's people like you [the editors] who really have filthy minds.

Yu Luojin, 1984

Wedding Night

Yu Luojin

"Let's get to bed!" It was barely nine o'clock when Zhiguo hurried me in this way.

There was something shifty about the slightly coy and bashful expression in his eyes—it made me uneasy. What was the hidden meaning behind that look?

Right up to this day, we hadn't exchanged a single word about love; we hadn't even held hands! It was a perfect case of "marry first, love later"—typically Chinese! I myself was Chinese, and had nothing against Chinese custom. But that wasn't to say that I was happy about it either. I didn't love him at all.

Tonight, I would have my first lesson in marriage—what was to be the content of this lesson? What form would it take? What would it feel like? My mind was a complete blank on the subject. I'd never read medical books; my parents had never talked to me about it; my schools had never taught me anything about it; my friends were all like me, we'd never discussed the topic.

It wasn't until I went to the labour camp that I got any inkling of what it was all about, from the foul language the louts hurled at each

Yu Luojin's outspoken novel A Chinese Winter's Tale, *telling the story of the persecution and death of her brother Yu Luoke, and of her own unhappy marriage, first appeared in the journal* Contemporary Literature *in 1980, in a heavily expurgated version. All passages containing explicit sexual references were removed, as were several sections considered politically offensive. Other arbitrary editorial changes were made on literary grounds. This extract is translated from Ms. Yu's complete original text, and all the expurgated passages have been restored and printed in italics. In December 1985, the People's Literature Publishing House in Peking published the novel in book form, restoring some but not all of the excisions. At approximately the same time, Ms. Yu, who was on a visit to West Germany, sought political asylum, and was granted permission to stay in the West.*

other when they were fighting amongst themselves, hollering loud enough for the whole compound to hear. It was unfortunate that I'd received my first "sex education" from their dirty mouths! But our "reactionary" group didn't live with them or work with them; and the people in our group never talked about it. So it was no wonder I was still a complete ignoramus in this respect at the age of twenty-four.

And here I was, suddenly married. I was making the bed, when all of a sudden the foul talk from the camp came flashing into my head— was it really like that? But I quickly put a stop to this unpleasant train of thought—*surely a decent person couldn't act like that? Zhiguo certainly wasn't a lout.*

"Put the quilts together," Zhiguo ordered when I'd just finished making the bed—again, that strange look in his eye.

I rearranged the bedding compliantly, feeling more and more uneasy. Zhiguo was washing his feet in the outer room. I took off my jacket and lay down without waiting for him.

This was the experience every young girl had to go through. Was it really my turn today? My heart was beating wildly.

Was there any joy?

. . . no.

Was I shy?

. . . no.

Happy?

No.

Content?

No.

Afraid?

Yes.

Worried?

Yes.

Was I in pain? Did I have any illusions? . . . I turned my face to one side, not wanting to see *the lust in* Zhiguo's eyes as he came in— it was so coarse! I closed my eyes, and quietly, lost myself in my own fantasy . . . .

. . . We were sitting under the warm quilts in our pyjamas with our jackets draped over our shoulders, in a tender embrace. . . . I was expecting nothing, there were no thoughts in my head. I felt only happiness and contentment; I was as happy as an innocent child. All

*my past suffering was going to be tenderly soothed away in this one
night* .... All my suffering .... I had lost my job,—my four years
training as a toy-maker had been wasted—I'd been labelled a "reactionary"—I'd been put behind bars—the spark of my first love had
been quenched before it could break into flame—my family had been
deprived of its happiness—my beloved brother had been shot—and
on top of all of this I had been compelled to abandon all sense of shame
and sell myself in the Great Northern Wilderness—oh, after all this,
after all this suffering, didn't I deserve some tenderness from my
husband—from the man who'd "bought" me? Even though our union
might look like some sort of deal, I wasn't a maid, a servant, or a
whore! My marriage had been a humiliation, but still I cherished the
hope that my humiliation would be dispelled by his tenderness, and
that I would find some reason, however small, to love him.

    ... I imagined us lying under the quilt, holding hands in friendship
—it was the first time we'd ever touched each other. He took me gently
in his arms, stroked my hair and my face and gazed at me fondly,
treating me like a poor little child. It was right that he should comfort
me like this, because he had suffered much less than I had. And I felt
a deep contentment and a sweet happiness in this wordless expression
of love. All the unhappiness and pain in my heart was melting away
into nothing .... The pleasant sound of his breathing was cleansing
me of all my humiliation and pain .... I was falling asleep in this
tender embrace, dreaming sweet dreams the whole night through. And
then the next day, the day after, and many more days would pass by,
and this person who'd "bought" me treated me so tenderly that I came
to love him more and more with each passing day, until the time came
when I felt I must prove my love for him. And then, I said to him, "I
want to have your child"—and after that, we would be truly married
.... How beautiful that would be! We just needed a bit of time, to fall
in love! ...

    ... I imagined my gratitude and respect for him growing ever
stronger with all the tenderness and love he gave me; no matter how
many faults I might find in him, I would excuse them all, if only for
the memory of these first nights ....

    Suddenly, a large foot landed on the quilt beside me, and I opened
my eyes, leaving my fantasies behind. It was a size 46 foot, enormously
large! I looked up at him timidly, and there he was—a six foot giant

standing on the kang *undressing himself. He was bending slightly to loosen his belt. The lustful glint in the corner of his eye when he glanced at me was* a million miles from the gallant knight of my dreams!

He sat down to take off his trousers, and proceeded to strip himself stark-naked, looking at me all the while.

What an ugly sight it was! I involuntarily closed my eyes, drew myself in, and clutched at my padded quilt, my heart cold as a sheet of iron.

I could feel his large hand lightly lifting up the quilt before he slid under it. *His ice-cold feet and his hard, bony legs hurt me.* My beautiful dreams were gone like fire-crackers, exploding into nothingness.

He began thrashing around with his arms and legs, roughly and clumsily stripping off my pyjamas and underwear and throwing them hurriedly aside; I just lay there like a terrified puppet, like a fish about to be killed, offering no resistance. Why did my life have to be so full of pain?

Before I could gather my wits about me, the whole weight of his body was pressing down on top of me; two large rough hands were

Yu Luojin (right) and her first husband Zhiguo.

gripping my head. I closed my eyes. Oh God, his sticky tongue was frantically trying to push its way into my mouth! Oh God! . . . I struggled with all my might to turn my face away, but I couldn't escape his "passion" however hard I tried. I felt a sudden pain in my crutch, as if I'd just been brutally attacked . . . . This indescribable agony only lasted about a minute, when suddenly he loosened his grip and collapsed onto the pillow, panting convulsively. I tried to get myself free of him and then sat up, my whole body a mass of pain. I leaned forward and spat on the ground over and over again—my mouth felt

---

Whose Dirty Minds?

If you insist on removing this passage, I would rather you didn't publish the book at all. You have all read it with great glee, and you have not been poisoned; so why are you so worried about it "polluting" its readers? You insist on tampering with my text, you blur the original meaning and make the whole thing ambiguous, and all you do is force the reader to go off into flights of fancy of his own. This is the real poison, your feudal distrust of other human beings! It's people like you who really have filthy minds. Authors should be left to bear the responsibility for their work. If there are readers who think they have been poisoned by the book, and if they wish to rebuke me for it, then let them by all means go ahead and do so. We can have a public debate. We can discuss the best way of writing a work of this kind. They can come out into the open and say exactly how they have been poisoned. And at the same time we should give the ones who have not been poisoned a chance to speak out too.

It is a tragedy, the way an author's rights are trampled on! If you have no respect for the author, how can you possibly talk of respecting the reader?

Please do not remove a single word from this passage. I am quite prepared to take the entire responsibility for it. The editors of Contemporary Literature *removed this entire passage and I was very angry about it. If they can read it without being "poisoned", what possible justification can they have for saying that the average reader cannot do the same? Handbooks like* The Facts of Life *describe such things in far greater "detail" than I do, and they are used as textbooks in school. So, what I want to know is, where exactly is this "poison" you all keep talking about?*

from Yu Luojin's manuscript note to the
publisher of *A Chinese Winter's Tale*

unspeakably dirty! I was about to put on my clothes and go and rinse out my mouth and wash myself, when I suddenly saw a patch of wet blood on the bed—I was horrified!

"What's that?" I gasped in alarm.

Zhiguo raised his head. When his weary eyes alighted on the blood, he burst out triumphantly:

"Do you really not know?" Suddenly he became all excited again, he clutched me in his arms and pressed me down on the kang, murmuring in my ear:

" '*The Golden needle pierces the flower of the peach.*

The Silent maiden frowns to stifle her screech.'—or so the saying goes! Ha, ha, ha!"

Even as he laughed, his wet tongue was coming at me again. God! I pushed him off with all the strength I could muster, and got down from the bed.

"You . . . !" I kept spitting on the floor, my face going white and then red with rage. "What are you saying! You filthy brute!"

I washed myself thoroughly with hot water, and found some clean pyjamas to change into. Zhiguo stared at me in bewilderment all the while, with his mouth open. I didn't want to look at him at all. One more look at him and my eyes would be blinded by the filth.

But however much I might wash myself, I felt that I would never be clean again, as if countless poisons were eating into my body. I could never be clean again! What was inside my body was no longer completely my own; there was also something of him. And what did he represent for me? Love?—No! Shame and vulgarity, meanness and filth! I had hoped for love and tenderness that night, but instead I got a double sense of shame and humiliation! Pain and disgust, foul language, repulsive kisses, those were his gifts to me! Was marriage really like this? Would every night from now on be like this? I would rather die, I would never give in!—Just thinking of this, all the blood in my body seemed to be welling up inside—that cursed moment! *How I wished I could strangle him! I simply could not bear the thought of his continued existence!* In an instant, I opened the lid of the trunk and whipped out a pair of scissors which I'd recently bought for making clothes—the sharp blades flashed a ferocious blue in the silvery moonlight. Grasping the scissors in my right hand, I leapt onto the kang glaring fiercely at him, and spit out these words one at a time:

"Now listen here, Zhiguo. If you dare lay a finger on me ever again, I'll kill you!—even if it means paying for it with my own life. You'd better beware!"

His mouth opened wide with fear and astonishment, and he stared at me dumbfounded as I pulled my bedding away from his side and put it at the other end of the kang. It was a long while before he got his breath back and mumbled in a baffled and choked voice:

" . . . what have I done? . . . you're a strange one!"

I put the scissors under my pillow—from now on, they would never leave my side! I buried myself from head to foot under the quilt, *but was constantly aware of the big black hairy ape sleeping at the other end of the kang.* I didn't even want to hear the sound of his breathing. My mind was hopelessly confused, I couldn't think straight, I couldn't disentangle a single one of my thoughts. Sleep just would not come . . . .

It felt like a long time before I calmed down. The big ape seemed to be asleep. I slowly lifted the quilt and sat up. Soft moonlight filled the entire room. I looked at him with disgust; his mouth lay slightly open in his sleep, it still made me feel sick. Even sleeping, he still wore that stunned and puzzled expression. I quickly turned my face towards the window and looked out into space . . . .

Moon! Was this the happiness you had in store for me?

What did he know of love? Absolutely nothing! *This was all he'd wanted out of me when he'd hurried me to bed—as if this was all the love he had to give, as if he wanted me to know that this was how he would be loving me for ever after.* And in return, all I had for him was my pair of scissors—if I even chose to live after this. *That moment was the sum total of our union; it was also the beginning of our separation* . . . . I would never acknowledge him as my husband, and I would never consider myself to be his wife . . . .

A hundred years of bitterness and humiliation were contained in that cursed moment! How he had defiled the word "kiss"!

Ever since I first started nursery school at the tender age of three, the teachers were always telling us that the mouth was a breeding-place for infections and germs. I vividly remember when I was five, my father once kissing my cheek and leaving some drops of saliva on my face. I immediately ran to the inner room to wipe at it again and again with a wet towel, feeling very angry but at the same time afraid that my father would be hurt if he saw what I was doing . . . . So far as I knew, the mouth was for eating, for talking, and for singing. At the labour camp, I'd learned that it could also be used for swearing, for words you couldn't even find in *The World Dictionary*. I'd read in novels that the mouth could also be used for kissing, but I'd never imagined it would be like this!

There were quite a few kissing-scenes in films and novels. They neither offended me, nor excited me. I doubted the accuracy of the "burning hot lips" described in books—how could the body's heat be concentrated in the lips when someone was aroused? Had anyone ever measured them with a thermometer to prove that they were "burning hot"? This kind of cliché only reflected the personal taste of those particular authors. (Of course, it is my personal feelings on the subject that I'm writing about now; but I have no intention of imposing my views on others.)

Supposing we accept "burning" or "hot", I'd still not come across a single sequence in a film or a single passage in a novel which indicated the need to use the tongue when kissing! Where had Zhiguo got that from? Did some people go even further? Did something as sacred and as pure as love have to take place in a hotbed of germs? Was that the only thing that gave it excitement? Ugh! It took an oaf to love in this oafish fashion!

What was love in Zhiguo's case? For him, animal desire had taken the place of love, brutishness the place of tenderness, and coarseness the place of nobility. But the blame for all my bitterness could not really be laid at Zhiguo's door. I myself had chosen to come to the Great Northern Wilderness! I could only hate myself, be disgusted with myself. Who else could I blame?

Oh, moon! Surely our society ought to bear some of the responsibility for all this? We are like simpletons as far as sex is concerned! Even mentally we are unprepared—we are so naive about sex for people of our age! Surely we should have been taught something about it, as part of our general knowledge?

I remember my mother once telling me about these special colleges that were set up in Japan a long time ago, to teach young unmarried women a few basic facts about married life; and a girl wasn't allowed to marry without a certificate from one of these colleges— it wasn't a bad idea! But we learned nothing about sex, either from our

parents or from our schools. The very mention of the word was some-
thing shameful and immoral, almost a crime. All of us women are going
to experience that night, so why should any understanding of it be kept
hidden and secret from us? Why should a motley collection of men be
left to teach us instead, each in his own particular fashion?

Surely there is a more decent, a more pleasant way? Surely, in-
stead of feeling ashamed and cheapened by men, it should be possible
for us to recall happy memories of their tenderness and nobility when
we speak of that first night?

Since Liberation, there's been no "sex education" whatsoever—
worse than that, we've not even had enough of the most ordinary
education, enough food for our most basic spiritual needs as human
beings.

Those leftist fanatics, their heads full of one thought only—
never-ending struggle . . . . What have they given to the people?!

from A Chinese Winter's Tale

Whose Truth?

In dealing with the theme of marriage, the author acts as the hand-
maiden of the bourgeoisie. . . . We must also mention [Yu Luojin's]
unhealthy political tendencies and incorrect literary aesthetic as revealed
in her "speaking the truth". Other flawed aspects of the novel include the
way the author colours her observations and descriptions of her own past
with unhealthy political sentiments; and the very form in which she has
chosen to express herself—the so-called school of "telling it like it is". . . .

The author is a great admirer of literature which "tells it like it is".
She actually believes that all past literature is either entirely or partially
dishonest, and thus has chosen to write something in diametric opposition to
the fiction of the past. We support the belief that in their works authors
should be true to themselves in terms of both facts and feelings, and condemn
all writing which smacks of either dishonesty or deception. We also believe
that Yu Luojin's view of all past literature as either wholly or partially dis-
honest is gravely flawed, and that it only serves to demonstrate her perversity
and ignorance. Yu Luojin equates artistic truth with the realities of life, and
mistakenly believes that the courage to "tell it like it is" is in itself something
beautiful.

Cai Yungui, writing about Yu Luojin's other autobiographical novel
Spring Tale, *in Huacheng, 1982.3.*

Of Hogs and Whores

Li Ang

Li Ang is a Taiwan writer in her thirties. Her novel Butcher, *from which these extracts are taken, was awarded the prestigious* United Daily *fiction prize in 1983. It is included here both for its intrinsic interest, and because it demonstrates the difference between what was printable in the Mainland* (A Chinese Winter's Tale), *and on the other side of the Taiwan Straits. Interestingly, just as this anthology was going to press, the popular Shanghai quarterly* Shouhuo *reprinted* Butcher, *with some deletions.*

CHEN HEAVED a sigh of relief as he left the slaughterhouse. It was still early, only a few minutes past seven in the morning, but the sun was already blazing down. From force of habit, he started heading straight towards the red light district in Back Lanes; then as he was nearing the pond, he remembered that he had a new wife waiting for him at home. He was still wondering whether to go on anyway as he usually did and sleep with Jinhua in her snug cocoon of a bed, when suddenly he remembered the gratifying way his wife had screamed for him the night before, and turned with a glint in his eye onto the road that led back to the Village.

When he reached home, Linshi had evidently just got up. She was combing her hair, leaning against the bed, with her back to the door. Chen was struck by the darkness and lustre of her hair, which seemed somehow incongruous on such a skinny woman. He stole up on her from behind, fondled her hair for a moment, then seized a handful of it and yanked it viciously. She shrieked and fell flat on her back, and without further ado Chen clambered heavily onto the bed and lay on top of her. She stopped screaming when she saw who it was, but when he started pulling off her things, she realized what she was in for and began to struggle and scream again, which only aroused Chen all the more.

This time it did not take him very long. He relished her torment, he enjoyed having the woman howling helplessly under him and screwed up his puffy sunken little eyes in a nasty laugh.

When he came, there wasn't much there. But the instant of ejaculation rid him of the bloated feeling in his stomach, which had made his palms so clammy and shaky since the early morning. He felt an enormous sense of relief and exhaustion, and immediately fell asleep.

Linshi had an excruciating pain in her groin. She got up and felt around with her hand, and found blood all over it. The dirty brown bedstead had dark round patches of congealed blood on it, and amid the bloodstains she was shocked to see Chen's long shiny butcher's knife, which he must have dropped when he got onto the bed. Linshi crept to the other side of the bed, to be as far away from the knife as possible. She could still feel the blood trickling from her crutch, and did not pull up her pants for fear of staining them. This time she had a feeling she would die.

It was noon when she woke again. The sun was shining brightly into her eyes through the one small window, and against its light she could see a figure standing by the bed, holding out a large bowl of food. She reached instinctively for it, and recognized the figure as Chen.

The bowl only contained the leftovers from the wedding feast the night before, but there was fish and meat, and Linshi was ravenous and ate the heartiest meal of her life. When she finished she noticed Chen staring at her with rather a strange expression on his face. She looked down at herself and saw that she was almost naked. Her pants were down around her ankles. She had eaten the whole meal in this state. Terrified that Chen was going to assault her again, and shocked by her own nakedness, she quickly pulled up her pants and sat up on the bed. She didn't dare stand. Chen took one more look at her, then strode out, announcing that he would be back later.

(from Chapter Two)

CHEN CAME BACK later than usual that evening. There was a dark look on his face as he walked through the door, and he started drinking straightaway, yelling at Linshi for some food to go with the drink. Linshi answered fearfully that there was nothing left. She was afraid

of getting another beating, but Chen was already too drunk. "Fetch
me a pig's trotter then, and chop it up," he commanded her without
a second thought.

A huge wave of terror engulfed Linshi. "But they've been offered
as a sacrifice to the hanged ghosts!" she stammered.

"Ghosts—bullshit!" Chen waved his hand. "I'm not a spineless
fisherman. I don't believe in all that crap."

Linshi hesitated.

"Look how many hogs I've slaughtered! And nothing's happened
to me!" Chen boasted with a sneer. He was talking half to himself. "Let
the ghosts come and get me. Let them do their worst!"

Chen's bravado seemed to lend Linshi a little courage. She fetched
a pig's trotter as he had ordered her, and started cutting it up. The skin
was cooked, but the inside was still dripping with blood. It was dark
and thick, it reminded her of the blood in her dream, the blood that
would flow from the seven orifices of the body. Another wave of
ominous fear swept over her.

She boiled the pieces, then took them out one by one and put
them in a big bowl, her stomach heaving all the while. She looked away
and set the bowl on the table. She refused to touch any of the food
herself, but Chen started chewing noisily. He was puzzled that Linshi
had not even picked up her chopsticks. "You're a great one for sneaking a bit of meat," he taunted her. "You're not usually so picky, in
fact. How come you're holding back today? Don't you want any?"

Linshi would not answer, and still refused to eat. Chen tried
everything he could to persuade her to eat, but to no avail. Suddenly
he flared up and started pounding the table, setting the plates clatter-
ing. "Eat!" he threatened her, "or I'll beat you!"

Linshi picked up a piece in her chopsticks and put it into her
mouth. It didn't taste of much. She chewed it and felt a glutinous
substance fill her mouth. It didn't taste anything like as good as she
had imagined, in fact it was mostly skin and sinew and fat, and it was
tough and tasted like old fish skin. She swallowed her second mouthful
down in one gulp, without even chewing it.

Chen found the concentrated frown on her face while she was
eating highly amusing. He laughed hilariously and dumped more in her
bowl. She struggled on piece by piece. Luckily the end of the trotter
was mostly bone, and she was soon able to finish it.

Chen became more and more excited as he watched her. He stumbled drunkenly into the kitchen and took a big chunk from near the fleshy end of one of the trotters. He threw it at Linshi and barked: "Eat it, eat it—go on! See how generous I am! I'm letting my woman eat a whole trotter!"

Only the skin was cooked. The meat was still rare, dripping with blood at the centre. Linshi looked at the great bloody hunk of meat that Chen was putting in her hand and started vomiting. She brought up all the meat she had just swallowed, and went on retching until she had nothing more to throw up but bile.

The vomiting left her weak and out of breath. That night she tossed and turned in bed, haunted by strange fragmentary dreams. She would wake up in horror, only to find that she had already forgotten the content of the dream. She heard the faint crow of a rooster in the darkness outside, and fell into a deep sleep.

Not long afterwards she felt someone pulling down her pants. She was so tired, and had no desire to wake up. "I'm having my period," she mumbled. She was immediately thumped twice. She opened her eyes in shock, and heard Chen sneering: "Don't try fooling me with that again. I won't fall for it this time."

"But this time it's true," she argued feebly.

In the darkness Chen gave an unpleasant laugh. He soon had his way with her. This time he did not hit her, nor was he especially violent about it, but he kept on for a very long time. Linshi lay there on the bed, seized with the fear that this time he would surely kill her. He had never before assaulted her like this when she was having her period. She was in such pain she could only cry and groan. The pitch darkness outside the window began to lighten. When Chen got off her, in the first light of dawn he saw that his member was smeared with dark blood, and noticed the rusty brown clots of blood in the woman's crutch and on the bed.

(from Chapter Five)

DAWN WAS already breaking mistily in the sky when Chen finally showed up at the slaughterhouse. He didn't stop to change into his rubber boots, but walked straight up to the first stand, amidst the jaunts and jeers of his mates, and before anyone knew what was happening, four or five hundred catties of hog let out a long, desperate squeal, and the beast started convulsing.

The instant Chen withdrew his hand, the pig's head flopped to one side and a column of blood thick as a rice-bowl spurted into the air. It did not rise very high, seven or eight inches, but a massive amount of it came frothing out. A woman was standing ready with a receptacle, but some of the blood was still spilled and splashed onto the stand, as the howling pig put up its desperate last struggle. A minute or two later, when the blood had mostly drained away, and the squealing and struggling had died down, the assistants lifted the pig up and heaved it from the stand and down onto the ground. The beast still twitched and blood still continued to flow from the opening in its throat, staining the entire surrounding area scarlet.

This had always been Chen's big moment. When he retracted the knife and the blood came, he had a sense of climax, it was as if a warm stream from within his own body had been somehow transformed into thick white semen and was being ejaculated, pumping itself into the darkest and deepest recesses of a woman. The gushing blood was his orgasm.

But that morning Chen could not help associating the blood spewing from the pig with the brownish clots of blood on his marital bed. He was trembling with some obscure fury, some chilly sense of apprehension. Menstrual blood was widely believed to bring a man bad luck, and Chen was particularly sensitive about this superstition, since he himself dealt in blood as part of his profession. It had definitely been a bad omen . . . Chen cursed himself silently. Somehow he couldn't forgive himself for having been so careless, and kept muttering: "How could I be so fucking stupid!"

. . . They were in a hurry to get the carcasses ready, so Chen went to the small room to help chop off the heads. He was severing a big meaty one straight through the joint at the neck, when suddenly he turned to the little middle-aged man standing beside him: "Flatty, this head's yours, isn't it? Have you sold it already?" Flatty shook his head. "Then can I have it?" asked Chen. "O.K. Normal price." Flatty slapped Chen on the shoulder. "I should really be asking more today. It's Ghost Festival and all that. You can use the head for one of the three main offerings."

Chen tied a length of cord securely through the pig's mouth and left the slaughterhouse with the head swinging back and forth. The sun was already high in the cloudless midsummer sky, blazing down, burnishing the paddy-fields by the slaughterhouse, where the rice was already beginning to ripen. A light breeze stole across the open fields, soft and warm.

It was going to be another hot, humid day. As Chen walked down the small path, the bamboo leaves stirred in the breeze. He couldn't decide where to go, and stopped and leaned against a bamboo stem, thick as a rice-bowl. Where could he go at this hour of the day? Where else except home? And at home there was only Linshi and that long face of hers, that shifty look in her eyes, that panicky expression. The very thought of her made him sick. Then a better idea came sneaking back into his mind: Jinhua, and the bed she'd been keeping warm through the night.

Jinhua's place was in Back Lanes, about ten minutes away by a path that meandered through the paddy-fields. Back Lanes was nothing more than a street behind one of the main thoroughfares. It had ten or so houses on either side, mostly low wooden buildings, and one two-storied nineteenth-century structure, which rejoiced in the name of Pleasure Terrace . . . . The trips paid to the Terrace by men-of-letters and men-of-taste, and the high-class courtesans that they patronized, had once been the talk of the town. But to Chen, that kind of thing was totally without interest. Whatever glamour or glory may once have attached to the Terrace, it was nothing compared to the pleasure of having a good wench pinned beneath him with her legs spread open— a pleasure further enhanced of course if the wench in question could scream and howl with a satisfactory degree of abandon. In his opinion, the young things at Pleasure Terrace knew nothing.

Chen's haunt was Venus Court, and in particular he enjoyed the delights of Jinhua and her warm bed. His colleagues in the slaughtering trade used to tease him and say that he had found in her a true mother-figure, someone to suckle him. But years had passed, and he still kept coming back to Jinhua. In the end it became common knowledge among the women of Back Lanes that what Chen really loved about Jinhua was her lewd way of screaming.

. . . At Venus Court the old two-panelled wooden door was still shut . . . . Chen waited for a while. When there was no answer to his knocking, he began to grow impatient. He raised his hand and was about to pound again, when the door opened with a creak. He stepped forward. The bright summer sunlight could not penetrate the intense darkness of the interior. Chen dimly distinguished the outline of a woman's body with a shirt thrown over her shoulders. Then the woman opened the door fully with her hand, exposing to the light two huge breasts that dangled down to her navel. He knew immediately that it was Jinhua.

"It's me, Jinhua," he said hastily. He stepped into the house, reached at once for the huge breasts and began fondling them and squeezing them. The woman stood there casually, neither advancing nor retreating. When Chen finally let go, she led the way to her room.

She turned on the dim light. It was rather a small room, about six or seven feet wide, with a wooden bed and a bamboo chair. On the bed was a white cover with a red turnover: the cover was soiled, greyish, with several darker stains here and there. The woman stepped onto the bed, throwing off her shirt as she did so, lay down on her back and pulled the cover up over her belly. She spoke slowly and calmly: "It's nice to sleep with nothing on in the summer. But it's easy to catch cold."

Her voice was low and coarse. She spoke with a strong local accent, and many of her words ended in a rising intonation.

Chen hung the carefully tied pig's head securely to a nail on the wall. Then he threw off all his clothes, exposing his fat hairy body, and jumped onto the bed next to Jinhua, covering his lower limbs with a corner of the sheet.

When Chen was settled, the woman continued: "You haven't come here for a long time." She paused and then went on in a monotone: "Now that you've got a woman at home, you won't be coming any more."

Chen did not answer, but turned the woman onto her side to face him. He buried his face between her huge breasts and took a few deep breaths. He had roused her from sleep, and a nocturnal warmth and sweetness lingered on her body and in the bed. "I'm going to sleep now," he said, pillowing his head on her breasts. And indeed he fell asleep immediately.

The woman lay quietly on her side with her eyes open. She had a broad, flat face, large eyes, thick lips. At first glance she looked stupid, but there was a certain lazy sweetness about her, perhaps a natural product of her occupation. She had a strong body, the body of a labouring country woman, and her hands were big and rough. The onset of middle age and all her years of easy living had made her body flabby, but it still had the underlying firmness and strength of a peasant woman. She looked relaxed and her skin was still brown from the sun. Her whole body was like a paddy-field flooded with water after the autumn harvest.

She lay there with her eyes wide open. After a while, when she saw that Chen was sleeping heavily and would not wake up for a while, she too closed her eyes and listened to the quiet morning sounds that drifted in from Back Lanes. The early hawkers' cries could be heard in the distance. Inside the room it was stuffy and warm. She soon fell asleep and began to snore softly.

Some time later, she felt Chen moving at her breast. She was half asleep and thinking that he wanted her, turned over onto her back and instinctively spread her legs apart. But Chen did not make another move. Instead he said in a friendly tone: "Had a good sleep. Made up for a few bad nights." Jinhua did not open her eyes or speak, but remained in the same posture. "Don't you want it?" she asked, when she noticed that Chen was still making no move.

"I fucked my woman this morning and got her period all over me."

"You're so impatient," she chuckled. "Of course, it's not all your fault. Folks say your woman is quite something, the way she gets so excited each time and can't stop screaming. They can hear her a mile away!"

"She still can't scream the way you do." Chen leaned his face good-humouredly against hers.

"But with me it's just play-acting." Jinhua laughed heartily, showing her healthy white teeth. "You haven't come for such a long time, I'm out of practice. Perhaps I won't be able to do it for you any more."

"Silly woman," he said softly.

. . . They lay side by side . . . . Intermittent hawkers' cries could be heard: a high-pitched old man's voice indistinctly crying "Bean—curd —cream . . . . Almond—tea . . . ", pitchless and slow. As he passed by, the people next door began to talk. Chen and Jinhua heard a door being opened and things being moved around. Chen yawned, stretched and sat up. "I've got to go."

Jinhua hurried up too, and handed him his clothes from the bamboo chair. Chen put on his fluffy black trousers and his blue jacket. He left the jacket unbuttoned, with his pot belly protruding.

. . . The sun was rising higher and higher in the sky, and it was growing humid in the room. Jinhua did not even put on her shirt this time, but stood there naked without a trace of make-up on her face, her legs apart, her belly sticking out slightly, like a tired, gigantic country woman.

Chen went out. The bright sunshine on the stone paving hurt his eyes. He squinted and cursed. "Fuck!" He stumbled off with the pig's head dangling from its cord. He knew his way out of Back Lanes with his eyes closed.

At home, Linshi was lying on the bed, her skinny little body all curled up. She was dressed in grey, and looked like a heap of rags. The only touch of colour was provided by her bruised cheeks. She looked terrified, and in considerable pain. Lunch was set neatly on the table. Chen sat down to eat without paying her the slightest attention . . . .

(from Chapter Six)

from the novel Butcher *(Taipei, 1983)*

From the Horse's Mouth

Zhang Xianliang

Zhang Xianliang is a middle-aged writer who, like Liu Binyan and many others of his generation, was a political outcast for twenty years. He received national acclaim with his novel Mimosa, the story of an intellectual sent to a labour camp for his bad class background and for expressing anti-Party sentiments. Zhang has stated that this novel is the first instalment in a nine-part autobiographical epic, The Apocalypse of a Materialist—good news for any reader who enjoys turgid prose spiced with long and frequent quotations from Das Kapital and the works of famous world writers.

Halfman, the second volume in Zhang's epic, is also labour camp literature. The prurience with which he disguises his positive political theme made what is an otherwise unremarkable and poorly written novel an instant success. The author plays on the temporary impotence of the main character, Zhang Yonglin—the hero of Mimosa—which he attributes to political and psychological causes, and describes "sex scenes" in what for mainland Chinese audiences is a fairly explicit manner. The following excerpt is from one of the more memorable though less racy episodes of the novel: the dialogue between the impotent protagonist and a gelding. Halfman is important only because it shows that such overt reference to sexual matters in mainland China requires some political justification; and although 1985 may have been hailed as the year in which writers finally introduced sex themes in their works, the simple fact is that sex too has now been bludgeoned into the service of Party literature.

As indicated in the appended critique by Wei Junyi, the aging female director of the People's Literature Publishing House in Peking, the book was one of the major bestsellers of 1985. It became the object of heated debate and criticism late that year while Zhang Xianliang was travelling overseas. He returned to China claiming to have refused the offers of KMT agents to grant him asylum in Taiwan. He was subsequently lauded for his patriotic stance, and accorded a hero's welcome in Ningxia, his home base. The notoriety afforded him by the publication of Halfman did nothing to hinder his career as a government writer or his promotion to Vice-Chairman of the Chinese Writer's Association.

Zhang Yonglin is sent off to undergo labour reform for the second time during the Cultural Revolution. Having endured persecution and humiliation, he discovers after getting married that he is impotent. After a day in the fields, he cannot bring himself to go home and face his wife. He wanders in the wilds, dejected and desperate . . . .

"I know you don't really want to go back home." A grey horse tossed its head and looked me straight in the eye. "Take a look at yourself—here you are after only a month of married life and you're scared of sleeping with your wife. That's right now, isn't it? You're scared; scared of the night. As scared as I am of being harnessed to a cart."

"You can talk!" I was so shocked that I fell flat on my arse, wetting the seat of my pants on the soggy turf.

The horse snorted in derision.

"If you could only see yourself now. You seem to have forgotten that blaring loudspeaker that hangs just outside my stall, and all the big-character posters I've munched in my time. The ink wasn't that nourishing, but the paper was good vegetable fibre, and tasted a lot better than some of the rubbish we're given to eat. I've come to realize that I was born into an unprecedented age of verbalizing. You humans may indeed be going downhill in every other respect, but you're all quite expert at manipulating language. It was no big deal for me to acquire the power of speech. Just a process of natural osmosis."

"Oh," I stammered, absolutely dumbfounded. "It's just . . . so very odd."

"That's what's wrong with you people," he commented. "Try to be like me, and learn the virtues of cool and silent observation. That's the way to survive peacefully in this world."

"Then what made you decide to open your mouth just now?" I queried.

"I know you don't want to go home," he snorted, "and it so happens that I don't want to either. At times like these I too feel the need to get away from everyone. We need to think things over in peace and quiet. Philosophy encompasses everything in the world, and, after all, the laws of nature that govern men and horses are much the same."

"If you say so," I agreed hesitantly. He was right: deep down I really didn't want to go back. I felt like staying out in the wilds to work things out for myself.

"Perhaps I can be of some help," the horse offered in a clinical tone. "I may not have your 39 years of human experience, but in equestrian terms I'm an old nag, and as the saying goes, 'an old horse knows the way'. So maybe I can give you some advice."

"Since you're so perceptive, perhaps you'd like to give me your analysis of my situation."

He smacked his lips eagerly. "I feel for you. Let's face it, we're both victims of a similar fate: as you probably know human beings castrated me too."

"I see, but I *haven't* been castrated. My member is still hale and hearty; it's simply stopped doing its duty. But why?"

"Before they got to me, all it took was the neigh of a filly or a whiff of her hind parts and I'd be head over hooves and off running. Nothing could hold me back. My tool never failed me, and I can assure you it always threw me into fits of ecstasy. But when they were through with me I lost all sense of sexual stimulation and I became completely indifferent to everything . . . . "

"But I still feel the urge!" I cried. "When she first wanted to sleep with me I could get it up all right—the first, second and even a few other times . . . . It's only recently that I've lost interest. I get frightened by my own impotence."

The horse neighed a series of strange chilling laughs.

"You set far too much store by such things; doesn't it make you feel crude and vulgar? Sexual impotence must inevitably destabilize your whole personality. You're an educated man; you must be aware of the fact that every man is an integral part of a complex ecosphere, and that it is necessary to analyse every individual system within the context of the whole. If one part of the system goes haywire, it only stands to reason that all the other systems will also be thrown out of kilter. At least you can fall back on your political beliefs, your ideals and lofty aspirations, can't you?"

"But I'm pretty sure none of that has anything to do with my condition," I replied halfheartedly. "Sima Qian, the Grand Historian of the Han dynasty, was castrated by imperial command as a punishment, yet he went on to write his great masterpiece . . . . "

"Hah, hah . . . . " The horse let out a raucous laugh and then snorted loudly, "Quite the scholar, aren't you, my dear herdsman? You may be well read, but unfortunately in this case I'm afraid you're guilty of faulty logic . . . . The 'palace punishment' they dished out to the old boy was a horribly wicked form of physical torture, but more likely than not it spurred him on to complete his chronicles. I'd even go so far as to speculate that if it hadn't been for his castration he would have never written the book. The world may have lost a set of genitals, but it gained a masterpiece. It's an example of that Mao quote you hear so often on the radio about 'some good coming out of something bad'.

"And here you are as strong and healthy as one of my own kind. They dragged you out to the execution ground but you came away unharmed. Physically you're perfectly healthy, it's just your mind that's all screwed up. The shock you suffered has left its mark on you and affected your entire nervous system. Do you honestly think you can compare yourself to the Grand Historian?"

"You're right, I know." I lowered my head. "But please continue."

"This is the very thing we have in common," the horse said to me with a sympathetic gleam in its eye. "My castration has robbed me of the urge to have sex, and I have had no choice but to abandon even the luxury of fantasies. It's because I'm not like the normal run of animals that I have been able to liberate myself from animal dumbness. In a way my achievement is not unlike yours. No one can deny the fact that during your long years of forced labour in the fields you have been able to familiarize yourself with the quotations of Marx, Engels, Lenin, Stalin and Mao. But on the other hand, *you* haven't had anything cut off—excuse me if I'm not expressing myself properly—well, at least not like the Grand Historian. However, like me you suffer an impairment; though mine is physical and yours mental, the end result is the same: we are both doomed to lives of under-achievement. We are fated to be subject to the whims of others, to follow their lead, to be whipped into compliance and to be rode over roughshod.

"Hee, hee, we're quite a pair: a eunuch and a castrated horse!— Do forgive me, I often have considerable trouble keeping a rein on my sense of humour. Even in this respect we resemble each other. We both enjoy being ironical and indulging in caustic satire. We like to give ourselves over to harmless humour, irreverent rantings and wild exaggerations.

"I'll even go so far as to say that you intellectuals have allowed yourselves to be lobotomized, or rather that you have suffered the ill-effects of the linguistic acrobatics of the age. If only one out of ten Chinese males were a real man, this country wouldn't be in the mess it is. I don't know how you feel about it, but I'm bored stiff listening to that loudspeaker all day long. Do you really mean to tell me that with your highly developed linguistic prowess you humans can't come up with something better for your broadcasts?"

"So you mean, I'm done for," I finally said in a mortified tone.

"What do you mean done for?" the horse asked me sternly, raising its head. "You've had your go at life. You've worked, seen many things, eaten lots of meals, heard about all kinds of strange happenings: watched a head of government turn into a common criminal, and a petty hooligan become vice-chairman of a political party with tens of millions of members overnight, just to give a few examples. And after all that you drop dead. It's the same for everybody. And you've been relatively lucky; at least you've had the good fortune to live in an age of unprecedented absurdity. What more can you possibly ask for? Ah, perhaps you also had hopes of helping produce another generation?"

"No, I don't have any illusions on that subject. But as you just said yourself, if the country is endlessly staging farces, even if I did have offspring they would be condemned to re-enact the mean tragedy that has been my life. It would be better for them not to be born at all." I put my hands to my head. "What I am trying to say is that a person should strive to make some contribution to the world, do something creative for his fellow men . . . . "

"In heaven's name, get rid of the desire you have to create, whatever you do. Resign yourself to your place in the world. Be like me."

"According to what you say my wife's right. I'm useless, only half a man." I felt my cheeks, they were icy cold with tears.

"Ah . . . that's right." He let out a long, deep sigh . . . . Why do men castrate us? Because they want to deprive us of the power to create, so we'll be entirely at their beck and call. If we weren't castrated we would still have our own free will. As it is, we often outsmart you humans. If we were whole how would you be able to manipulate and exploit us? Why go on with all this rubbish about creativity?"

I was speechless. I felt maligned and my stomach churned uncomfortably.

The horse suddenly tossed his head back in horror. His nostrils flared and he took a few deep breaths.

"I smell a hint of carnal desire. It's not something coming from you, but it envelops you like an aura. How very odd. Beware, herdsman . . . . We should be going now. I don't want to see you suffer any further misfortunes. After all, you're one of the kinder ones . . . . "

adapted from Halfman

Tales of Halfman

The swift publication and widespread popularity of Halfman *is a landmark development in the recent history of serious literature in China. It is a phenomenon that shocks and disturbs me, making me fear for the future of our literature.*

In the normal course of events the immediate publication in book form of a novel that has just been serialized in a literary journal should be a cause for rejoicing. If only all books could enjoy such a happy fate! Unfortunately, they do not. Serious literature is facing a crisis: bookstores refuse to order our books, print runs have fallen off dramatically and vulgar popular literature has flooded the market. Despite this, Halfman *is a bestseller. Young readers have grabbed it from the shelves of bookstores without any prompting from the reviewers. It is sold out everywhere. It is a book that even seems to be able to hold its own against* kungfu *fiction, as well as the works of popular literature that are populated by bloody corpses and menacing ghosts. This is a surprising phenomenon, and one that I find deeply dissatisfying.*

We are duty bound 'to take a closer look at just why so many young people have bought this book. The talk one hears about town is that it is a novel all about "sex". Naturally, most people aren't so frank about the enticements of Zhang's novel, preferring to describe it instead as "a book all

HALLUCINATION, Xia Xiaowan

about that, *real interesting!" The fact that so many readers have been attracted to this work is by no means an indication that popular aesthetic
standards have improved overnight. We cannot simply assume that this
novel's popularity is an indication that the crisis facing serious literature is
easing; in fact, it seems to prove quite the opposite.*

*I am not saying that the writer's sole intention was to cater to vulgar
tastes. Nor would I go so far as to say that this is a pornographic or dirty
book. However, it is a novel that contains too many naturalistic descriptions
of the relations between men and women; especially in the latter half of the*

work when the author abandons his legitimate and serious theme of how normal human needs are suppressed in a labour camp to dwell on a detailed depiction of the mental anguish and domestic discord resulting from Zhang Yonglin's impotence. By being confronted with such things the reader loses sight of the original scope and import of the novel, or at least is forced to make them take a back seat .... The novel itself must take the lion's share of responsibility for the negative social repercussions that have resulted from its appearance. Readers shouldn't be the only ones held to blame.

As a female reader I must admit I find the author's naturalistic descriptions [of sex] quite unacceptable. I'm sure many young girls would feel the same. This has nothing to do with the fact that traditionally the majority of educated Chinese women are compulsive about cleanliness, generally regarding their own ideals, purity, personal independence and work as the most precious things in their lives. We find it offensive to be seen as nothing more than sex objects, living only for the opposite sex. Any argument that supports such a claim is downright insulting.

No writer can be expected to take sole responsibility for the social effects of his or her writing. Especially in China today literature is no longer something exchanged privately among friends, now it is the preserve of huge numbers of readers .... However, it is the duty of every author to carefully consider how their works can put beauty before vulgarity, depth before superficiality. At times writers must take great pains to make sure readers will not discover vulgar associations in their works ....

from *Literary Gazette*, December 28, 1985

The Deep Structure of Chinese Sexuality

Sun Longji

Suckled by Sodality*

THE CHINESE as a whole show a marked tendency towards oral fixation. In the Chinese language, population is expressed as "number of mouths" (renkou). The Chinese tend to relate to the world with their mouths.

Chinese adults still need to be suckled at the breast of Sodality. Within the network of Chinese Sodality, there is a great need for interdependence, and this relationship is usually cemented by the exchange of material things such as food. And, in typically infantile fashion, when a man's "somatized" needs are satisfied by another person, then he must surrender his Heart-and-Mind. Thus the individual comes to obey authority. In this way, the Chinese adult never totally outgrows childhood. Throughout Chinese history, the Chinese common man has been the little child of a paternal but dictatorial ruler.

Even when their darlings are well over thirty years old, Chinese parents, especially mothers, still feel obliged to stuff them like little children. When dining together, the older generation will force the younger to consume more food. This is the most direct way of expressing concern, through the mouth. Visitors are plied with candies and biscuits like children. Older people seem to think that younger people will stay at the oral stage forever.

Sexual Identity

THE OLDER GENERATION constantly treat the younger as babies, whose sexual organs are not yet developed. They never disclose anything about sex, with the result that the young remain ignorant and

*For a definition of this term, see p. 32.

bewildered. And yet the old tend to create a terrific fuss when the young make friends with the opposite sex. They usually think their children are too young for this. In the mainland, university authorities regularly intervene in love affairs between students. Even a woman over thirty will be cautioned when going out with a male friend.

The Chinese consider adultery "the sin of all sins"! To maintain social harmony they must "desexualize" the individual, that is, make him unaware of his own sexuality. This also helps to maintain harmony between the generations. If an individual is allowed to be an independent being, he will eventually break away from his elders. This is the basis of Freud's theory of the Oedipus Complex. Sexual maturation brings about the rebellion of the individual against authority. The father is the symbol of authority, and of course he will be the target for adolescent rebellion. At the same time, if an adult no longer allows his mother to feed him like a baby, but treats her as just another person of the opposite sex, then the mother is no longer indispensable.

Though the parent-child relationship seems so close in Chinese families, Chinese parents seldom disclose anything about their personal or sexual lives to their children. Sex itself is of course a taboo topic in every family, but parents also refrain from discussing any kind of personal experience or emotional problem, even with adult offspring. This attitude on the part of the parents undermines the childrens' sense of identity. They don't know how to express their feelings (or wonder whether they have the right to do so). Some are seriously affected by their parents' attitude, and become apathetic and dull as people. In fact, to lose contact with one's own sexuality is to run the risk of losing one's sense of identity altogether. In China, each generation is a generation without an identity.

Fathers, not Men

Generally speaking, the Chinese individual is not a dynamic and developing being, but forever an inert body requiring and receiving external care. Maturation is not a process of growth, but of ageing. Youth has been eclipsed in the Chinese developmental process.

The elimination of adolescence has of course a direct link with the desexualization of the Chinese people. If marriage is only a perpetuation of life and an investment against old age, then eroticism and passion are unnecessary in a relationship between the sexes. Often sexual intercourse is merely a means of procreation, rather than a source of personal enjoyment. In the mainland, when the government allocates jobs, marriage is never taken into account. Husband and wife may live miles away from each other and meet only once a year. In a political system like this, sexuality is of course repressed. The role of the family is replaced by that of the community.

Chinese tend to oralize their sexuality. It is assessed in terms of whether it injures or benefits the health. Sex, like food, strengthens the body, but too much of it, like too much food, is harmful, especially to the genitals. Such a concept inevitably leads to the suppression of sexual desire in men, and hinders them from full development as human beings with a normal sex life. If a man is not fully developed as a mature being, it will be impossible for him to produce other "men". Lu Xun once remarked: "(The Chinese) as a rule are tools for the production of children. They are not fathers of 'men'. Even if a Chinese has children, he himself is still not a 'man'."

RED AND BLUE, Wu Shaoxiang

Anal Fixations

ALTHOUGH THE CHINESE do not have a concept of personality development, nonetheless a Chinese does grow physically from childhood to adulthood. But many of the problems of childhood remain unsolved.

In the mainland, and to a lesser extent in Hong Kong and Taiwan, you still see people spitting, picking their noses, scratching, farting in public and throwing bones on the dining table or floor. They also dump litter and slops in public places. In their public lives, some of them are regularly late for appointments, break regulations, refuse to queue up, or simply fail to co-ordinate their bodily functions (bump into others or swing their feet). This is all evidence of poor training in childhood.

The anal stage follows the oral stage. It is concerned with toilet training. Generally speaking, the development of autonomous muscular control marks the beginning of the formation of a concept of individual identity. But the Chinese have formed a double habit at the anal stage of polluting the external environment with their waste and at the same time allowing others to impose their will on them. This is clearly a continuation of the egocentricism of the oral stage of development. At the stage when Western children are beginning to shape their identity, their counterparts in China are being trained *not* to develop their individuality. In short, from the very beginning, a Chinese is defined by a bilateral relationship with another person.

Sexual Unawareness

TO HAVE A WELL developed ego, a man has to proceed from the oral and anal stages towards the genital stage. In other words, he has to recognize his own sexuality. This is not to say that physically a Chinese never reaches sexual maturity. But in the Chinese conception of man, the genital stage has been deliberately eradicated and there is, therefore, a greatly distorted concept of sex.

Yet with most Chinese, sexual repression does not lead to hysteria as it did with their Western counterparts in the Victorian age. The real problem with the Chinese is not sexual repression but "desexualization"—unawareness of sexuality. The average Chinese is not "ignorant and innocent as a child", he is merely ignorant of how to channel his libido so as to attain self-actualization in spirit and body. Otherwise, as an adult being, he would not be able to tolerate the lack of sexuality.

Sex is Dirty

WHEN PEOPLE are fixed at the anal stage, they may try to moralize about sex, to debase it as something ugly and dirty. This may be a defence mechanism. They themselves may be secretly obsessed by sex. They are quick to point an accusing finger when they sense that a man and a woman are having an affair. They want to control others, to deprive others of sex, while they themselves may be secretly masturbating.

WAITING, Wu Shaoxiang

Sculpture should be symbolic, pregnant with meaning. Forms should be smooth and clear, yet allow for a broad range of interpretation. Henry Moore's sculptures exemplify these qualities. He uses the forms of reclining women to communicate highly personal perceptions .... The artist should avail himself of metaphor and subconscious associations to create works that will make people think.

Wu Shaoxiang

To regard sex as something dirty is to confuse the sexual organs with the excretory organs. An adult should not commit such an error. But an anally fixated person may. In this respect, the Cantonese are the most seriously fixated. In the Cantonese vulgar language, many words connected with the female sex organs have the connotation of rotten and smelly, and are used as coarse expletives. Even Mr. Wu Zhihui, a veteran KMT revolutionary, once declared: "Politics are like a woman's genitals. The dirtier they are, the more you want to touch them." If a man regards sex as dirty, then he will only go through the motions of intercourse in order to impregnate the woman. Any other aspect of sex will revolt him.

Concubines for Cadres

PEOPLE—MAINLY FEMALE— have told me that some high ranking cadres have as many "concubines" as the emperors once did, and yet they deprive the common people of their sexual rights; the whole social system—the interference on the part of the leaders, the lack of physical privacy, the lack of respect for privacy, the jealousy—it all seems to work to this end.

from Deep Structure

VII: MISTS

These misty poets poison the minds of their readers. Theirs is a lone, funereal voice, bewitching readers with its morose, despairing tone.

Zang Kejia, 1981

Actually, our poetry is not misty at all . . . . Some areas are in fact becoming gradually clearer.

Gu Cheng, 1983

Out of the Mists

One of the most exciting developments in Chinese literature during the past decade has been the emergence of a new generation of poets. They first published their work in the samizdat *magazine* Today, *launched during the brief period of the Democracy Movement (many of the magazine's editors and contributors were acquainted with political figures such as Liu Qing and Wei Jingsheng, and derived much of their impetus to create from the movement). Since the closure of the magazine in 1980, the writers have gone on to develop their own personal styles. They have also continued to draw the fire of the literary establishment, who first branded them as Misty (the veteran poet Ai Qing protested that their work was incomprehensible and did not serve the people), and later denounced them as "spiritually polluting". However, they continue to dominate the Chinese poetic scene, and to be in great demand by the reading public. As Mandelstam wrote in 1937:*

> *The people need poetry that will be their own secret*
> *to keep them awake forever*
> *and bathe them in the bright-haired wave*
> *of its breathing.**

*tr. Clarence Brown and W.S. Merwin, in Osip Mandelstam, *Selected Poems*, Harmondsworth: Penguin Books, 1977.

Misty Manifesto

Hong Huang

A new kind of poetry has been born.

It is flowing in the winds and waters of our land, in the blood and breath of a new generation. Some call it a revolution; others an invasion of the world of Chinese poetry by Western monsters. But its birth is an incontrovertible fact.

It has been given a variety of names: symbolist, surrealist, "misty", even impressionist. In fact, it is none of these. We should rather call it a new embodiment of our national spirit, the voice and pulse of the thinking generation, a reaction against the poetic disease of the past two decades.

A truly vital self, one endowed with human dignity, intellect and a complex inner life, has appeared in poetry; poetry is no longer hack literature, no longer the mouth-piece of politics; now we are standing face to face with our land, imbued with suffering and yet full of hope; we muse on this sorrowful but radiant dawn; now we need our own stance, our own voice.

The poets and critics refuse to take us seriously. That Rose on the tomb of Homer remains unconcerned and indifferent to the Nightingale singing fresh songs, would rather see youth wither in the parchment pages of the *Iliad*. But the Nightingale will continue to sing, to conjure an oasis of moisture and fragrance out of this wilderness ravaged by wind and sand.

Peking 1980

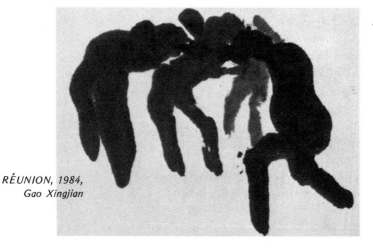

RÉUNION, 1984,
Gao Xingjian

Bei Dao

The Answer

Baseness is the password of the base,
Honour is the epitaph of the honourable.
Look how the gilded sky is covered
With the drifting, crooked shadows of the dead.

The Ice Age is over now,
Why is there still ice everywhere?
The Cape of Good Hope has been discovered,
Why do a thousand sails contest the Dead Sea?

I come into this world
Bringing only paper, rope, a shadow,
To proclaim before the judgment
The voices of the judged:

Let me tell you, world,
I—do—not—believe!
If a thousand challengers lie beneath your feet,
Count me as number one thousand and one.

I don't believe the sky is blue;
I don't believe in the sound of thunder;
I don't believe that dreams are false;
I don't believe that death has no revenge.

If the sea is destined to breach the dikes,
Let the brackish water pour into my heart;
If the land is destined to rise,
Let humanity choose anew a peak for our existence.

A new juncture and glimmering stars
Adorn the unobstructed sky,
They are five thousand year old pictographs,
The staring eyes of future generations.

All

All is fate
All is cloud
All is a beginning without an end
All is a search that dies at birth
All joy lacks smiles
All sorrow lacks tears
All language is repetition
All contact a first encounter
All love is in the heart
All past is in a dream
All hope carries annotations
All faith carries groans
All explosions have a moment of quiet
All deaths have a lingering echo

The Old Temple

The fading chimes
form cobwebs, spreading a series of annual rings
among the splintered columns
without a memory, a stone
spreads an echo through the misty valley
a stone, without memory
when a small path wound a way here
the dragons and strange birds flew off
carrying away the mute bells under the eaves
once a year weeds
grow, indifferently
not caring whether the master they submit to
is a monk's cloth shoe, or wind
the stele is chipped, the writing on its surface worn away
as if only in a general conflagration
could it be deciphered, yet perhaps
with a glance from the living
the tortoise might come back to life in the earth
and crawl over the threshold, bearing its heavy secret

Gu Cheng

Résumé

I am a child of sorrow
from cradle to grave undergrown
from the northern grasslands I
walked out, followed
a whitish road, walked into
the town stacked with cogs
walked into narrow lanes,
lean-tos—every trodden heart;
wrapped in indifferent smoke I
still tell my green tales
I believe my devotees
—the sky, and
the spuming drops of water on the sea
will shroud me completely
shroud that insituate
grave, I know that
at that time, all the grass and small flowers
will all crowd round, in
the glimmer of the dim lamplight
softly softly to kiss my sorrow

No one likes sorrow; we have all passed that way.
I drifted to a stretch of grasslands; raised pigs. I could not go to school
—no books, not even the clatter of people eating. The only thing
that comforted me was the silently rising cloud at the edge of the
grasslands.
Walking, I dreamed of someone I could talk with; the footprints on the
alkaline land were white.

I rambled into the city, and in a roar became a carpenter. My three masters, their ages combined, were 220 years old. They liked me; tenderly teaching me how to make latticed windows. They also liked to smoke (one had smoked opium), liked singing The East Is Red, *definitely did not believe the earth to be round (because water always stays in the water vat). Later, came a sister apprentice. Every day she added to her collection of boy friends, occasionally removed her false eye to show others.*

Who could I talk to? Tell that looking-glass forest's fairy tale.

One time, I cleaned the only window—a broken one, so, while working, I could see the tiny patch of blue sky. I asked myself, "Why this way?" "It can only be this way." "What for?" "For everything I love."

I answered. I wrote this "Résumé".

I will tell tomorrow, tell tomorrow's newborn flowers: in the past, in a small smokefilled room, there was a heart which had loved them.

NAISSANCE, Gao Xingjian

Gao Xingjian is more widely known as a playwright, author of the controversial plays Bus Stop *and* The Primitive. *These ink paintings were exhibited in Germany in 1985.*

Misty Mondo

We have paid an enormous price, and we have begun to understand that neither politics nor materialism can substitute for everything. If a nation wants progress, it needs more than electronic technology and scientific management; it needs a highly advanced spiritual civilization, and that includes the creation of a modern, a new aesthetic consciousness. Beauty will no longer be prisoner or slave, it will shine with as much light as the sun and the moon. It will rise high in the heavens to drive away the shadow of evil. Through the windows of art and poetry it will cast light on the hearts of both the waking and the sleeping.

Gu Cheng, 1983

PALACE LADIES, Ah Xian

MASTER AND DISCIPLE, Shen Qin

A host of young artists have invaded the art world. Their arrival is like a flash flood inundating a stagnant pond. Artists like Shen Qin have been educated in traditional Chinese painting, but they have broken away from it. This is the first giant step . . . . Fresh perspectives and new materials offer us the chance to start the revolution in Chinese art anew. The young artists who talk of remaining faithful to tradition while attempting to create a new art, are doing nothing more than following "The Middle Way" of the past . . . . Integrity, courage and reckless daring are the greatest virtues of the modern artist. As Lu Xun once said, those who keep to the Middle Way will, of course, never be cast into Hell; but Heaven will also be denied them.

—Li Xiaoshan, art critic

Xu Jingya
The New Poetry: Door of the Soul

Feeling is the soul of poetry. The single most important characteristic of these poems is that they vibrate with the spirit of their times.
The new poets stress the subjectivity and individuality of poetry, they
call on it to witness the whole variety of life's emotions. For the young
poets of the 1980s, poetry is a mirror with which to see oneself, it is
the history of the human soul. The poet creates his own world. This is
the new manifesto.

The result is not mere poetic imagining, but the poet's instantane-
ous response to reality. Once the door of the soul and the door of
nature have been opened, the world is no longer monotonous and drab;
the richness of the soul imbues it with a renewed splendour.

1982

PATH TO HEAVEN,
Zhang Qun

Editors' note:

Xu Jingya's long essay defending the New Poetry, from which these lines are taken, became one of the main targets for attack during the campaign against Spiritual Pollution. He was finally obliged to make an abject self-criticism in March 1984:

> *Recalling the writing of my essay, I feel that I came to make all these errors because during that period liberalism was rampant and I neglected the study of Marxist theory. And later I did not promptly grasp the essence of a whole series of Party instructions on literature and art. For a long time after the writing of the essay, I was not aware of the erroneous viewpoints contained in it. As a result, some of my uncorrected errors spread again in theoretical and poetic circles, doing harm to the cause of literature and art.*
>
> *From now on, I will consciously expend more effort on the study of Marxist theory of literature and art, will firmly take the socialist road, will go deep into life, close to the people—this is the resolution that has formed itself in my mind.*

Shortly after this, Xu moved to the Shenzhen Special Economic Zone, across the border from Hong Kong, where he works on the staff of the Shenzhen *Youth Daily*.

THE GRASSHOPPER
"The moment he's caught, he nods like mad."

Huang Yongyu

Jiang He

Begin from Here

Begin from here then,
Begin from my own story, begin from the human aspirations
Of millions, dead and alive;
Begin from the name that thrilled through me before my birth.
That the forgotten,
the injured,
the lone,
May stretch from their huddled, fearful numbness
stretch out for life.
Ice breaks, language begins to reconcile;
Each plain name is title for a poem,
flowing with the grand melody of life.
Begin from here then, blood
quickening,
fragrance of every flower, every child, every wisp of kitchen smoke
rising as one into the spring time, every brown tree swaying
branches and leaves
lifting ripened fruits, fuller than a mother's breasts.
White clouds hang big in the sky,
passion a cumulus within the heart, building,
every contact, every lightning, every kiss
frees me from loneliness, unites me
with all beating hearts.
Love cannot be withheld, the earth hungers and thirsts.
Begin from the rain then, begin from the teeming river
Begin from stone bridge, steel bridge
Arm stretched from earth to earth, from hill to hill,
leading every brother and sister
connecting every valley and riverbed.
Let the moon, sickled by night, image no more the father's
     crooked spine,
let the bent ears of grain be grasped taut as a bow in the sons' hands,
let the waves stirred by bird and fish, the wind,

be strong to blow sail, spread net,
highways grid the wilderness and hills,
cities like knots
pin the net, roads of sunlight quiver
in the ditches, in the streets, the flowing water, the crowds
forever blue.
Let me uncover the pattern latent within action,
honeycomb it, instil order in my dwelling-place;
let light etch the borders of shadow,
and shadow slowly drain into noonday;
my gloom, my silence, my suffering
fade into joy, as
I, homo aureus, the golden-skinned,
join all pigments of the planet
to make life glow with the colours of light.

Mang Ke

The Vineyard

A small vineyard
    was my sweet home.
The autumn wind burst in, rattled the gate,
    filled my garden with grapes of tears.
Over the walls that had long darkened the yard,
    a few pigeons flapped in panic.
Frightened children hid their grubby faces
    in a corner behind the house.
Dogs that used to slouch around
    vanished.
A clutch of red hens puffed up a dust-bath,
    clucking busily.
I watched the grapes fall to the ground,
    blood flowing amid the fallen leaves.
The peace we sought was denied us,
    and our daily sunlight.

Yang Lian

Birth

In my premature solitude
Who can tell me
The destination of this road singing into the night
To what shore its flickering ghostfires lead?
A secret horizon
Ripples, trawls distant dreams to the surface
Distant, almost boundless
Only the wind rousing a song
In place of the broken sundial buried in the earth
Points to my dawn

We must rediscover, explore and secure once again those things in our history that answer our own aspirations; we must pick out from the numerous and diverse sources the "inner core" that is still strong and vital; this is the vitality and strength that Yeats called mature wisdom. Wisdom is not intelligence, the essential difference between them being that intelligence moves from the simple to the shallow, while wisdom moves from the complex to the profound. Intelligence may dazzle for a while with innate flair and novelty; but the origins of wisdom lie in breadth of experience, and its fruit grows through painstaking pursuit to firmly structured conception. Without this inner substance, so-called feeling seems to me to be an illusion. It is only in the works of those comparatively few artists who have matured in this way and who possess this firm consciousness, that bright imagery is endowed with a precise and emotionally convincing meaning. This is the only real kind of "creation".

from "Tradition and Us", 1983

Homage to Poetry

Freedom will return, bringing its little shell,
And within it the deafening roar of the storm.
Daybreak will come, the key of dawn
Turn in the tangled trees, ripe fruits flame.
I will return, reopen the furrow of suffering,
Begin to plough this land deep in snow.

Torches

Many have sung the praises of the torch
Eulogized those days of light
Stars of hope

Today I come here
No language but my heart
No road but my heart
The head of the sierra sinks into night
The forest grows quiet and still
Like love slowly cooling
Bare rock, buckwheat rippling
My heart leaping, searching—on this festival night
To find a fellow glimmer of light upon this earth

Again and again I ask eyes sluggish with mountain-shadow,
At the windows of impoverished souls.
No lamplight—like a long-spent firepit,
Like a looted village,
Stripped bare, deserted; the wind,
Starving vagabond, leaning against the banging door.

I search for the torches: from eye to eye
A tortuous road, from soul to soul
A slow senilescence, as if this land

Had drawn off all my blood, dripping
To the feeble candle of men
Hollowed with toil, flickering.

Oh ancient people, it is your very lifeblood, frozen,
Silent in the dark abyss.

Aftermath of shattered dreams—the torch is out;
An infinite wasteland as far as the eye can see.

No dreams:
In a quest like this
I would gladly die.

from Norlang

Suntide

The plateau like a raging tiger
        burns at the shore of creation's torrent
Light! There is only light;
        the setting sun floods over you
        in a perfect sphere
        earth hangs in space

The cliffside trail has collapsed
        there is no path along the precipice
        the sundial in the cave is black
And the heavens of the ancient shaman once again reveal
        the riddle of the seven lotus flowers

—the sun waits
        in ecstasy
        for the meteoric
        apocalypse

My light
    illumines you
    even in your meteoric
    fall
A golden summons
    returns anguish to the sea
    the never-tranquil sea
Over the black night
    over oblivion
    over the twittering, faint cry of dreamtalk
Now
    in the centre of the universe
    I say: live on—
Heaven and earth have begun.
    Birds are calling. All
    nearly
    a revelation

These are a few lines taken from a long poem. "Norlang" is the name of a Tibetan male deity.

An Objectionable Poem

Since the publication of his long poem "Norlang", the young poet Yang Lian has been criticized for being too obscure and esoteric and ideologically unhealthy. The poem beautifies the ugliness of hooligans, scoundrels and "sexual liberationists". In order to enhance the supreme sanctity of this "male deity", the broad masses are portrayed as muddle-headed and insensitive.

The author takes pleasure in natural disaster and man-made calamity, and deliberately sings of a "ravaged beauty". The Fascist Japanese bandits no doubt felt the "harmony of the universe", and enjoyed a similar feeling of "ravaged beauty", as they raped and pillaged their way through China in the 1930s and 1940s.

This is not the cry of a nation, not the call of an era; it is the voice of one individual over-riding a whole nation and a whole era. Its incantatory riddles express a presumptuous will to dominate.

from *Literary Bulletin*, March 1984

The Pursuit of Ugliness

Sun Longji

THE HUMAN MIND is mysterious. There are crazy people in the world who do nothing but destroy works of art. But for a culture that suffocates individuality, this kind of destruction becomes a collective neurosis. A culture that prohibits people from developing "the beauty of individuality", must regard the people who possess this beauty as a threat; a culture that forbids people to create beauty, and forces everyone to consider ugliness an honour, must regard beautiful people as immoral; a culture that does not allow people to bloom, must be against life, must worship death. People who cannot be "alive" themselves will try to deaden those who are.

from Deep Structure

DISPERSION, Gao Xingjian

VIII: YELLOW EARTH

The makers of this film have thought deeply and seriously about society and life; and even if their feelings are vague and obtuse at times, they have gone far beyond the social analyses and statistics of our philosophers and sociologists.

Huang Zongying

... cinematic innovation must keep pace with what the masses can accept and enjoy .... If we let things go, there will be an unconscious drift towards "art for art's sake" and "innovation for the sake of innovation".

Xia Yan

Yellow Earth
—an Unwelcome Guest

WHEN THE FILM "Yellow Earth" was screened at the Hong Kong International Film Festival in March 1985, it was immediately hailed by local and international film critics as representing the long-awaited breakthrough in Chinese cinema. It was subsequently invited to festivals in Europe and America, and bought for commercial release in many countries, making it internationally the most popular Chinese film made since 1949.

"Yellow Earth" was completed in late 1984, and initially refused international release by China's film censors amidst considerable controversy. Many critics found the perspective of the director, Chen Kaige, and Zhang Yimou, his cinematographer, to be politically suspect, condemning the film for using mass art as a vehicle to "display the backward and ignorant aspect of the Chinese peasantry." Chen was regarded as being too young to understand what Yan'an was all about, and he was accused of distorting the Communist spirit. The striking simplicity of the plot and stunning cinematography—both rare achievements for a film culture that has if anything become more theatrical and contrived since 1949—were roundly decried for being "arty" and "naturalistic". In fact, "Yellow Earth" was only one of a number of controversial films made by new directors—the so-called "fifth-generation" of film-makers trained in Peking since the Cultural Revolution. However, it was the popularity of Chen's work with young urban audiences and the international attention that brought the debate surrounding the new cinema into the open.

On a deeper and, for orthodox Communist viewers, more disturbing level, "Yellow Earth" reflected the vision of the Urbling generation of the Cultural Revolution, the dispossessed young people sent to be "re-educated" by the peasants. The director as well as most of his film-crew belong to this group, and the understanding of Chinese realities that their exile afforded them is in striking contrast to the distorted and blinkered vision of the older Party and cultural leaders.

Although critics made much of the tragic fate of the heroine, Cuiqiao, it is perhaps in the character of her younger brother, Hanhan, and the deceptive silence with which he preserves his individuality, that we can find the most striking message of the film.

The dispassionate yet pessimistic picture presented by the makers of "Yellow Earth" and its relevance to China today struck the film's supporters as well as its opponents. Huang Zongying, one of the most open-minded members of China's film establishment, demonstrated her understanding of the real significance of "Yellow Earth" when she said: "I am convinced that the next generation of film-makers will leave us all far behind. But what worries me is that the conservative stodginess of our veteran film-makers is making the young despise them."

In the following we offer a short synopsis of the film and a pictorial introduction to highlights of the work, along with a selection of contrasting comments from a discussion of "Yellow Earth" by the committee which chose the Golden Rooster Awards (China's Oscars), in 1985.

For Chinese film audiences and critics alike, the arrival of "Yellow Earth" was quite unexpected. It was like a pleasant social gathering where people are awaiting the arrival of a friend: the doorbell rings, the door opens, but the person who steps in is a stranger that no one recognizes. The interloper and the guests gape at each other, a lively conversation that has been in progress gradually dies out and there is an awkward silence. If the unbidden stranger apologizes, says he has come to the wrong place, then turns and leaves, the matter could end there. However, if he is stubborn, and declares that he is going to join the party anyway, there could be some trouble. Two things could happen: he might be rudely ejected, or he may be grudgingly accepted and become a friend.

—Li Tuo, film critic and novelist

Synopsis

SPRING 1939, North Shaanxi. As part of a mass effort to mobilize the peasants against the Japanese invasion, the Communist-led Eighth Route Army propaganda teams are engaged in collecting and disseminating folksongs in the north-west.

Gu Qing, a soldier in the Eighth Route army, is walking to each of the villages on the loess plateau by the Yellow River, when he sees a wedding procession and follows it into a village, where he is invited to join the feast. The peasants are so poor, however, that wooden fish are offered instead of live ones to the guests.

The Village Wedding Feast

A young girl, Cuiqiao, has come to watch the wedding, anxious to learn something of her own fate. Afterwards she goes to the Yellow River to fetch water, and sings to the tune of a local folksong:

In the sixth month the ice in the River hasn't thawed,
It's my own father who is dragging me to the wedding board.

Of all the five grains, the bean is the roundest,
Of all the people, daughters are the saddest.

Up in the sky pigeons fly, one with the other,
The only dear one that I long for is my mother.

That night Gu Qing stays at a peasant's cave home. The father is in his late forties but looks much older, and he lives with his two children: fourteen year-old Cuiqiao, and her brother Hanhan, who is about ten. Gu Qing explains that he has come to collect folksongs, and asks them if they can sing, but they are non-committal. He learns that the bride he saw earlier was only fourteen. He tells the family that the Communist Party opposes child marriages, but the father is not impressed.

The next morning Cuiqiao brings water for Gu Qing. He starts mending his clothes, explaining that in the Eighth Route Army the women are soldiers just like the men, and the men mend their own clothes. On the doorframe outside, Cuiqiao sticks up the New Year couplets. Gu Qing is surprised to see that instead of Chinese characters there are only black circles. Cuiqiao tells him that there is no one in the area who is literate. She also explains that her father is suspicious of Gu Qing's notebook.

Gu Qing climbs up the ridge to the family's field, desolate in the spring drought, where he finds the father and son. He lends a hand, and the family is surprised at his skill. The father reveals that his wife is dead; his eldest daughter married into a family that he thought could support her, but since her marriage she has often gone hungry.

Cuiqiao comes with the midday meal: millet gruel. Before eating the father says a short prayer. Gu Qing laughs, and is rebuked. Gu Qing asks the father if he can sing. He answers that he only feels like singing when he is happy or sad. Gu Qing asks how people can learn all the

Gu Qing with Cuiqiao's Family

local songs. The father replies: "When you have had a hard life it's easy to remember and understand." Gu Qing explains that folksongs help to raise the soldiers' morale. He also explains that in the Eighth Route Army, all soldiers are taught to read and write, including women.

Later that day, Hanhan sings for Gu Qing:

> When the pomegranate flowers, the leaves start showing,
> My mother sold me off to him, witnout me knowing.
>
> All I ever asked for, was a good man to wed,
> But what I ended up with was a little wetabed.*

* A child bridegroom.

When you pee, I'll also pee,
Curse you, you can pee with me.

In spring next year, when flowers blossom red,
Frogs will start croaking, under the bed.

Right to the East Ocean, flows a river of pee,
To the Dragon King's palace, under the sea.

The Dragon King laughs, as he hears the pee:
"This little wetabed's in the same line as me."**

** The Dragon King produces rain.

Hanhan Singing for Gu Qing

In turn Gu Qing teaches him a Communist ditty.

Cuiqiao returns home to find the matchmaker has come to settle her betrothal. Her father tells her that she is to be married in the fourth month, and she'll be better off than her sister: her husband is older, and therefore more dependable. He explains that the bride-price he gets will pay for a wife for her brother. Cuiqiao doesn't want to let Gu Qing know what has happened. She asks him how far it is to Yan'an, the headquarters of the Eighth Route Army, and how women soldiers there live. Gu Qing tells her that he will be going away the next day but will return in a few months. He leaves some money to cover the cost of his food and for her to buy new clothes.

Cuiqiao's father is concerned that Gu Qing might get into trouble if he fails to collect enough folk songs, so that night he sings for him.

The next morning Hanhan accompanies Gu Qing as far as the ridge. Further along the way, Cuiqiao is waiting for him. She wants to go with him to join the army, but he replies that he must first get permission. He promises to come back to fetch her.

Time passes; it is the fourth month, and the marriage procession arrives to take Cuiqiao to her new home. On her wedding night, she shrinks from her new husband.

Yan'an; Gu Qing arrives back to see a peasants' send-off to new recruits. The recruits perform a waist-drum dance.

Back in the village, it is now Hanhan's task to fetch the water. One evening he sees Cuiqiao by the river bank. She tells him she is going to cross the Yellow River to join the army, and bids him to take care of his father. She hands him a pair of hand-sewn shoe soles to give to Gu Qing on his return. He gives her the sewing kit with a red star on it that Gu Qing had given him.

Cuiqiao rows the small boat into the turbulent Yellow River. The next morning her body is found washed up on the opposite shore.

Gu Qing arrives back at Cuiqiao's old home. Finding no one there he goes down to the village. The peasants, led by Cuiqiao's father, are praying for rain:

> Over the fields let the good rains fall,
> Oh Dragon King, come save us all!
>   Come save us all!

> East Sea Dragon, let the crops grow tall,
> Oh Dragon King, come save us all!
> Come save us all!

Hanhan sees Gu Qing, and runs towards him, but Gu Qing is too far away. The film ends with the sound of Cuiqiao singing as the camera focusses on the yellow earth.

—Bonnie McDougall

The Debate

We wanted to express a number of things in "Yellow Earth": the boundless magnificence of the heavens; the supporting vastness of the earth. The racing flow of the Yellow River; the sustaining strength and endurance of a nation. The cry of a people from the depths of primitive obscurity, and their strength; the resonant paean that issues forth from the impoverished yellow land. The fate of a people, their feelings, loves and hates, strengths and weaknesses. The longing those people have for a brighter future, a quest hampered by ignorance but rewarded by an earthy goodness. In fact, the actual physical objects we could film were extremely limited: there was the earth, cave-dwellings, the Yellow River itself and the four characters. We wanted to use our "limited artistic tools to paint a vast canvas of life; to use our 'inks' to paint a world of resounding power."

—Zhang Yimou, cinematographer

. . . in terms of cinematic structure, I want our film to be rich and variable, free to the point of wildness; its ideas should be expressed with great ease, without any limitations or restrictions. However, most of the actual contours of the film must be mild, calm and slow . . . . The quintessence of our style can be summed up in a single word: "concealment".

—Chen Kaige, director, addressing his film crew

If the trickling streams of the upper reaches of the Yellow River can be said to represent the youth of the river, and the thunderous surge of its lower reaches its old age, then Northern Shaanxi sees the river in its prime. For here it is broad, deep and unhurried. It makes its stately progress through the hinterland of Asia, its free spirit and serene depths somehow symbolic of the Chinese people—full of strength, but flowing on so deeply, so ponderously. By its banks an unbounded expanse of hills rises up, land which has not seen rain for many years. The Yellow River flows through here in vain, unable to succour the vast barren wastes which have made way for its passage. This sight impressed on us the desolation of several thousand years of history . . . .

. . . In a more sombre mood if we meditate on the fact that this river gives life to all things, but by the same token can destroy all things, then we realise that the fate of Cuiqiao, who lived among the people of old China, had an inevitably tragic cast. The road she chooses is a very hard one. Hard, because she is not simply confronted by the malign forces of society in any narrow sense, but rather by the tranquil, even well-meaning, ignorance of the people who raised her . . . .

—Chen Kaige

The loess plains of Shaanxi are the birthplace of the Chinese people. It is an old liberated area, but even today it is poor and backward . . . . The question is how should we regard such a place? The most important thing is to change the environment, or as the Party Centre has directed "to plant grass and trees" . . . . [In the case of cinema] it is a question of how to get people to see the problem of the loess plains in the proper way. Should the audience come out of the film thinking that Shaanxi is a dreadful place, or should they go away feeling that it deserves their affection?

We're not scared of telling the truth; we're not afraid of revealing the obtuseness and backwardness of that region in the past. But this is not our aim. By revealing these things we are calling on our people to wipe out this ignorance and overcome their backwardness. We do not approve of artists revelling in such things simply for the sake of it. Needless to say, we thoroughly disapprove of an attitude that delights in the ignorance and backwardness of the masses.

—Xia Yan, critic and doyen of Chinese film

All I have to say is that the cinematographic achievements of the film are divorced from its content.

—*Ling Zifeng, veteran director*

I don't think this is such a faultless film. [The film-makers] have ignored the fact that our audiences, especially people in the country-side, cannot possibly cope with a film like this . . . . They've paid a great deal of attention to the composition of a lot of the shots and visually the result is stunning. But what happens in these scenes has absolutely nothing to do with the inner working or actions of their characters. All in all, it's a bit like a foreign art film. There are a lot of shots in which the camera simply doesn't move, and the characters remain immobile and silent for long periods. You can't really tell what they're supposed to be thinking.

—*Yu Yanfu, director*

A Scene in Cuiqiao's Cave Home. One of the many quiet and brooding scenes that baffled older critics.

Cuiqiao Working Outside Her Home

This film brings to mind the Italian director Antonioni's documentary "China". I'm not going to get involved here with the question of whether the criticisms made of him in the past were justified or not; let me simply say that his film depicted the backwardness of China: women with bound feet, spitting, as well as the insular ignorance of many people. All Antonioni did was present an objective account of the realities of China. He didn't attempt to show China as it should be, and his work revealed no desire or ability to change the realities which confronted him. In comparison it is obvious that "Yellow Earth" is not an objective, dispassionate study of the ignorance and backwardness of its subject. Nor does it take an indulgent stand in regard to these things. Rather it assumes a serious and historical perspective with the aim of awakening people to these realities.

—*Deng Baochen, science documentary film-maker*

And that boy seems to be too much of a simpleton. He's always standing around and doesn't say a word for ages. This is completely unrealistic. Everyone knows that the universal characteristic of children is that they are energetic and lovable, regardless of whether they are from rich or poor families. The doltishness of the boy in the film is clearly something imposed on him by the director.

—Han Shangyi, veteran art director

Cuiqiao's Father

Hanhan

The peasant who sings the folk songs in the film is very ugly. Why did they have to go and choose such an actor? The duty of film is to reflect life as realistically as possible, and to retain its true face. But we must not encourage naturalism, nor let our film-makers waste their energies by indulging in voyeurism and the depiction of the remnants of the primitive past . . . . Generally speaking, innovation inevitably involves exploration, and when exploring we must be prepared for both success and failure.

—*Chen Huangmei, critic and cultural bureaucrat*

I think we should encourage the innovations of the young, but surely we should actively discourage "creative endeavours" that no one wants to see.

—*Han Shangyi*

It may not do very well at the box-office, but I can assure you that the classmates of these film-makers would give them a comradely slap on the back and say, "You've got a winner there." "Yellow Earth" has shown me what our young film artists are capable of. This group of young creators have poured their heart's blood into this film. It sparkles with warmth and enthusiasm, and it reflects their historical sense and aesthetic view. They have thought deeply and seriously about society and life; and even if their feelings are vague and obtuse at times, they have gone far beyond the social analyses and statistics of our philosophers and sociologists.

Let me put a question to all of you: why hasn't the Peking Film Studio which is situated at the "very feet of the emperor", or Shanghai Film Studio, a studio strategically located in the commercial and cultural centre of China, or any of the other "senior" film studios for that matter, produced a few good films by young directors? Just how many films made by young people have you made to date? Surely, it is within this context that we are forced to recognize the impact and power of "Yellow Earth". I am convinced that the next generation of film-makers will leave us all far behind. But what worries me is that the conservative stodginess of our veteran film-makers is making the young despise them.

—*Huang Zongying, writer, film producer*
and actor Zhao Dan's widow

All right, if the director likes the peasants as much as you say, then how come he never gave a thought to making a film they really want to see? I'll go out on a limb here by saying that I don't think the broad masses of peasants would necessarily like such a film . . . they like light comedies, war films, *kungfu* movies and historical dramas . . . but they can't accept what some experts call "new cinema" . . . . What are you supposed to do if you've got a mass art form that the masses don't understand? How can the making of such films be an expression of your love for the peasants? Why do you have to give them something they don't understand?

— Yu Min, screen-writer

One of the old peasant's many pregnant silences

Our films are made for hundreds of millions of people to see, and it is for this reason that cinematic innovation must conform with what the masses can accept and enjoy . . . . If we let things go, there will be an unconscious drift towards "art for art's sake" and "innovation for the sake of innovation", as well as other types of artistic self-expression.

—Xia Yan

... [Surely,] there is a spark that sets light to the young girl's [Cuiqiao] heart, but as for the broad masses—those countless people kneeling on the ground praying for rain—they haven't seen the faintest glimmer of that spark .... I simply fail to understand how people so close to Yan'an could remain completely untouched by the new spirit that came from Yan'an ....

—Xia Yan

Why can't you tolerate such things in a film? Let me tell you something: it's our own children who can no longer tolerate the unchanging realities of China, the stagnant productive forces of the peasants as well as the dead film language we use. They have the courage to break all the rules and they have rubbed you oldies up the wrong way. But the future is on their side.

—Huang Zongying

Drum Dance at Yan'an

Praying for Rain

Chen Kaige: These two scenes [the drum dance and the rain dance] were the result of very careful thought and planning . . . . The Chinese people can throw themselves enthusiastically into a lively drum dance, or equally give themselves over heart and soul to a blind and superstitious prayer for rain. This is symbolic of the two sides of the Chinese national character.

Reporter: Some comrades are of the opinion that the prayer for rain scene exaggerates the ignorance of the people. One even hears the comment that this sequence is somewhat voyeuristic in tone. What do you think of such comments?

Chen: Praying for rain is one of the most ancient rituals of our people, and it survives even today . . . . People often begin praying for rain just as it is about to start raining. Thus it is not simply an expression of superstitious ignorance, for there is also an element of enjoyment in the dance. Our aim in filming this scene was not at all "voyeuristic", or calculated to show up the ignorance of the peasants, but rather to express the formidable energy and force of the peasants —although that energy is still blind and undirected, as long as it exists it has great potential if properly tapped and directed.

—*Chen Kaige*

On the scales of artistic criticism "Yellow Earth" is a hefty weight; and regardless of whether it achieves official recognition, it is a milestone in the development of youth cinema, and its place in the annals of Chinese film is assured.

—Huang Zongying

Cuiqiao's last meeting with her brother by the Yellow River

"Yellow Earth" is an outstanding work. If nothing else it is a controversial film. Its appearance means that we can no longer simply sit back and take things easy. After today's discussion everyone is going to have a hard time getting to sleep .... It has made us all reflect on many things, most of all on the future of Chinese cinema.

—Zhu Xijuan, actress and producer

IX: FIRE BEHIND BARS

Our society is not a park [like Hyde Park], where everyone can voice his opinion and when everything is finished no harm has been done, no flowers have been injured, and everyone leaves the park and goes home.

Hu Qiaomu, June 1980

Farewell—Democracy Wall

Ling Bing

Farewell—Democracy Wall.
What can I say to you?

A few more days.
And maybe I'll be sitting
Beneath a window, behind bars,
And people will stare, hard as ice,
Will cross-examine me,
Will not understand
That you and I are one.

But I believe
That you will never vanish,
Will never die . . . .
Remember,
While humanity lives,
You will never die.

from Peking Spring, *April 1979*

In the following pages we introduce four of the leading personalities of the Democracy Movement—Wang Xizhe, Wei Jingsheng, Liu Qing and Xu Wenli—all now serving long prison sentences. Their ideas (as can be seen from the brief extracts we have included) range from the more pronounced liberalism of Wei Jingsheng to the more moderate East European-style Marxism advocated by Wang Xizhe. They are among the many talented young people whose persecution has disillusioned even such sympathetic and hopeful observers as the Hong Kong intellectual Lee Yee (see pp. 274-6).

The accompanying poems are all on the theme of imprisonment, though they date from different periods: Zeng Zhuo's from the years when the KMT controlled the prisons, Niu Han's from the height of the Cultural Revolution, Jiang He's from its last years—while Ling Bing (above) is actually witnessing the democratic debacle itself.

Wang Xizhe and Socialist Democracy

Wang Xizhe is a native of Sichuan province. He is a convinced Marxist-Leninist, and an articulate theoretician. He first became known as one of the authors of Canton's famous Li-Yi-Zhe poster (1974), which advocated democracy and the rule of law. He and the other two authors were sent to work "under supervision" in the Guangdong countryside, and were subsequently (1977) imprisoned as counter-revolutionaries. They were released and rehabilitated in 1979. Wang then joined the Democracy Movement.

Wang was re-arrested on 20 April 1981 at his factory (ten days after Xu Wenli), and is reported to have been tried on 28 May 1982 and sentenced to 14 years' imprisonment and four and a half years' deprivation of political rights. He is said to have been charged with: (1) "inciting the masses to resist arrest and violate the law and statutes of the state"; (2) "counter-revolutionary propaganda and agitation"; and (3) "actively taking part in a counter-revolutionary group". The first charge referred to Wang's open letter about Liu Qing, which (according to reports) was quoted at the trial as evidence that he had incited violations of the law. The second charge was apparently based on the political views he expressed in his speeches and articles, and the third charge on his close association with other democrats, in particular Xu Wenli. According to the unofficial text of the ruling in Xu Wenli's case, Wang Xizhe was accused of taking part in Xu's "counter-revolutionary" group and of participating in "secret meetings" in Peking between 10 and 12 June 1980. These were allegedly aimed at the eventual creation of a "new form of proletarian political party" with the intention of "destroying the one-party dictatorship".

Socialist Democracy

Socialist Democracy is not something that can be bestowed on a society artificially by passing some kind of law; it can only arise organically out of certain new economic relations, on a new economic foundation. It is nothing other than the political form that naturally corresponds to those new econo-

mic relations.... Shouldn't we investigate for ourselves different forms of socialism and roads of socialist development? And shouldn't we perhaps learn a bit from our Yugoslav comrades?

The Tiananmen demonstration was a courageous attempt by the people to regain control over a party and a state that had become increasingly alien to them.... The Party suppressed the demonstration. This was not some accidental result of a seizure of power by the Gang of Four. It was a public confirmation of the estrangement of the Party from the people!

The system of economic management established by the Anshan Constitution (1960) and known as "workers' participation in management" must be transformed into direct, democratic management by the workers .... This is what the Paris Commune sought to accomplish, and is still the goal that every true socialist should strive for.... True socialism can only be realized in a situation where the associated workers are directly united with the means of production. Only then will the people really be able to control their own destiny. Only then will the whole web of mysterious social relations that once seemed to envelop them and dominate their lives be smashed. Then they will know that they have finally become human beings, and they will look upon all forms of superstition and worship—including worship of the Gang of Four—as relics of their ignorant past.

Wang Xizhe, from *For a Return to True Marxism* (1980)

An Appeal on behalf of Wang Xizhe
Lee Yee

THE WRITINGS of Wang Xizhe are a source of hope for the countless Overseas Chinese who are concerned for the future of their homeland. Though some of his views differ greatly from the pronouncements of the Communist Party, his writings inspire us with hope for both China and socialism. In addition, the incorporation of some of Wang Xizhe's ideas into official government policy has strengthened confidence within the Overseas Chinese community about China's future.

Thus Wang Xizhe's arrest was a great shock to us all. It seemed that Chinese politics had taken a turn down a painfully familiar road .... Wang's arrest has made me even more doubtful about the future of socialism in China.

Wang Xizhe differs from the Russian dissidents and other members of the Democracy Movement in China, most of whom tend to be advocates of Western liberalism. Wang is an accomplished Marxist theoretician. Wang's writings, from the Li-Yi-Zhe big-character poster in the early 1970s, to the theoretical articles published more recently, offer a thoughtful analysis of Soviet and Chinese Communist history. He maintains a critical stance toward Western liberalism and decries the exploitation characteristic of capitalism. It is within this context that he supports what he would refer to as the *true* "four basic principles"*, though his interpretation of them, and in particular his condemnation of the means by which the Communist Party has put them into practice, is at variance with official policy. His writing displays a mastery of Marxist theory, and tight logic. His realistic approach to China's present problems, his idealistic attitude and strong sense of patriotism strike a sympathetic chord in Chinese intellectuals everywhere.

In short, Wang Xizhe's writings are a ray of light for those of us whose ideals have been shattered by the events of the past decades, but who still have hope for socialism in China. We can admire his patriotism, his wisdom and courage. His writings are proof of the talent that exists among the present generation of young people in China.

Ultimately the responsibility for the future of China must rest

Lee Yee (Li Bingyao), who also writes under the penname Chi Hsin, was born in Canton in 1936, and moved to Hong Kong in 1948. In 1970 he founded The Seventies, *a Communist-supported current affairs monthly popular among Overseas Chinese intellectuals. Lee's persistent support for the Democracy Movement and his defense of Wang Xizhe resulted in his break with the Communist publishing authorities of Hong Kong in 1981. He renamed his magazine* The Nineties *in 1984. Lee Yee is now regarded as one of the leading independent analysts of Hong Kong and Chinese affairs.*

*"The four basic principles" are: (1) following the socialist road; (2) upholding Proledic; (3) respecting the leadership of the Party; (4) supporting Marxism, Leninism, and Mao Zedong Thought.

with these young people, who represent sixty-three per cent of the population, and in particular with such exemplary individuals as Wang Xizhe, who are so courageously breaking new ground.

I can appreciate the need for a policy of "stability and unity" in China at the present moment. But if temporary stability and unity are achieved by persecuting talented young people (who are only seeking to realize their ideals), then it will become more and more difficult to regain their trust and confidence in the future. Wang Xizhe has confined himself to writing, and has participated in very few demonstrations. His writings have also for the most part conformed to the "four basic principles". It is for this reason that his arrest appears to be so much more blatant a suppression of freedom of speech than the arrests of Wei Jingsheng and Fu Yuehua. Whatever the details of the case may be, even if Wang Xizhe has broken the law, I appeal to the Chinese leadership to make positive use of the extraordinary talent and high aspirations of young people like him, and to treat them with greater magnanimity.

1981

Education and Punishment

The relationship of ruler and subject is essentially that of father and son. The ruler must educate his subject, and the subject must obey his ruler, or he will be punished . . . .

. . . From early childhood, the Chinese are taught to learn from others, that is, not to form their own values. Punishment goes hand in hand with education. Labour camps are a form of punishment. Such punishment is not necessarily based on legislation. The Chinese people are just like children. They must be educated by a parent government. This education includes punishment for the disobedient. If the people are to be served, they must also be educated. If they are to be educated, they must be punished.

Sun Longji, from *Deep Structure*

Wei Jingsheng and the Fifth Modernization

Wei Jingsheng was an electrician, from an Anhui cadre family. He was for a time a Red Guard, and spent four months in prison during the Cultural Revolution. When the Democracy Movement was launched in 1978, he founded the magazine *Exploration*, and was one of the most vocal and radical democrats.

He coined the term The Fifth Modernization, arguing that Deng Xiaoping's Four Modernizations were insufficient, and that China needed a fifth political modernization, based on democracy and human rights. Whereas most of the dissidents supported socialism, Wei is at best a half-hearted socialist. He was arrested on 29 March 1979, and sentenced in October to fifteen years as a "counter-revolutionary" and for revealing "state secrets" to a foreigner.

The Fifth Modernization

The leaders of our nation must be informed that we want to take our destiny into our own hands. We want no more gods and emperors. No more saviours of any kind. We want to be masters of our own country, not modernized tools for the expansionist ambitions of dictators.... Democracy, freedom and happiness are the only goals of modernization. Without this fifth modernization, the four others are nothing more than a new-fangled lie.

Following his trial Wei Jingsheng was reported to have been held for several years in solitary confinement in the Detention Centre adjacent to Peking Prison No 1. According to a former prisoner who was held in the same prison during 1980 and 1981, Wei Jingsheng was then detained in isolation in Cell 11, Block 2—a block reserved for "major criminals". Wei went on hunger strike once during that period, and in April 1981 he was suddenly moved from his cell because he was constantly "making trouble" and it was feared that his rebellious spirit would influence the other prisoners.

Dissent

Dissent may not always be pleasant to listen to, and it is inevitable that it will sometimes be misguided. But it is everyone's sovereign right. Indeed, when government is seen as defective or unreasonable, criticizing it is an unshirkable duty. Only through the people's criticism and supervision of the leadership can mistakes be minimized and government prevented from riding roughshod over the masses. Then, and only then, can everyone breathe freely.

The Marxism I have opposed is in no way the Marxism of Marx and Engels. Marxism's fate has been similar to that suffered by a number of religions. With the passage of time, the revolutionary substance is quietly abandoned, while the doctrines are selectively adapted by those in power as tools to deceive and enslave.

China's struggle for democracy is bound to provoke resistance, but I am prepared to make any necessary sacrifice.

In mid-1983 Wei was reported to be still confined in isolation in his cell, being allowed out for exercise only once a month and not permitted to meet other prisoners or receive visits from his family. In May 1984 it was further reported that Wei had twice been transferred to a hospital as his mental health had suffered, and that he needed treatment for schizophrenia. It was also rumoured that he had been transferred to a camp in Qinghai province, but this remains unconfirmed.

Q1—a Twentieth-Century Bastille

Wei Jingsheng

IF YOU GO a short way down the main road in Changping County, in the countryside due north of Peking, you will come to a hot springs resort area set in the most picturesque scenery. This is the famous spa, where, according to tradition, the Manchu Empress Dowager used to come to take the waters.

Continue further north a few minutes, and by the roadside you will see a large sign in several languages: Foreigners Prohibited. The innocent traveller will take this to be a military zone and go on without giving it another moment's thought. But anyone who knows the truth will instantly experience a sense of terror, for just beyond the sign lies China's top political prison: the infamous Qin Cheng No. 1—Q1.

You won't find Q1 on any map, and you will only ever hear it referred to as No 1. The local farmers know nothing of this huge maximum-security complex. There is only a vague sinister rumour circulating that the Japanese once constructed a prison in the area.

To the north a lonely but well-maintained asphalt road leads straight to the prison. The main entrance and the gate house beside it seem perfectly ordinary. A stranger wandering by would suspect nothing unusual. A huge screen wall inside the open gate makes it totally impossible for the casual passer-by to catch even the slightest glimpse of the "view" beyond . . . . On this huge screen is inscribed a single quotation from Mao Zedong, on the subject of Proledic—the Dictatorship of the Proletariat.

Behind the screen wall is a building of several storeys with an archway in the middle of it, beyond which lies the main part of the prison proper, enclosed within a three-metre wall, topped by electrified barbed wire. The rusty iron gate inside the archway is a chilling sight. Just reflect for a moment on all the people opposed to Mao and his dictatorial policies.who passed in through this gate never to return; or on all Mao's former followers, who were sent here under a cloud of suspicion; many of them entered here, but few were fortunate enough to re-emerge. Even the shock of release could be fatal. After 1975 it became the practice to put newly released political prisoners in hospital for a short stay before their actual release, in the hope that this would make the transition less violent. Those who enter through this double iron gate are usually atheists, but the ones lucky enough to leave have had a taste of what it's like to be cast into a "modern hell". People even jokingly call it the Atheists' Gate to Hell.

There are sentinel boxes on either side of the gate. If you have permission to visit the Underworld, you will be allowed to continue from this point on down Hell Alley, a T-shaped asphalt road that lies within the enclosure. It slopes gradually towards the north. The land to the east and west is laid out with symmetrical compounds, all painted the same colour. A lot of the compounds to the west have fruit trees growing in them, and to the east, further down the road, is an area of newly-constructed housing. These new buildings were put up after the Cultural Revolution to accomodate the rapidly increasing number of high-ranking political prisoners. They are one of the prison's showpieces of "modernization".

Each building has a small door that opens directly onto the road. The road leads to a hillock covered with chestnut trees, and in the spring and summer it is a scene of lush greenness. The buildings are neatly laid out. In fact the environment has a natural beauty and tranquillity that make it ideal for rest and recuperation. And yet it is in this place that indescribable suffering is inflicted on countless Chinese families. Their loved ones have come to this beautiful and secluded spot to be subjected to the cruellest torture imaginable; former inmates and their relatives are left with harrowing memories of what happens within the walls of the compound, and their agony leaves its imprint on their features for the rest of their lives.

Q1 is completely isolated from the outside world. Only former prisoners, their families and close friends ever know or talk about it. The prison is run by Section 5 of the Ministry of Public Security, and it is even kept a secret from the regular police force. The guards are very carefully selected, and have to be below a certain age. Prisoners report never having seen guards over twenty. They are replaced in batches at frequent intervals.

Prisoners are divided into four categories, according to the level of their monthly keep—theoretically 8, 15, 25 or 40 *yuan*. In actual practice widespread corruption means that no prisoner receives his entitlement. For example, a prisoner's official monthly ration of grain may be 17.5 kilos, but because he never takes any exercise, he cannot possibly eat even half of it. The entire amount is still purchased, however, and according to one version the guards use the surplus to feed their pigs, which are in turn sold to supplement the guards' own diet. Such stories of corruption and embezzlement abound. The whole situation could be summed up by saying that the "legal" expropriation of the prisoners' allowances has come to be considered a routine and reasonable practice at Q1—and at other prisons. Some of these "routine practices" double as punishment: starvation, for example— the lightest and most common form of punishment meted out at Q1. First the prisoner is starved, then he (or she) is given a bowl of cold noodles with great blobs of fat floating in it, to "make up" for all the missed meals. Ninety-percent of prisoners fed in this manner suffer from diarrhoea and nausea as a result and have to miss the next few meals until they recover.

This superficially "civilized" form of torture has been institutionalized at Q1: it serves as a punishment and at the same time as a means of enriching the warders' diet. Small wonder that it is carried out with such zeal.

Each inmate has a separate cell, one metre by three, containing a sink, a chamber pot, and a plank bed with a thin cover. Their black prison uniforms are replaced every six months. When the winter uniform is issued, the summer one is called in. With the delays in the clothing department, this often means that prisoners are still sweltering in their padded winter clothes in May. There is a small window in the door of each cell, which serves as an observation hole, and as an opening through which food, a needle and thread, or the newspaper can be passed. Some prisoners are allowed to read the Marxist-Leninist classics, or the *People's Daily*, but this is considered a great privilege. Ordinary prisoners who "co-operate" are allowed to engage in a number of unpaid activities such as making rope or straw-hats, to keep themselves from becoming stiff. But the ones who make a bad impression on the prison staff are subjected to all sorts of punitive or restrictive measures. They may, for example, be denied the right to exercise, whether outside or within their cell, for as long as six months at a stretch. A former deputy director of the PLA Academy, who had been deputy chief of staff during the Korean War, was kept immobile for six months, after which he was no longer able to walk at all.

The exercise area is approximately one hundred metres square, and is quite separate from the cells. It is laid out in rows of connected squares, like rice paddies in Southern China. The endless walking and running has worn the grass into a circular dirt track. The exercise area used to be divided by bamboo partitions, but these were replaced in the late 1960s by a high brick wall which separates two rows of connected compounds, and is patrolled by guards with rifles.

The inmates' lives are governed by all sorts of irrational regulations. They have to sleep facing the door. It is forbidden to turn the other way, and if a prisoner happens to do this while sleeping, he is woken up, repeatedly if necessary, until he learns to face the observation hole. There was a Tibetan who had to sleep on one side of his face for more than ten years. One of his ears became swollen and numb, and finally infected. He tried sleeping on the other side, but was repeatedly woken up and abused by the guards until, driven beyond endurance, he finally went berserk and tried to strangle one of them. In the end he was granted special dispensation to sleep facing the other way.

Sanitary conditions are very poor. Soap is not provided at all, and bathing is permitted only once a month, regardless of the season. A few privileged prisoners are given semi-annual physical examinations.

Living conditions at Q1 are enough in themselves to destroy an ordinary man's will. If one did not know that most of the inmates were among the finest people that modern China has produced, one could easily mistake the place for a lunatic asylum, or a penitentiary for prisoners sentenced to death. What an irony! These prisoners are gifted individuals who joined the Communist Party to fight for the freedom, prosperity and peace of China and of all of mankind; they devoted the better part of their lives to achieving and maintaining power for the Party. Many of them were imprisoned in the past by the party's enemies: now they are being detained by the very party they helped to create. They are at the receiving end of modern techniques of torture. Every day they face psychological and physical destruction.

The torments of daily life are not enough to break the will of these stalwart people. Q1 is therefore equipped with modern instruments which cause terrible pain in the head during interrogation. When the pain becomes unbearable, and the prisoner is writhing around on the ground, the pain suddenly ceases; only to resume again just as suddenly, and so on, until either a confession is extracted or the interrogators conclude that their techniques are proving ineffective. There are other more antiquated but still highly effective methods of torture. For example, the exposing of a prisoner night and day to a strong light; after a while this can cause severe mental disturbance, even complete insanity.

One of the people tortured at Q1 was Wang Guangmei [widow of former head of state Liu Shaoqi]. She had been given the bright light treatment over a long period, and suddenly one day, while eating her bread and cabbage soup, she is said to have gone out of her mind. She was visited by an old friend, the wife of a high official, who said she looked so terrible that she could hardly recognize her. She was haunted by the sight and, at considerable risk to herself and her family, she protested to Chairman Mao. Her letter to Mao, together with the general indignation among high-ranking cadres, eventually led to a change in command at the prison. The public security people were replaced by PLA Unit 8341 [the Palace Guard of Mao and the Central Committee] and Q1 became a "relatively civilized" institution.

Someone may object that I have only cited extreme cases, and that none of these are the really common forms of torture. That is perhaps true. The most common torture of all is simply to beat the prisoner up. Normally he is called out and surrounded by a group of men who then proceed to kick him and beat him up until his head bleeds, and he can hardly breathe. One high-ranking cadre who was released from Q1 had scars all over his head. Another even more common form of torture is to forcibly administer heavy doses of drugs —under the pretext of some mental disorder. The drugs themselves in fact produce a state of grave mental imbalance. Sometimes the inmate has to be sent to hospital for "further treatment". One person who had this treatment recalls that after being given the drugs he began talking to himself all the time, for days on end, even while he was eating. Naturally, these monologues were recorded for use during future interrogations. Among the hospitals that cooperate in such practices are the Fuxing Hospital [this is the hospital where Wei Jingsheng himself is reported to have been subsequently "treated"], Hospital 301, and Anding Hospital in Peking. The relevant sections of the hospitals are officially called "clinics for senior personnel". The Anding "clinic" is in the suburban area outside Desheng Gate and it is simply called Clinic 5. A visitor there once saw a stocky middle-aged man with a zombie-like expression on his face, his whole head pitted with scars, walking somnambulistically forward in a straight line. If he had not been pulled to a standstill by a guard he would have walked straight into the wall. These prisoners, who fought against dictatorship from youth, who dedicated themselves to the cause of freedom and human rights, have now been subjected to these "advanced" methods of investigation, and have been brutally tortured, to the point where they have lost all sense of reality.

The KMT special agent in the film "Red Crag" was a bungling amateur when compared with the adepts who work in Q1. The techniques of torture used by the KMT in the 40s were advanced for their times; the techniques employed by the Communist Party since the 70s are positively futuristic.

Someone may in all innocence suggest that this is not unlike what happens in the Japanese film "The Chase". Actually, it is quite different: one is a film, the other is real life. In "The Chase" the villain commits his villainy by stealth but gets caught and punished in the end; in Q1 the villainy is being perpetrated in broad daylight by the government, and high-ranking officials periodically receive "invitations" to "inspect" the premises. Nearby, foreign tourists are sampling the delights of the Great Wall; but the Chinese officials who have the fortune to visit Q1 are enjoying recreational activities of a radically different kind.

These inhuman methods naturally provoke violent reactions among the prisoners. Some inmates, unable to endure the hardship inflicted on them, attempt suicide. Others go on hunger strike. The Panchen Lama once refused to eat. He declared that he had no wish to live any longer, and he requested that his corpse be "delivered to the Central Committee". The guards will not countenance such defiance. They show no sympathy for cases like this. Usually after a prisoner has been on hunger strike for about a week, he is given a severe beating, may have a few teeth knocked out, and then he is forced into a "pacifying suit"—a tight rubber straight-jacket, which is extremely narrow at the shoulders and chest, and joined together at the sleeves and legs. The suit is then inflated, making breathing virtually impossible. These suits are particularly effective in immobilizing refractory elements. If these methods are still not effective, prisoners are force-fed large quantities of liquid.

Prison terms at Q1 generally run for more than ten years, and many die there while serving their sentences. Hardly anyone was released before the 1970s, which is why one never heard the place mentioned. It was extremely rare for anyone to be allowed to visit.

Before the Cultural Revolution generally one was not notified when a person was thrown into Q1. Relatives did not know where their loved ones were or whether they were alive or dead, or what condition they were in at all. Even warders are ignorant of the names of their prisoners, who are identified by number rather than name. When they fail to obtain information from the Ministry of Public Security, relatives normally consider that the person has permanently disappeared. Likewise, prisoners are given no information about their families, though they generally assume that since they are in prison the party authorities on the outside will certainly be giving their families a hard time. They will have every obstacle put in their way, every trick the bureaucracy can manage will be played on them, and they will have no one to help or protect them. The anxiety a political prisoner experiences can only be comprehended by those who have been through the same thing themselves.

A human being is more than just flesh and bones. Even atheist materialists must recognize the existence of the human spirit. But what kind of spiritual existence is there for the inmates of Q1? Some former inmates recall not being allowed to converse with anyone at all. Sometimes, even at the risk of being punished for "troublemaking", an inmate may abuse a warden just to provoke him into conversation. Interrogation provides inmates with their only opportunity to talk. One man, after ten years of confinement, was so overwhelmed when he heard his name spoken during an interrogation, that he was literally unable to speak. Many strong-willed men still show deep-seated symptoms of psychological damage after their release, even though they have not actually been subjected to prolonged physical or mental torture. After a decade of solitary confinement, some still cannot speak properly, even a few years after their release.

But even in this oppressive spiritual environment, the human mind continues to function. Whoever invented the various forms of "mental therapy" employed in Q1 understood that a prisoner in circumstances like these is bound to be concerned for his family and friends, to worry about his wife and children. The most effective way to break a prisoner's will, to destroy his spirit, is to keep him in an unbalanced state of mind: to make sure that he is unable to obtain information about his family and friends, so that he torments himself with the thought of how they are being discriminated against on his account. The aim is to keep the prisoner mindful of his own impotence to help them, and to cause him to torture himself with the knowledge that their suffering is a result of *his* offences against the authorities.

The proverbial saying, "force is the tactic of the petty man; psychology the way of the adept", is borne out by reports from many released prisoners. During their confinement they were told things like: "Your wife has remarried and is getting on very nicely in her new home . . . . Your son has committed an offence against socialist order, but he was not jailed. Instead he has simply been sent to a labour camp for re-education . . . . That most attractive daughter of yours has been receiving a lot of attention from young men . . . . Your other children have been ill, but the government is 'doing everything possible' to treat them . . . etc, etc." Afterwards prisoners often discover that the stories were completely untrue. So why were they told such lies in the first place? Just so as to inflict further pain and anguish.

In some important cases, they find a woman who is physically similar to an inmate's wife, and get her to flirt with the man. It is one of the oldest stratagems in the book, although perhaps it is employed as nothing more than another form of torment . . . . Anyway, the people at Q1 resort to every conceivable means to squeeze the "last drop of surplus value" from these hapless souls.

In 1975 many long-time Party members suddenly had what they thought was a stroke of good luck. As part of Deng Xiaoping's "rehabilitation" movement, they were released from Q1. But such sudden and overwhelming joy can be dangerous, even fatal . . . . To "ensure the safety and well-being" of these people, the Central Committee adopted a policy of temporary exile. Those who left Q1 that year had first to spend a period of time in hospital to absorb the shock of re-entering society. Then in 1977 hospitalization was no longer considered necessary. Instead, the prisoners were sent to remote towns in the countryside, where the quiet surroundings would likewise "soften the shock" of liberation. The places of exile were selected according to the Three

Nots for the relocation of political unreliables: 1) *not* in Peking or any large city; 2) *not* near any major transportation junction; 3) *not* in a place where the prisoner concerned had once lived or worked. Most political prisoners have probably been exiled in accordance with these regulations, with the exception of such rare cases as the Panchen Lama and a small number of people close to Party leaders.

Release is no easy or pleasant affair either. Before leaving Q1, the prisoners are confronted with a number of groundless accusations. A final "case summary" is then drawn up showing why your decade of incarceration was well deserved. Upon release, you were expected to express gratitude for Chairman Mao's leniency: after all, your case, which in fact represented a "contradiction between the People and the Enemy", was now being treated as an "internal contradiction within the People" [Maoist gobbledegook for the conversion of a serious political crime into a pardonable offence]. Therefore you are not expected to complain if your activities are restricted and you are sent off to a faraway village. Former Peking Mayor Peng Zhen, former State Planning Chairman Bo Yibo [both key Party leaders once more], and many other prisoners were dealt with in this manner. Bo Yibo was more courageous than most. "In the past I erred by following the directives of the Central Committee," he declared and promptly added: "If I obey the Central Committee this time, shall I be committing another error? To avoid the possibility of any further errors, it would be best if I declined to carry out the Central Committee's decision altogether." Bo simply refused to leave Q1. Since then, so it is said, the preliminaries have been dispensed with, and political prisoners are sent directly into exile.

Once he sets foot in Q1, a prisoner loses all sense of normality; when he leaves he assumes that exile will be comfortable by comparison. But is there really much difference between being in Q1 and being in exile? The food ration still operates on a four-tier system—200, 120, 80 and 60 *yuan*. In Q1 prisoners are constantly guarded by armed wardens; in exile they are constantly watched over ["taken care of" to use the official expression] by local workers. Take for example the Russian widow of Li Lisan. She was accused of being a Soviet spy and sent to Q1 for seven or eight years. Upon her release she was exiled to Yuncheng in Shanxi Province, where the local commune provided two young people to "take care of" her. As she was an old woman, she requested a transfer to Peking, to live with her daughter and grand-child. Permission was finally granted in December 1978.

Or take the case of one of the organisers of Tibet's earliest com-munist organisation—the East Tibet Democratic Youth League. Because of his contacts with the Soviet and Indian Communist Parties in the 1940s, he was falsely accused of having illicit relations with foreign countries and was imprisoned at Q1 for eighteen years. In 1978 he was released and sent to a small town in Sichuan province. Even to go to the doctor's he needed to be accompanied. He had to be constant-ly "looked after" by someone assigned to him by the United Front Ministry—although he had a son and daughter living with him who were quite capable of seeing to his needs.

These two instances are relatively mild. Some exiles, it is said, are still not allowed to receive visits from their friends and relatives. For them exile is nothing more than an extension of Q1, a further extension of the Party's consistent and all-embracing policy toward prisoners.

I have revealed the brutal terror of Q1 not merely as a plea for the innocent prisoners incarcerated there. These young men and women who dedicated their lives to the Chinese revolution and dared oppose Mao's barbaric dictatorship, do indeed deserve our respect and emulation. But the most profound lesson to be learnt from Q1 is that the dictatorship of the proletariat does not exist in our country. Instead what goes by the name of the proletarian dictatorship, this Proledic, is manipulated by a small group of tyrants as a tool to oppress the proletariat. The tool has been used so effectively that all of the dic-tator's opponents have been eliminated, even his "close comrades-in-arms" from the era of the Long March.

It is inevitable that dictators resort to barbaric measures. Dictator-ship cannot justify its oppressive methods; it can therefore only main-tain itself by the use of force. The instruments of repression are not only directed against the masses, they must be used to quell any and all internal opposition. Dictators show no mercy even towards comrades who once fought at their side. One can almost say that those who lost their lives during the revolution were the lucky ones. They are honoured as heroes who fought for freedom and peace; and they have attained true peace of mind. They have been spared the fate of being tortured by their comrades, and did not live to see their relatives being maltreated. They need not constantly tremble in fear at the thought of the next day's torment.

Dictators can create any number of political excuses for eliminating their opponents. They talk glibly of "class enemies", "counter-revolutionaries", "rebels", and "traitors". Dictatorship needs these labels, and it needs prisons like Q1. Or to put it the other way round, if political imprisonment was somehow made impossible, then one of the indispensable tools of dictatorship would have been removed. So we are dealing here not just with the humanitarian implications of imprisonment for the individual, but with the significance that such imprisonment has for the basic rights of the people as a whole. In order to avoid the disastrous consequences of dictatorship, one must first eliminate the conditions that create it and sustain it, including the dehumanizing system of political imprisonment and persecution.

from Exploration, *March 1979*

Deviation and Conformity

The Chinese individual is indeed extremely weak and vulnerable—he needs the warmth of Sodality. In such circumstances, his only option is to give up his freedom of choice. The Chinese consider people who hold different views deviant. To deviate is unfriendly. It damages the relationship with the group, it wounds the very people who care. The Chinese want conformity. Those who refuse to conform are enemies. Contradiction leads only to open confrontation, and ultimately to chaos.

Sun Longji, from *Deep Structure*

Iron Bars and Fire

Zeng Zhuo

The tiger paces his cage.

In his cramped cage,
Silently he paces
Quietly growls
Ignoring the jeers
The alms outside.

Weary, he lies
Behind the bars
A mass of blazing stripes,
A ball of fire!
He stands,
Eyes burning,
Fangs bared,
Tensed to pounce;
Shrieks of terror from beyond the cage!

Lowering his snout, he takes in
A deep breath of the wilderness scent
That lingers still on his body,
Remembers
Mountain, forest, valley . . .
Years of freedom,
Dignity.

Late in the night
He paws the bars;
A longdrawn roar of rage and grief
Shatters the night air
Dies in the darkness
          like a lightning flash!

Fire
Behind iron bars!

1946

Zeng Zhuo was born in 1922. He was first attacked in the early 1950s as a member of the "Hu Feng clique". He is now a writer in the city of Wuhan.

Tiger

Niu Han

In Guilin
In a small zoo
I saw a tiger.

Pressed in the crowd,
Outside two rows of iron bars,
I peered at the tiger in his cage
For a long, long time.
But could see nothing
Of his brindled face
And flaming eyes.

The tiger in his cage
Turned from the cowardly, hopeless crowd,
Lay calmly stretched in a corner.
They pelted him with stones,
They goaded him with cries,
They coaxed and lured him,
But he ignored them all,
Slowly flailing the floor
With his long, rough tail.
Tiger, O caged tiger!
Are you dreaming of the vast mountain forest?
Is your stout heart twitching with shame?
Or are you thinking of lashing
        the sad, laughable crowd
        with your long whip of a tail?

Your sinewy legs
Are stiffly splayed.
Each broken claw
Blood-encrusted.
Were they
Wrenched out

As you lay trussed and bound?
Or, did you yourself,
Out of wrath and despair,
Crush them with your splintered, bleeding teeth?

On the grey cement wall
Beside the cage,
Runnels of blood
Blasted my eyes like forked lightning.

Finally I understood . . . .
Leaving the zoo in shame,
I seemed to hear a sound,
An earthshattering roar:
A soul unbound
Had soared above my head.
I saw the fiery stripes,
I saw the flaming eyes!

June 1973

    *Niu Han was born in 1923. He was first attacked in the early 1950s as a member of the
"Hu Feng clique". He is now an influential publisher and editor in Peking.*

Notes from Prison

Liu Qing

My "Arrest"

VERY STRANGE WEATHER for November. A beautiful autumn afternoon, with not a trace of chill in the air; then in the evening, the temperature suddenly dropped. It looked like we were in for a cold spell. We hurried through the biting wind to the waiting room of the Peking Municipal Public Security Bureau (PSB). Our teeth were chattering with the cold. I explained the situation to the officer in charge and made my complaint [about the seizure of the transcripts of Wei Jingsheng's trial, and the arrest of other democrats]. He replied brusquely that he would telephone his superiors in due course. Apparently his superiors were more concerned about us than he was: before he got round to telephoning, a call came through from them asking about us—obviously the station on Chang'an Street had reported us and our whereabouts. After the call the officer decided to take us more seriously; he came out of his office and chatted with us in the waiting room. We questioned the legality of the way the Peking PSB had been making arrests and seizing books, and he graced us with his thoughts on the subject. His view was that if the PSB seized things or arrested people, then it had to be legal. Obviously, in the mind of this administrator of justice, the law was created by the PSB. I tried to bate him by asking Yang Jing [another Democracy Movement activist, who had recently become co-editor of *April Fifth Forum*, and was himself subsequently arrested] to write down what he had said, and threatened to quote him on some future occasion. He seemed a little put out by that. But with proverbial Chinese compassion and common sense, he observed: "Go on, write your essays! Make a few speeches! It won't get you anywhere! At most you might get them published abroad. That's not going to hurt the PSB one bit. But if you get caught making trouble, you'll get fifteen years. Think about it carefully."

We waited there a long time, hungry and cold.

The Chinese PSB habitually regards itself as being in the right. It represents the Dictatorship of the Proletariat; it is Proledic, it is the law. And its officers have cultivated a correspondingly crude and high-handed way of operating. It never even occurs to them that they might be wrong; in every case, their victims must confess, must bend down and let the PSB step over them. The PSB must come out of everything smelling sweet. They had probably met very few people who actually refused to run and hide, even after having taken a licking from Proledic, or who even had the nerve to argue back. The PSB simply couldn't conceive of admitting that they'd been wrong, that they had acted illegally. It would be altogether too embarrassing. Our society has made these people so brazen, they have become so accustomed to throwing their weight around, that any attempt to defy them just fills them with blind fury. They respond by using all the power at their disposal; they forget the very laws which they above all are bound to observe; they set the whole machinery of Proledic* in motion against their enemies.

I'd always had a low opinion of the PSB and the way it had used Proledic to intimidate people. This time I had finally lost my patience. The way they seized books and made arrests, their barbaric, coarse, thick-skinned, vicious attitude was just too much for me. I wasn't going to bend to them now, just because they were in a fix; I wasn't going to let their anger cow me into submission; I wasn't going to make things easy for them. They'd made the mess, they'd tried to put on a great show, and it had flopped, and now they should be the ones to bow out. Why should I show any mercy to these officers of the law, when they themselves had broken the law? Surely China has suffered enough? Every one of us should be alert, should argue every single point; we must keep up a spirited resistance if illegality like this is ever to be reduced. If we are weak or afraid, and look for personal security, all we are doing is providing further opportunities for this kind of illegal behaviour.

*For a definition of Proledic, see p. 65.

Liu Qing was born c. 1945. He graduated from Nanjing University in 1977, and then worked as a mechanic in a nearby factory. He moved to Peking, and in November 1978, founded, with Xu Wenli, the magazine *April Fifth Forum*, one of the most influential Democracy Movement publications. The next year Liu published the transcript of Wei Jingsheng's trial, and was subsequently arrested (November 1979). He spent several months in the Detention Centre of Peking Prison No. 1, the first five months in solitary confinement. In mid-1980 he was sent to a camp in Shaanxi for three years "re-education through labour". In late 1982, he was reportedly transferred back to Peking, and secretly tried there in August 1982.

His 196-page "Notes from Prison—An Open Letter" (from which the following extracts are taken), describing his arrest and detention, and including many miscellaneous observations on the Democracy Movement and Chinese society and politics in general, was published outside China in late 1981. It is largely for having had this document smuggled out of prison that Liu Qing is reported to have been sentenced to seven years' imprisonment.

A man walked into the room with a yellow padded jacket slung across his shoulders. He was about 40, and looked like some sort of official. He was very worked up and red in the face. "Liu Qing," he shouted at me, "this is an organ of Proledic! It may be easy enough to get in, but you'll find it *very* hard to get out! Don't fool yourself you're anything out of the ordinary. We've got plenty of ways of dealing with small fry like you! You'd better answer our questions, or you can forget about leaving."

I looked him straight in the face. "May I know your name?"

"None of your business!" he screamed.

I told him that since he already knew my name and who I was, then he must tell me who he was. I wasn't going to talk to an "unknown quantity". I also asked him not to shout at me.

He summoned up all his strength. "Do you know what this place is?" he bellowed. "Do you know where you are? This is Proledic! Now, you'd better stop trying to be so clever! Liu Qing, you're nothing special! What's special about you? We know how to deal with you: we have ways. So you claim that Wei Jingsheng is not a counter-revolutionary? You claim he was unjustly treated? You do, do you?"

What could I say? I thought I must have stumbled into Anding Mental Hospital by mistake. I suggested to Mr Wang, who seemed to

be the senior official present, that the state this man had worked himself up into might not be beneficial to the solution of our problem. Mr
Wang did not seem to agree with my point of view. "This is an organ of
Proledic!" he barked. I rested my head on the desk and dozed off. The
room went on reverberating with the shouts of this agitated functionary
for what must have been fifteen minutes. His face turned purple, and
he started foaming at the mouth. Then suddenly in the middle of one
of his tirades, he stopped and rushed out of the room.

At about midnight Yang Jing and the others came in. "Let's go
home now," they said. I made to leave but the officer in the waiting
room blocked my way. My imprisonment had begun.

The Peking Detention Centre

THE COLD SPELL had arrived all right. It was freezing that night. I was
only wearing a sweater and almost froze to death. Two policemen in
overcoats had been detailed to watch over me. The second day I complained that my detention was illegal, tantamount to a kidnapping, and
I went on hunger strike in protest. At noon, a man in his forties came
in. He was accompanied by a young woman in her twenties and the
man with glasses who'd taken notes the night before. The leader of the
group sat across from me and stared, while I curled up on the armchair motionless. After a couple of minutes, he asked me my name
in slow deliberate tones. Then after another pause, he said they had
decided to detain me. I stirred a bit in the chair and asked: "On what
grounds?"

At this point he suddenly leapt to his feet and shouted: "Stand
up! And listen to me while I read the decision reached concerning
your case!" He took out a sheet of paper and read it to me. I asked to
see it. It was newsprint-quality paper, and the text on it was mimeographed in black. My name had been entered in the space after the
words "decision to detain"; the reason given was violation of social
order; the duration of detention, fifteen days. I handed back the paper
without saying a word. He seemed to be waiting for a reaction. I was
racking my brains for every bit of legal knowledge I possessed; I needed
to think it through carefully, to make some deductions. I didn't react
immediately, so he motioned to the other two, "Take him away!"

We got into a very smart sedan; I was between a policeman and Glasses. I said to Glasses: "Give me some paper and a pen. I intend to exercise my rights and charge the PSB with arbitrary persecution." Glasses sat there as motionless as a log.

We arrived in front of the iron gate of the Peking Municipal Detention Centre and the young woman went running busily to and fro for at least twenty minutes before the car was eventually allowed to squeeze its way in. It was like a painful labour. Once inside, we had to wait again for over an hour; the driver got out of the car and went into the building to warm himself by the fire. Finally I was called into the building, given the customary frisking, registered, and casually led by a young policeman to my cell. As he left, I heard him say to the policeman in charge of registration: "We'd better find some bedding here and send it over. They may not accept him in the main building. He's temporary. We'll have to make an exception!"

My "Detention Order"

FROM THE VERY first I had doubted the validity of that so-called detention-order. Now I was sure that the document they had shown me was a fabrication. The Peking PSB had embarked upon this illegality, and now in order to save face, they would have to go through with it to the bitter end. That was why they were trying to intimidate me.

Later, during my long period of solitary confinement, I learned from what the guards said that my first doubts had been completely justified. One of the chief guards in Block 6 verified my suspicions. "I don't know," he said, "if your detention procedures were legal or not." (Of course he knew.) "They processed you at the front gate, so I accepted you. That's the way it is."

One of the younger guards in Block 6 was even more revealing. He said, right in front of all the prisoners in Cell 9: "We don't always do things legally. There are exceptions. When the head of the PSB, or the Mayor of Peking, or a Party secretary, or a standing committee member gives the order for an arrest to be made, we have to lock the person up, even if the proper procedures haven't been followed."

Later I talked to people with more experience in these matters, and what they told me proved beyond doubt that the piece of paper the PSB had shown me was not a real detention-order at all. Formal detention-orders have to be properly printed on bond paper, not mimeographed on newsprint, a cheap process which anybody can imitate. The "order" on cheap paper was apparently a sort of internal document used by the PSB. It had no external validity whatsoever. Even an order printed on regulation bond paper was only valid if it bore the official seal of the judicial body that authorized the detention. The paper shown to me had no such official seal. And the order also had to be signed or initialed by the detainee, whereas my "piece of paper" had had my name on it before it was even shown to me, and I was never even asked to sign. Finally, the detainee is supposed to be given a copy of the detention-order. I was never given one.

The reasons given for my detention ranged from the absurd to the shameless. The regulations and punishments for the maintenance of "social order" have become the most efficient possible blunderbuss for the PSB. As a boy, I had read an illustrated edition of these regulations; so far as I could remember, I had not violated any single item on the list. But memory is fallible. I could not be absolutely sure. So I tried to find out from my interrogators, their minions, and the guards, which rules I had actually violated. They were either embarrassed, and tried to change the subject, or were plainly startled and rendered speechless by my questions.

Solitary Confinement

AT FIRST, I was put in Cell 2, Block 12, Building K. I was on my own, in a room about fifteen metres square. It was at the end of the corridor, and always cold. I had to huddle up in the cotton quilt and curl up in a corner to keep warm. For a time, I had severe pain in my left foot, and every step I took was agony . . . .

Block 2 was the most unusual block in the Detention Centre. The guards used closed-circuit television; or so it was said. I was never able to verify this. All I know is that the guards knew immediately if I touched the windows. There may have been an alarm system. The guards in the duty office could open the doors by pushing an electric buzzer, which made a very loud startling noise. They could also communicate directly with any of the prisoners through an intercom system. If you needed to call a guard, all you had to do was push the buzzer on the cell door. The radiators and lights were recessed into the wall and covered with heavy iron grates. The lights burned twenty-four hours a day, and the brightness could be regulated. Sometimes they were so bright they hurt your eyes; at other times they were so dim you couldn't even read a newspaper.

In Blocks 12 and 2 I was always kept in solitary confinement— nearly five months altogether. While I was in Block 12, a young guard asked me if I was bored and if I would like to have someone in my room to keep me company. Naturally I did not object to the idea, and he said he would talk to his superiors about it. The next time we saw each other, he simply gestured with his hands to indicate that it was hopeless. Solitary confinement is a violation even in the case of legally sentenced criminals. In 1979, the Public Security Minister, Zhao Cangbi, issued a document stating this clearly. This is the least one would expect in a humanitarian society. Solitary confinement seriously impairs physical and mental health. It is a gratuitously inhuman and cruel practice.

For a while I was put in the same cell as a man called Hong Tao. His name was mentioned in court during the trial of the Gang of Four. He was put in solitary confinement for eight years; then he was given three years labour re-education. After his release, and before he'd been home for a week, he was re-arrested and had been imprisoned at the Detention Centre for almost two years. Although it was more than five years since his solitary confinement, he still could not speak clearly. His tongue was stiff, and he found it very tiring to speak at all. The psychological damage done to him was even worse. He told me that when he was in solitary confinement his guards tried to poison him with arsenic. He tried to keep some, to incriminate them after his release. But the most dreadful thing, according to him, was the high-voltage instrument which the prison authorities installed in his cell. This instrument was able to control his thoughts, it could actually lead him in the direction of the evidence needed by the authorities, it could even record his thoughts for use the next day in his interrogation. He said that they were using it all the time to drive him to suicide. When he was not talking about such things, he was quite normal.

His mental state reminded me of an old friend of mine called Guo

Lusheng, who some ten years earlier had been quite popular with young people because of a poem of his called "Faith in the Future." Lusheng had been imprisoned for a long time, and had been totally brainwashed. In the end he became schizophrenic. He was supposed to have been cured, but he was still noticeably abnormal. Several days after Wei Jingsheng was sentenced, Lusheng's schizophrenia flared up again, and he was sent to Anding Hospital. He had been very close to Wei Jingsheng; they had lived together; they had even been to the same primary school.

My own time in solitary confinement was relatively brief, and I was of course not so badly affected. But I didn't come out unscathed. One day I noticed large tufts of matted hair on the cotton blanket I was lying on. I went to look in the small mirror on the door and discovered that my hairline had receded right back to the top of my head. It was very damp in the cell and I'd been crouching in a corner for long periods of time. Perhaps this was why my left foot was so swollen, and ached so much. I was quite short-sighted to begin with; now my eyesight deteriorated rapidly. I began talking to myself; sometimes I carried on feverish debates with an imaginary opponent. And I tried to remember formulae in mathematics, physics, and chemistry. I made deductions and drew diagrams on the wall. Please don't laugh at me— I missed my mother very much. It hurt me deeply to think of the sadness I'd brought her in her old age. In April, looking up through the broken window in the toilet, out at the high perimeter walls and the electrified barbed wire, I saw a small green leaf of devil's ginger pushing its way up through the black soil. Such a dazzling green! I felt a burning desire to be out beneath the blue sky.

Prison Friends

MY PRISON FRIENDS took good care of me. I have never been much good at keeping an even keel in my everyday life. I often neglect the practical things that need to be done, I fail to keep myself neat and tidy. I might forget to do my laundry when my bedding and clothes were dirty, because I spent so much time reading the newspaper or just sitting idly, or debating issues with other people. My cell-mates often helped me give my things a thorough clean. It was very moving to see the enthusiasm with which they set about spreading out my bedding and clothes to wash them, the patience with which they darned the holes in my socks. They even sponged me down a few times. It was such a nice feeling to be clean again and to be wearing clean clothes; it cheered me up, and my mind functioned better as a result.

I appreciated their support most of all when I got into conflict with the guards by refusing to obey the humiliating rules they inflicted on us. I don't know whose idea it was, but suddenly there was this rule that prisoners had to walk with their hands folded near their lower abdomens whenever they were let out for fresh air or to relieve themselves; in some cell blocks they were even made to lower their heads as well. I immediately protested to the authorities that I could not observe this rule. For two reasons: (1) I was not a criminal; I was being illegally detained by the PSB, and the rules of the Detention Centre did not therefore apply to me. (2) Even convicted criminals should not be humiliated by rules such as this. This was clearly stipulated in the relevant laws. All my friends announced a campaign of disobedience in my support. Of course, the guards put such pressure on them that in the end they gave in. But when they saw how I was beaten for my defiance, they were filled with rage. In the condition I was in, the guards did not dare put me back in cell 9 [a communal cell] in Block 6; they returned me instead to my small cell. Every time my old friends in cell 9 passed my cell on their way to the latrine, they always knocked on my door or said a few words to show their concern and to comfort me.

They gave me a nickname: Chicken. I was short-sighted, and once when Yue Zhenping was holding up a picture of two chubby babies, I'd mistaken them for two chickens. So, when they passed by my cell they often shouted out "Chicken!" It was quite a coincidence, because my friends at *Today* [the seminal literary magazine founded during the period of the Democracy Movement by Bei Dao and Mang Ke] had also nicknamed me Chicken. They said I was fond of arguing, I was a "fighting bird".

Other Democrats in Prison

WHEN I WAS put back in the small cell, my entire body was black and blue from the beatings. I was made to wear a gas mask which made breathing very difficult; and the handcuffs cut deeply into the flesh on my back. This time I was not alone in the cell; there were two others. One of them was a man called Wei Rongling, who claimed to have been a deputy section chief in the General Political Section of the PLA, and for a long time had been in charge of protecting Zhang Chunqiao and Jiang Qing. This Wei Rongling had been in Cell 9 with me once before. He'd spent a whole year in the death block (Block 23), and told me all sorts of stories about people who'd been sentenced to death. When he learned who I was, he told me something about Wei Jingsheng. He said that when Wei Jingsheng was convicted, they didn't send him to the camp to serve out his sentence, but kept him in solitary in the death block. Wei Jingsheng had been able to hand him some material he'd written, and asked him to deliver it (if he ever got out) either to me or to my friend Lu Lin. Unfortunately, the material was found by a guard and he (Wei Rongling) was severely punished. I couldn't quite believe his story, because it was already seven or eight months since the Higher Court had finished with Wei Jingsheng's trial. The regulations were that once a criminal was sentenced, he had to be sent to the camp to serve his sentence; how could Wei Jingsheng possibly still be in the Detention Centre? But Proledic is infinitely flexibile. Wei Rongling's story turned out to be true. On July 1, 1980, when I was returning from being let out for fresh air, I came face to face with Wei Jingsheng; he was pale and thin. When he saw me, there was an expression of bewilderment on his face; he was led by two interrogators and walked very close by me.

I also met Zhang Wenhe, the most radical member of the original Human Rights League. In prison, he was still very defiant. He protested incessantly and disputed with the guards, and was given a hard time for it. He had his hands hand-cuffed behind his back for several months at a time; this made it very difficult and painful for him to eat, to go to the toilet, to sleep, to scratch his body (which itched all over), and to change his clothes. He was also made to wear a tank-hat and a gas mask. He was badly beaten many times. They locked him in Cell 1, which was diagonally across from my Cell 9. When we were let out for fresh air, our two cells were unlocked one after the other; we deliberately walked slowly so as to be able to stay together for a little while, to say a few words or to shake hands.

Proledic

I DON'T AGREE with the basic premise of Proledic. I don't approve of the way in which the concepts of revolution and counter-revolution are being used in our society. They only cause harm. They artificially exacerbate social conflict; they take precious human energy, energy which should be being used to create prosperity, and divert it into the "manufacture" of social tragedy. China's low productivity, the poverty, the injustice, the false accusations, and the unfair sentences that have affected the lives of over a hundred million people (if family members are included) have all been undertaken and accomplished in the name of Proledic, in the name of revolution . . . .

When I look back at history, I see long, dark shadows: Yu Luoke, Zhang Zhixin, Ma Mianzhen, Shi Yunfeng . . . . They didn't say or do any more than I have, and yet they were put to death. I have been treated more mercifully. I have only been given three years of labour. It is an irony that pains me. History moves forward. The blood of these heroes will not have been spilled in vain . . . .

When I look into the future, I see our nation carrying the heavy burden of history, and enduring the interference, the traps set for it by powerful cliques; I see the forces of conservatism trying their utmost to drag our nation back. History still needs people like Yu Luoke and Zhang Zhixin. My heart is very heavy. I know that this life-blood propels history forward; but I am dejected, very dejected . . . .

Xu Wenli and Human Rights

Xu Wenli was an active participant in several unofficial democratic publications, including *April Fifth Forum*, and one of the more moderate of the democrats, advocating co-operation with the authorities.

In interviews in 1980, he stressed the need for reform and democracy under the leadership of the Communist Party. He told journalists that he considered himself a Marxist; he also insisted that "democratic socialism" could not be "achieved by police action". Xu denied the insinuation voiced at that time by Vice-Premier Deng Xiaoping, that the Democracy Movement activists were anti-socialist. Xu is also reported to have appealed to the authorities on 10 January 1981 about Liu Qing's detention.

According to Chinese sources, Xu Wenli was taken from his home by the police at midnight on 10 April 1981. The police reportedly confiscated his tape recordings and personal papers.

Xu is reported to have been held in the Detention Centre of Peking Prison No 1 since his arrest. According to various sources, he was tried on 8 June 1982 and sentenced to 15 years' imprisonment plus four years' deprivation of political rights for "organizing a counter-revolutionary group" and for "counter-revolutionary propaganda and agitation".

His account of his own trial and self-defence (from which the following three extracts are taken) and various letters of his written in prison were brought out of China and published in Hong Kong in December 1985.

Human Rights

The question of human rights is a very sensitive one in China at the moment. Deng Xiaoping refused to discuss it when he was in the United States. The situation now has nothing in common with the one under the Gang of Four. However, I prefer to talk of "civil rights", since if you say "human rights" you are regarded as an agent of Carter. Some people say that the main thing now is to work to modernize China, and that there will be time to discuss civil rights after that. For the time being we should not bother about affairs of state. But in that case, how are the people to express their power? Is the aim to turn the Chinese into conveyor-belt workers, like in

Chaplin's Modern Times*? What then is the point of human intelligence? Ever since there has been a more open policy towards the outside world, Chinese intellectuals have been able to go abroad. Many have not come back. That is a very clear sign. A person who cannot think freely feels wounded. Only a minority are allowed to express their views. It is impossible to modernize the country unless you let the intelligence of a thousand million individuals unfold. So the problem of freedom of thought is more serious than that of physical attacks on people, although it is true that such attacks are very widespread in the countryside . . . . Carter is not going to solve this problem. We must rely on the Chinese people to do it themselves.*

Xu Wenli, February 1980

All prisoners of conscience like Wei Jingsheng, Ren Wanding and Liu Qing should be immediately set free. People imprisoned in the past for political offenses should be given retrials. The vague and ambiguous articles of the penal code dealing with counter-revolutionary activities should be amended. The administrative ordinances that permit the PSB to exercise judicial powers should be abolished. The freedoms to speak, assemble, associate, publish, march, demonstrate and strike, which citizens have on paper, should be guaranteed in practice.

The focal point of all reforms should be human liberation, and the respect for human value and human rights. The free development of each individual is the basis for all social progress. Military-style authoritarianism must be replaced by government by moral persuasion; all government must act strictly within the law. Administrative units should no longer have control of dossiers on individuals. Instead, there should be a system of passports, and the state should set up archive bureaus from which individuals can get their identity papers. Employment agencies should be set up, and staff should be engaged on the basis not of central allocation but of job advertisements, exams and proper selection methods, with the signing of short or long-term contracts. Provision should be made for job allocation in case of unemployment. Restrictions on residence permits should be progressively relaxed so as to eventually guarantee freedom of resettlement.

Xu Wenli, Autumn 1980

Trial by Proledic

Xu Wenli

Challenging the Judge

BEFORE THE hearing started, two clerks came to explain the relevant regulations to me once again, though I told them I already knew them.

They had learned a lesson from Wei Jingsheng's case, during which there had been too many people in the court. My case had been limited to a selected audience, yet the big room was still crowded with people. The case was heard in the foyer of the court, which had been decorated especially for the event. It was all very solemn and awe-inspiring: two cameras were set up with magnesium lights and spotlights; there were three big tape recorders lined up and a dozen or so electric fans. There were about fifty people in the audience, mostly petty officials of the court and some others who looked like journalists; admission was by ticket only. I recognized two "routine" interrogators who entered with a young man.

First, Ding, the presiding judge, asked me: "Is there any member of the court whom you wish to challenge?" (He clearly assumed that my answer would be no.)

"Yes!" I replied. Ding was taken aback. Before he could recover his composure I hit him with a question myself. "Your Honour, I would like to ask whether or not you came to talk to me several times before this hearing?"

"Yes, I did," he answered. (I dare say he was wondering what I was up to.)

I didn't give him a second to think and pressed on. "Your Honour, did you or did you not tell me each time we met that it would be in my own best interests to confess my crimes, and that I would be treated leniently if I did so?" Now I was interrogating him.

"I did," he answered, lowering his guard somewhat—perhaps he thought I was trying to play up to him by praising his professional skill in front of all these important people.

I didn't explain the legal basis of this line of questioning straightaway. I knew I had to press on while his defences were down, so I continued clearly and precisely: "So, the person I would like to challenge is you, Your Honour!"

I stared at him. He went pale, his dull gaze moved over to the "puppeteer" sitting in the first row behind me on the right. From now on the "puppet judge's" eyes were fixed nervously in that direction.

Obviously he received some sort of a signal, and declared in a flurry: "Clear the court!"

The audience had been sitting bolt upright in their seats. Suddenly they relaxed and the camera lights went out with a "poof!"—like the air going out of a balloon.

Furious voices rose from the court. "He's making a mockery of the court. Challenging the judge! Who ever heard of such a thing? Who can carry out the interrogation if the judge is forced to withdraw? What utter nonsense! They should throw the book at him and give him a really heavy sentence."

But the more sensible members of the audience must surely have realized that a toady like this judge was incapable of presiding over a proper trial. The Standing Committee of the People's Congress announced long ago that in China a person is considered innocent until tried. If you tell someone that he is guilty, then why bother to try him at all? In my case the judge had convicted me and passed sentence before the trial had even started. The trial was just a sham. And as for my sentence, I stood no chance at all of being justly treated.

Some people may say that I'm stating the obvious. They may think it pointless to go on like this. I disagree. I believe that what I am saying is of some significance. It may be obvious to everyone, but the point is, by speaking out, I can draw people's attention to the fact that a law enforcement officer has no right to break the law. If he does, then he should be exposed. The law can cut both ways. The educated people of the present generation understand the law, and they won't allow themselves to be manipulated any more! Although law enforcement officers may be able to get away with illegal conduct in the short run, this situation will not last long. No one may speak up now, but it will be recorded in the chronicles of Chinese judicial practice for future generations. They will study and consider it, when they come to

rationalize our legal system. My actions today are based on this conviction about their value in the future.

Faking the Evidence

THE HEARING resumed after a ten-minute recess. My request to have
the judge replaced had, of course, been refused. I tried briefly to explain in legal terms why I had made my challenge, but Ding interrupted
me and I had to give up. The audience could ponder the question themselves. I would be content if just a few people gave the matter some
thought. You can't change everyone's way of thinking at once.

The moment the examination commenced, Ding dealt his knock-
out blow. They knew perfectly well that according to the letter of the
law they would have to prove counter-revolutionary motivation before
they could convict me as a counter-revolutionary. Although they sifted
through all of the *prima facie* evidence they had, including the material
recorded by their "electronic earwigs", they still lacked a single piece
of evidence to prove my counter-revolutionary intent. This should
have been enough to call a halt to the proceedings, but they continued,
for reasons best known only to themselves. The procurator seized on a
passage in Xu Shuiliang's article which they had cleverly edited, claiming that I was its author. The argument was flimsy and easily disposed
of, so Ding came up with another trick. He used a "secret weapon" that
hadn't been mentioned till now.

Ding: "Is there any reactionary content in the publications you
edited?"

Xu: "No, definitely not."

Ding: "Did you edit this?" A court assistant showed me a copy of
the second issue of the *Journal of Studies*.

Xu: "Yes, I was editor of the magazine, but this particular issue
was edited by Wang Xizhe, because it was carrying an article by him."

Ding: "Did you read it?"

Xu: "I did. If there is any problem in the contents, I accept my
share of the responsibility."

Ding: "In this article it says that the dictatorship of the proletariat
[Proledic] is a bloody dictatorship. Is that so?"

Xu: "Definitely not. I certainly don't recall that. Could Your

Honour please read the original?"

Ding read the relevant passage out loud.

Xu: "Very well. Could you now read the paragraphs immediately before and after this passage?"

Again Ding read.

Xu: "That should make it clear. What Wang Xizhe is saying is that some comrades have an erroneous idea that since land-owners and capitalists once treated the proletariat in a bloody fashion, the proletariat, after seizing political power, has the right to treat them in an equally bloody fashion. He states that this does not conform with the principles of Marxism and is inhumane. It should be criticized and brought to an end. The article says, moreover, that years of practice have proved that the existence of many so-called 'enemies' is quite illusory. In writing this Wang was upholding Marxism and criticizing the fanatics of the extreme left. Surely this is not the same as saying that Proledic is a bloody dictatorship? I could just as well accuse you of being a counter-revolutionary, and charge you with calling Proledic fascistic, just because at some time or other you have used the words Proledic and fascistic. It is almost six years since the fall of the Gang of Four; how can you still use their methods and trump up charges by quoting out of context?"

Ding was at his wit's end. He quickly changed the subject at a sign from his "puppeteer".

The Sweating Prosecutor

VARIOUS CLUES alerted me to the possibility that the statement I had originally prepared in my defence might be photocopied, so I abandoned it and wrote an entirely new one, making a new draft on rough toilet paper. I put it in my pocket and kept it with me day and night, taking care not to let even my cell-mate notice it (though I told him everything later). This hurried redrafting naturally weakened the structure and strength of my defence considerably, so in court I had to rely to a large extent on the inspiration of the moment and on my own self-confidence. I was still able to conduct my self-defence successfully and to deal with the ensuing cross-examination.

On the other hand, my change of defence threw the prosecutor into complete confusion.

They were aware that I knew about my statement being surreptitiously copied, but they had not reckoned on my being able to write a new one in the short amount of time left to me. There were about thirty papers piled on the prosecutor's desk in readiness for the cross-examination, which began immediately after my statement. It was the prosecutor's task to refute my statement on the basis of the notes he had taken while I had been speaking. But he was in a hopeless muddle. As I had completely reorganized my original defence, he couldn't locate his refutations of the points I had raised, since he had arranged them in the order of my original statement. He became increasingly flustered and frantic, as he sifted through the pile of papers on his desk. He broke out in a muck sweat. Such is the fate of petty thieves.

When it was my turn to speak again I pointed out to the audience, not without a touch of sarcasm, that it seemed odd to me that the prosecutor should have been privy to the contents of my defence and should have made preparations accordingly. I asked pointedly why he had been thrown into such a state of confusion at the last minute?

The prosecutor blushed in embarrassment. He attempted neither to deny my implied accusation, nor to defend himself in any way.

Surveillance

The leader of a production unit is not only in charge of production, he is also responsible for the "thought" and "moral conduct" of the people under him. College students who have not yet been assigned to a work unit have a "political instructor" to keep an eye on their thoughts and prevent them from falling in love. The instructors' assessment at graduation has a decisive effect on the students' job assignment, so these instructors become the objects of much fawning and flattery. Quite a few students volunteer to act as informants, and report on the private lives of others.

This intrusion into and control of private lives has no other function than to eradicate individual personality. Ironically, this practice developed to its extreme during the most "revolutionary" period, that is, from the Anti-Rightist Movement to the Cultural Revolution. Thus, the concept of "revolution", as used in the East, needs a new definition.

Meekness and Apathy

Disorganization of the self easily leads to a weakening of the will. In similar fashion, the rule of law is difficult to achieve in China because the Chinese do not enact appropriate legislation. They are too easily influenced by personal relationships or power. Today in the mainland when "the Party looks after everything for the individual", the disorganization of the self has reached a critical stage. At home, at school, at work, a man cannot organize things for himself. He is forever looked after by an over-protective mother.

Some people think that the present Chinese policy of one child per family will result in a highly individualistic generation. In fact the opposite may happen. Chinese parents tend to encourage dependence in their children, and if they concentrate all their attention and concern on one child, the Chinese may become even more lacking in personal organization in the future. A man must be fully developed before his life can be a dynamic process; only then can he attain self-actualization in body and mind, can he organize and control his life, his work, his future, his thoughts, his con-science, his interpersonal relationships, etc. Only to such a man are human rights important.

The majority of the Chinese are unsure of their own rights. They submit meekly to oppression, and allow others to encroach on their rights. The meekness of the Chinese people makes them particularly receptive to authoritarianism.

Sun Longji, from Deep Structure

To the Execution Ground

Jiang He

Cheating winds muffle windows and eyes.
At this hour, killing is going on.
I cannot hide in the house.
My blood cannot let me remain this way.
Morning-like children cannot let me remain this way.
I am thrown into the prison.
Handcuffs and blood weave into a net upon my body.
My voice is cut off.
My heart is a ball of fire, burning silently upon my lips.
I am walking toward the execution ground, looking with scorn
Upon this historic night. In this corner of the world,
There is no other choice. I have chosen the sky
Because the sky will not rot.
Nothing but execution for me, otherwise darkness has nowhere to hide.
I was born in darkness, in order to create sun rays.
Nothing but execution for me, otherwise lies will be exposed.
I am all the people being milled by ancient rules and laws
Painfully watching
Myself being executed
Watching my blood flow, wave upon wave, till dried out.

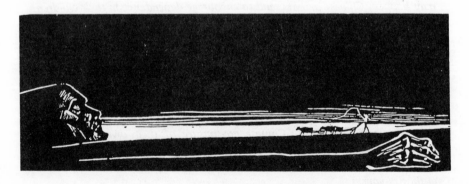

BLACK & WHITE III, Ma Desheng

X: THE SHADOW'S FAREWELL

Forget me and live your own lives—if you don't, the more fools you.

Lu Xun, September 5, 1936

If Lu Xun were still alive

Zhang Yu'an

If he were still alive I don't know
How people would address him.
If he were still alive
What instructions would he give to the young?

Perhaps he would be holding high office,
Or perhaps just one of the rank and file.
In high office he would not forget to be like an ox to a child,
If humble he would not fawn or be servile.

Perhaps he would have been heaped with honours,
Or perhaps he would be just out of jail.
Honoured, he would feel new outcries, new hesitations;
In jail he'd have written new "Permitted Conversations"
                              and "Pseudo-Free Letters."

He might not still wrap his lecture notes in flowered cloth,
But he certainly would not stride arrogantly around.
He might have to go to important meetings,
But not with three bodyguards and two secretaries.

He might ride in a modern car,
But he would not close the curtains to cut off the sights of the roadside.
He would stretch out his hand to every vagrant,
And listen patiently to the complaints of well-read jobless youngsters.

Perhaps he would splash his ink around to praise the "new life"
But perhaps too he would try to cure the ills of the age.
He might be rather happier and more cheerful,
But he might too have felt new unease and wrath.

October 1980

One Autumn Night

Yau Ma Tei

Scene One

Lu Xun's tomb in Hongkou Park, Shanghai.

An autumn evening. The eerie blue sky is dotted with stars twinkling like ghost's eyes.

The park lights glimmer in the dusk, and the leaves scurry along the ground. A bird of ill-omen shrieks as it flies past into the night. At the stroke of midnight the sound of laughter is heard, a muffled cackle, as though reluctant to rouse people from their sleep. But it draws echoes of laughter from all around. Suddenly a ghostly shadow emerges from the tomb, and approaches the statue of Lu Xun.

It is the spectre of Lu Xun. His hair is short but scruffy, the features drawn. He is wearing a long grey scholar's gown and his hand dips (as it always did) into his pocket for a packet of Capstan cigarettes. Removing one, he lights it and exhales a puff of smoke. He gazes up at the bronze statue on its pedestal, and floats out of the park.

The autumn wind continues to chase the fallen leaves....

Scene Two

Morning in the Great Hall of the People in Peking.

A grand meeting is being held to honour the centenary of Lu Xun's birth.

The Spectre enters just as Party Secretary Hu Yaobang begins his speech.

HU YAOBANG: "Comrades and Friends: Lu Xun was a great hero in China's modern revolutionary history, a great fighter on the cultural and ideological fronts . . . (drone, drone)

"If we allow weeds and flowers to grow side by side in China's literary garden, and do not purge poisonous influences,

> *Party Secretary Hu Yaobang celebrated the one hundredth anniversary of Lu Xun's birth with a lengthy speech that unwittingly brings to mind an observation made by Lu Xun himself: "Although bedbugs are unpleasant when they suck your blood, at least they bite you without a word, which is quite straightforward and frank. Mosquitoes are different. Of course, their method of piercing the skin may be considered fairly thoroughgoing; but before biting, they insist on making a long speech which is irritating. If they are expounding all the reasons that make it right for them to feed on human blood, that is even more irritating. I am glad I do not know their language."*
>
> *Today, Chinese intellectuals and writers are not so lucky: they unfortunately know all too well the language of their Great Mosquitoes.*
>
> Simon Leys
> from *The Burning Forest*

chaos will reign in our literature and art . . . . (drone, drone)[1]

"Some writers persist in their erroneous ways [by creating works that reek of bourgeois liberalism] because they lack a correct understanding of our people and the great cause of modernization undertaken by our nation. The situation we are faced with today is a complex one. Some writers have a distorted concept of their relationship with the masses. To use Lu Xun's own words, they have opted out of the people's actual struggle. They dream up a few stories, and turn the revolution to their personal advantage . . . . "

(*The* SPECTRE *smiles wryly.*)

HU YAOBANG: "Then there are people of another type who have an ingrained hatred for new China, socialism and our Party. Such people exist in our new society. As Lu Xun said, even a lion is prey to pests. Some disguise themselves in order to stab others in the back. Lu Xun's words again . . . . "

---

[1]Hu Yaobang took advantage of the celebrations marking the centenary of Lu Xun's birth in 1981 to attack the "bourgeois liberalism" of Chinese writers, in particular the screenwriter Bai Hua. Other figures such as the poet Sun Jingxuan were also condemned at this time (see pp. 120-130 of this book).

(The cadre at the end of the table is holding a copy of Bai Hua's screenplay Unrequited Love—upside down.)

Ma Long

(*The* SPECTRE *of* LU XUN *merely observes the proceedings with a smile.*)

HU YAOBANG: "As Lu Xun so rightly said, no one in ancient or modern times has ever been defeated by mere abuse. It is not abuse that leads to a person's downfall, but the exposure of falsehood and pretence."

SPECTRE (*smoking as he laughs*): "Hah-hah!"

HU YAOBANG: "Comrades, friends, I now call upon the chairman of the All-China Creative Artists' Association and the first deputy chairman of the Committee for the Celebration of the Lu Xun Centenary, Comrade Zhou Yang, to address us . . . . "

(ZHOU YANG *mounts the podium amidst thunderous applause.*)

ZHOU YANG: "Comrades, friends!"

SPECTRE (*with a sneer*): "So it's you, eh, Zhou Qiying.[2] Hah-hah!"

ZHOU: "Lu Xun was an outstanding patriot. He was someone who could come to grips with things foreign and learn from their good points; but he never lost his highly developed sense of national dignity or his consciousness of national destiny . . . . We must carry on Lu Xun's tradition and struggle and inculcate his revolutionary and scientific spirit in ourselves . . . . "

SPECTRE: "Sounds good." (*With this he drifts out of the hall.*)

Scene Three

A room in a Peking hospital.

The white-haired and shrivelled figure of Hu Feng, Lu Xun's old friend and disciple, persecuted for over thirty years, is lying on the bed staring into space.

The Spectre materializes at his bedside.

HU FENG (*muttering to the spirit*): "The founding father of the People's Republic distinguished between true helpers and hangers-on. True helpers he involved in important matters of state, and appointed as ministers; hangers-on were just kept on to write verses of praise and to entertain like modern-day court jesters. If you had lived on, what would you have been? A grandee or a jester? Where would you be now? In prison, or on the execution ground? Death or jail? They even called me a KMT spy! . . . That young writer friend of yours, Xiao Jun, he's old and grey now— he calls himself an archaeological relic . . . . Well as for me, Sir, I'm little more than a living corpse. His sword, Sir, is the insanity of despair; each thrust is a kind of murder! . . . . "

(*The* SPECTRE *leaves the room brooding.*)

HU FENG (*crying*): "Sir, sir . . . . "

(*A nurse rushes in.*)

NURSE: "What are you making all that noise for, you old loony?"

---

[2] Zhou Yang's real name. Zhou was one of Lu Xun's most implacable enemies in his last years. After 1949, Zhou became China's leading cultural bureaucrat, a position which enabled him to reinterpret and thus manipulate the spirit of Lu Xun's works.

Scene Four

The Spectre comes to the Spark Tobacconist's.

He hands over some money and points to a packet of Qianmen cigarettes.

SHOP-ASSISTANT (*takes the money and cries out in surprise*): "What's this old stuff you're trying to palm off on me? Issued by the Communications Bank? You must be joking. (*looking at the* SPECTRE) Listen here old man, this is the New Society. What are you doing in that old-fashioned gown? I know, you must be an enemy agent, a Taiwan spy! Comrades, come here quickly, help me catch this spy . . . . "

(*A crowd of people comes running to her assistance. The* SPECTRE *flees in a panic.*)

Scene Five

The Prairie Fire Café. It's empty.

(*The* SPECTRE *floats in and sits down at a table.*)

WAITRESS A: "So I said to him, if he wanted to get married, then it'd be all right with me, but that I'd be expecting a 28-inch colour TV, a stereo, a sewing machine, a refrigerator, washing machine, eight thousand *yuan* in foreign currency, a house, and RMB¥38,000 . . . . "

WAITRESS B: "If you ask me I'd say you were letting him off lightly. I'd ask for at least . . . . "

(*The* SPECTRE *tries to catch the attention of one of the waitresses with a smile and beckons to her with his hand.*)

WAITRESS B (*taken aback*): "Where did he pop up from? Just sitting over there, looks like a right old fogey . . . . You go and ask him what he thinks he's playing at."

(WAITRESS A *saunters over with a cold expression on her face.*)

WAITRESS A: "All right you old dog, what do you want?"

SPECTRE: "A catty of Shaoxing wine . . . and some food: ten pieces of fried bean curd; and make sure you put lots of chilli on it."

WAITRESS A: "We're closed, and anyway we don't sell Shaoxing wine or bean curd. Just noodles."

SPECTRE: "Very well, give me a bowl of noodles then."

WAITRESS A: "A bowl is it? Got any ration coupons?"

SPECTRE: "Sorry? Any what?"

WAITRESS A: "You are Chinese aren't you? C-O-U-P-O-N-S!"

SPECTRE: "What's that?"

WAITRESS A: "Good heavens, old man, what hole did you crawl out of? You trying to give me a hard time here, or what? (*To* WAITRESS B) Call up the PSB and tell 'em we've got an old pervert on our hands. (*Taking a closer look*) Hold on, he's wearing one of those old gowns.... (*To the* SPECTRE) You look just like someone in that play about the old society, 'Teahouse'. Uh-huh, I get it: you're a throw-back. Bet you must be an old landlord or some sort of baddy."

SPECTRE: "I don't understand a word you're saying."

WAITRESS A (*to* WAITRESS B): "Hurry up with that call."

WAITRESS B (*grabbing the phone*): "Hello, is that the Public Security Bureau? This is the Prairie Fire Café in Xidan. We've got a very suspicious character here."

SPECTRE (*to himself*): "This is my wish, friend—To journey alone to a distant world of darkness, without you, without all shadows. I will be there alone, sunk in the darkness. That world will be all mine."[3]

Scene Six

At the entrance to Lu Xun's childhood home in Shaoxing.
The Spectre of Lu Xun floats into view.
An old woman in rags appears out of an alleyway. In one hand she has a bamboo basket containing a chipped, empty bowl; in the other, a bamboo pole, taller than herself and split at the bottom.[4]

OLD WOMAN: "So you've come back?"

SPECTRE: "Yes."

[3] This is a quotation from Lu Xun's prose-poem "The Shadow's Farewell", from the collection *Wild Grass* (1926). For a full translation, see below, pp. 322-3.

[4] The old woman is Xianglin's Wife, the main character in Lu Xun's short story "The New-Year Sacrifice", written in 1924.

WOMAN: "That's good. You're a scholar. You've travelled and seen the world. There's something I want to ask you—(*She draws two paces closer and lowers her voice.*) Do dead people become ghosts or not?"

SPECTRE: "Quite possibly, I'd say."

WOMAN: "Then there must be a hell too?"

SPECTRE: "What, hell? Hell? Logically speaking, yes—but not necessarily . . . . Who cares anyway? . . . "

WOMAN: "Then will all the members of a family meet again after death?"

SPECTRE: "Well, I'm not really sure . . . . In fact . . . . "

WOMAN (*shakes her head in disappointment*): "A lot of help you are, comrade."

(*The* SPECTRE *gazes at the receding figure of the old woman as she staggers off.*)

Scene Seven

One autumn night in Hongkou Park in Shanghai. The wind chases the fallen leaves.

The Spectre of Lu Xun drifts back to his tomb.

SPECTRE (*stares at the bronze statue of himself for a while, shakes his head and recites one of his poems*):

> "There's nothing you can do about a hostile fate:
> You bump your head before you even turn.
> When in the street I pull my old hat down;
> My leaky wine-boat drifts along the torrent.
> Coolly I face a thousand pointing fingers,
> Then bow to be an infant's willing ox.
> Hiding in our little house, sufficient to ourselves,
> I care not what the season is outside."[5]

With this chant the Spectre vanishes back into the tomb.

The autumn wind continues to howl, and a light, misty rain dances in the chill air . . . .

from Playhouse

[5] This poem is entitled "Self-Mockery". See *Lu Xun Selected Poems*, translated by W.J.F. Jenner, p. 57.

The Shadow's Farewell

Lu Xun

IF A MAN should sleep to a time when time is no more, then his shadow may come and bid him farewell, saying:

There is something about Heaven that displeases me; I do not wish to go there. There is something about Hell that displeases me; I do not wish to go there. And there is something about your future Golden Age that displeases me too; I do not wish to go there either.

What displeases me is you.

Friend, I do not wish to go with you. I will not stay.

I will not.

Alas! Alas! Let me drift in the land of nothingness.

I am but a shadow. I wish to bid you farewell and sink into darkness. The darkness may engulf me; or I may dissolve in the light.

I do not wish to drift in the twilight, between light and darkness. I would rather sink into the darkness.

And yet I drift in the twilight, between light and shadow. I do not know if this is dusk or dawn. I raise a grey hand in pretence of a salutation. I will journey alone, to a distant place, at a time when time is no more.

Alas! Alas! If this is the twilight, then black night will engulf me; if not, if this is the dawn, then I will dissolve in the light of day.

My friend, the time draws near.

I shall move into the darkness, I shall drift in the land of nothingness.

You would still have a gift from me. What is there I can give? If there must be a bequest, then let it be darkness and void. I would rather give you darkness; or dissolve in the light of your day.

Best of all things I would give you the void, and occupy no space whatsoever in your heart.

This is my wish, friend—

To journey alone to a distant world of darkness, without you, without all shadows. I will be there alone, sunk in the darkness. That world will be all mine.

September 24, 1924

Huang Xinbo

MORE STONES, MORE SEEDS

Introduction

The events of late-1986 and 1987—the student demonstrations in major Chinese cities and the devastating campaign against Bourgelib, or "bourgeois liberalization", that followed in their wake—confirmed the premises of this book. Many of the writers and artists represented here came under attack and in many cases were unable to publish at all during 1987. Ironically, the purge has only served to disseminate more effectively the spirit of the Democracy Movement of the late 1970s. It has allowed us to hear more voices of conscience.

The four new sections that follow reaffirm the themes of the first edition of *Seeds of Fire*. They reflect the events of 1987, and give some indication of the importance of those events in contemporary Chinese history and their connection to the underlying problems, or the deep structure, of Chinese society.

The first section, "Dissent", contains the interview conducted by the *Der Spiegel* correspondent Tiziano Terzani with the astrophysicist Fang Lizhi in June 1987. In this interview Fang declared that he was continuing where the jailed democracy activist Wei Jingsheng left off, making himself the first establishment intellectual openly to defy the government after being purged. He reiterated Wei's call for "The Fifth Modernization", democracy.

"Bourgelib" takes as its theme the latest of Mainland China's political campaigns, the "struggle against bourgeois liberalization". This is a process that Chinese leaders have declared will continue well into the next century. Its aim is to attack and denounce intellectuals, writers and artists who defy the leadership of the Party by indulging in any form of solipsism, or the culture of the self. Selections are given of speeches and writings of establishment Mainland writers purged during 1987. To these are added comments by Bo Yang whose speech "The Ugly Chinaman" was also denounced, and by the Hong Kong satirist Hah Gong.

In the section entitled "Pressure Points", artists, writers and a Chinese pop star speak on the difficulty of creating a world of their own in the prison culture of China. There are occasional advances, defeats and further advances, all of which depend on the force the State applies to the pressure points (the metaphor is taken from acupuncture) of the individual artist.

"Böd", the final section, reflects some of the impact that the changes in Han China have had on the unique and powerful culture of Tibet. As a victim of the erratic developments within China, Tibetan culture and life has gone from being an object for attack and "reconstruction" to become on the one hand an exotic oddity exploited for tourist dollars, and on the other a victim of Han cultural vandalism. At the same time, for many of China's younger writers and artists Tibet is also a powerful symbol which they use to adorn their own quest for the self.

XI: DISSENT

In overcoming ignorance we must exert our utmost efforts to seek out knowledge. We have no time to ask whether this knowledge is Chinese or Western, whether it is new or old.

Yan Fu, 1902

I think we scientists must be able to admit the facts of science. To make progress we must have the courage to admit failures. In terms of the socialist system, what we have done in the past thirty years has, I think, been a failure.

Fang Lizhi, 1986

Technology can be imported. But bourgeois thinking, theories and ideology are to be kept out; they're polluting . . . In my opinion, we should import all these things as well . . . To introduce their [i.e. Western] technology but reject their ideology is like importing the hardware without the software. It's an empty gesture.

Wang Ruowang, 1986

The astrophysicist Fang Lizhi was born in Hangzhou in 1936,
graduating in physics from Peking University twenty years later. Like
countless other intellectuals of his generation he was denounced for his
outspoken criticisms of Party rule in 1957. Following the Cultural
Revolution he was appointed Vice-President of the Chinese University
of Science and Technology in Anhui, one of the most prestigious new
seats of learning. Fang became an increasingly controversial figure on
China's university campuses during 1985-6 when, refusing to restrict
himself to his area of specialization, he began giving public lectures in
which he called on intellectuals to agitate for democracy and freedom.

Fang named and criticized certain government leaders in his
speeches, but it was not until students in cities throughout the country
took to the streets to demonstrate in favour of the Party's policies of
reform and democratization in late 1986 that the leadership decided to
take action against him. Fang was accused of rabble-rousing and
encouraging an intellectual atmosphere which fostered political instabil-
ity. He was expelled from the Communist Party, sacked from his job in
Anhui and removed to Peking as a research scientist.

Fang's call for democracy harks back to the spirit of Wei Jingsheng
(see pp. 277-89). But as Fang is an internationally recognized scientist
and also highly regarded in China, the government has been wary of
taking further punitive action against him. The outspokenness of a man
like Fang, an establishment intellectual who has benefited directly from
the "Open Door Policy", has surprised some foreign observers.

Within days of its publication in West Germany, the following
interview was translated into Chinese and read by Politburo leaders.
Yet no action was taken, in part, it would seem, because the
government is confident that they have succeeded in silencing Fang
within China itself.

Ninety years ago, Yan Fu, the late Qing Dynasty translator and
thinker, pointed out to the reformists of his day: "The faith cannot be
preserved, and if one asserts that we should advance even while
preserving the faith, it is not the original faith which is being
preserved."* Fang has told the reformist patriarchs of today very much
the same thing; but whereas Yan Fu's critique was aimed at Confucianism, Fang's target is Marxism, the moribund faith of today.

*From a letter to Liang Qichao written in 1897. Quoted in Benjamin Schwartz, *In Search
of Wealth and Power: Yen Fu and the West*, Cambridge: Belknap Press, 1964, p. 48.

Fang Lizhi:

An Interview with Tiziano Terzani

By special permission of acting Party chief Zhao Ziyang, Fang Lizhi left China in late April 1987 in order to take part in a symposium on physics in Trieste, Italy. Tiziano Terzani, who had known Fang from the days when he was a Peking correspondent, met with him in Florence, where Fang wished to see Galileo's house. This interview took place during his three-day stay in Terzani's house in the countryside.

Professor Fang, among Chinese students you are a hero. The international press has hailed you as China's Sakharov. Deng Xiaoping, on the other hand, calls you a "bad element". China's Communist Party maintains you are a victim of the disease called "bourgeois liberalization". What are you really?

A little bit of all of these. But in the first place I am an astrophysicist. The natural sciences are my religion. Einstein once said something of the sort. Previously I did not understand him. Now I know: we scientists have a belief and an aim, we have an obligation towards society. If we discover a truth and society does not accept it, this weighs on us. This is what happened to Galileo. That is when, as scientists, we have to intervene. With this mission I step into society.

What kind of a mission do you have in China?

Democratization. Without democracy there can be no development. Unless individual human rights are recognized there can be no true democracy. In China the very ABC of democracy is unknown. We have to educate ourselves for democracy. We have to understand that democracy isn't something that our leaders can hand down to us. A democracy that comes from above is no democracy, it is nothing but a relaxation of control. The fight will be intense. But it cannot be avoided.

First you have attacked local Party cadres, then the Municipal Party Committee of Peking. Recently you attacked the Politburo. What is your next target?

Next I will criticize Marxism itself.

You go very far.

It is an undeniable truth that Marxism is no longer of much use. As a scientist I can prove it. Most answers given by Marxism with regard to the natural sciences are obsolete, some are even downright wrong. That is a fact. What Marxism has to say about the natural sciences stems from Engels' book *Natural Dialectics*. On nearly every page of this book one can find something that is either outdated or completely incorrect.

For example?

In the 1960s, with the aid of Marxism, the USSR and China repeatedly criticized the results of modern natural sciences. In biology they criticized genetics, in physics they criticized the theory of relativity and extended their criticism from cosmology to the development of the computer. Not even once has their criticism been proved correct. Therefore, how can one say today that Marxism should lead the natural sciences? It's a fallacy.

Have you ever believed in Marxism?

I certainly have! Immediately after Liberation [1949] and in the 1950s I firmly believed in Marxism. In 1955, when I joined the Party, I was convinced that Marxism would lead the way in every field and that the Communist Party was thoroughly good.

When, in 1958, during the Anti-Rightist Campaign, I was expelled from the Party, I made a very sincere self-criticism. I was convinced that I had wronged the Party. Now the Party has expelled me a second time, but this time I know that I was not in the wrong. Therefore I have refused to make a self-criticism.

Deng stated in 1979 that, in conformity with the Chinese Constitution, every citizen should be guided by the Four Basic Principles: the socialist road, the people's democratic dictatorship, leadership of the Party, and Marxism-Leninism and Mao Zedong Thought.

Marxism is a thing of the past. It helps us to understand the problems of the last century, not those of today. The same is true in the case of

> *I have read Fang Lizhi's speeches. He doesn't sound like a
> Communist Party member at all. Why do we keep people like him in the
> Party? He should be expelled, not just told to quit.*
>
> Deng Xiaoping, December 30, 1986

physics. Newton developed his theory 300 years ago. It is still valuable,
but it does not help to solve today's problems, such as those related to
computer technology. Marxism belongs to a precise epoch of
civilization and that era is over. It is like old clothing that must be put
aside.

*Hearing you talk, one must admit: this time the Party was right to
expel you. Would you like to found a new political party yourself?*

I've asked myself this question. But under the present circumstances it
would be impossible. Perhaps in 30 years time. Perhaps by then we
shall be in the position in which Taiwan finds itself today, with more
than one party.

*Aren't the Four Basic Principles a sort of strait jacket that prevents
China from developing into a democracy?*

Yes, if the principles remain rigid. But the leadership itself said that
Marxism should develop. I read this sentence in the *People's Daily*.
We can hold onto the principles provided they can evolve.

*But how can fundamental reforms be achieved within the present
power structure?*

One could keep the form, but change its content. The Protestants
broke from the Catholic Church during the Reformation, but they
went on using the same Bible. In China we could do the same: outside
the butcher's shop dangle a sheep's head, but inside sell dog's meat.

*You consider a communist system to be reformable—but until now
this has never been achieved.*

It is difficult, but if any country stands a chance, that country is China.

A better chance than the Soviet Union under Gorbachev?

Of course. We find ourselves in a much better position—for a simple reason: in the Soviet Union the Communist Party has achieved a few successes, for example, in terms of military defense and the sciences. Their intellectuals enjoy much more freedom than we have ever had. In China, on the contrary, the Communist Party cannot boast a single success. It has achieved nothing of value during the past 30 years. That's why leaders at all levels are worried. That's why even among the highest cadres there are some who admit that nothing of value has been achieved. This couldn't be said as easily in the Soviet Union.

Is there really not a single success that China can boast of?

It depends what you mean by success. Sure, in ping-pong and volleyball we have been successful, but not in any other field. That is why the need for reform is being felt so acutely at all levels of society. Belief in the Party has vanished in our country, particularly among the young.

I have an older friend who is also a physicist. He has been a member of the Communist Party since before Liberation, when he fought in the underground. In 1958 he was labelled a right-wing deviationist, but never complained about it. Only recently has he publicly stated: "I have believed in the Party firmly all my life. Today I realize that this faith was only a dream." Many intellectuals think as he does.

You seem to consider it a matter of course that the intellectuals should be the vanguard of society. Isn't that the old Platonic idea of philosophers becoming kings?

Intellectuals are no kings, but they are the main force pushing society ahead. They should be independent and free. Intellectuals ought to have a big role to play.

Up to now it has been the Party that has decided on the role of the intellectuals. During the Cultural Revolution they were forced down to the lowest, "stinking ninth" position of the "nine bad categories" of people. Today, under Deng Xiaoping, they have climbed up again to the third position, after peasants and workers. But they are still not independent.

Quite right. Mao described the dependency of the intellectuals with the saying: "The hair clings firmly to the skin". The situation remains unchanged. Intellectuals continue to be looked upon as tools. Now is the time for them to show their strength. No one should be intimidated. That is democracy. If we fail to achieve this, China can hardly expect to become a truly developed, modern country.

In 1978 something similar was said when the worker Wei Jingsheng wrote on a wall in Peking, which later became known as Democracy Wall: "Without democracy, there will be no modernization!" He got 15 years in prison for it. You, Professor Fang, are still free. Is it because you are a well-known scientist, whereas Wei Jingsheng was nothing but an electrician?

Of course. That's how things are in China. A worker who says something objectionable can easily be removed. Workers' unrest does not worry the government; workers are easily dealt with. Right now there are quite a few [workers'] disturbances, but the public is not aware of them. One knows nothing of them overseas, for these people have no international contacts.

Are things different in the case of the intellectuals?

Whenever it is students who demonstrate, the government is more concerned. It does not dare to take action as easily against students. That is why I maintain that the power of the intellectuals is relatively great. That is why I keep telling my students: he who has knowledge also has influence, and cannot be disregarded by the government. I advise my students not to say too much at first, but to study diligently. Those, however, who have successfully completed their studies must speak out. Wei Jingsheng spoke out ten years ago. Today I speak like he did. In another ten years perhaps other scholars may also speak up. People should be allowed to criticize their leaders without fear. This is a sign of democracy. Should I have refrained from criticizing Hu Qiaomu just because he is a member of the Politburo? It's the people up there who have themselves said that Mao was a human being, not a god.

What about Hu Qiaomu?

In 1986 I wrote an article on quantum cosmology. Hu Qiaomu criticized it and branded me a "subjective ideologue". He attacked my thesis that the universe is finite, on the basis of Marxism, for Engels once wrote in the draft of a book that the universe surely was infinite. While I welcome well-founded criticism, what does Hu Qiaomu know about cosmology? He knows nothing. I would be more than glad to discuss it with him if he did. Otherwise it is meaningless. Unfortunately, he is not in a position to say anything whatsoever.

What about human rights in China?

It is a dangerous topic. The question of human rights is taboo in China. Things are far worse than in the Soviet Union. Wei Jingsheng is a famous case, but there are thousands of others whose names are not even known. At least in the Soviet Union there are name lists. Not so in China.

Is democracy really a necessary condition for the development of a country? States like Taiwan, South Korea, Singapore and the Crown Colony of Hong Kong have made enormous economic progress without being true democracies.

First of all, in the countries you have named there is far more democracy than in China. Secondly, those countries are under American protection, and the USA wants their economies to develop. Things are different in the case of China. Moreover, it is particularly difficult to separate economic from political democracy in China.

Deng holds a different view. He has told the Chinese: "Get rich; to be rich is glorious. The Party will take care of the rest."

In China the Party wants not only to manage politics. It wants to control everything, including people's lifestyles and thinking. Today, factories are being run by managers, but the real power still lies in the hands of Party cadres. Peasants enjoy a free market system, but the cadres tell them: You still need our rubber stamp and for that you still have to buy us! And here lies the root of the new corruption. In order to create a true economic democracy in China, one ought to abolish political controls. And that is exactly what the Party fears most.

Hasn't Deng Xiaoping with his economic reforms opened a Pandora's box? Doesn't he equally want democracy?

No. In the short term Deng's reforms are intended to stabilize the system. What he wants to do is avert a total collapse of the system. The Party is in a quandary: if it introduces reforms then it has to reduce its own power; if it fails to reform then its power will be undermined even faster.

Deng Xiaoping is the hero of the West. In 1985 Time magazine elected him Man of the Year. The West views him as an ally on the international stage.

It would appear that the West has a very superficial understanding of China.

Doesn't Deng have a comprehensive, even if not explicit, plan for China?

No. Deng has no such plan. We Chinese find ourselves standing in front of a massive river, and we are trying to cross it, like blind people, by feeling our way over the stones. We do not know the river and constantly risk ending up back where we started.

Could Deng ever rescind his reforms?

I doubt it. The economy would collapse and the Party would disintegrate. In 1963, millions of people died in China because of economic mistakes. Mao's prestige was the only thing that kept the country together. Today, no one leader has comparable prestige.

But haven't a lot of Deng's reforms been successful?

Many people, in particular people overseas, believe so. There have been some successes in agricultural production, but in the cities, in industry, reforms have not really started yet. The reform of the wages and price structure has been unsuccessful.

You cannot deny, however, that people in China are better off today.

They have more TV sets and refrigerators. The reforms produce more money which is being put into consumer goods.

Isn't that progress?

Certainly, but the progress of a society should be comprehensive. The

Fang Lizhi's Expulsion

On January 17 [1987], the Disciplinary Inspection Committee of the Anhui Branch of the Communist Party of China came to the decision that Fang Lizhi should be stripped of his Party membership.

Fang Lizhi was formerly the Vice-President of the Chinese University of Science and Technology. On January 12 he was dismissed from his post. In their report, "Regarding the Decision to Expel Fang Lizhi from the Party", the Disciplinary Inspection Committee pointed out that in recent years Fang Lizhi has on various occasions publically encouraged Bourgelib [see the following chapter], opposed the Four Basic Principles, defied the leadership of the Party, denied the socialist system, caused dissension between intellectuals and the Party, and incited student demonstrations, resulting in serious disturbances.

People's Daily, January 20, 1987

With regard to Fang Lizhi's errors of word and deed, the relevant Party organizations have subjected him to severe criticism many times, but he has always merely feigned compliance, admitting to some mistakes on one hand and on the other continuing in his bad old ways, becoming in fact even more unbridled in his attacks on the four Basic Principles and in his advocacy of Bourgelib. He has thrown Party discipline to the winds. Not to eliminate from the Party someone who has been so outspoken in his opposition is something that neither the Party nor the people can tolerate. Fang Lizhi is a middle-aged intellectual who has been nurtured by the Party. The Party had high expectations of him and had, moreover, entrusted him with an important post. He has disappointed the Party and disappointed his people, however, by falling into the muddy ditch of error, from which he is incapable of extricating himself. Now, although he has been dismissed from his post and expelled from the Party, the Party and government have arranged a position in scientific research for him, thus allowing him to bring his specialised vocational skills into play. If his actions indicate he has made a genuine change for the better, he will be welcomed back by the Party and the people.

Even though people like Fang are only a tiny minority within the Party, their negative example reminds us of the importance and urgent necessity of educating Party members at large to abide by the Party Regulations, and to implement Party discipline, particularly within the new historical conditions created by the policies of Reform and the Open Door to the outside world.

People's Daily, January 21, 1987.

economy is an important indicator, but it is not the only one. The Arab states are very affluent, but they remain socially underdeveloped. I believe that education and cultural standards are important facets of a developed society. Eating and drinking are very important, to be sure, especially in a poor country like China. But it is equally important for a human being to be able to realize that he is a human being.

You do not agree, then, with the present target that by the year 2000 every Chinese should have an annual income of US$800?

To be rich is, of course, better than being poor, but it is not a be-all and end-all.

Today China is importing western technology in order to push forward its own modernization. Do you think this is right?

Certainly. But it is not enough just to import things in a piecemeal fashion, to buy a few big computers. In order to become truly modernized, we have to import the spirit of western civilization into China. Chinese civilization has achieved many profound insights, but it ignores logic. For the sake of our development, we must adopt the western spirit.

The Party has accused you of being polluted by western ideas, and of advocating the wholesale westernization of China. Is this true?

We must open our country in all directions, then many positive things will come in, while our own values will not be lost. I have never said that we should repudiate those Chinese traditions which are good. However, the feudal relationships of Chinese society are bad and must be done away with. True, western morality is different from ours, but that doesn't mean it is worse.

By inviting the Communists to reform the system, aren't you asking the Party to commit political suicide?

One cannot ask the Party to relinquish its power. The Communists must hold onto their totem [*sic*]. Therefore one must consider whether there isn't some way around it. Couldn't it be that one day the totem will vanish all by itself?

If it does, China will be without an alternative power structure.

Wouldn't there be the danger of the country falling into chaos, of warlords taking over the country?

That danger always exists in China.

What is going to happen after Deng Xiaoping dies?

In the short run we might be worse off; in the long run, better. It's possible that after Deng's death Mao Zedong Thought will no longer be considered valid and then we will finally be able to make a radical reassessment of the past thirty years. That is probably just what General Secretary Hu Yaobang, who was demoted in January, planned to do. He once said that not one portrait of Mao should be left hanging in China. The last one hangs on the Tiananmen Gate, but Mao's Thought continues to dominate us.

Could the army play an important role in the future?

In our society, the army does play an important role. But it is no monolith. People at different levels hold different views. I, for one, have received numerous letters of support from members of the army.

How many have you received in all?

Thousands. Often simply open postcards with the name and address of the sender — a brave deed in China. On one it even said: "If this postcard does not reach its destination, then there is no democracy in China". When, on the day of my departure, I passed through customs, the policemen on duty in the booths stopped working and came over to talk to me. "Are you Fang Lizhi? Are you all right now? Are you allowed to travel overseas? That's good!"

Are you sure that after you return to China you will not be arrested or exiled to some far away place?

I'm prepared for that possibility.

You could emigrate . . . .

I have seriously considered it in the past. Now it is impossible. Should I leave now, I would be abandoning my students and friends in China.

I have been denounced by high-level cadres, yet I haven't emigrated, whereas the children of high-level cadres go abroad to study although they've never been criticized . . . .

What's happened to the students who took part in the demonstrations?

As far as I know, no students from the well-known universities have been arrested. However, we do know that all of them have been photographed and had their names registered [by the police]. Later, they will make them "wear small shoes",* as we say in China.

The campaign against "bourgeois liberalization" continues . . . .

That campaign has shown us just how strong the resistance to the reforms is. It has shown us that we badly underestimated the strength of our opponents. We have been too optimistic. On the other hand, the campaign has convinced more and more people of the necessity of reform. We do not want a revolution, which would in the first place be

*To make someone "wear small shoes" means to persecute them by making life as uncomfortable as possible.

FANG LIZHI

Tiziano Terzani

very difficult to achieve, and secondly would not necessarily be a good thing. Therefore, the only way left for China is reform. Democracy, education and intellectual freedom are the absolute and indispensible prerequisites of this reform. Without these last—be it with or without democracy—China has no future.

Professor Fang, we thank you for this interview.

When Fish Start to Talk

Paris taxi drivers are notoriously sophisticated in their use of invective. *"Hé, va donc, structuraliste!"* is one of their recent apostrophes—which makes one wonder when they will start calling their victims "China Experts"!

Perhaps we should not be too harsh on these experts: the fraternity recently suffered a traumatic experience and is still in a state of shock. Should fish suddenly start to talk, I suppose ichthyology would also have to undergo a dramatic revision of its basic approach. A certain type of "instant sinology" was indeed based on the assumption that the Chinese were as different from us in their fundamental aspirations, and as unable to communicate with us, as the inhabitants of the oceanic depths; and when they eventually rose to the surface and began to cry out sufficiently loudly and clearly for their message to get through to the general public, there was much consternation among the China pundits.

Simon Leys, "The China Experts," The Burning Forest

XII: BOURGELIB

Our sages have always profoundly feared the word freedom.
Yan Fu, 1895

Why should freedom be such a terrifying thing, even today?
Liu Binyan, November 1986

We cannot do without dictatorship.
Deng Xiaoping, December 1986

Some cultures have no history. They may be the happier ones, but it is hard to tell, since we usually forget to ask before destroying them. Some cultures have a linear history, like ours, for instance. We forge ahead with gusto and dynamism, we move forward faster and faster; only we are not too sure where exactly we are heading. Let us hope it is not into a brick wall or a black hole. Some, like the Chinese, appear to have a cyclical history. This simplifies the task for the historians. Yet if these idle bystanders enjoy watching the merry-go-round, it can in the long run produce some dizziness among its hapless passengers . . .

The outline of the story is rather simple: the old Leader (whom foreigners generally consider to be a Humanist, a Poet, a Progressive, a Liberal, etc.) wants to get rid of the very man he had previously picked as his heir-designate. To provoke the downfall of his most trusted acolyte, he engineers civil disturbances by manipulating the widespread and permanent discontent of idealistic youths. These young people finally realize that they are being used, but when they attempt to take a stand on their own, it is already too late, and they are crushed. Order is being re-established by "killing one chicken in order to scare all the monkeys." The chicken is found in the cultural circles, since writers and artists are always expendable (you only need to keep a few domesticated specimens for the purpose of Cultural Exchanges and International Congresses; as for the rest, with communism on tap in every household, who needs culture anyway?). While prominent intellectuals are duly gagged and ritually humiliated in the big cities, the merriment takes a more casual style in remote provincial corners that are conveniently sheltered from outsiders' eyes. There, local officials eager to show their zeal, send a few cartloads of their own private enemies to the execution grounds.

Such is the basic plot. It needs only to be told once: erase all the individual names, fill in the blanks with new names, and every ten years or so the old story will be ready for recycling.

Simon Leys, "China's New Math", The New Republic, March 2, 1987

1979-1987
A Chronicle of Purges

1979

March   Having initially supported the Democracy Wall in late 1978, Deng Xiaoping warns in a speech to old cadres that some of the ideas expressed in posters on the Wall are excessive and that there are "bad elements" among the authors. Deng elaborates his four Basic Principles and denounces "liberalization".

      Wei Jingsheng publishes his famous attack on Deng, "Do we want democracy or a new dictatorship?". He is subsequently arrested and new regulations restricting the rights of citizens are promulgated by the Peking Municipal government. The purge of democracy activists begins, bringing an end to the Peking Spring.

June   The Four Basic Principles are written into the Chinese Constitution by the National People's Congress.

November   Liu Qing is detained by the Peking police.

December   Trial and sentencing of Wei Jingsheng.

1980

January   Hu Yaobang starts a campaign against freedom of expression in literature.

      Deng emphasizes that for the realization of the Four Modernizations an atmosphere of "unity and stability" is required.

1981

February   The *People's Daily* attacks those calling for democracy and freedom, calling them political dissidents and supporters of the Gang of Four.

April   Starting in this month a nation-wide operation to arrest and jail democratic activists begins; Xu Wenli and Wang Xizhe are among the victims.

THE FOUR BASIC PRINCIPLES

Party Central is of the opinion that for China to achieve the Four Modernizations it is imperative to adhere to the Four Basic Principles in the realm of ideology. These principles are:

1. *Adherence to the socialist road;*
2. *Adherence to the dictatorship of the proletariat;*
3. *Adherence to the leadership of the Communist Party; and,*
4. *Adherence to Marxism-Leninism and Mao Zedong Thought.*

As you all know, none of these principles are new; our Party has been resolutely adhering to them all along.

Deng Xiaoping

What then are the Four Basic Principles? The very idea is ludicrous, they are like manacles and irons on the arms and legs of every Chinese.

What is "the socialist road"? Although Comrade Marx couldn't define it we're expected to believe that those comrades who've locked themselves away in Zhongnanhai divorced from the people—men who spend their time dreaming of quadrupling per capita income by the turn of the century—know what it's all about.

What is "the people's democratic dictatorship" (also known as "the dictatorship of the proletariat")? It's all about a country having been turned into a police state by the PLA, the Ministry of Public Security, the militia and a network of spies.

What is "the leadership of the Communist Party"? It's all about a pack of Party cadres, illiterates or semi-illiterates, people decried for having "no better than a primary school education", leading the people like a blind man on a blind horse racing towards an abyss.

What is "adhering to Marxism-Leninism and Mao Zedong Thought"? It's the situation you're faced with when the nation has been impoverished in the name of a pack of blue-eyed red-bearded foreign devils like Marx, Engels, Lenin and Stalin—men whose portraits have been put up in Tiananmen Square as though they were the ancestors of the Chinese people.

Hah Gong

August   A campaign against the writer Bai Hua and Bourgelib is officially begun at the behest of Deng Xiaoping and
Hu Yaobang, continuing well into 1982. Among the
writers attacked are Dai Houying, Sun Jingxuan and Yu
Luojin.

1983

October   Deng calls for the elimination of Spiritual Pollution.
The largest political campaign since the Cultural Revolution is carried out. Among the writers singled out for
attack are Bei Dao, Gu Cheng, Wang Ruoshui, Xu Jingya
and Yang Lian.

Spiritual Pollution, 1983-4

*Deng Xiaoping accused certain Party ideologues, literary critics
and cultural workers of purveying what he said were "all kinds of
corrupt and decadent ideas of the bourgeoisie and other exploiting
classes," declaring that Spiritual Pollution consisted of those ideas and
works which spread "distrust of socialism, communism and leadership
of the Communist Party." On October 12 he said: ". . . . Spiritual
Pollution can be so damaging as to bring disaster upon the country and
the people. It blurs the distinction between right and wrong, leads to
passivity, laxity and disunity, corrupts the mind and erodes the will. It
encourages the spread of all kinds of individualism and causes people to
doubt or even to reject socialism and the Party's leadership . . . . Unless
we take it seriously and adopt firm measures right now to prevent its
spread, many people will fall prey to it and be led astray, with grave
consequences."*

*The term was subsequently replaced by the more prosaic phrase
"bourgeois liberalization"—Bourgelib. Apparently, in early 1984 Deng
was informed that the term Spiritual Pollution had a somewhat
unsavoury history: Adolf Hitler had used it to condemn decadent
bourgeois and Bolshevik culture in his famous speech on "Aryan art" in
1937.*

*Deng's remarks in 1983 resulted in a nation-wide purge not only of
ideological aberrations, but also of innovative and popular literature,
cinema, pop music, and even western-style dress. This "Mini-Cultural
Revolution", as it was dubbed, was called to a halt in early 1984 by
leaders who were justifiably fearful that it would derail China's
economic reform policies, scare off foreign investment, and revive
Maoist extremism.*

1984

November   Deng is rumoured to have called for a moratorium on ideological campaigns for three years, dating from late 1983.

1985

January   At the Fourth All-China Writers' and Artists' Congress, Hu Qili states that creative freedom is to be permitted.

February   Hu Yaobang reminds editors and writers that all news publication must serve the interests of the Party; journalists are the "mouthpiece" of the Party.

November   The play *WM* is banned.

1986

December   Student demonstrations in favour of political reform and democracy throughout China.
Deng calls for the purge of Fang Lizhi, Wang Ruowang and Liu Binyan from the Party.

Students burning the Peking Daily, *January 5, 1987*   *AFP, C. Henrieth*

1987: Year One of Anti-Bourgelib

January   Deng orders a nation-wide struggle against Bourgelib and Hu Yaobang is forced to resign.

A Second Cultural Revolution?

Since I was five years old, every political campaign has directly affected my family and myself. It has been a rough road. Every step has left its mark . . .

In the midst of all this endless aggression and insult, I have never been able to convince myself of the existence of such a thing as a Rule of Law in China! What is the function of our so-called legal system? How much longer will it remain a meaningless ornament? When have humanity and human rights ever been respected in our country?

If we refuse to speak honestly, if we force ourselves to enjoy our punishment, if we insist that this country of ours, which is capable at any time of wantonly killing its own people, must be obeyed like a mother, then, I think, a second Cultural Revolution is on its way . . .

Thirty-nine years of political purges have left me frightened, disillusioned and sad. I can never think of that lawless country of ours without being seized with terror . . .

I don't want to be a victim of the "second Cultural Revolution". Nobody can guarantee that it won't happen again. Look at the Campaign against Spiritual Pollution. All those Krats went leaping into action, hacking off high heels, cutting off long hair . . . It was well under way, and would have taken off properly, if the Party hadn't changed its mind at the last minute . . . Purges like that get started so easily, because there are always people wanting to climb up, and they know they can use a purge to put paid to others. They've seen that the persecutors of the past have never really been punished. So long as this is the case, so long as the persecutors are left unpunished, there will be more purges: to promise otherwise is futile . . .

Seeking political asylum is a way of protesting against China's policies, not just for myself, but on behalf of the thousands of educated people who have suffered persecution . . .

In China policies change three times a day. If one day they allow you to go abroad, you'd better jump. Because you never know when the next directive is going to arrive, telling you you can't go after all. It might be the very next day. I virtually fled from China.

Yu Luojin, April 1986

"The problem is that there has been some confusion in our ideological work and students have not been given strong, effective guidance . . . . We should expose those people who have acted out of ulterior motives, because this time they have adopted slogans that clearly express opposition to Communist Party leadership and the socialist road. Certain individuals have made exceedingly pernicious statements, trying to incite people to action."

Deng Xiaoping

February   "The Constitution stipulates that citizens of the People's Republic have the freedom of association and demonstration. Then those Party hacks concocted 'new regulations' claiming that the student demonstrations had disrupted traffic. Now demonstrators have to apply for permission five days in advance, provide the authorities with a list of names of people taking part, a detailed map of their proposed route and the reasons for their demonstration. Isn't this proof that the comrades in charge of Public Security use the Constitution as toilet paper? But it'll only give them piles.

"There's nothing you can do if you get sores like that. If you're going to sit on the Constitution, it's like putting your bum on a time bomb; it can explode at any moment. But do those comrades who are illiterates, semi-literates, or who 'have no more than a primary school education' understand any of this? No way. They even expelled Fang Lizhi, Wang Ruowang and Liu Binyan from the Party."

Hah Gong

March   Over 2,000 Chinese students studying in America sign an open letter to the Chinese government protesting against Hu Yaobang's fall, the expulsion of Fang, Liu and Wang from the Party, and the new political struggle. Some 700 of these students take the unprecedented step of signing their real names.

Thirty-six Chinese writers and scholars in America send a similar letter of protest to Deng Xiaoping, as do editors, writers and sinologists from a number of countries and regions, including Hong Kong and Taiwan.

April   "For the whole period of the realization of the Four Modernizations, at least for the ten or so years remaining in this century plus the first thirty of the next century, there will be a need to continue to oppose Bourgelib. If we don't emphasize our opposition to Bourgelib then the political situation of unity and stability will be lost."

Deng Xiaoping

May   Zhao Ziyang attempts to contain the campaign against Bourgelib as it threatens to get out of control. However, in an important speech he reiterates the point that Deng Xiaoping has made since the beginning of the year: the struggle against Bourgelib will continue up to the middle of the next century.

     "Bourgelib thinking has been deprived of an audience. There are fewer people who are calling for a rejection of Party leadership and socialism. Anyway, the press won't publish them . . . ."

Zhao Ziyang

Zunzi

An Old Tale Retold
A: What are you here for?
B: I opposed Hu Yaobang. And you?
A: I supported him. (addressing C) What about you?
C: I'm Hu Yaobang.

June   In interviews with foreign and Hong Kong journalists Fang Lizhi and Wang Ruowang declare their opposition to Party purges of intellectuals.
    "As long as the spectre of Mao Zedong lingers, as
long as it goes uncriticized, then we may have another
'earthquake' at any moment. This is because extreme

Bourgelib Defined

"Bourgelib" is an abbreviation of the term "bourgeois liberalization". Deng Xiaoping is perhaps the most reliable guide in providing a
definition. In late December 1986 he stated categorically: "Bourgeois
liberalization means rejection of the Party's leadership."
    As early as March 1979, when he denounced Wei Jingsheng [see
pp. 277-89], Deng said that by rejecting the leadership of the Party,
members of the Democracy Movement were guilty of "liberalism". In
fact, Deng was echoing the words of Mao Zedong who had said in
"Combat Liberalism", his famous speech of 1937, that "Liberalism is
extremely harmful in a revolutionary collective. It is a corrosive which
eats away unity, undermines cohesion, causes apathy and creates
dissension . . . . It is an extremely bad tendency." To think and act
independently of the Party—either to ignore it or to preempt its
decisions—is to be guilty of Bourgelib.
    Bourgelib has appeared in many forms since the Cultural Revolu-
tion. Wei Jingsheng's call for democracy in 1978-9 was denounced as
"liberalism"; the alleged lack of "social responsibility" in literature and
the theatre in 1980, the "crisis of confidence" in the Party and the Bai
Hua Incident in 1981-2, the "Spiritual Pollution" denounced in 1983-4,
as well as the debates on Chinese culture and political reform in 1985-6,
have each in turn occasioned either a political or cultural purge.
    Hu Yaobang, the General Secretary of the Communist Party who
was forced to resign his post in January 1987 for reportedly encouraging
Bourgelib, was also denounced for interfering with the Anti-Spiritual
Pollution Campaign of 1983-4.
    Chinese leaders have repeatedly declared that the struggle against
Bourgelib is not a transient political strategy, but rather an ideological
necessity for China's Open Door and Reform policies. In fact, regular
campaigns against Bourgelib are the hall-mark of post-Mao Proledic
rule. Chinese leaders find it essential to invent phantom ideological
opposition. Ironically, intellectuals and writers used as official
scapegoats and denounced for Bourgelib may in time actually become
dissidents or opponents of the ruling élite.

leftists are still active, in power and treated like the Party's darlings. Remember, only recently they [Deng Xiaoping and Zhao Ziyang] announced that Bourgelib would have to be attacked for twenty, seventy, even eighty years to come. As long as this slogan remains in place then the rotten stench of extreme leftism will remain, ever ready to set off new shock waves. This slogan is like a piece of elastic, it can change length at will, it can be wrapped around anything. But one thing is for sure: it is the product of extreme leftist thinking."

Wang Ruowang.

August   A further purge of Party intellectuals and writers takes place. The playwright Wu Zuguang, himself instructed to resign from the Party, writes a letter of protest to the Party.

September   "Political movements are used to control ideology. This latest business, Anti-Bourgelib, is also a small-scale movement; the Anti-Spiritual Pollution Campaign was also a movement. Although they make a point of saying that it is not a movement, in fact they have never ceased to use movements, large and small, what one could define as 'non-movements'. Take the University of Science and Technology, for example. All students are required to write a report on what they think of Anti-Bourgelib. In it they must state their support for the Four Basic Principles and their opposition to bourgeois tendencies. Making people write things like that is tantamount to carrying out a political movement."

Fang Lizhi

October   The Thirteenth Congress of the Communist Party of China is held in Peking. Zhao Ziyang, now Party General Secretary, marks the end of the latest Anti-Bourgelib purge when he states in his report to the congress that: "The struggle against Bourgelib is developing in a healthy manner. It has enhanced the political awareness of the people, and has helped us further accumulate experience in the area of using positive education and correct criticism to attack erroneous thinking instead of carrying out political campaigns. During the profound changes brought about by full-scale reform, it is of the greatest necessity to maintain unity and stability; this is also a very difficult thing to do."

November   The congress concludes with the "retirement" of many older cadres including Deng Xiaoping. These elder statesmen still hold their key advisory positions, while Deng retains control over the army.

"Comrade Xiaoping's position and role as the paramount decision-maker in the Party and the State has been proven by the test of time. This is recognized both inside and outside the Party, both in China and overseas. To consult him will facilitate our work. What possible reason could I have not to ask for his guidance in all important matters in the future?"

Zhao Ziyang

Deng "retires" after a ten-year rule during which he has supervised five major campaigns against intellectual and literary freedom in China.

"We have witnessed the dawn of the most brilliant age in the thousands of years of Chinese history."
Cao Yu

Liu Binyan:

The Loyal Minister

Liu Binyan [see pp. 65-7] was highly outspoken in his call for greater press freedom and democracy in China throughout 1986. As a popular writer and a veteran reporter for the most prestigious Party newspaper People's Daily, *Liu was invited to speak at many universities and publishing houses in late 1986. Confident of high-level support within the Party machine, he was also vocal about the two periods of Party history that are covered by a taboo: the Anti-Rightist Campaign of 1957 during which Mao purged China's intellectuals; and the Cultural Revolution. As Deng Xiaoping had been intimately involved with the 1957 purge, he regarded Liu's call for commemorations of its thirtieth anniversary with great hostility.*

Liu had made many enemies in provincial Party organizations through his reportage on Party abuses, many of which had their origins in the Cultural Revolution period. Although regarded by many as a faithful Party man and an enthusiastic supporter of Party reform, his honesty in the speeches he had made was seen as an abuse of his privileged position. Along with Fang Lizhi and Wang Ruowang, Liu was accused of being one of the main public figures to have incited, directly or indirectly, the student demonstrations of December 1986.

Speeches and quotations from speeches made by Liu Binyan in late 1986 were published in internal Party pamphlets as part of the Anti-Bourgelib Campaign in the early months of 1987. The following extracts are taken from those pamphlets.

Man Without Conscience

To put it simply, man isn't treated as a human being. Can we claim that this way of thinking has been eradicated? I would be only too delighted if it had. The ultra-"leftist" line [of the Cultural Revolution] dehumanized man. It made slaves out of men who should have enjoyed freedom. It turned independent minds into servile tools. It transformed men into animals, and in the process men, that is the Chinese people, abandoned their conscience. They lost their sense of remorse. Now many traits germane to human beings—independence of thought, the concepts of honesty and trust—have disappeared. Well, anyhow, conscience is lost, comrades. Perhaps to say it is "lost" is going a bit too far. Let's just say it has degenerated greatly. And what has taken its place? Hostility, suspicion, and cruelty. Who can deny this? Cruelty and hatred have become virtues . . . So few people have written their confessions. And yet we must be honest about our nation's weaknesses. Not all the Chinese people, of course, are guilty. But suspicion and cruelty were the cornerstones in the reign of terror: a violent and all-powerful terror, a terror that served our leaders. Injustice stared us in the face, yet we stood by watching with folded arms, or simply gave in to it. People were prepared to see the whole world destroyed, just so they could preserve themselves . . .

September 13, 1986

On Bourgelib and Freedom of Expression

Take this whole opposition to Bourgelib, for example. Even now they talk of it and won't hear of it being discarded.

It is a question of the freedom to speak and write. Some countries use a more inclusive term: freedom of expression, which includes such things as demonstrations, marches, and strikes—a way for the masses to express their will. This type of expression is part and parcel of the freedom of speech. This is something to which I paid particular attention when I visited America. There is a great deal of published material dealing with the subject there. The First Amendment to their Constitution states that the most sacred thing is [freedom of] speech, belief, and so on, and that neither government nor Congress can curtail it. Isn't there a lot of talk about the "Double Hundred" Policy [i.e., letting a hundred flowers blossom and a hundred schools of thought contend] in China? It's just a shorthand for the freedom of speech, creativity and scholastic research. There has been a silent debate on this subject raging all along throughout our vast land; it is a debate that has been bathed in blood and tears. In my opinion the freedom of expression is not only necessary for the solution of some major problems, it is bound up with the whole state of a nation's vitality. There are many things the politicians don't even dare think of, and they won't let you think or talk about them either. Why should they let you waste your time thinking about such things? Over a period of time this attitude corrupts the nation, everyone becomes a mediocrity. The whole race becomes mediocre.

November 2, 1986

Socialism or Sham

Aren't we supposed to be adhering to the Four Basic Principles? One of them is socialism. Well, what is socialism? Is what we had from 1953 to 1976 real socialism or just a sham? If that was genuine socialism, then is everything we've been doing since 1979 nothing but a sham? If, however, what we're doing now is genuine socialism, then the socialism of the past can't have been very real. At best it was a sham. One or the other must be a sham; it's a simple matter of elimination. If I was forced to say which period was real socialism, I know I couldn't. Even our official ideologues haven't been allowed to discuss this.

November 7, 1986

Rivers of Blood for a Few Slogans

We have been deluded for a very long time, and have made numerous sacrifices for a handful of beliefs. I'd venture to say that we've broken the world record: a nation that has continued to shed rivers of blood generation after generation, just for the sake of a few slogans, a few concepts! Isn't this just what has happened? What's the name of that river running through Guangxi and Guangdong? The North River? It's been blocked by a dam of corpses: tens of thousands of lives sacrificed so as to uphold slogans and concepts that were wrong, muddle-headed, even reactionary . . .

November 7, 1986

The Inhumanity of Ultra-leftism

What, in the final analysis, are the essential elements of the Chinese leftist [i.e. Maoist] line? What lies at its heart? In my opinion, it has to do with its whole concept of humanity. Was not humanism a "forbidden zone" in China until quite recently? The essence of the leftist line is its contempt for humanity, and the destructive cruelty it displays towards human beings. Man is not regarded as human. He needs nothing: neither schooling, nor travel, nor the right to think for himself. What does he need then? All he's allowed is a belly, and even that shouldn't be filled too full. He needs slogans so he can shout at class-struggle sessions. And then there's labour: hoeing and ploughing with an ox in the fields. That's the sort of animal man is supposed to be.

Stagnation and Degeneration

Why should freedom be such a terrifying thing? It still is, even today. The constitution clearly states that people have the freedoms of speech, publication, meeting and organisation. Yet there are those who partially or completely doubt the wisdom of such a stipulation. Freedom is not always such a good thing. There is something rather frightening about it, something rather dangerous. Why? What happens when you don't let a person air his views? Well, first, he stops thinking; and second, he stops seeing what is going on around him. He stops caring about lots of things. Nothing concerns him any more, he leaves everything to the leadership.

In 1979, when I was in Harbin, I heard a scholar talk about what life had taught him. The experience of twenty years, he said, had proved to him that anyone who wants a carefree existence in China must never say anything to contradict the authorities; and, furthermore, must never make any suggestions on how they can improve *their* way of doing things. I was horrified. What a country this has become! Of course things have stagnated and degenerated. It would be a wonder if they hadn't.

Dead-end

There's just one thing I want to say: since 1957 [the purge of intellectuals by Mao Zedong, the "Anti-Rightist Campaign", of which Liu was also a victim] the path open to China's youth and her intellectuals has been extraordinarily narrow. If you aspired to be an upstanding and honest man politically, then you would inevitably end up as a counter-revolutionary, so there's been no way out there. If, on the other hand, you felt you had some talent, in science or technology, and you were hopeful of making some contribution to the country, then it wouldn't be long before you were attacked for "apolitical specialization" and "bourgeois individuality". That would provide no way out either.... So what was left for China's intellectuals? Really only one path, or only one that was relatively safe and comfortable: that was to become a political opportunist. This was how limited the possibilities had become. Batch after batch of intellectuals took this way out, and of them quite a number became the power base of the Cultural Revolution, and it is these people who are the obstacles in our way today....

If I hadn't become a Rightist what could I have done? There were three possibilities. 1. I could have avoided saying or writing anything

---

Liu Binyan's Expulsion

On January 23 [1987] as the result of Liu Binyan's serious errors, the Disciplinary Inspection Committee of the People's Daily *Branch of the Communist Party of China came to a decision to strip Liu Binyan,* People's Daily *reporter and Vice-Chairman of the Chinese Writers' Association, of his Party membership in accordance with the Party Constitution.*

In their "Decision Regarding the Expulsion of Liu Binyan from the Party", the Disciplinary Inspection Committee pointed out that Liu has seriously violated the Party Constitution, Party discipline and Party decisions. He has often used public speeches and articles as a means of opposing the Four Basic Principles and encouraging Bourgelib.

People's Daily, *January 25, 1987*

Apart from doing his utmost to vilify and oppose the leadership of the Party, Liu Binyan has carried out a thoroughgoing attack on the Four Basic Principles. He has declared that they are "a rigid and outdated dogma that has repeatedly led China along the road to disaster. They may sound very fine, but their contents are conservative, even reactionary." Adhering to the Four Basic Principles is the basis of the State. There are specific stipulations regarding this in both the Constitution and the Party Constitution. They are a conclusion that has been reached by the history of China, they are the expression of the heartfelt wishes of the various nationalities of China. Liu Binyan's defamation of the Four Basic Principles was a way to prepare the public for capitalism in China....

Of course, we hope that following his expulsion from the Party Liu Binyan will make a thorough self-examination and use positive actions to prove that he has seen the error of his ways, keeping within the boundaries of the Constitution and the law. If he does so, the Party and the people will welcome him back.

People's Daily *commentary, January 25, 1987*

that would have landed me in trouble, and I would have weathered the storm to become a well-off, even if somewhat reclusive, fellow, a cultural bureaucrat increasingly divorced from the people of China. 2. I might have been a borderline case and only written things when conditions permitted, in which case in the Cultural Revolution I would have been persecuted for everything I'd done in the past. I wouldn't be alive today. 3. I could have been an enthusiastic supporter of the Cultural Revolution, become the head of a faction, and ended up in Q1 [see pp. 279-289].... Just think about it for a moment. What other possibilities were there for me? None. No matter how energetic I may have been, or how talented, what could I have possibly written of worth in those twenty-two years [from 1957 to 1979]? In an age in which the truth was outlawed, what could a reporter or a writer possibly do?....

November 21, 1986

LIU BINYAN . Mi Qiu

. . . After his expulsion Liu lived for months in fear that he would be brought to trial for libel, because of certain factual errors in his work "A Second Kind of Loyalty" [see pp. 65-7]. He calculated that, if successful, his enemies could have him jailed for up to nine years. It was not until August 1987 that this threat was finally removed. Before then he had said to visitors he would not publish anything for three years, an expression of his indignation with his expulsion from the Party. Liu felt the reasons for his purge to be unlike that of Fang Lizhi and Wang Ruowang, men whose statements and demands were far in excess of what the Communist Party could accept.

Observers both in China and overseas have often cast Liu in the role of a literary Superman who would take on everyone from local thugs to Provincial potentates. His heroism did not unsettle people who believed in China's glasnost for the simple reason that he was a man doing right without really rocking the boat, a man who could question every disastrous move of the system without ever doubting that system itself. The West also needed Liu: he bolstered the hope that China was becoming more liberal, more like the West. He had become a vehicle for wish-fulfilment both inside and outside China. Many believed that the highest echelon of Party leaders, the supposedly enlightened "reformers", Hu Yaobang, Zhao Ziyang, and sometimes Deng Xiaoping himself, implicitly, and at times even openly, supported Liu's quixotic crusades against the darker side of the apparat. With Liu in the Party the regular cultural purges, massive anti-crime campaigns and their concomitant waves of executions seemed somehow explicable: pardonable excesses in a regime reforming for the better.

Then Liu's erstwhile backers ordered his expulsion from the Party and the nation's media carried out a vicious campaign of denunciation. Throughout 1987, Liu, now as free of Party constraints as Fang Lizhi, took his political ostracism in the spirit of a martyred loyal minister. He handled himself with the unprepossessing grace of Rubashov in Darkness at Noon. Superman emerged from the phone booth dressed as Clark Kent.

In late July 1987 the Taiwanese writer Chen Ruoxi [see pp. 46-61] visited Liu during his dolour, and came away from the interview with the remark that despite everything he remained "the model of a loyal Party man". By the end of the year he was expressing confidence that the latest developments in China's political snakes and ladders augured well for the future and that he had faith in the positive nature of the Party.

Wang Ruowang:

Out of Control in Shanghai

A Foul State of Affairs

The lack of democracy within the Party and the system of arbitrary rule by one person has nurtured a deformed sort of administrative talent. It is a system in which power and hierarchy determine the pros and cons of any question. If you have power then truth is on your side. (According to the same principle, power is greater than the law and power can overthrow the law.) The leadership is eternally correct; nobody is permitted to doubt it or express differing views, and if they do they will be attacked for anti-Party crimes. Since the Third Plenum [in December 1978] this foul state of affairs has improved only marginally. In numerous cases this unwritten law proves itself to be mightier than either the Party or State constitution. This has done nothing but encourage bureaucrats with big titles to abuse their power, act wantonly and manipulate affairs to their personal advantage. One of our ideological chiefs can make a statement on the basis of personal bias and his underlings will react as though it were an imperial command. This kind of "rule from the bureau" is the result of a system that permits personal arbitrariness, it stems from a belief among those in power that they are always correct and far superior to everyone else.

This quotation from Wang Ruowang was printed in the Shenzhen Youth Herald, *September 30, 1986. The paper was closed down during the early phase of the Anti-Bourgelib Campaign in 1987. It was accused of numerous ideological errors, one of the most serious, although unspecified, crimes of its editors being the publication of an article encouraging Deng Xiaoping, China's new patriarch, to retire. Among those stigmatized by the closure was the literary editor Xu Jingya [see pp. 242-43].*

People say that our political system only breeds mutes, and will lead to the extinction of the lark. That's something worth thinking about.

Deng Xiaoping has said himself that our system of leadership encourages bureaucratism. I think he should add a line: "And furthermore, it gives rise to personal arbitrariness in which only one person has a say."

Like Fang Lizhi, Wang Ruowang, a veteran Party member and novelist born in 1917, was not silenced by his expulsion from the Communist Party. Following the nationwide criticism of Wang, his apartment was raided by the Shanghai Public Security Bureau, officers of which confiscated personal manuscripts, letters, notes and address books. Despite this he gave an interview to the Hong Kong magazine Pai-shing Semi-Monthly *in July 1987, in which he candidly discussed his fate. He also gave the magazine a number of articles for publication in which he was highly critical of Party ideologues. In a preface to one essay in which he criticizes both Hu Qiaomu and Xiong Fu [see p. 271 and the chapter "Pressure Points" respectively] Wang wrote:*

The Communists have declared that my presence [in the Party] can no longer be tolerated as I have propagated Bourgelib. According to the Communist policy of realizing "two systems within one country" [Deng Xiaoping's formula for the solution of the Hong Kong question] Hong Kong and Macao may continue to be inundated by Bourgelib. It is as though a nature reserve has been established and the hunters banished from it. I'm taking advantage of this loophole to publish articles in Hong Kong and Macao. I presume that by so doing it is unlikely that I can again be found guilty of "inciting students to demonstrate"!

On the 1987 Anti-Bourgelib Campaign

We admit that for a time after the Third Plenum [in December, 1978] the Communist Party seemed to demonstrate that its major policies were different from those pursued by Lin Biao and the Gang of Four. The people of China were delighted by this and relaxed. Why then from the very first day of 1987 have people been crying out that "the cold winds are blowing" and declaring despondently that "silence rules once more"? Is it not simply because from the first day of 1987 the Communist Party has shown itself to be acting in a way that is no way "basically different" from Lin Biao and the Gang of Four?

It's plain for all to see that overnight there has been yet another call to rout a Three Family Village [i.e. Fang Lizhi, Wang Ruowang and Liu Binyan. The original Three Family Village being the writers Deng Tuo, Liao Mosha and Wu Han, who were persecuted at the beginning of the Cultural Revolution]. On the basis of one speech by the country's senior leader the whole Party and country was mobilized, and all propaganda tools were turned to the task. The "accused" who were being struggled were not allowed to defend themselves, nor were dissenting views allowed to be published. Great criticism articles filled the media, despite the prestige their targets have in the fields of science and the arts. They could no longer be referred to as "comrade" in the press, and they were stripped of their freedom of expression and creative freedom—freedoms guaranteed every citizen by the Constitution. The editors of newspapers and journals that had previously published their works were investigated and attacked, some were fired, others forced to close their publications. And the style of the denunciations, both in terms of their irrationality and language, were no different from those of the Cultural Revolution period. They invariably started off with a "directive" from the Party Leader, the crimes of the accused were all explicated in terms of the Party's political slogans, and the quotations selected from the damned were taken entirely out of context and drastically abridged. The writer of this article had his apartment searched and he was taken to the Public

---

Wang Ruowang's Expulsion

On January 13 [1987], the Disciplinary Inspection Committee of the Shanghai Municipal Branch of the Communist Party of China came to a decision to strip Wang Ruowang, Member of the Directorate of the Chinese Writers' Association and the Shanghai Writers' Association, of his Party membership.

In their "Decision Regarding the Expulsion of Wang Ruowang from the Party", the Disciplinary Inspection Committee pointed out that, since 1979, and in particular over the last two years, Wang Ruowang has often used public speeches and articles as a means of encouraging Bourgelib and opposing the Four Basic Principles, and he has repeatedly failed to correct the error of his ways despite repeated attempts at re-education....

Xinhua News Agency, Shanghai, January 14, 1987

Security Bureau under custody "for questioning". Meanwhile, they [the authorities] declared that the student demonstrations that had occurred in all of China's major cities undermined unity and stability and therefore had to be crushed mercilessly....

However, it should be said that there are differences between the present criticism movement and the Cultural Revolution. For example, they have changed the nomenclature: they call this a "struggle", not a "political movement", as if this could fool anyone. Moreover, they hold struggle sessions which they won't allow the person being struggled to attend. Finally, when they attacked people in movements in the past they would always print some of their "poisonous weeds" in full, or show their reactionary films in order that they could be more effectively struggled against by the masses. This time, however, they've only printed selected quotes from tape-recorded speeches by the evil-doers. Unfortunately, such thrift in no way indicates an improvement on the part of the Communists, in fact, quite the opposite. Our present leaders are much weaker and less sure of themselves than Mao Zedong ever was. They are scared that the people will see right through them. Because they know that what we have been saying is the truth they have no choice but to deal with us in this fashion. The reason they cannot allow the accused to take part in their struggle sessions is because they are scared people will not toe the line or that the accused may attempt to defend themselves. This would not only prove very embarrassing, but would spoil the hopes of some people to be rewarded [for their activism]. The reason that these "differences" between the two movements exist is because nowadays there is an invisible but powerful "psychological block" operating in the minds of the people. In the days of Mao Zedong, the people, cretinized by the "deification policy" of the Party, went around wishing "Long life!" to the leadership. They hadn't yet formed this new style of self-defence....

Both Stalin and Mao Zedong mobilized the whole Party and the whole people to achieve a communist society. Events have shown that both of these remarkable heroes not only failed to help their countries advance, but actually succeeded in dragging them into poverty and backwardness. Perhaps it is no coincidence then that at virtually the same time in 1986 the current leaders of both countries declared that after decades, or more than half a century, of building socialism, they remain today still in its "initial phase". Even Deng Xiaoping has recently been forced to admit that the superior nature of China's socialism will only become apparent in the middle of the next century.

> *Wang Ruowang is absolutely out of control there in Shanghai. I said long ago that he should be expelled [from the Party], why hasn't anything ever been done about it?*
>
> *Deng Xiaoping,* December 30, 1986

Historical facts have proven that the subjective will to realize communism quickly has finally collided smack into the wall of historical materialism.

Given that wholesale westernization is impossible, what about wholesale sovietization? Mao went all out to achieve this in his day, but the results were similarly disastrous. In the end he made enemies out of the Soviets and continued to denounce them for a good fifteen years. But even then, sovietization was just another type of westernization: Marx, Engels, Lenin and Stalin were all westerners after all, and the Chinese Communists have thus been carrying out theories introduced from the West. Even when they established their peasant guerilla bases they gave them foreign names: the "Chinese Soviet Government" (or simply "Soviet"). In every other aspect too the Chinese Communist Party faithfully adopted the Soviet work style: we too have political commissars; Party secretaries; Party branches; Party control of elections; a one-party dictatorship; the elimination of opposition through Proledic; the renaming of collective farms as communes, with the result that there were smaller harvests every year; the impoverishment of the people, at the same time as the establishment of special privileges for Party cadres (the corruption of these people and the way they misuse their power to feather their own nests is virtually the same in both countries); and, of course, strict control over culture and the media. If the Chinese Communists really wanted to seek truth from facts, then they should make a massive criticism of Mao Zedong's wholesale sovietization (or better still, let's just call it Stalinization). This would be far more to the point, as well as being highly beneficial to the reforms and the opening up of China....

In late April news leaked out of Diaoyutai [the State Guest House in Peking and venue for many important secret Party meetings] that there were plans afoot to criticize "leftism". The speech Zhao Ziyang made before going overseas [to Eastern Europe in May; the speech was on the subject of propaganda work] was a criticism of those unspecified people who tried to push the Anti-Bourgelib Campaign beyond its [officially delineated] boundaries and into the fields of economics, the arts and publishing. One would imagine that following this criticism the champions of "leftism" would have restrained themselves somewhat. However, we cannot say that this was a turning point, although we do admit that it brought about a slight improvement. The thing that prevents us from being optimistic is the fact that there has been no attempt to examine the reasons why "leftism" has been able to develop to the extent it has. Unless there is a determined effort to eliminate "leftist" disruption at the leadership level, unless there is a public recanting of the mistaken approach [taken by the leadership] to the student movement of last year, then all criticisms of "leftism" will remain nothing more than a propaganda slogan, or even worse, a ploy to present a fresh image. Although we have noticed that the Communist leadership has made a little progress, we hope to see more in the future.

The reasons behind this little bit of "progress" are complex, but the first and foremost is that the leaders have been confronted with the unsurmountable Great Wall of the popular "psychological block" [against political movements]. This new Great Wall is evidence that the Chinese people are politically mature and generally self-aware. This type of psychological protection mechanism is still at the passive stage, it has yet to become a social force. If the present high-pressure policies continue to be enforced relentlessly and the Anti-Bourgelib struggle is intensified, then people will become active instead of passive in their resistance. However, Zhao and the others have realized that the blind stupidity of their much beloved leftist commissars has created a powder-keg. Another reason is that in the first half of this year, both industrial and agricultural production fell off sharply while prices continued to skyrocket. Popular discontent naturally identified the Party's policies as being at fault, and this forced the leaders to loosen a few screws in the machinery of the movement. The third reason is the extent of international pressure and the disaffection of large numbers of Chinese students studying overseas. A number of major western investor nations have been unwilling to continue investing in China. Because of all of these social and economic drawbacks, the Communist Party leadership has been forced to make a few necessary adjustments to their policies, to restrain their own excesses. Rather than saying that this is the start of a turn-about, it would be more advisable to see in this the flexibility of pragmatism, for the root-causes of "leftism" remain untouched.

It will be very hard for the Chinese government to regain the trust or understanding of the people just by denouncing "leftism" in slogans. What is required is that the Maoist Anti-Bourgelib paradigm be abandoned entirely, and true freedom of the press, expression, creativity and publication be realized; furthermore, Hu Yaobang should be given back his original position [as General Secretary of the Party] and the student movement of last year should be publicly rehabilitated, as should the students who have been expelled from universities for being involved in it, and so on.

July 1987

Wang Ruowang has boasted that he's proud to be known as the patriarch of Bourgelib. Well, we feel ashamed on his behalf. From now on he might try acting as a good citizen within the boundaries permitted by the Constitution, and write a few things that are beneficial to the people. In this way he will be able to regain his integrity in his last years.

Chen Yi, Wang's former commissar and retired head of the Shanghai Ministry of Propaganda, in the *Guangming Daily*, 19 April, 1987

WANG RUOWANG   *Bao Naiyong*

Wu Zuguang:
A Disaffected Gentleman

The playwright Wu Zuguang, father of Wu Huan [see pp. 103-4] first paid for his outspokenness in 1957 when he was sent to the Great Northern Wilderness to undergo labour reform. Among other things he was condemned for saying that Party leadership was not the key to a flourishing cultural scene. After all, he asked, did the famous Tang poets Li Bo and Du Fu have commissars looking over their shoulders?

Ever since joining the Communist Party in 1980, he has been a vocal critic of the Party's erratic cultural policy. In 1983, while travelling in America, Wu went against Party discipline by criticizing the Anti-Spiritual Pollution Campaign and, upon returning to China, he organised a petition calling for a halt to all such ideological purges. In 1986 he championed the cause of the banned play WM [see pp. 102-117]. He criticized the doctrinaire ideologues who called for this and other bans, and berated them for being too spineless to admit openly that they had done so.

Cultural Assassins

The crux of the matter is that it is all too common for people in power to say one thing but do another; or even do the exact opposite of what they've said. Then they get away scot free, regardless of how disastrous their actions may have proven to be. Ours is a land with thousands of years of feudal history behind it, where people habitually accept the right of might rather than the importance of democracy and law. The leaders and those they lead are often in a relationship of obvious inequality. Add to this the fact that over the last few decades it has been the "fashion" to denounce and purge people. For example, just after the "Double Hundred" Policy was announced [by Mao Zedong in 1956], encouraging intellectuals to make political statements and criticize the Party, a nationwide movement aimed at obliterating the very intellectuals who had done just that was launched, with the most frightening consequences. The number of people who suffered is incalculable, and this was but the first in a series of vile campaigns. There's a famous saying of the feudal philosopher Mencius: "If a lord treats his ministers like dirt, then his ministers will regard him as a bandit and enemy". It shows that Mencius understood the relationship between the rulers and the ruled. Surprisingly, even after all these years, there are many leaders who don't understand this simple principle. They treat the masses like dirt, see them as slaves and fools; at the same time they train a group of opportunistic flatterers, vicious, double-faced rogues, as their intimates and strong-arm men. Decades of this situation have led to the near-extinction of integrity. The atmosphere of duplicity at one point brought New China to the verge of collapse, and it has still not been dispelled.

From my experience, the aims of any level of feudal dictator [in the apparat] are completely incompatible with the aims of the so-called "Double Hundred" Policy. These dictators are like Qin Shihuang [the first emperor of China), they can't countenance any opposition within their sphere of control. They can only accept fawning and compliance. They appear stern and powerful on the surface, but in reality their every moment is spent in dread that they may lose their grasp on power. So it is inevitable that they feel threatened by anyone who does not agree with them entirely, worst of all the intellectuals, who think, speak and write.

Intellectuals have suffered like this for the past thirty years. Every political movement has been aimed at intellectuals first. The arts world in particular has been the first victim in every campaign. This is because intellectuals are not trusted . . .

But have the extreme leftist elements in the cultural world given up now and disappeared from the scene? Far from it. Let me illustrate this fact with a few comments about the play *WM*. It was first subjected to various types of pressure and finally done away with. This process is in itself both fascinating and highly dramatic.... There is a popular saying in cultural circles that sums up the situation: "They used to execute plays in public, now they carry out assassinations in private. Party officials have been forced underground."

June 1986

This extract is from a speech made at a meeting to commemorate the thirtieth anniversary of Mao's "Double Hundred" policy speech. Although subsequently published in China, Wu's speech was edited so as to remove all references to the case of WM.

In 1987, when Wu Zuguang again called for an end to the Party's pervasive system of censorship, perhaps the most outrageous of his many acts, and derided the Anti-Bourgelib Campaign, the apparat called for action.

Although Wu was on a second "black list" drawn up after the expulsion of Fang, Wang and Liu from the Party in January, nothing was done until later in the year. On August 1, 1987, the Politburo member Hu Qiaomu [see p. 271] was sent to visit Wu Zuguang at home. He read him a Central Committee document demanding that he resign his Party membership or face expulsion. Ten days later, Wu wrote "A Letter to the Discipline Commission of the Central Committee of the Communist Party of China" which he sent to Hong Kong for publication in September. In this letter he gave the reasons why he had relinquished his Party membership so readily.

Three Good Reasons for Quitting the Party

Although entirely unmoved by the criticisms of my "errors" and dumbfounded by the extraordinary fashion in which I was requested to quit the Party—privately and without any scope for discussion—I acquiesced to Comrade [Hu] Qiaomu's request on the spot. I had three reasons for doing so:

1. Respect for the aged is a glorious Chinese national tradition. I have always treated my elders with respect. Comrade Qiaomu is a man rich in years and frail of health. To be the humble object of his magnanimous attention, indeed to be the cause of such exertion on his part—he had to climb up the four flights of stairs to reach my unworthy hovel—caused me the greatest unease. For this reason I said to Comrade Qiaomu: "This decision has taken me completely by surprise, and I cannot understand it. But, as you have come here to present this request to me in person, I will accept it."

2. At the time my first thought was: as a Party member it is my duty to uphold the credibility of the Party. In the documents issued by Party Central this year, and in many speeches of the leaders of the Centre over the last months, it has been repeatedly stated that following the expulsion of those three people [Fang Lizhi, Liu Binyan, Wang Ruowang] earlier in the year, no other comrades would be expelled from the Party. Only two weeks ago, on 16 July to be exact.... Comrade Qiaomu . . . repeatedly emphasized that there wouldn't be a fourth expulsion [from the Party]. "Who said there would be a fourth?

Who is the fourth?" The words still seem to be ringing in my ears. Needless to say, I felt both devastated and sick at heart when I realized that I could inadvertently become that fourth man. The document [read to me by Hu Qiaomu] stated that if I did not relinquish my Party membership voluntarily, I would be expelled. I didn't refuse, since that would have forced the Party to expel me, and once again the credibility of the Party would suffer in the eyes of the people of China and the whole world. Because of the extremely unconvincing nature of the document [demanding my resignation] I realized that it would lead many people in our society overly to sympathize with me. Again this would be highly deleterious to the Party. Indeed, in the past ten days I have become the object of numerous well-wishes, something that is very painful for me. The last thing I want is to become a news-maker. Of course, there are also some comrades who will have nothing more to do with me.

3. There is one more reason, one that I am most unwilling to give voice to, and it pains me much to do so. I have decided to resign from the Party because I am disillusioned with some of its decisions.

The Communist Party of China has a glorious tradition. It has achieved great things; it revived the confidence of our nation, it is a Party to which the people of China are deeply grateful. It was founded and grew to strength at a time when it was surrounded by the threats of capitalism and feudalism. It went from isolation to widespread support, from weakness to strength, and finally having sent the united forces of imperialism, warlords and landlords packing, it united China (apart from Taiwan). The Communist Party defeated capitalism, this is a fact that is plain to all. So I see absolutely no need to exaggerate the threat of the bourgeoisie today, for it is no easy thing for them to infect the body of the proletariat. The Chinese people have been educated and immunized by the Communist Party for many years; they are capable of warding off the infections of capitalism. We won't be corrupted by the bourgeoisie. To my mind the Communist Party of China was always an energetic and fearless organization, not one that was scared of criticism or lacking in self-confidence. Capitalism and the bourgeoisie are nothing to be scared of, nor for that matter is the student movement. After all, the two great student movements of modern Chinese history, the May 4 and December 12 Movements, were both led by the Communist Party of China....

The Communist Party of China always had the magnanimity to accept criticism humbly. Only when all manner of ideas and the wisdom of the broad masses are accepted can the great task of reunifying China be achieved. I first came under the guidance of the Party in the 1940s, so I have had personal experience of this. "When a gentleman is told of his faults he is delighted, when he hears of the goodness [of others] he pays them his respects"—this is one of the traditional strengths of the Chinese. However, starting in the late 1950s, some leaders in Party Central would only listen to pleasing words of praise, and became increasingly annoyed by criticism. For many years now, it is the most loyal and outspoken intellectuals who have been denounced, their lives destroyed. The numerous political movements have had an inestimable and devastating effect on a huge number of China's most outstanding talents. The results have been tragic. Although the Party has attempted to change, it is all too evident that up to now it hasn't been able to do so.

August 1987

> *Wu's expulsion brought him sympathy from many quarters. He was invited to take part in the Twentieth Anniversary of the Iowa International Writers' Program in October, and during his trip to America remained critical of the Anti-Bourgelib Campaign. In one interview he commented: "I know I can be a good human being, but it's impossible for me to be a good Party member too."*

WU ZUGUANG   Mi Qiu

Under a Curse:

Bo Yang in Conversation with Lee Yee

During the heady months of 1986, the unthinkable (see p. 169) occurred: Bo Yang's speech "The Ugly Chinaman" was published in Mainland China.

At the end of 1986, Lin Ruo, the Secretary of the Guangdong Province Party Committee, heard that a local publisher was planning to print Bo Yang's full-length book The Ugly Chinaman. *Lin commented: "What's all this about ugly Chinamen, eh? Well, I'm not ugly!" And with this he banned publication of the work.*

In a trip to Hong Kong in March 1987, Bo Yang and Lee Yee (see pp. 274-76) met for the first time. Just prior to their meeting the Mainland press had denounced "The Ugly Chinaman". They discussed this and the Anti-Bourgelib Campaign.

Lee Yee: What's the most common question you've been asked by Hong Kong reporters?

Bo Yang: Most reporters have concentrated on the criticism of me published in the *Guangming Daily* on March 1st. I've been at a loss as to how to reply to their questions. They tell me that apart from denouncing Hu Shi forty years ago and the present attack on me, the Mainland has never denounced scholars or writers outside Mainland China. They asked me for my thoughts on the subject and what the motive has been. To be quite honest I have no idea what their motives are. I'm surprised that reporters have been directing their questions at me instead of asking the people who've attacked me. Having said this, I'd like to ask you what you think is behind all of this? Are they "killing one to warn a hundred"? Or is it due to a change in attitude to Taiwan?

Lee Yee: In my opinion, that article printed in the *Guangming Daily* was only meant for internal consumption. If they'd wanted to make an issue of it to the outside world then it would have been carried by the Xinhua News Agency or the China News Service. The main readership of the *Guangming Daily* is the Mainland intelligentsia. One of the direct causes and targets of the present campaign against "bourgeois liberalization" is Fang Lizhi's advocacy of wholesale westernization. This is despite the fact that what Fang meant by wholesale westernization is that countries should be free to learn from each other, and that China should open up to the outside world without reservation. This view of Fang's is directly related to a major trend of thought that surfaced on the Mainland last year. Following the ten tragic years of the Cultural Revolution, people were satisfied at first with simply attacking Mao Zedong and the Gang of Four. But later they started to look more closely at the system itself. It was only one more step from there to conclude that the problems of the system were also related to China's cultural traditions. It is just like the period in the 1920s and 1930s when Lu Xun was reflecting on Chinese culture and the Chinese national character. Over the past few years many articles dealing with these questions have been printed on the Mainland; they call this trend "cultural reassessment". Some of the things that have been discussed happen to be the very notions you raised in your essays on the "soy-sauce vat of Chinese culture" over twenty years ago.

The process of cultural reassessment attempts to dig deeper into the origins of China's tragedies. The conclusion is that such tragedies are a natural corollary of China's cultural tradition. If there hadn't been a Gang of Four there would have been a Gang of Three, or a Gang of Five. If no Mao Zedong, then there would have been a Zhang Zedong, or a Li Zedong. In other words, it is a problem of traditional Chinese political culture. This reassessment wasn't your doing, they started it themselves. But it started off as a highly theoretical debate, not a popular one. Then last year "The Ugly Chinaman" made its appearance on the Màinland. The clarity of your argument and your approachable style immediately found a large audience. Even some high level people in charge of propaganda, culture and publishing liked it. They were competing with each other to publish it, and before long local publishers were producing countless reprints and pirate editions. The result was a "Bo Yang craze". The old men of the Communist Party have always used patriotism to keep the country united. They view wholesale westernization as a form of national nihilism; and, of course, the things you say in "The Ugly Chinaman"

> *I have also lifted a curtain on certain aspects of our ugliness. In this respect I'm similar to Bo Yang; but different also since I don't blame our people, or even our cadres for that ugliness. I have located the root cause of China's backwardness, economic decline and mass poverty elsewhere: the errors of the leadership of our Communist Party.*
>
> *Wang Ruowang, June 1987*

are seen by them as a threat to the ideology that they use to rule the masses. Thus the present criticism of Bo Yang is, in fact, aimed at Fang Lizhi and the entire process of cultural reassessment that has been occurring amongst the middle-aged and younger generations of the Mainland. It isn't aimed at you personally, its purpose is to maintain Party control.

Bo Yang: The Chinese have been scared of talking about peace ever since the Southern Song; peace means betraying the country. In fact, negotiation is a highly sophisticated form of knowledge. It's harder than engaging in war. Democracy is a kind of ceaseless negotiation in which endless concessions are made; endless demands and compromises.

Lee Yee: Do you feel that since you started criticizing Chinese culture in the 1960s there's been some progress?

Bo Yang: Yes. At least in Taiwan they can tolerate *The Ugly Chinaman;* no big problems resulted from its publication. This is proof that the ability of the Chinese in Taiwan to reassess themselves is far superior to that of those on the Mainland.

Lee Yee: In the preface to *The Ugly Chinaman* you used a hypothetical conversation to express the idea that the greatest fault of the Chinese is a desire to conceal their faults; and that at the root of this lies a fear that someone's going to come along and try to cure them of their faults. Every nation has its good points and its faults, but other races don't seem to suffer from this particular problem as much as the Chinese. They are not just scared of "doctors" when they are ill, they even want to kill them, or at least throw them into jail.

Bo Yang: Where does this fear come from? In my opinion it's due to mental illness and lack of confidence. People who are paranoid often suffer from an inferiority complex. For example, you might ask someone out for a meal and they decline because they're engaged. If you are convinced that this is actually because they look down on you, it's a sign of mental aberration. Chinese people often require the sacrifice of others to affirm their own sense of self-worth. As in the case I've just cited, you'd expect the person to give up their previous engagement so as to humour you; otherwise you might make out that the person who has declined your invitation is, in fact, completely worthless, thereby proving your own worth. Another characteristic trait is the refusal to admit one's own faults. These are typical traits of a personality that lacks confidence and is ashamed to admit mistakes.

Let me give you another illustration. Say, for instance, that you Mr Lee are a proofreader and that you have missed five words. I say to you: "Mr Lee, you've missed five words." You immediately respond by shouting: "I didn't make any mistakes yesterday, but I didn't hear a word of praise from you. Nor, for that matter, did you say anything about my good record the day before. And here you are hounding me over five lousy words. Do you know what type of impression this could make? No one would have known a thing if you hadn't opened your mouth, now the whole office knows and everyone looks down on me. Once it gets out that there are five misprints in the paper then sales will fall off: too many mistakes! And before you know where you are we'll all be out of a job. Do you want to see us all starve?" Heavens! Why the hell do I have to smother you with praise for your spotless record before I can make the slightest criticism? *(laughter)* What's all this fear of admitting one's illness when a doctor turns up?

Lee Yee: Do you think this is the reason why China repeatedly re-enacts the same tragedies?

Bo Yang: When I heard that they had crushed the student demonstrations in the Mainland I was deeply upset. I had thought, there's a sign of hope, not hope for you or me alone, but hope for us as a nation. And then, in an instant, it was blotted out. I've been hearing of the appearance of some new hope, and then its destruction, over and over again since I was seven or eight . . . . I can't help thinking that maybe the Chinese as a nation are under a curse . . . Cursed never to be able to organize a modern government or to become a modern state. Condemned never to be able to unite, and doomed forever to live in a dirty, disordered, noisy and acrimonious environment. Our descendants will be doomed for all time. Isn't this just the predicament we find ourselves in now?

The Chinese people are under a most foul curse. I believe this to be the truth. Otherwise, how could we have become as we are? There's no way we can preserve any of the extraordinary achievements of our ancestors. In Taiwan some sort of new model has appeared, with the greatest of difficulty, but even then there is a dark spectre hovering over the island. The Chinese, nearly every one of them, are using the most destructive means at their disposal to love China, to express their love for their own people . . . . You could say that the Chinese are the most patriotic people in the world; but at the same time they are the most anxious to become foreigners.

Some months after this, General Secretary of the Party Zhao Ziyang commented that Bo Yang's speech was patriotic and that he meant well. It is unclear, however, if this means that "The Ugly Chinaman" will be officially reprinted in the Mainland. Nonetheless, when the speech was published in China in 1986 many editors chose to preface it with a comment that although the phenomena described by Bo Yang exist, it is only under the ideologically sound leadership of the Communist Party and within the process of socialist modernization that the Chinese national character can be reformed.

It is interesting to note that although Bo Yang's satirical writings are available in Taiwan, as is the book The Ugly Chinaman, *the major KMT newspapers cannot print his name, articles by him, or in some cases even advertisements for his historical works. Bo Yang's comment on this ironical situation is: "Maybe this is because I'm the only Ugly Chinaman on either side of the Taiwan Straits!"*

Hah Gong:

Dizzy With Success

> *Hah Gong finally launched his own satirical magazine,* Emancipation Monthly, *in January 1987. His editorial to the very first issue made reference to the first Hong Kong edition of* Seeds of Fire. *He wrote: "I am a seed of fire.* Emancipation Monthly *is a seed of fire; so are the student demonstrators. Such seeds of fire shouldn't be underestimated. The warlords were scorched by the fire of the May 4 Movement, the Anti-Hunger Movement of 1949 burnt the KMT. Who can honestly say that the seeds of fire of today's student movement won't scorch the new rulers of the Mainland?"*
> *Hah Gong died on June 15, 1987.*

Comrade Hu Qili was shooting his mouth off at a recent board meeting of China's major political corporation.

He called Fang Lizhi "China's Sakharov", and demanded his expulsion from the Party. He added that, if need be, Fang could be sent into exile to play Sakharov in some foreign country. Liu Binyan and Wang Ruowang were just as bad . . .

From the sound of it, Hu's in a real fighting mood. In fact, I can't remember anyone carrying on quite like that since the "Great People's Holocaust" [the Cultural Revolution], when there was all that talk of Liu Shaoqi being "China's Khruschev" and the "timebomb at Chairman Mao's side".

But if it comes to being a truly powerful and awesome figure, Hu Qili can't hold a candle to Zhang Chunqiao and Yao Wenyuan [two members of the Gang of Four].

At least they had omnipotent Aunty Jiang Qing to back them up. Who's Hu Qili got?

Everyone's speculating these days, whether the three Venerable Hus [Hu Yaobang, Hu Qiaomu and Hu Qili] are going to lose their

STABILITY AND UNITY—
with Chinese characteristics

Our socialist construction can only be carried out under leadership, in an orderly way, and in an environment of stability and unity.

Deng Xiaoping, December 30, 1986

rice bowls at the next Party congress.

Now Big Hu, Bossman Hu Yaobang, has a penchant for saying the first thing that comes into his mind. One minute he's decked out in a suit and tie [and wants the whole country to imitate him]; the next he's telling everyone that the only way to be hygienic is to use knives and forks. Then he claims that the Chinese can only become as strong as Westerners by boozing and eating hunks of beef.

Hu Number Two, Hu Qiaomu, the "intellectual" of the Politburo, knows fuck-all about anything, except, of course, cleaning up "spiritual pollution". And there's his son—an expert at fraud and an accomplished rapist [Hu Shiying, reportedly detained in 1986 for the misappropriation of state funds and on multiple counts of rape, both capital offences. He was subsequently released by order of Deng Xiaoping].

What about Hu the Third, Hu Qili? Well, he's obviously just full of hooey. I bet he doesn't even have a clue who Sakharov is.

Fang Lizhi, Liu Binyan and Wang Ruowang all love their country. Why else would they have bothered speaking out against government policy? They did it for the sake of China and the Party. They could easily have behaved like the new Minister of Culture, the writer Wang

Meng, putting on airs the moment he became a bureaucrat. They too could be enjoying the good life.

So my friends the Pink Panther *et al* have asked me to give Comrade Hu Qili a few words of advice. Be as smug as you like about your success, just be careful not to become too dizzy with it. And whatever you do, don't go apeing the ways of the Gang of Four. Oh, and while you're at it, Comrade, why not pass on a few words of warning to the leaders of "the State and the Party"? Tell them from us: whatever they do, they'd better not start playing the deadly games of the Gang of Four again. You know, one day I denounce someone, the next day someone else denounces me; that sort of thing. We all know where that'll land you all: first there'll be the purge of a new Gang of Four, and then there'll be another Gang of Four, and another, and so on until you've squandered all your time denouncing, arresting and purging each other. In the end there will be nothing left of the beautiful rivers and mountains of China but a blighted wasteland.

January 9, 1987

"Big Hu" was ordered to resign less than a week later, accused of fostering Bourgelib.

Ba Jin:
A Cultrev Museum

Ba Jin, a novelist in his eighties, is the grand old man of Chinese letters and the President of the Chinese P.E.N. He is famous for his early work Family, a novel about the destructive and malevolent aspects of the feudal Chinese extended family. Since the cultural Revolution he has written a series of essays which he has entitled Random Thoughts. They are inspired by Alexander Herzen's memoirs My Past and Thoughts, which Ba Jin has translated into Chinese. Although an enthusiastic propagandist for the Party up to the time of the Cultural Revolution, Ba Jin entered a period of self-reflection after the death of his wife in 1973. His recent essays are, as he puts it, his final testament, a personal confessional, or, as he wrote in a preface to the collected articles in June 1987, his own "Cultural Revolution Museum". Although he remained conspicuously silent throughout the 1987 purge, Ba Jin's attitude to such political movements is more than clear from the essay presented here.

In one of my *Random Thoughts* essays written some time ago I recorded a conversation with a friend. In it I suggested that they should build a Cultural Revolution Museum. Now, I have no well thought-out plan or detailed proposal for such a building, but I do firmly believe it is something we should do, something for which every Chinese should take responsibility.

That's all I want to say; I'll leave the details to others. I'm sure few of those who were baptised in the blood and fire of the Cultural Revolution will wish to remain silent. Everyone has his own story to tell. One thing is certain: no one will make out that the "cow sheds" [makeshift jails for intellectuals and cadres] were "heaven", or say that the violent and ruthless murders that took place were really part of a "Great Proletarian Revolution". People may have differences of opinion, but I'm sure we are of the same basic mind: none of us wish

to see another Cultural Revolution in China. Another disaster like
that would mean the destruction of our nation.

I don't think I'm being alarmist when I say this. Everything that
happened twenty years ago is still clearly before my mind's eye. Those
endlessly long and painful days, the degradation and torture that so
many were put through, the distortions, deceptions, confusion of good
and bad, true and false, and all the frame-ups, the endless injustices.
You cannot tell me we should forget all about it, or forbid people to
talk about it? That would only make it possible for another Cultural
Revolution to take place in twenty years time. By then people would
somehow think it was something new.

"Another Cultural Revolution? Impossible!" I can already hear
voices raised in protest. But is it really so unimaginable? I've given the
matter a lot of thought over the last few years, in the hope of finding a
clear answer to this question. Without an answer I shall never be able
to sleep soundly at night. But no one can give me any assurances. I
shall never be able to sleep in peace, I shall be forever in danger of
tumbling out of my bed, waving my arms in the grip of some new
nightmare.

It's not that I don't want to forget; it's simply that the gory spectre
of the past has me in its grip and won't let me go. How I let myself be
disarmed, how the disaster crept up on me, just how that tragedy
unfolded, and the hateful role that I played in it all, walking step by
step towards an abyss. It is as though it were all only yesterday. But I
survived, even though I was left a shell of a man. How many talented
people were destroyed in front of my very eyes! How many dear
friends were torn from my side!

"It will never be repeated. Dry your tears and look to the future,"
my friends urge, soothe me. But I remain only half convinced, and
think to myself: we must wait and see. And I did wait, right up to the
time they started calling for "the elimination of Spiritual Pollution".

I was in hospital at the time. It was my second stay in hospital, for
treatment of Parkinson's disease. I was in the neurology ward. My left
leg, which I'd broken the year before, was better, though three
millimetres shorter than it used to be. I was out of traction and could
walk with the help of a stick. It was a great effort for me to read, so I'd
got into the habit of listening to the morning news on the radio, and
watching the television news at night in the lounge room. I was
allowed visitors after three in the afternoon, and they often brought all
types of strange news with them. I'd only been in hospital a few days
when things started getting tense. Every day the radio would broadcast

speeches by various provincial leaders denouncing "Spiritual Pollution". At night, artists and writers would appear on television and pledge themselves to the fight to wipe out Spiritual Pollution. On the surface I remained calm and collected, but when I returned to my room each night I was haunted by visions of those early days of the Cultural Revolution in 1966. I couldn't help feeling that another tempest was brewing, another disaster was stalking us. I wasn't scared for myself: what do I have to fear at my age? I simply couldn't understand why they had to start another Cultural Revolution and cast us once more into that abyss. Still there was no one to answer my question.

Rumours abounded. It was as though I could see a giant broom sweeping back and forth in front of me [one of the early slogans of the early Cultural Revolution was "sweep away all cow demons and snake spirits"]. I counted the days and waited. What a long and painful wait that was! I could see the dark storm clouds gathering, the war drums thundered closer all the time. But this time I kept clear-headed, I was able to make a comparison between the last Cultural Revolution and the details of this campaign as it unfolded. I heard no cries of "Long Live", no one was "taking the right stand" or capitulating in the face of the onslaught. But somehow the process continued to unfold, the thunder could be heard in the distance and the first drops of rain were just beginning to fall. And then, within one month of it all starting, someone [Hu Yaobang, the Party General Secretary who was subsequently purged) spoke out, and their brooms were unable to get at "the dust". I don't know where all the storm clouds were blown to, but those bellicose drummers had no choice but to fall silent. We had been spared another holocaust.

I was invited to attend the forty-seventh International P.E.N. Conference in Tokyo in May 1984, and wrote my speech in hospital. I spent another peaceful six months in the hospital [after that]. I had a stream of visitors, and they always brought with them new rumours, the reliability of which they left to me to sort out.

I should be thankful to the people who have kept their memories of the Cultural Revolution alive for the fact that I was left undisturbed in my hospital room. They had refused to let their blood be used to nourish the "buds" of another Cultural Revolution. Such attractive buds, but oh so poisonous once they blossom! All it would have needed would have been one new flower and I would have been dragged out of my hospital bed and denied treatment.

After a year of reflection and analysis I came to realize that neither the soil nor the climate existed for a second Cultural Revolution. It was quite the opposite, however much everything seemed to be in place for such a thing to happen. And yet if that "one month" I spoke of above had been a little longer, say two months, or four months, then things might have reached the point of no return. Because there are a lot of people around who are capable of manipulating a Cultural Revolution to their own advantage . . . .

I've said more than enough. I received many letters from friends and readers; the papers printed articles in approval. They spoke in a far deeper, more thorough and forceful manner. They have even more intense recollections than I have, they suffered more. They have made themselves heard: "Never again will we allow that dark and evil period of history to repeat itself!"

The building of a Cultural Revolution Museum is not the responsibility of one person. Everyone owes it to their children and the future to leave a monument to the harrowing lessons of the past. "Don't let history repeat itself" should not be an empty statement. Everyone must be made to see clearly, to remember fully. That's why it would be best to build a museum, one in which concrete and real things could be collected, emblems of the terrifying events of the Cultural Revolution, displayed so that people can see what actually happened here in China twenty years ago. Let people be confronted with the whole process and meditate on what we Chinese did throughout that decade. Force people to take off their masks, to show their conscience and to face themselves as they really are. Let them repay the debts of the past. Those who aren't selfish will not be scared of being deceived, those who dare speak the truth will not easily fall for lies. Only by remaining mindful of the Cultural Revolution will people be able to prevent history replaying itself.

It is extremely important that we build this Museum, for only by remembering the "past" can we be masters of the "future".

August 1986

I still haven't changed my mind about opposing Spiritual Pollution.

Deng Xiaoping, December 30, 1986

XIII: PRESSURE POINTS

I can sum up what's wrong with Chinese writers in one sentence: They can't create themselves, they simply don't have the ability, their very lives don't belong to them.

Liu Xiaobo, December 1986

Theirs is an abomination that has grown in the body of our socialist culture, suckled on the milk of various western schools of the irrational and mysticism.

Xiong Fu, April 1987

I said to a friend: I'm seeing our generation slowly die . . . . I should have added: But there's no turning back. We have already exhausted all possibilities of retreat.

Yang Lian, October 1987

All I want is peace, and a chance to be a shepherd.

Gu Cheng, December 1987

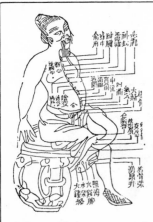

The Chinese Velvet Prison

After decades of rule by Proledic, external political coercion and the internal pressures of the Chinese deep structure meld to create a new self-censoring cultural figure, the state artist. The degradation of the individual, in particular the intellectual, in such a situation is often thought of by the Chinese as unique to their cultural tradition. In fact, the artist under Proledic is common to all socialist systems. The Hungarian dissident-poet Miklós Haraszti describes the phenomenon in his samizdat classic The Velvet Prison: Artists under State Socialism.

As Mainland China enters the phase of "soft" technocratic socialism, the parameters of the cultural Velvet Prison are being measured out in everyday practice. But this does not mean that there is no resistance to a new higher level of co-option, conformity within the deep structure of the State. Individual artists struggle to maintain or achieve their independence. Each campaign against Bourgelib disaffects sections of the intelligentsia and increases the number of marginalized intellectuals and writers seeking to develop their own self-referential system of values and artistic norms. But they are faced with a choice of suffering complete cultural ostracism or accepting the State's efforts to incorporate them in a new social contract, one in which consensus replaces coercion, and complicity subverts criticism.

It is in the borderlands of permissibility that contact between alienated or marginal writers and the State takes place. They barter endlessly, using different rates of exchange—freedom to publish, or the right to remain unmolested, permission to enjoy the privileges of the cultural élite or even to travel overseas. Deals are cut, or fall through as the case may be. The sensitive pressure points of the individual are laid bare, in the antechambers of the Velvet Prison.

PRESSURE POINTS: one of a series of oil paintings by Guan Wei, a young Peking high school art teacher of Manchurian descent. In 1986-7 he abandoned his earlier attempts at collage and conventional oils to work on a series of paintings based on the acupuncture or pressure points of traditional Chinese medicine. Many of his paintings play on the deeper significance of these points; some are of his own whimsical invention. The titles (for example, Xia Guan: "Lower Pass", the Seventh Point of the Stomach Meridian, which physically controls the facial muscles, the ears and teeth) are often simply the names of traditional acupuncture points. The paintings also evoke the nightmarish world of the artist as inmate.

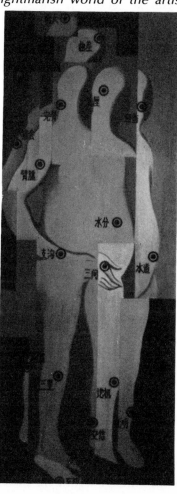

Inside-Out:
Bei Dao in Paris

Ming Lei, Paris special correspondent for the Hong Kong-based
Chinese monthly Cheng Ming, interviewed the "misty" poet Bei Dao
(see pp. 2-16 & 236-7) in Paris on August 2, 1987. These are extracts
from that interview.

*Because of your past history you are often under pressure in China. I
was concerned for you as soon as the present Anti-Bourgelib
movement began; then, as expected, I heard you'd been blacklisted by
the Chinese Writers' Association. Following your departure from
China, certain circles in Peking were buzzing with a rumour that you'd
defected. Could you tell me why you are overseas and about the
process of getting out?*

I received the invitation [to visit Durham University for a year] at the
height of the student demonstrations in China. That was followed
immediately by the Anti-Bourgelib Campaign, so my application to
travel overseas created a lot of problems. As you know, every time I
apply to leave China I have many problems and have to face a lot of
pressure. The first time I left China, when we met here in Paris the
first time, Hu Yaobang had to give his personal approval. The second
trip was approved by Hu Qili [the Politburo member in charge of
ideology and culture]. This time things were different, more difficult
because of the political situation. The Durham invitation was for a
year starting on 1 April, 1987. Despite all the difficulties I managed to
arrive in London on 27 March.

*I know many people in China and overseas have been anxious to help
you. Was this also the case this time?*

Yes. I had the help of a lot of friends, but for their own sake I can't say
who. Quite frankly, this time it was particularly difficult, and rushed.
As to the rumour that I had defected, I didn't hear this until I was
overseas. A friend told me. I was very angered by it. I'm sure this
rumour was started on purpose, with the aim of making me too scared
to return to China, to prevent me from going back. They've even
spread stories about me having contact with Taiwan. This means if I
do want to go back to China I could be in serious trouble.

Why are these people against you?

They've never liked me. They call me a dissident. I've said in public that I am an anarchist, because by their very nature artists are anarchists. Of course, I respect the laws of the State. If I'm a dissident in the Chinese context, then that's equally true when I'm overseas, for there are many things about the western system that fail to impress me. A person can't feel completely satisfied with any system, especially an artist.

In June 1985 you were accepted as a member of the Chinese Writers' Association, but you've never been assigned work. What about now?

I've never been a full-time State-employed writer, nor do I have any chance of becoming one. I can find other employment in Peking if I so wish, but in my opinion a writer should concentrate on writing.

The conservatives in China are of the opinion that the effects of Bourgelib are extremely serious in the arts. The present campaign has hit the cultural world very hard. As a modernist poet could you tell us what it has been like for you?

I was deeply saddened by the political developments in China in January of this year. My grief doesn't result from any one isolated political movement, but rather the historical circumstances of political upheaval. The vicious cycle of political unrest in China has made me realize many things about the history of the Chinese nation. When the political situation deteriorates I become very depressed and feel there is no hope, that our land may well be as Bo Yang has said: cursed by God. Yet when I suffer any misfortune due to political changes all I feel is personal outrage It is impossible for me to distance myself completely. In interviews with British reporters I have stated my views on this movement. As I don't have a work unit in China, I have not been put under any pressure or suffered any constraints this time. But at the same time I feel completely hopeless about China and her people.

Will this hopelessness lead you to abandon China?

No, it's not my fate to do that. I'm 38 this year. My life, my past history, is tied up with China. If I were younger then I could change that history, live a different life, make a new start. I've met many young

Chinese studying in the West. They can adapt to a new life; for me it's impossible. I'm bound up with China, no matter how hopeless I may feel about it. This has got to do with my psychological attitude, my language, my history, the way I live. It is not a question of good or bad, it's a fate that can't be altered.

Last year the Secretariat of the Writers' Association ordered that the literary monthly China *stop publication. It was an extremely interesting magazine. You were a guest editor and did a lot of work in the magazine. What is your opinion of this incident?*

Last year, before the Anti-Bourgelib Campaign began, when the cultural world was in a state of ferment, there were many things that foreshadowed such a purge. My resignation from the Creative Committee of the Writers' Association last June was directly linked to [the activities of] conservative elements. There were complex reasons for the closure of the magazine *China*. However, the main reason was that it had published a great many works of artistically high quality. The leadership and editors were furious when they were ordered to stop publication. I had begun work with the magazine in 1986, so I joined the other editors in resigning. In fact, the Writers' Association didn't move to the "left" after the Anti-Bourgelib Campaign began, it was there already. That's not to say that the leadership of the Association is in favour with the [political] conservatives at the top. They've had their share of "internal" criticism. It's all relative. In my opinion, the Association itself is a conservative force, distinguishable from the [political] conservatives only in its degree of conservatism. The writers' organizations I've come across overseas are just a type of union, their main function being to help writers who are having difficulties and to support them in their creative pursuits. In China, the Writers' Association is another yamen, it functions as a restraining or a supervising force on writers, and it controls all the literary journals and magazines. This is directly related to the nature of traditional Chinese culture. Chinese intellectuals can only think of themselves in relation to the patronage of bureaucratic rulers. As soon as the bureaucrats loosen up a little they're delighted and grateful. This is the reason why the Chinese cultural world appeared so excited last year.

Last year, a literary critic by the name of Liu Xiaobo publicly declared that it was farcical to lavish praise on post-1979 Chinese literature. They dubbed him the "dark horse" of the literary scene. He may have been somewhat excessive in some of his comments. They

Old Whine in New Bottles

At a national conference held in April 1987, Zang Kejia (advisor to Poetry *magazine and veteran poet, see p. 233) said: "There is excessive praise for middle-aged and young writers on the literary scene at the moment. A situation exists in which such writers are being used to oppress veteran writers. Not all the works that get literary awards are necessarily up to scratch; some even make light of the need to have a strong theme. That stream-of-consciousness stuff is completely incomprehensible. And just look at these writers, they're intoxicated with themselves. They think that the more incomprehensible a work is the better. The classics and realist works have all been attacked as conservative and passé. Then one has these younger writers who are constantly flitting overseas; while it is becoming extremely difficult for older writers to get a look in. We even have difficulty getting work published. Our hope is that all workers in the arts will undertake a renewed study of Chairman Mao's* Talks *at the Yan'an Forum on Art and Literature thereby furthering their own ideological reconstruction and strengthening their struggle against Bourgelib."*

were certainly controversial. But I'm in agreement with his basic analysis of the central problems of Chinese literature at the moment. Many members of the leadership cannot tolerate his views, but that's because he negates the "literature of the new period" [1976-86]. Liu's first article was published in *China*, the fourth issue of 1986. He sounded a warning for Chinese literature. The tenth issue of *China* last year published an academic article of his which took Li Zehou, the leading authority on aesthetics in China, to task.

Unfortunately, there are some political fat cats in the Writers' Association itself who know just how to destroy art, because they were once writers themselves.

How do you see the future development of Chinese literature? Do you, for example, see a Chinese writer being awarded the Nobel Prize for Literature in the foreseeable future?

I answered this very question in an interview with a Finnish reporter last spring. I said that at the moment Chinese literature is heading in the right direction, but it is nothing more than a start. It is far too early to talk of [a Chinese writer] being awarded a major international literary prize. For that we'll have to wait at least ten to twenty years. After that interview was published I learnt that my reply had offended the leaders of our literary world. That's because last year they were enthusiastically discussing the Nobel Prize. Upon my return to China, the leadership [of the Writers' Association] rang me and criticized me for talking the way I did to foreigners. I replied as follows: "I am an anarchist. I certainly don't see myself as being responsible to the Writers' Association, nor to the State, and I only take personal responsibility for what I say. I say what I think, and if you let me go out again I will do the same!"

Nowadays a fair amount of Chinese literature is being translated into western languages, and a lot of sinologists are involved in this work. But, to be quite honest, the situation does not permit optimism.

Are you in favour of "wholesale westernization" in the cultural sphere?

(Laughing) I know you've been speaking to Fang Lizhi . . . . It is my opinion that our ancient Chinese nationality has had too little exposure to outside cultures. As a result of this, the [recent]

YUN MEN: Cloud Gate

intermingling of Chinese and foreign culture has spawned many "cultural abnormalities". I think that without doubt Chinese culture needs to be exposed to more foreign influence. As to how people should come to terms with western culture, everyone has their own view. In England or France there is no feeling whatsoever of a need to reject outside cultures. But throughout Chinese history this has been a serious problem. The Chinese have always been fearful of foreign cultural influences. It is like a phobia, an illness, in the race. In China it is very serious indeed to be accused of propagating "westernization".

Now a second generation of modernist poets has emerged in China. How do you evaluate these young modernist poets?

The present variety of poetic genres and the high profile of their exponents is a phenomenon unique in the history of modern Chinese literature. They undeniably represent a new system of values. In a sense, they have made a more drastic break with the Chinese cultural tradition. Although they all have different styles, they do have a common creative tendency in that they emphasize the significance of action in itself, eliminating the distance between art and life. For example, in their works you often find such lines as "I drink coffee", "I walk along the street", "I sleep with a woman", and so on and so forth. In the 1960s and 1970s a similar poetic trend appeared in the West. In reality, it is a reaction to modernist poetry. Generally speaking, I take a wait-and-see approach to the new poetry; I have my doubts about it.

Thinking of You

Chen Lin

In the dusk
I'm all alone
With my shadow
Not saying a single word

No
I did not think of you
You are already someone else's wife

Your home is not far from the school
Right?
You gave me a photograph once
Right?
You wrote to me once
Right?

I'd rather not think about
What happened in the past
Not think
Not think at all

Tonight
Not eating
Not eating
You are already someone else's wife

Tonight
Not eating
Not eating

Chen Lin is a young writer of the Hunan "Angry School" of poetry founded in 1985.

A Dark Horse

from an interview with Liu Xiaobo

Liu Xiaobo is a young scholar and literary critic from North-East China. A classmate of the editor, poet and critic, Xu Jingya (see pp. 242-3), he came to prominence in 1986 when he wrote a series of controversial articles on contemporary Chinese philosophy and aesthetics. His comments on Chinese literature made him unpopular with writers and critics of all persuasions. The following quotations are taken from an interview conducted by Geremie Barmé in Peking, December 1986.

I No matter how famous someone might be in the Chinese literary scene, or among artists, the fact is that the quality of the cultural environment of China is so inferior and people's cultural background is so poor, that it is impossible for any really outstanding things to appear. I've been working in literary theory and aesthetics for years now, and I'm more than aware of the truth of this. Sometimes there's something you've been thinking about for ages and you reckon you're really hot, that you've got something new to say so you should write it. Before you even set pen to paper someone goes and translates a book and you discover that it's all been said before, and far better than you could ever say it. Of course, it's deeply upsetting. The only thing we can do in China is accept modern Western culture, establish our own contemporary mentality, and from that point review and re-evaluate what's been happening here.

II Western culture leads the rest of the world. At the base of it lies a sense that there is nothing but a vague, unknowable future ahead. Only when you have a consciousness like this can you have a literature in which there is no need to have a fixed audience or purpose, can there be a sense of nihilism. It is very difficult for the Chinese to understand real nihilism, that's why the new literature [post-Cultural Revolution literature] is so shallow. It inevitably finds itself [to quote from Mao Zedong] "walking on two legs": searching for a way out in traditional culture, or through simplistic, inane and blind imitation of western culture. China is caught in a paradoxical situation: on the one hand we

lack cultural sophistication, which makes it impossible for us to experience the type of perception inherent in modern western man. On the
other hand, we Chinese are excessively vain. This gives rise to a desire
to insinuate ourselves into the ranks of the world's advanced cultures.
It allows us to believe that we can artificially put our culture and art on
a parity with the most advanced cultures on earth. The eagerness with
which the Chinese yearn for a Nobel Prize for Literature or an
Academy Award is part and parcel of this hypocritical approach.

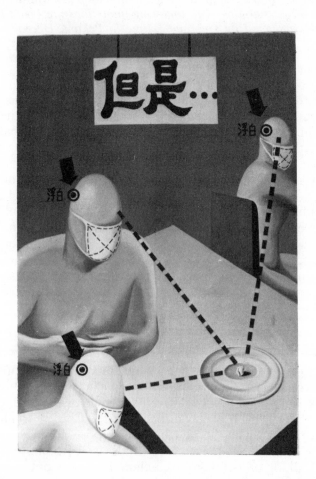

FU BAI : Floating White

III The inertia of the old is so great, the roots of the past so deep, it's almost impossible to guarantee that anything new you attempt will, in reality, be new. We're caught in the quagmire of the past, so everything we create is saturated with the very essence of the old. One of the crucial aspects of our national inertia is that the Chinese are always wanting people to show them a way, to create a new system of values for them. This is an extremely traditional way of looking at history and man: the belief that there is a model way along which man develops, and that the nature of the relationship between people is unchanging. In fact, it's still very hard to say just where we're all going. In the West no one could have guessed that WW II would break out; in China certainly no one thought that after 1949 there would be a Cultural Revolution. Both man and history are charged with the unexpected.

IV I can sum up what's wrong with Chinese writers in one sentence: They can't create themselves, they simply don't have the ability, because their very lives don't belong to them. So when young people go off to get involved in politics and all that rubbish, taking part in demonstrations, I see it as something completely superficial. In my opinion true liberation for the Chinese will only come when people learn to live for themselves, when they realize that life is what you make of it. They should establish this type of a credo: "Everything I am is of my own doing. If I become famous, that is due to my own efforts; if I'm a failure it's my own fault." If a person is really self-aware then none of these things matter. What has brought about the present state of affairs is group consciousness. People feel that they can't rely on themselves, they can't prove their own unique worth, that self-esteem only comes when you've thrown your lot in with the group. But, if you act independently, even if people think you are absurd and that what you do is of no social relevance, if it's something no one else has ever thought of or done before, and you do it, then I believe your life hasn't been wasted.

Landscape in a Room

Yang Lian

Thirty-two, I've heard enough lies
No more landscapes can move into this room
Visitors with corn-cob faces
Stand at the door hawking crumbling rocks
Sticking out their coated tongues.
  eternity ground between teeth

  They
  you
  all so cold
  so cold it feels like
Vomit
Like a sacrilegious picture on the wall
Memory a single file of faded addresses
The stubble of autumn
  death on a bare foot of gold
Who is it leaning at the window sill
  hearing the stars disappear?
The wind this night
  like pears fallen from heaven
The empty room thrown out

Wandering in your bare flesh
Dismembered
  like sky and water
Wet sun
  crying wounded and forgetting all
No other landscape can move into this
To kill you

Until the last bird flies skyward, escaping
Colliding in that hand
   frozen into a blue vein
Where you have locked yourself
There will remain
   an empty echo
Reciting darkness
Burying the only landscape in your heart the only

Lie

1987

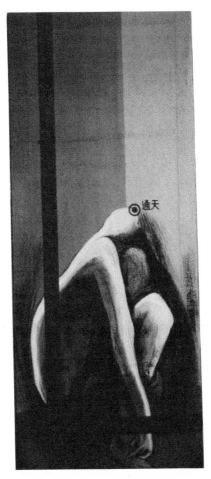

TONG TIAN : Reaching Heaven

Cui Jian

Cui Jian is the lead singer and composer for Peking's one and only rock band, "A-Do", a group made up of both Chinese and foreign instrumentalists. In his mid-twenties, Cui played the trumpet with the Peking Philharmonic Orchestra until he was cashiered at the height of the Anti-Bourgelib Campaign in April 1987.

Cui Jian performed the song "Nothing to My Name" in public, dressed in army and peasant garb from the Yan'an period of the 1940s. The lyrics of the song displeased the leadership of the Peking Municipal Party committee—"How can one of our young people sing about having nothing when he has socialism?" they argued—and Cui was subsequently banned from performing for local audiences. By the end of the year, however, "A-Do" was allowed to give in-house concerts for university students, and Cui Jian had signed a recording contract with CBS Records.

In "It's Not That I Can't See" we hear what a younger generation has to say about the questions raised by such poems as "The Answer" (see p. 236). Cui Jian's music and lyrics reach a much larger and less intellectually-minded audience than the works of writers like Bei Dao and his misty colleagues.

Nothing to My Name

It's ages now I've been asking you:
When will you come away with me?
But all you ever do is laugh at me, 'cause
I've got nothing to my name.

I want to give you my hope
I want to help make you free
But all you ever do is laugh at me, 'cause
I've got nothing to my name.

When will you come away with me?

The ground is moving under your feet
The waters of life are flowing free
But all you ever do is laugh at me, 'cause
I've got nothing to my name.

Why do you always laugh at the pack on my back?
Why do I always keep on going?
The old horse stands before you; here I am
With nothing to my name.

When will you come away with me?

Tell you this—I've been waiting a long time.
Tell you this—my final plea:
I want to grab you by the hands
And have you go away with me.

Your hands they are a-shaking
Your eyes awash with tears
Do you really mean to tell me
You love me as I am?

Come with me then

Come with me then

It's Not That I Can't See

Never used to know what it meant to take it easy,
Just couldn't see how weird the world was growing.
The future I'd been seeing sure isn't here today,
But now I think I know which way it's going.

Of everything that's said and done,
I can't tell good from bad,
Which year was which, the times I've had.
The things I thought were simple.
Makes me feel like I've been had.
Suddenly it seems as if the world's no place for me.

Twenty years and all I've learnt is patience, holding on.
No wonder all the comrades said my head was in the clouds,
I got myself together, made myself stop dreaming,
Now I'm awake and I can see
This world's as weird as weird can be.

Looking out at all the highrise buildings there
    like fields of rice and wheat,
Looking out and all I see is waves of people
    traffic in the street.
Looking left now right, front, back,
I'm so busy I can't keep track.
This 'n' that, that 'n' this
    the more I see the weirder it is.

Never used to know what it meant to take it easy,
Just couldn't see how weird the world was growing.
The future I'd been seeing sure isn't here today,
But now I think I know which way it's going.

It's not that I can't see,
The world's too weird for me.

It's not that I can't see,
The world's too weird for me.

CUI JIAN

AFP Gianini

These Are a Few of My Least Favourite Things:

Comrade Xiong Fu Speaks

Xiong Fu, editor of the Chinese Communist Party's major theoretical organ Red Flag, *gave a secret speech at a meeting of propaganda apparatchiki held at Zhuozhou, a city near Peking, in April 1987 at the height of the Anti-Bourgelib Campaign. Along with a number of other speeches by propaganda leaders, this document was leaked to the Hong Kong magazine* The Nineties *which published it in June 1987. The following is an extract from that speech.*

Personally, I know very little about the situation in the arts world. It is, however, an undeniable fact that since the Third Plenum of the Party [December 1978] the socialist art and culture industry of our country has seen considerable developments. But when I read, hear or come into contact with certain things, I feel as though I am having a nightmare. They both horrify me and make me feel extremely isolated, for it has become virtually impossible to hear the voice of Marxism. To date I have been unable to do anything about the situation. I feel dejected and guilty. Even to talk of it makes me feel extremely ashamed.

I am disturbed:

By the advocacy of abstract human nature and humanism, the excessive praise for "self existence", "self awareness" and "self worth" and all the other aspects of the value systems of extreme individualism of the bourgeoisie; the advertizing of existentialism, social Darwinism, Freudianism, and Nietzsche's philosophy of the "Superman";

When our writers take to writing works in which they lavish praise on free sex and sexual liberation;

Whenever I come into contact with those works of literature that are brimming over with pornography, all manner of bad taste, in pursuit of absurdist surreal episodes divorced from time and place, divorced from history; the mysticism that reflects contemporary life in a distorted way melding man, beast and god in one form, and all that extravagant encouragement of the anti-rational works of modernism in which ugliness and depravity are extolled as beautiful—works that fill the pages of our magazines and books;

Whenever I read those flattering passages that fly around, extolling all of the types of works that I have mentioned above, eulogies masquerading as literary criticism, riddled with technical terms taken from the natural sciences, exulting in an abstruse and incomprehensible style;

When I read those works of criticism in which the writer takes a nihilistic approach to our Chinese national cultural heritage, both national and historical nihilism, distorting and belittling as they do our national history and culture in every possible fashion, taking as a target in particular the revolutionary and progressive cultural movement led by the Party since the May 4 Movement [of 1919], which they denigrate and distort, claiming as they do that since the May 4 there's been a break in our cultural development. They call it a field strewn with ruins, or a desert, declaring that all that one can find of worth among those ruins or in that desert are little tufts of grass like [the writers] Xu Zhimo, Zhu Xiang and Shen Congwen;

When I read the new schools of literary theory which spend all their time establishing an aesthetic which extols "consciousness of the subject" or "consciousness of the self", saying this is the highest form of imagination. They advocate Nietzsche's voluntarism and Bergson's

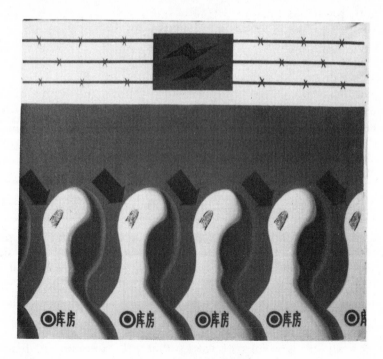

KU FANG : Repository

intuitivism, and insist that only when the mind attains intuition of the self can the *extremum* of beauty be realized. They have carelessly gleaned things from the aesthetic trends of western bourgeois modernism and contemporary philosophy so as to denigrate Chinese culture and champion western culture. In fact, they have a completely poverty-stricken understanding of the historical development of both

Not-Not

Zhou Lunyou and Lan Ma

Not-Not: a blanket term covering the object, form, contents, methodology, process, way and result of the principles of Pre-cultural Thought. It is also the description of the primordial mien of the universe. Not-Not is not "no".

After deconstructing the relationship between man and objects to their pre-cultural state, there is nothing in this universe that is not Not-Not.

Not-Not is not the negation of anything. It is only an expression of itself. Not-Not is aware that liberation exists in the indefinite. Not-Not reveals itself in constant flux. Not-Not knows no time. It communicates via intuition and pre-culture, because Not-Not is non-sentient, unalloyed. Transparency is one of the goals of Not-Not. The reduction of the lofty—irony is the hallmark of Not-Not, but that is not all that Not-Not is. As a new form of artistic perception, Not-Not is a type of revelation, a method . . . .

The starting point of Not-Not thinking is a profound mistrust of language . . . .

from "The Not-Not Manifesto", May 4, 1986, Chengdu, Sichuan

cultures and with this mishmash have come up with a systemic structure of self which demands that objective reality conform to subjective thought . . . .

Recently I heard of a new genre of poetry called "Not-Not". They have published a manifesto, a "Guide to Pre-Culture". I got hold of a copy of this and discovered that theirs is nothing but a banner concealing an admixture of irrationalism and mysticism. They negate the rational and all culture, including written culture; they call for a return to a pre-cultural primitive naturalism, and they believe one should rely on intuitive feelings by means of which one can be privy to the revelations of the spirit. They employ undefined language to

Chairman Mao: I'll Never Forget You

Yang Li

The sun dazzles this afternoon
I turn around, walk toward
A massive boulder in the distance
A few girls sitting on the edge
Relaxed
Their colourful clothes
Sparkling

Afternoons like this are rare
As I walk I'm thinking it might rain
Drops of rain will fall on the boulder
Where will the girls go for cover?
But now there's not even a hint of wind
The sun shines down silently
It's so beautiful! That boulder
And behind the boulder
In the distance, the dazzling sky

express the undefined intuition of the self, which they call true beauty. Theirs is an abomination that has grown in the body of our socialist culture, suckled on the milk of various western schools of the irrational and mystical.

An Old Chinese Story

Wu Zuguang

As part of the activities organized to celebrate the twentieth anniversary of the Iowa International Writers' Program, a seminar for Chinese writers was held on October 18, 1987. The writers attending that seminar were asked to talk about why they had taken up writing. Wu Zuguang, only recently forced to resign his Party membership (see the previous chapter), had the following to say:

I'd like to tell you all an old Chinese story. Once upon a time, there was a small township in which traditionally all the men were scared of their wives. One day the local magistrate thought he'd put this to a test. He summoned his underlings and after having them all line up asked for those who were scared of their wives to stand to one side. All except one did so immediately. The magistrate was much impressed with the man who hadn't moved. He asked: "Are you not scared of your wife?" "No, it's not that," came the reply. "It's just that my wife told me to keep away from crowds."

I suppose I'm like that fellow, I'm terrified of my wife and scared of crowds too. All of us men are like that, where I come from. So I thirst for freedom. Why exactly are we scared? Because they won't leave us alone. So I long for an environment where I can be left alone. That for me is freedom . . . .

I'm seventy years old. I hope to keep writing for the sublime cause of freedom.

XIA GUAN : Lower Pass

Cultural Ministrations

Wang Meng

New Thinking that is in keeping with the progressive flow of society directs the experience of Reform, and the experience of Reform in turn provides an inexhaustible source for New Thinking. Because of our sensitivity as intellectuals, many of us are thirsting for Reform, fantasizing about Reform, moving beyond the present period and attacking various problems at the same time as calling for Reform. But because of a lack of experience, a lack of in-depth appreciation of China's unique national situation, a lack of practical and personal experience, some of our number invariably tend to idealize, conceptualize or simplify Reform. They think that just by importing a few new and foreign ideas, or by asking a few "rigid conservatives" to depart, everything will be perfect; that they will be able to transcend the present period and bring forward the realization of modernization. When they are frustrated or come up against various complications, on the other hand, they tend to use the classic excuse of having been born "too late", or "in the wrong place", and with this cheap rationalization they shake their heads and sigh, becoming dejected and hopeless. To get to the point, these people who support Reform, discuss Reform, have their heads in the clouds about Reform, are precisely the ones who in the face of real Reform see nothing but a world of difficulties and uncertainty in which they fail to find a place for themselves. This is truly a tragic situation that we must come to grips with.

November 17, 1987

Wang Meng, celebrated writer of "modernist" fiction with a Marxist message, is Minister of Culture and a member of the Central Committee.

POETRY OF THE SUPREME ULTIMATE

School founded March 1, 1985
Members include Daozi, born 1957

STATEMENT

It passes, it passes, and the substance of decay increases. Supreme Ultimate Poetry has fashioned from the mysterious culture of the Orient a vessel for transcendence. It has bred a poetic scorpion from the historic centre of chaos. The many forks in the road, like the phenomenal world, wear differing models of running shoes, each reaching its own truth.

This recognition of the Supreme Ultimate in the modern transformation is certainly not what contemporary people comprehend as "nostalgia" or "revival of the past". Even less is it a shallow "seeking of roots". It is a symbolic universe: all things in heaven and earth, society, nature, history, individual life, all of this forms in our poetry a continual chain, a repeated double helix.

In the process of Change, all is process. And every process contains its own negation. This negation is indeed the outward manifestation of the Life Force.

Change is the motion of Non-Change. From Non-Being to Being and again to Non-Being. Both contrary and utmost extremes.

The directions of Change have no goal.

All beings in the world are evolved from the Supreme Ultimate, are identical with the spirit of the Supreme Ultimate causing the subjective heart-and-mind and the objective Ultimate to merge into one substance.

In order to meet heart with heart and to sympathise with the Universal Mind, one must pass through Stillness.

The Supreme Ultimate school of poetry exists on a solitary island, in a wonderful ancient sea, pure and alone.

Daozi, early August 1986,
at the Not-Not Studio,
Li Shan

Being within Non-Being

Daozi

(eighth of a series of eight poems entitled *Endland*)

The dried marsh reveals
The snake stirs insects
The emblem flies
The stars ripen
Rotten on the ancient secret-covered pond
The black spirit speeds past —
    close-up of doomsday

Awakening a wilderness of wolfbones
    sad beauty
Ten thousand leagues of hatred
    unfurled
Mollified by a chromosome

Ants mawing hair and nails
Bringing rotten news from below ground
The forest fades
The wooden man sloughs his stump
The cave expands

Every ring whorls the ripples
    below eye
You have already been
    in lifelong unrequited love
    with the narcissus
    from the depth of eyes
Attempting to remove the face
    from the mirror-moon

The moon is in midsky
    the beauty
    the fere
Darkles love
    in the eternal gloom

October 85 — March 86
Li Shan, Chang'an

There is a Beginning;
There is that which has not yet begun to begin;
There is that which has not yet begun
    to begin to begin;

There is that which is;
There is that which is not;
There is that which has not yet begun
    not to be;
There is that which has not yet begun to begin not to be.

Zhuangzi, "On the Equality of Things"

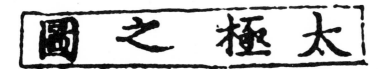

Performances

Mu Dan

Impassioned protestation, indignation, eulogy, laughter
Eyes in the dark have long awaited
These performances, the latest cast
Compounding anew its grand emotions;

Actors and audience grown so accustomed to the sham
That innocence and nakedness seem strange,
Unaccountable discords.
"Prune 'em away, hush 'em up, revise, revamp 'em!"

To achieve abnormality every wit is strained,
Each form polished and perfected.
"This is Life," and violates the laws of Nature,
Despite the actors' artful artlessness.

And countless hearts of gold have been betrayed.
A counterfeit coinage circulates,
Buying, not a true response,
But numb indifference beneath assumed applause.

Mu Dan (see p.166) wrote this poem shortly before his death in 1977. Though written over a decade before the latest campaign, it captures the essence of the Chinese artist-inmate's predicament, caught in the false dialogue between the commissars and the crowd.

XIV: BÖD

It may happen that here in the centre of Tibet the religion and the secular administration will be similarly attacked from without and within, and the holders of the Faith, the glorious Rebirths, will be broken down and left without a name. As regards the monasteries and the priesthood, their lands and properties will be destroyed. The officers of State, ecclesiastical and lay, will find their lands seized and their other property confiscated, and they themselves made to serve their enemies or wander about the country as beggars do. All beings will be sunk in hardship and fear, and the nights will drag on slowly in suffering . . . .

The Thirteenth Dalai Lama (d. 1933)

Potala, can this really be you
Solemnizing the dusk,
    more mysterious than the song of the shamaness

Yang Lian, February-March 1984

These Tibetan elements of the primitive are being used in China as a spiritual raft during a transitional period of weakness, frustration and vacuity.

Li Xianting, February 1987

Tibet under Proledic

On October 1, 1987, the Thirty-eighth National Day of the People's Republic of China, crowds gathered in the square outside the Jokhang Temple in the centre of Lhasa and demonstrated for Tibetan independence. This was but one of many such disturbances that have occurred in recent years. Like other expressions of local Tibetan sentiment, it was crushed ruthlessly by the police. This time, however, as the result of China's "Open Door Policy" and the accessibility of Tibet to tourists, foreign observers were on the scene to record the violence. The Chinese government was quick to denounce the exiled Dalai Lama, spiritual leader of the Tibetans, for having incited the demonstrators.

Over the years Tibetans who call for the independence of Tibet, or who have refused to give in to the decades of Sinification of the region, have, like so many Chinese, entered the dark world of Proledic. Their experience both parallels and adumbrates that of such writers as Bao Ruowang (see pp. 70-8). Tenzin Choedrak, one of the Dalai Lama's personal physicians, spent seventeen years in the Chinese gulag, imported as it was to Tibet to deal with "counter-revolutionaries". His record of those years is included here to show the omnipresence of Proledic. Monks and laymen arrested during the various disturbances in Tibet have shared, or are still sharing, these experiences. Ironically, China's prison-province Qinghai was originally a region of Tibet called Amdo, and the birthplace of the present Dalai Lama.

Tibetan independence may be a political impossibility given the strategic and territorial importance of the region to China. However, in cultural terms, Tibet stubbornly remains a unique entity and has refused to be assimilated by what the Chinese government has itself repeatedly called "incorrect policies" pursued for over two decades— forced resettlement of Tibetans, rule by Han Chinese commissars, the physical destruction of Tibetan Buddhism, bans on Tibetan education and publications, severe economic dislocation, and so on. Indeed, so effectively has the Tibetan spirit survived, that many younger Chinese writers today find in Tibet a source of inspiration denied to them by their own culture.

The poet Yang Lian, having already found inspiration in the lesser ethnic minorities of Central and Western China (see pp. 246-9), finally travelled to Tibet in 1983, spending several months there and writing on his return a powerful cycle of poems entitled simply "Tibet". For him, the "Tibetan experience" was an important stage in his quest, a new "secret horizon", a centre of spiritual energy and rebirth (as of course it has been for generations in the West).

Similarly, other Han poets such as Cai Chunfang have found in the Tibetan landscape an inspiration for their own Snow Sea Poetry; while artists such as Yu Xiaodong and Pei Zhuangxin have gone to teach in Lhasa, discovering there an independent artistic tradition that has changed the direction of their own work.

Much of this new work is thought-provoking and liberating, both for the artists and writers themselves and their audience. Much, however, is as exploitative of Tibet as the activities of the Han in the region since the 1950s, although it is certainly less destructive. We offer works of this kind by two novelists: Ma Jian, originally a young Han photographer from Peking, and Tashi Dawa, a Sino-Tibetan writer resident in Lhasa.

YU XIAODONG: The First Man

Ma's story, which became famous in early 1987 as the first literary target of the Anti-Bourgelib Campaign, is part of a phenomenon well described by Li Xianting, editor of *Fine Arts in China*, the most controversial Chinese art weekly: ". . . . we see [the Han] approach the question [of Tibetan culture] with a sense of overriding superiority. It's all well and good to say that the very elements of primitive colour, strength, mystery and even barbarism, are just what is lacking in Han civilization. This fascination with 'frontier culture' is understandable. But what is happening, in fact, is that these Tibetan elements of the primitive are being used in China as a spiritual raft during a transitional period of weakness, frustration and vacuity. They enable the oppressed self to be temporarily liberated from the constraints of society."

Tashi Dawa, a Tibetan imbued with the ideology and literary trendiness of the Chinese, uses Tibet's religious culture in the service of Marxist-Leninist Modernism. The selection from his story "Tibet: Soul Tied to a Leather Buckle" represents the nature of the Sinification of Tibetan culture, an insidious Proledic of the soul.

Jiuzhen Prison: A Tibetan Account
Tenzin Choedrak

as recounted to John Avedon

Doctor Tenzin Choedrak, one of the Dalai Lama's four personal physicians, was arrested in Lhasa in 1959 following the March uprising against the Chinese occupation of Tibet. He was finally released in March 1976. He is now living in exile in Dharamsala, India.

On October 15, 1959, the prison's [the maximum-security PLA prison in Lhasa] seven hundred inmates were drawn up in long files surrounded by Chinese troops, in the southern quad. Seated at a small table before them, the camp commander spoke. "Among you there is a very stubborn group who persist in telling lies and refuse to recognize the truth," he said. "We have decided to send them for further study in China. Conditions are far better there than here. Food is more plentiful, and their needs will be amply provided for." The results of seven months of interrogation were then read out: 4 prisoners were to be released and 21 would be sent to work at the hydroelectric plant at Nachen Thang. The 76 men bound for China were to leave within two weeks. The prisoners, however, were not told who had been selected for the last contingent until three days before their departure. At that time, on the morning of October 29, Dr Choedrak was informed that he had been picked. Because neither charge nor sentence had been given him, he didn't actually believe he was going to China. Instead, he assumed that the selected prisoners were to be taken somewhere nearby and, under one pretense or another, executed, their separation having been for this purpose only.

The next day Tenzin Choedrak's handcuffs and leg irons were removed and, along with the seventy-five other men, he was driven to the Norbulingka [the Jewel Park, the old summer palace of the Dalai Lama]. Quartered there for two nights and a day, Dr Choedrak gradually made the acquaintance of his new prison mates—all of whom had held high positions in Tibetan society and government. The men were of one mind: even if China was, in fact, their destination, singled out as they were, there could be little doubt that their remaining time was limited. Their fear increased when, on the morning of their departure, they were permitted to bid farewell to their relatives. As dawn broke the prisoners were brought near a wall, from where two or three at a time were called to a window for a strictly allotted few minutes with their families. Despite Chinese threats to cancel the meeting if a single Tibetan showed emotion, everyone wept. The guards then ordered those who had yet to go forward to console their relatives. They were fortunate. They were going to the motherland itself—to receive education. On the far side of the wall the families—all of whom had brought food, clothing and blankets—were assured that their relatives would be living under the best possible conditions in China. Nonetheless, the prisoners were permitted to accept the gifts.

When Dr Choedrak's name was called, he walked to the window and saw his elder brother Topgyal. In tears and unable to speak, Topgyal took Tenzin Choedrak's hands in his. Dr Choedrak then said, "Now it's best that you forget about me forever. You must go back home and take good care of yourself". Topgyal offered him *tsamba* [parched barley], a woollen sleeping rug, two blankets, some clothes, a food bowl and a washbasin. He bent over and unlaced his tall Tibetan boots, but Tenzin Choedrak refused to take them, insisting, "You'll need to walk in these boots. I won't".

Their farewells completed, the prisoners were directed into two roofless troop trucks, a soldier mounted on the corners of each. A truck bearing a machine gun aimed at the Tibetans led; another, carrying ten soldiers and a second machine gun, took up the rear. With no room to sit, the thirty-eight prisoners in each truck stood shoulder to shoulder and stared in silence as the engines started and they were driven off, their wives throwing dust and crying after them the traditional phrase for dispelling sorrow, "Let all of Tibet's suffering be gone with you! And now be done!"

Dr Choedrak and his companions were indeed en route to China. November 1 had been earmarked for a massive transfer of prisoners from the capital; numerous convoys had already set out ahead of them and as they passed Drepung, the road behind filled with six more trucks, transporting three hundred young monks from the monastery, all thirteen and fourteen years old. Grown to ten trucks and over four hundred people, the convoy headed north for Damshung, and its first major stop, Nagchuka. For the entire journey, the prisoners, forced to stand, were whipped by the late-autumn wind as they repeatedly crossed 15,000-foot passes. Night-time provided little respite. Jammed into the largest quarters available in whichever village they stopped in—often, for convenience sake, a single room—half the men had to sit on one another's laps for lack of space. Every night was punctuated by loud yells as arms or legs were trampled. Those who had to relieve themselves could do so only in their bowls, which they then had to hold so that nothing would spill. Irritability was heightened by the drastically reduced rations, now down only to a cup of boiled water and six steamed flour dumplings a day.

On the eleventh day, the column halted on the north shore of Lake Kokonor. Herded into boxcars on a railroad, the prisoners rode east, toward Lanzhou, the capital of Gansu province. Though few had seen a train before, they were too exhausted to care. Together, they sat in silence bunched against the cold, watching the light dance between the slats of the cars' walls. After one day they arrived at Lanzhou, and the two groups were separated. While the young monks remained on board to continue farther into China, Dr Choedrak's group was placed in trucks and driven north once more. Though Lanzhou had been the jumping-off point for the Great Silk road for centuries, the surrounding countryside was empty, perennially ignored by the Chinese and populated only by the Hui, Moslem people, now a minority themselves. On the city's northern edge, the silt-filled Yellow river ran west to east. Beyond lay Mongolia, its alien nature attested to by the ruins of the Great Wall and the edge of the Gobi Desert.

It was toward an outcrop of the Gobi, the Tengger Desert, that the prisoners were driven. A giant tract of flat rocky debris, the Tengger served as a springboard for windstorms and fierce winter gales which rifled the featureless land between it and the Wall. This forlorn expanse was traditionally spoken of as having "three too-many's"—too much wind, sand and rock—and "three too-few's"—too little rain, grass and soil. It had always been an area of transit—Mongols passing through, north to south and back on pilgrimage to Tibet, traders moving east or west on the Silk road. The Communists, however, had found a new, seemingly ideal use for the region—as a vast zone for prisons.

The number of prison camps dotting the barren landscape of northern Gansu and Amdo (renamed Qinghai by the Chinese) was known only to those in Peking. Nevertheless, the general estimate was that these two provinces contained a vast sea of prison camps housing up to 10 million inmates, a "black hole," as a 1979 *Time* magazine article dubbed it, "from which little information ever reached the outside world or even the rest of China."

Owing to its 300,000 square miles of inaccessible terrain, Qinghai had been designated, soon after 1949, as the future site of most of China's prisons. In the early fifties, small camps, holding a few hundred prisoners, had begun as tent compounds surrounded by barbed wire—sometimes electrified. As their first task, the inmates had constructed their own prison walls out of brick or mud. By the middle of the decade, these had given way to colonies of prisons—fortress-like compounds lining dirt roads for miles at a stretch. Containing from 1,000 to 10,000 inmates each, the archipelagos provided the backbone of the system. The strip north of Lanzhou, for which Dr Choedrak's group was destined, was considered the worst. It was followed in severity by four zones, two north and one south of Qinghai's capital, Xining, the fourth, four hundred miles due west, on the way to Xinjiang. Prisons and labour camps, though interspersed with nomad flocks, distinguished the entire countryside.

At sunset, the Tibetans passed through a ragged village of packed-mud houses, by a few stunted trees. Five miles beyond, they caught their first sight of Jiuzhen Prison. Four fortress-like stockades, set a sizable distance from one another, constituted the camp. Approaching one, the trucks passed staff quarters and a group of outbuildings behind which the prison's twenty-foot-high five-foot-thick brick walls stretched a half-mile long by 1,000 feet wide. Two guard towers rose on either side of the red flag raised over the gate in the eastern wall; one was positioned at the centre of the western wall. Within stood seven cellblocks, housing 1,700 prisoners, in either fourteen- or twenty-seven-man rooms, built in files down the central yard. The kitchen ran along the western wall; the toilets were in a block in the southwest corner. A single notice board hung to the left of the gate. In the main, the prisoners were Chinese and Hui of high social standing: ex-officers of the Moslem warlord Ma Bufang's army, as well as doctors, professors, judges, civil servants and other members of the intelligentsia now marked as reactionary. It was clear there was no hope for escape: the area was far too barren and remote to live alone in for more than a few days . . . .

The day following their arrival the men were acquainted with Jiuzhen's rules. Communication, save for practical necessities, was forbidden. "This is a maximum-security camp for those who have committed the worst crimes," the guards informed them. "No spreading of reactionary rumours will be tolerated." On the basis of recommendations by the officials who had accompanied them, a "progressive" leader was appointed from each group of ten to fifteen prisoners. Although the leader lived side by side with his cellmates he was exempt from *thamzing* [Tibetan for "struggle", cf. p. 93]. In return, he was required to report the most minute occurrence down to potentially significant looks exchanged between their prisoners. Accordingly, from the first days of their new life in Jiuzhen, a second invisible prison held the men, a virtual moratorium on all human contact. The only statements made were for the informer's benefit and were stock phrases such as: "The new Communist leadership is so much better than the exploiters of the past." Or: "The conditions here are truly excellent, we are really enjoying it."

Each day, before dawn, the prisoners were mustered. Once in line before their cells, they were led in a rousing propaganda song, the first verse of which began: "Moscow has announced revolution so the imperialists are shivering with fear." They were then marched to work in the fields, returned briefly for lunch and, after the day's labour, required to sing again before dinner, which was served, as were all meals, in the cells by the kitchen staff. Following dinner, political "study session" lasted until ten o'clock, after which they slept. Every ten days each prisoner was subjected to a private interrogation session. In addition, prisoners were randomly taken to a small room in the staff quarters outside of Jiuzhen's walls where, for an entire day, four interrogators would question the man in turn, trying to wear him down by probing for "crimes" in the smallest details of his past life. Otherwise not a moment was spent away from the group, which was marched to and from the toilet as well as the worksite by armed guards.

It was the middle of the "three lean years", and Jiuzhen's produce was not for the prisoners' own consumption but that of the staff and the army units in the region. Guarded by the PLA, who shot on sight any man crossing his field's perimeter [cf. p. 66], each prisoner, equipped only with a shovel, had to break enough barren ground daily, including irrigation ditches, to be suitable for cultivating thirty pounds of wheat. The soil was turned a foot deep, covering an area of roughly 4,000 square feet. The task was so daunting that, even with clear soil, a strong man could barely manage to complete it. More often, the earth was hard and stony. In this case, after they had removed the larger rocks, the prisoners were ordered to fetch sand and clay from a nearby area in pairs; they used a long bamboo pole from which two baskets were hung suspended between them. The new earth was then mixed in with the old. Speed was of the essence. A point system rewarded those who completed their quota. Those who did not were punished. On returning from collecting sand, the inmate received a blue or a white slip of paper. Tabulated at day's end, the slips determined the number of baskets he had carried. The next day a red flag would be placed beside the field of the best team, whereas all those groups who had failed to approach its level were given increased labour time and a longer nightly meeting. Stretchers were always on hand for the frequent cases of collapse. If a field was close to the pickup point for sand, sixty trips could be made in a day, running both ways; if far, no more than twenty-five . . . .

With the arrival of summer, arid desert heat replaced the dry cold. Prisoners were issued baggy, gauze-like cotton uniforms. On the morning of May 1, 1960, six months after the Tibetans' arrival, the kitchen staff came to their cells bearing the usual basket of dumplings and a bucket of greens. The dumplings, though, were the size of an egg. When the prisoners asked why they were so small, they were told that rations had been cut from sixteen and a half to eight and a half pounds a month. Henceforth, three dumplings a day were given and they were no longer even made from wheat. To save yet more grain Jiuzhen's authorities had instituted the mixing of indigestible roots and barks with the food. Three types were most easily identified. The first was rotten bark taken from trees in an area of low-lying hills far from the camps. After it was powdered and mixed with the dough, the dumplings were tinged red; they left a heavy, painful feeling in the stomach. If ingested over too long a time the bark produced bleeding sores inside the stomach and intestines. After eating them for even a few days many of the men found blood in their stools. Chaff was also mixed in and, in the autumn, a further additive which destroyed the semblance of a bun altogether. This consisted of waste material from soybeans [cf. p. 71]. With the kernel of the bean removed to make tofu for the staff, its remaining skin was steamed to form a sort of porridge mixed with flour. The gruel was so loose, though, that the steamer itself had to be brought to each cell, where two spoonfuls per man were dispensed. Over the winter, meals had included the exterior layers of cabbage and other leafy greens, their interiors already taken by the guards. Now a native plant with flat green leaves topped by a yellow flower was used. Collected by periodic details, the plant was boiled in water and one ladle's worth for each man given out. Altogether, a single meal comprised little more than a mouthful of food.

Hunger governed the prisoners' every thought. Order broke down. The strong bullied the weak over who had received a large ladle of greens. Even when the Chinese took to skimming off each spoonful with a chopstick to make sure all the portions were of uniform size, the men's anguish about potentially unequal allotments focused itself as an obsession over the size of their bowls. There had never been a standard issue of containers. Thus, each man used what he had been permitted to retain from his relatives' gifts or, failing that, from containers he had somehow managed to pick up from guards. The assortment was varied. Dr Choedrak had brought a mug as well as a washbasin. As the mug proved too small to eat from, he secretly procured a pair of scissors from a brigade of ex-prisoners, kept on as labourers, who lived outside Jiuzhen's walls. With these, he cut down the high sides of the basin so that it fit fully over his face and could easily be licked clean. Most were not so fortunate. Some had cups, others tin cans, the rest metal ashtrays—given out by the Chinese. Those worst off possessed only pieces of wood in which crude indentations were carved. Eventually, the men devised a system for randomly exchanging containers after the meals were portioned out and just before they ate. In this way, some measure of peace was restored, though as the next month unfolded it mattered little.

With the beginning of summer, the first symptom of starvation appeared: extreme enervation. While walking, their knees frequently buckled, and a number of the men found themselves unable to stand once they had fallen. Even if they managed to sit, their legs would not carry them until after a few hours of rest. By July one and all resembled living skeletons. Ribs, hips and shin bones protruded, their chests were concave, their eyes bulged, their teeth were loose. Gradually their eyebrows and hair, once shiny and black, turned russet, then beige and then it fell out, the hair coming loose from the skin with just a slight pull. Each morning, those who could rise placed both hands against the wall and inched up, carefully balancing their heads in an effort not to fall. Once erect, they would edge dizzily through the straw down the back of the *kang* toward the cell door. From there they would go to the toilets by supporting themselves against the window ledges and walls of the buildings en route. From now on no one could walk securely, much less run for baskets of sand.

Leg joints felt locked in place; feet were dragged along, too heavy to lift. When the men returned to the prison at night, they lowered their bodies gingerly onto the platform, this time only one hand against the wall, the other used to steady the head; tilted to the side, its weight was sufficient to bring one crashing down, unable to check the fall.

The first man to die was a lama from Nagchuka. He had fainted many times in the fields, and was repeatedly carried by stretcher to the hospital room, where he was permitted to rest for a few days at a time. One day in September he could no longer lift himself from the sleeping platform. The prison guards arrived and demanded to know why he was not out working. He replied, "How can I work when I can't lift my legs or my head?" Then he added sarcastically, "Now I finally understand the policy of the Chinese Communist Party. It's very good. I'm a person who can't move and might live for just a day or two more—that's all—but I'm asked to go to work. This is truly a policy for the people." After this, he was taken to the hospital, where, as he had predicted, he died two days later.

This first death, which Dr Choedrak and the others had expected almost daily for a year and a half, was notable only in that it had taken so long to occur. It was greeted indifferently; no mental breakdowns had occurred since arriving at Jiuzhen, no expression of fear or depression, and none appeared now. Save for continued quarreling over food, starvation had stunned all other feelings into abeyance. The Tibetans now recognized, though, that they would not be executed or tortured to death; they were to die through forced labour, so that the authorities—by their own standards at least—could appear blameless.

Within just a few days, the next man died—a government official named Rongda Jamyang, whose sister later married an American and moved to the United States. From then on, an average of two to three prisoners died every week with the longest interval between deaths lasting no more than a fortnight. The process was always the same. Those who succumbed without complications, from starvation alone, would simply lie immobile on the kang. Their breath became softer and more shallow until, at the last moment, bubbles of saliva slipped over their lips and they died. In some cases, a man would linger for months. before passing away. The elder of the two monks from Tashikhiel, who had survived the demise of his 298 fellows, ultimately perished in this manner. For two months he remained prone, sustained by spoonfuls of gruel and water given by his fellow prisoners. After each feeding he regained some strength, looked around and even spoke briefly before relapsing into a semi-conscious state, saliva continually seeping from his mouth. For others, death would come after only a few days of lingering, as with another early victim, the ex-abbot of Gembung Lhakhang temple in Lhasa. Those who had died during the night were removed by the hospital staff, stripped of any useful possessions and placed in a pile in front of the toilets. Before dawn, the corpses were taken out of the camp by a three-man burial detail. The graveyard was a field not far from the prison walls. Its markers were made of handsized stones picked at random by the detail, who then wrote the prisoner's name in red enamel paint before placing the stone over the grave. The earth was so hard—frozen in winter, dry and tensile in summer—that only a shallow hole could be dug, into which, without ceremony, the naked body was thrown. Dr Choedrak saw Chinese families wandering through this field, searching to retrieve the bones of a deceased relative. Some had come to visit from as far away as Peking or Shanghai, only to be informed of their family member's death on arrival. Lent a shovel, they were told to find the remains and take them away if they wished—a gruesome and heartbreaking ordeal, due to the sometimes incompletely decayed cadavers unearthed.

For the prisoners, a death occasionally provided an increase in rations—for a single day at least. If they were lucky, the loss could be hidden from the guards and the deceased's ration obtained. Dr Choedrak himself benefited from this. Waking one morning, he noticed that the man lying next to him was unusually still. He nudged him, listened closely and realized that he was dead. By then, the prisoner on the fellow's far side had realized the same thing. By mutual consent, they managed to partially cover the dead man's head with his blanket, telling those around—and the Chinese, when they arrived—that he was too sick to move. By this, they obtained an extra portion of food, which they discreetly shared between themselves after the kitchen staff departed.

As the death rate increased the Tibetans began to consume their own clothes. Leather ropes, used to tie the bundles brought from Tibet, were cut into daily portions with stones and shovels. Each piece was slowly chewed during work, in the hope that some strength could thereby be gained. Small leather bags were put to the same use. Dr Choedrak owned a fur-lined jacket, which had proved invaluable through the first winter, but in the course of the following summer he was compelled to eat it. He began with the fur. As winter came again, he managed to secure a small quantity of brush with which to make a fire under the *kang*. Piece by piece, he roasted the rest of his coat.

Walking to and from the fields, prisoners picked as many plants—
dandelions were a favourite—as they could eat, scavenged leaves from
the few trees in the area, hunted for frogs and insects and dug for
worms. One worm was particularly sought after as a source of grease,
there being no fat of any kind in the diet. White, with a yellow head,
the inmates nicknamed it "Mapa", after the best, most tasty form of
tsamba mixed with butter.

    A more constant source of food was the refuse discarded by
Chinese guards. Crowds of prisoners would gather around bones or
fruit rinds thrown by the roadside. Those lucky enough to have arrived
first masticated their finds for hours to make them last. The results of
this scavenging, though, could be perilous. One day Dr Choedrak was
assigned—in company with a low-level government official named
Lobsang Thonden—to work on a garbage pile outside the prison walls.
It was in a large area where the camp's waste was mixed in with human
excrement before being taken to the fields as fertilizer. Together, the
two men shovelled the feces into trunk-sized baskets, which were then
carried off by their cellmates. As he shovelled, Lobsang Thonden
came upon a small baby pig—pigs were kept by the staff—dead and
almost completely decomposed. When the guards were not looking
Lobsang retrieved it and whispered to Dr Choedrak, "We should eat
this. It might help us." Wiping the excrement from it, he pulled the pig
apart to see if there was any edible flesh to be had. A portion about the
length of an index finger remained, still red, between the shoulder
blades. He then decided to take it back to the prison to eat more
palatably with the evening's greens. Dr Choedrak admonished his
companion to consume the meat immediately. On one count, Tenzin
Choedrak pointed out, he was so weak that it would be of instant
benefit; on the other, if it was discovered during the check at the
prison gate, there might be trouble. Lobsang Thonden ignored the
advice. Instead, he placed the meat in his back pocket, where, as Dr
Choedrak had warned, it was found a few hours later at the evening
check. The Tibetan's small piece of meat infuriated the prison guards.
That night he was threatened and abused; the next day work was
delayed and a public *thamzing* involving the entire camp was convened
in the prison yard. Lobsang Thonden was brought forward and tied by
the special method used to twist the shoulders in their sockets. The
camp commander shouted indignantly: "Taking such unclean food is a
grave insult to the Chinese Communist Party and to the nation itself.
Eating anything that can be found is a direct attempt to abuse the
government. The conditions and rations here are very good. Such an

insult cannot be ignored. It must be corrected by *thamzing*."
"Activist" prisoners jumped up to beat and "struggle" Lobsang
Thonden in the usual manner, repeating the charges against him.
Soon, however, he collapsed. Afterwards, he could no longer walk or
care for himself and was taken to the hospital, There, for the one and a
half inch of flesh, he died four days later.

Despite such harsh reprisals, the prisoners had nothing to lose and
were little dissuaded. On one occasion a group of Chinese inmates
attacked the kitchen staff—all of whom were fed to the point of being
portly—as they were leaving the kitchen carrying baskets of dumplings. Grabbing all they could, the men ate as they ran away; yet by
that night each had been identified and punished. Unprovoked cruelty
was common as well. While Dr Choedrak was in the toilet one day, a
Chinese prisoner came in to relieve himself. The man was so weak that
when he squatted down, he fell on the floor, foaming from his mouth,
unable to move. A guard entered. He began kicking the prisoner,
berating him for lying in the toilet until, in a minute's time, he died on
the spot. Taunting was a favoured means of abuse. Dr Choedrak
witnessed a Chinese inmate being dragged helplessly to the fields, the
guards reproaching him for being "too lazy to work." After moving
about listlessly for a few minutes, he simply collapsed and died. On
another occasion Chinese inmates were discovered eating a donkey's
head which they had retrieved from the same pile of feces and garbage
that Lobsang Thonden's pig had been in. Handcuffed and severely
beaten, they were brought in front of 900 prisoners for *thamzing*. The
prison staff railed at them, "You Kuomintang officials have badly
abused the poor people under you, and now you're even abusing the
Communist Party by eating a donkey's head. This is why you're dying,
because you don't know how to look after yourselves." Twice Dr
Choedrak himself received *thamzing* for "insulting behaviour" concerning food. In one instance he was caught eating cabbage leaves
from the manure pile. The other involved his training as a physician.
With the traditional Tibetan doctor's vast knowledge of plants, he
quietly advised prisoners what to eat and what not to eat in the fields,
despite the risk of such unapproved communication. Discovered, he
was brought to trial once more on the grounds that his actions were
premeditated provocation of the authorities, who maintained throughout that the entire camp was receiving "ample sustenance".

Dr Choedrak's advice, though, was badly needed. Prisoners ate
anything they came across. Some items were not so dangerous. One
cellmate managed to find the knee joint of a small sheep. There was no

meat on the bone, but for an entire month he kept it hidden under his bedding, taking it out each night for a few precious gnawings. On New Year's Day, to demonstrate magnanimity, a single mule was boiled for the entire prison. A friend of Dr Choedrak, a steward for a noble family in Tibet, noticed that the water the animal was cooked in had been thrown by a staff member onto a refuse pile not far from the kitchen. Though not the toilet proper, this was a place where prisoners also went to relieve themselves, and the whole area was covered with pools of urine. Regardless, Dr Choedrak's friend ran to the mound with his mug and collected all the surface dirt he could, in the hope that some of the boiled water could be strained out of it. He showed Dr Choedrak the soaked mud and asked if he thought this would benefit him. Like every prisoner, the steward had been suffering from an inability to sleep, difficulty with his vision and a constant loud rushing noise in the ear—all caused, according to Tibetan medicine, by the rising of "lung" or wind, which was produced by starvation. Dr Choedrak agreed that if he could succeed in getting some of the soup water separated from the mud and urine, it would help to repress the "lung". The man did so and actually felt better for a short while. But other cases were not so salutary. People were dying in the most horrible manner from abrupt dysfunctions in their digestive tracts. A prisoner named Gyaltsen Dagpa, whom Tenzin Choedrak was unable to assist, perished when his intestines burst. For weeks he had been indiscriminately picking and eating whatever wild grass he could find. Soon he had a bad case of diarrhoea and after a few days a viscous jelly-like substance emerged with his stools. Then, only water was ejected. At this point, whenever the man ate or drank he would scream from the excruciating pain. Soon the pain became constant, and he could no longer consume either liquids or solids. For two days he lay on the *kang* clutching his stomach, screaming, and then he died. Dr Choedrak deduced that the interior lining of the man's intestine had been scraped away by the roughage, accounting for the viscous substance. Once worn through, the intestine then burst—at which stage, when the man drank water, it passed into his abdomen, causing intense pain. At the very end, when nothing at all emerged, the internal wound had disrupted the digestive tract entirely and become fatal. Another man, named Teykhang Chopel, succumbed when his sphincter cracked apart due to the hard indigestible objects lodged in his intestine.

Though he knew what not to eat, Dr Choedrak could not endure such conditions long. As the anniversary of the Tibetans' first year at

Jiuzhen arrived, he too collapsed and was taken to the hospital—a place visited at one time or another by all the prisoners. It was here, during an intermittent stay lasting three months, that he gained a view of camp life outside the isolation of his own group's daily existence. The hospital itself—no more than a barren room—existed as such in name only. There was virtually no medical equipment or supplies except for a few ointments for applying to wounds and some Chinese herbs said to help digestion. On occasion, when a patient was in the most dire condition, a shot of glucose would be administered or a mug of carrot juice given. The main function of the hospital staff was to dispose of the dead, many of whom had perished on its premises. Staff members were mostly prisoners who had received the jobs as a reward for being "progressive". It was, in fact, a substantial dividend. Not only did the assignment replace gruelling field labour; it also provided a veritable cornucopia of extra food, the staff routinely disguising deaths and thus continuing to receive the dead men's rations.

The hospital was run by three so-called doctors, all prisoners, but only one of whom was actually a physician. There was little he could do. The other two were the only women in Jiuzhen. Both were rather remarkable. They belonged to the work brigade of semi-released prisoners who lived beyond the camp's walls. They too had once served terms within the prison, but, via a policy applied throughout the Chinese penal system, they were not released following completion of their sentences. Instead, their status was merely upgraded to that of "permanent labourer" and freedom forever postponed. Such labourers no longer received food, but had to toil, as did the population at large, for "work points," which enabled them to purchase rationed grain. In Jiuzhen, the 800 to 900 additional people so classified were mainly allotted the light labour of planting fields the prisoners had already broken.

Of the two women doctors, one was compassionate and selfless, the other driven and businesslike. The kind woman was a Christian, and fearlessly so: she openly wore a cross around her neck even after receiving repeated *thamzing*. An energetic and skilled worker, the guards had come to depend on her despite her attempts to thwart their practice of forcing patients back to field work. Her care was the sole sign of humanity in the prison. In one case witnessed by Dr Choedrak, a Chinese inmate, bedridden for months, developed severe bedsores over his entire body. Once infected, the sores filled with maggots. Each morning the woman arrived from outside the prison walls and sat by his side to pick the maggots from the sores one at a time. Going to the kitchen, she obtained ashes from the stoves which she carefully strained so that only a fine powder remained. Spreading this on a large cloth, she placed it beneath the man. Whereupon great numbers of maggots fell off. The patient eventually died, but until the end, she continued to relieve him in this way.

The second woman, named Wangchen, was, with the male physician, at the hub of a thriving black market. At night carrot juice was brought to the hospital by the kitchen staff—one carrot's worth for each patient who had been put on a list by the doctors. Coming into the room, the staff would announce, "Carrot juice is ready," at which point, Dr Choedrak noticed, the same three Tibetans always received portions though they were far from the worst cases. At the time, he could only guess the reasons. Suspicious themselves, the authorities called in the doctors and the patients concerned, and soon had it out that the latter had bribed the former with such articles as shoes and even a German fountain pen brought from Lhasa. But long before this was made public, Tenzin Choedrak himself was deeply involved in this new avenue for survival.

Wangchen's activities went far beyond small bribes taken from those under her care. The bulk of her business involved serving as go-between for transactions amongst the prisoners and the labour brigade. Whatever goods were dealt, she always took a large commission in kind. While the prisoners procured bits of clothing to trade, the labourers had worked out a technique for obtaining extra dumplings. To discourage theft of the grain given out for planting, Jiuzhen's guards coated it with poison before distribution to the labourers. Despite this precaution, because they were never searched, the labourers stole handfuls at a time, which they later washed. This they cooked for their own fare, reserving the dumplings they received from the prison kitchen, on the basis of their work points, to trade through Wangchen. Dr Choedrak offered Wangchen an old chuba[traditional Tibetan robe], the wool of which had been rubbed off. In exchange he received thirty dumplings: unfortunately, the kind tinged red from rotten bark. Of these, Wangchen took five as commission, and he obtained the rest two or three at a time over a month. But whatever the black market offered, it was still far less than that required for subsistence. Hence, the prisoners continued to eat whatever they could. One day Dr Choedrak saw a Chinese inmate holding a long red worm in his cup. Through a fellow Tibetan who spoke Chinese he asked where he had found it. The man replied that he had defecated the worm in his stool. Careful not to be caught by the guards, he had picked it out, washed it and brought it back from the toilet to eat—which he did that day mixed in with his other food.

The hospital also served as an additional place for interrogation. Shortly after a Tibetan was admitted, he would be visited by the security cadres, whose ongoing task was to question the prisoners. Their purpose was dual. While it was clear that the authorities considered a man's borderline state to be fertile ground for extracting a confession—hunger accomplishing what struggle sessions and beatings had, as yet, failed to achieve—interrogations also discouraged inmates from entering the hospital and thus kept them at work filling the labour quotas.

At the beginning of 1961, Tenzin Choedrak was released from the hospital and resumed work. His recovery was due not only to rest but also to his own form of cure. He had noticed one symptom shared by all those who died: severe diarrhoea. In most, a thin watery stool was constantly emitted; to absorb this flow, a rag had to be kept in the pants. In Tibetan medical theory, Dr Choedrak knew, the digestive power or heat of the stomach is the key to health, the level of digestive heat determining not only metabolism but, through it, the harmonic function of the three humours. In Jiuzhen, however, this heat had been subjected to a twofold attack: from the severe cold and the consumption of coarse, indigestible material with no grease or fat. To increase his digestive heat, Dr Choedrak quietly practised, for half an hour each night, an advanced form of meditation—called Tum-mo Bar Zar, literally meaning "Rising and Falling Heat". After his cellmates had gone to sleep, Dr Choedrak visualized purifying energy—in the form of white light—suffusing him, drawn in with each inhalation to a point just below his navel. Picturing a triangular flame the size of a rose thorn, he imagined it extending up the central channel of his body, through the tantric energy centres at the navel, stomach, heart, throat and crown of his head where, burning away the layers of mental impurity, it released a fountain of clear, nectar-filled light which returned, blissfully, down his body. He would then conceive all of the sufferings experienced in prison to be washed away, replaced by the ineffable joy embodied in the light. "In the beginning, one just imagines all this," he recalled. "But after five or six months there was an unmistakable improvement, a slight rise in body heat. I was very weak, but I never had any more diarrhoea or other digestive problems. Also, despite all the suffering we experienced, the meditation gave me more courage. I had no more fear, I just accepted my fate."

. . . . Despite the breakdown of conditions within their domain and the chaos without, the Chinese prison officials never deviated from their policies. With hundreds of prisoners already dead, executions—a constant feature of the camp—continued to be carried out. Charges were never specified. The names of those to be shot would simply appear on small posters periodically glued to the prison walls, beside such observations as "stubborn" or "suffers from old brains." When the executions had been carried out—they were not, as in other prisons, held publicly—a red check would appear next to the names of the executed, and the poster would be left up for some time as a warning. Then in the nightly meeting the officers would repeat a well-worn observation: "If one reactionary is destroyed, that is one satisfaction. If two are destroyed, that is two satisfactions. If all the reactionaries are destroyed, then you are fully satisfied."

Momentary Convergence

Cai Chunfang

Pilgrims
    at regular intervals
        to the right of the road
Performing prostrations,
    head to ground
Standing,
    moving forward
I saw their shadows crawling
Linked in a chain
A police patrol passes to the left
Marching,
    feet stamping
    the ground
Moving forward
    with equal
    conviction
I saw
Our shadows
Linked in a chain

*Cai Chunfang is a young
Chinese poet living in
Tibet, one of the founders,
in April 1986, of the
Snow Sea Poetry Group.*

PEI ZHUANGXIN   *Monks*

The Ruins of Gandan

Yang Lian

For so it is: man is a sacrifice. He is the morning offering.

The Upanishads

Everywhere
    stone pillars
        erect wings spread to fly
Everywhere
    solitary crenellations
        unfathomable paths and voices of wind
A rough stillness has frozen the shapes of violence
This high peak, trapped by death,
    backdrop to a small stage

September,
    my autumn barren as this
Save for that azure blue
    which would recede at a touch
The sun unfolds, on an emptiness
    scrawled with the calligraphy of ruin
Breakers of rubble
    disintegrating hate and sorrow
Dusk, packs of dogs
    poke wet noses into history
Sniffing out the broken images beneath the earth

(Yesterday never passes, it is enfolded in today
The stars revolve, a single glance and primordial terror
Tumbles out of the darkness
All things complete at the same point of departure)

GANDAN   *Juliet Nicholas*

Gandan Monastery, 70 km. east of Lhasa, one of the Great Three
(with Drepung and Sera), was established in 1409 by Tsong Khapa. It
was demolished by explosives in 1959 and further annihilated in the
1960s. It is now partially rebuilt.

Potala

Yang Lian

He who has knowledge of that which is oldest and greatest himself
becomes oldest and greatest.

The Upanishads

The cliff is shredded by the gale
But the hundred and fifty-six steps of earth still flow upward
A thick rattan trail, sombre grey leaves
Wilderness, grassland, history, the sky
Twisting, turning, awaiting me between the stones
Beneath the piled golden roofs, a Man, so small and lonely

Potala, can this really be you
Solemnizing the dusk
    more mysterious than the song of the shamaness
An existence, a mighty fluttering of prayer flags
Centuries of toil locked deep in your breast
A pool of blood
    cracked dry after the cry of battle
    blazing on the wall
The setting sun
paves the winding paths
with crimson shade
The Kyichu River spreads the silver of night
to the distant mountains

And you, beast of a thousand eyes, brood silently from above
A thousand circumambulations cannot solve this riddle
Ah! Sublime soul suffering soul
Though death is powerful, and life transient
Your light
your cliff
still shine
Children fear
old men brood
The forest cradles
a raging fire of leaves
—You possess us in your soul

The hundred and fifty-six steps of earth flow slowly upward
This sun of stone, makes each moment eternal

1984

POTALA   *Juliet Nicholas*

The Initiation

Ma Jian

The hills stretched for endless miles. In the sun they stood out
brazen, nude, silent and unmoving. At dusk when the setting sun had
transfused blood into this vast barren range of hills, they seemed to
undulate like flesh. And then in an instant the sun sank behind a peak,
and I started to climb, as the last glow lit up all between heaven and
earth. Later it pulled me inside out, bleached me, leaving me nothing
but a filthy, empty carcass. Cursing, I scratched myself all over. Then I
smiled, stood up and went back to the road.

It was the day after I left Kaga.* I hadn't been following the road.
I wanted to find a path over the desolate hills, see what this
motherfucker called life is all about. What else was there for me to do?
I wandered around for a day, nowhere to go, defeated, like a kid in
trouble. I cried.

Typical artist, everything always done in a crazy rush. Spirituality
suffuses every inch of the earth up here on the high plains; all is
enveloped in myth and legend. Modern civilization has robbed us of
sexual wisdom, it causes us so much suffering. Today I suppose I'm
writing down this story as a prelude to forgetfulness.

They found her the ninth day after the Tulku [Living Buddha]
Tenzin Wangjé died. She was nine days old. Her staring eyes kept
scanning the people and objects around her. She was born in a hut
made from bricks of mud and straw. The light from a butter lamp
illuminated her mother's breasts and the colourful strips of cloth on
the cushions. It was a poor family. When the mother heard a noise
outside she hid the baby inside her sheepskin robe. The door was
blocked by the strangers, who stood there like a dark pack of animals.
She stood up to ask them in. They were all prominent people, lamas
from the Dompa Monastery. The group was led by Tsrong Ripa.

He said: We believe your child was born nine days ago.

She replied in the affirmative. The other lamas joined their palms
and started chanting sutras. Tsrong Ripa sent a messenger back to
announce that the Tulku's reincarnation had been found. Then he

*All Tibetan names of people and places in this and the following story are approximations based
on the Chinese.

asked: Is it male or female? What's her name? Sangsang Drolma? From now on she will be called Sangsang Tashi.

Later they performed a solemn ceremony to celebrate the reincarnation, and Sangsang Tashi was removed to the Dompa Monastery.

By the age of fifteen Sangsang had read the *Five Major Treatises*, and she was studying medicine at Manrempa. The first time she left Dompa Monastery was to walk for an hour to Manrempa. For several months now she hadn't allowed anyone to accompany her; she liked to use the walk as an opportunity for reflection. Of late she had been unsettled by a strange, inexpressible feeling. For fifteen years she had spent all her time learning to read, memorizing the scriptures, practising yoga; this road she walked, a road which would wake her from her sleep, was one she'd often walked halfway down before. Opening the door of her meditation cell she saw the flagged stone path leading downhill, flanked on both sides by the courtyards of the provincial wards belonging to the theological colleges. At the bend in the path was a tall ochre wall behind which lay the heart of the monastery, a temple to Sakyamuni and the Sixteen Bodhisattvas. At the foot of the wall was a track for circumambulation, and an old woman who was constantly spinning a *mani* wheel; she'd been making her rounds for over twenty years. Tashi often bumped into her. When they met, the old woman prostrated herself on the ground. Opposite the wall was the entrance to the provost marshal's dwelling. There was usually a pack of dogs in there chasing after each other and humping. On the right a little further on, you could see the street outside the entrance of the Dompa Monastery. It was crowded with people during the festival of the Sunning of the Buddha, although normally it was full of merchants' tents. Stone-masons and beggars lived between the tents and the houses, in small hovels made of piled stones. Sangsang Tashi often bought bracelets and earrings from the Indian merchants here. To reach Manrempa she took the left fork. It was little more than a path that led away from the monastery, running between fields of buckwheat and peas. By the path horse-bell grew wildly among clumps of short willows, and the fragrance of flowers was blown along on the early morning breeze. She would often stand here and look back at the monastery. The platform for sunning the tapestry of Buddha was on the highest point behind the monastery, halfway up the hill. It was large, clean, pure. When the wind blew she could even hear the prayer flags flapping on the roofs. It sounded as though the fabric was tearing.

Hundreds of piles of *mani* stones lined the ridge of the hill. Further on was a stream that flowed down the hill and joined the Nechuk River, sparkling in the distance. Manrempa was on the other side of the Nechuk.

Every time she walked along this path she forgot entirely that she was a Living Buddha, the reincarnation of Tenzin Wangjé, that she was not an ordinary mortal. She was mesmerised by the fragrance of the fields. She just wanted to stand on the plank bridge looking at the grasses waving in the flowing river. Beyond the Nechuk was a barren mountain.

Tomorrow was to be the day of her final initiation, the ceremony of empowerment. Amitabha of the West would subjugate her covetousness and envy; she would be anointed for the last time, she would reveal her Buddha nature. It was autumn, and the devotees were flocking over the mountains to be here in time for her appearance as the Living Buddha, and for the alms giving. Tashi was not interested in any of this, she only wanted to be alone to think.

A Tongue-lashing

Ma Jian's story was published in early 1987 in a double issue of People's Literature, *one of China's most prestigious literary journals. In late February, the story and its publishers were denounced for Bourgelib. Liu Xinwu (see pp. 19-29), the newly-appointed editor-in-chief of* People's Literature, *was suspended from his job and forced to make a self-criticism. The* People's Daily *criticism was couched in the following terms:*

"'Stick Out Your Furry Tongue, or Fuck-all' uses the first person narrator to scavenge strange news and odd occurrences in Tibet. The narrator purposefully employs the most lurid language to distort the reality of life in the Tibetan region. He defames the image of our Tibetan compatriots, at the same time revealing his own complexes: an infatuation with sexual desire and a passion for money. This story is a piece of vulgar filth masquerading as 'experimental' fiction . . . [The editors of People's Literature*] have realized that to publish such a work is a serious breach of Party and State policies on national minorities and religion, as well as the fact that it has seriously offended the feelings of Tibetan compatriots and harmed the fraternal unity of the minorities. It represents an abandonment of the socialist direction in the arts, and has had a most negative effect, with repercussions that will be hard to eliminate. In reality, it is the result of Bourgelib and other erroneous ideologies being allowed to spread unchecked. . . . ."*

She went as usual straight to the main hall of the Master of Manrempa. It was a cavernous room with a corpse laid out in the centre. Today the Master would be lecturing on the positions of the psychic pulse in the human body. This was the very thing she was so anxious to know. The Master waited until an acolyte had laid out the altar before commencing his dissection. He cut open the chest, pulled out all of the vital organs one by one and placed them on a table. From these he picked out the heart and indicated the position of the heart's eye. The stench made Tashi feel nauseous. She was the only woman present, although, like the others, she was shaved bald. Géré Panché was standing next to her. He was looking on with undivided attention like the other ten or so disciples. He was a Geshé from the Parang Monastery, here for advanced spiritual training. He'd already completed instruction in the *Diamond Wheel of Time*. She liked standing next to him during the classes.

The Master instructed them all to close their eyes and to concentrate, to see if they could read his mind. After a time, four lamas spoke up and told what they had seen. The Master called on Sangsang Tashi. She was the youngest present, and a Living Buddha. She immediately entered a samadhic trance, but with only six years of training in yoga behind her, her mind's eye was still cloudy. She chanted a mantra to stabilize her tutelary deity, regulating her heart beat, but still she could not attain absolute concentration. Then suddenly she felt a burning heat in her toes, which gradually developed into a ball of fire, rose through her legs and entered her mind's eye. She hurriedly recited a mantra to herself to purify body, speech and mind, and before her there emerged a clear vision of what was in the Master's mind: it was a frozen river. Between the time she left her trance and perceived a brilliant light she saw herself standing in the frozen river without a shred of clothing on. She brought the vision to an end and told the Master what she had seen. He said that this was indeed what he had been seeing in his mind. The eye that sees into the future is not the mind's eye, he said.

The Master started to bore into the head of the corpse, through the temple. Sangsang was completely flustered. The Master hadn't told her what she was doing in the river. Was that her future? She was surprised how she looked in the nude, just like a Yidam in a religious painting. At that moment, the Master removed a piece of cartilage from just below the pituitary gland and said: "This is the eye for looking into the future. With practice you will be able to use this third eye to see the illnesses in other beings and the various malign spirits that surround them. When I saw Sangsang Tashi in the river a moment ago, I was looking into her future, for the astrologers have already selected a time in a few days for her to undertake this first part of the Austerities of Awakening. Listen to me, Sangsang Tashi: your present yogic abilities will enable you to endure the three days in the frozen river unharmed."

Tashi was utterly confused. She'd only ever seen that river in the distance, from the mountains. Although she could stay in the snow for a few days without feeling the cold, what would the river feel like? Then she thought of the warm current that had entered her body from her toes. It was not a result of her own yogic power. She looked to her side and saw an aura floating around the head of Panché. She smiled at him. She realized that his yogic powers were even stronger than the Master's, though he had never given any hint of this before now.

The Master held the piece of cartilage in his hand and explained that it was discoloured because the dead man had spent his life in ignorance and worldly confusion. If, however, one worked towards the birth of self-knowledge it would become translucent. The Zen, Orthodox and Tantric schools of Buddhism were, in the end, all concerned with this piece of cartilage. For only with this could one see the Buddha Land clearly, and perceive the spiritual substance of all things. Then he used his knife to cut open one of the corpse's eyes, and looking at the stream of dark liquid that came out of it, he said: "This is what the worldly use to see with. Because it is clouded over, worldly men are forever hampered by the Five Poisons and are unable to achieve enlightenment." Tashi was staring at the remains of the corpse. It had been a middle-aged man, his teeth were large and white; flies were now swarming around his exposed innards.

Tashi spent the afternoon sitting in meditation in her cell. She had been to see her mother, who was very ill. She used the medical knowledge she'd learnt over the past months at Manrempa to do what she could for her, but it didn't help much.

A month before she had transferred part of the spirit of her mother's illness to a dog, which had died immediately. Lobsang Gyamtso had said that all things had souls, so one should not move an illness to another body so lightly. Her mother was wasting away in front of her very eyes, and it weighed heavily on her. Tomorrow was the ceremony, and it would be the most solemn ceremony performed for her in the monastery since the passing of the Tulku Tenzin Wangjé. But her mind was somehow distracted. She had seen how all the hamlets had put out new prayer flags, how the monastery had sent people to repair the prayer-horns that hadn't been used for decades, and lamas were now practising on them daily. The lamps in all of the halls had been refilled with rancid butter and were burning day and night. But her mind was ill-at-ease, and she sat there staring at a lamp.

A ceremonial mandala had been constructed in the centre of the meditation hall and a Buddha image and various offerings had been put in place. The innards from the dissected corpse were included in the offerings, the intestines having been washed clean and heaped in a golden bowl; below the bowl a number of large cushions had been placed on the spot where she would perform the mystical union of Yab and Yum, and four burners had been filled with incense. The wall paintings in the hall had been decorated with strips of russet cloth and butter lamps burned in front of them.

The lama who would officiate at the ceremony was, as in the past, Lobsang Gyamtso, the brother of the late Tulku. The thought of having to perform the mystic union with him was suffocating. She could sense that he detested her, that he was displeased that his brother had reincarnated in her body. But he was an expert in the Tantras. He had instructed her in the study of the *Five Major Treatises* and had officiated at her initiation. Then she thought of his face: his forehead was heavily wrinkled, and when he looked at people the wrinkles moved around. His small eyes seemed to fill her own. He was extraordinarily large.

She thought of the wall painting in the meditation hall. There was a Diamond Copulating Bodhisattva sitting in the middle performing coitus with his female aspect. Tomorrow she would have to imitate the posture, climbing onto the Bodhisattva and putting her legs around his waist in the same way. She suddenly felt herself excited by a hot clammy sensation. Lobsang Gyamtso's face flashed before her; it wasn't smiling. She immediately forced herself to stop thinking of this and began meditating, repeating the Sakyamuni dharani to herself until she regained quietude. In her trance she saw three Yidam approaching her. They told her that tomorrow the Diamond Copulating Bodhisattva himself would preside, and the one dressed in red turned to her and smiled. Then her tutelary deity, the Bodhisattva Manjusri, manifested himself and sat in a mandala opposite her. She felt her body suffuse with heat and her cakras shine in her heart with a bright light—her buttocks, the sides of her thighs, her knees, soles and insteps all light as a feather. Just at this moment Panché appeared, and she was so embarrassed by her naked state that she came out of her trance. Again she felt flustered; she dissolved the Bodhisattvas of the four directions into her tutelary, but she was in a state of non-self and her mind echoed emptily with every sound outside her cell. She had no choice but to break off her trance again, thinking as she did so of what the three Yidam had said to her.

The fragrance of fried kapsai offerings entered the cell from outside. She felt hungry and beat her wooden fish. An attendant entered, and she asked her to bring a cup of butter tea, after which she locked the door. It was late at night. She looked at the black wick of the butter lamp, thinking to herself that she would look like that the next day. The very thought of herself lying there in the nude made her heart beat; for a moment she felt positively terrified. She did her utmost to banish such sacrilegious thoughts from her mind, and continued meditating. But no matter how hard she tried, she couldn't enter a trance again. She felt deeply unsettled. In all her years, this was the first time she had experienced such a feeling. She knew that she was contravening her vows, and this made her all the more nervous. Reciting a mantra under her breath, she relit the two lamps that had gone out. Gradually she entered samadhi.

She woke early next morning and, before it grew light outside, she sensed her own femininity in every inch of her body. The feeling began before dawn. It started in her blood; it coursed through every part of her body. Her breasts pressed against her inner garments, her thighs, her pelvis and the tender part of her stomach felt light and clammy. She sat up and her breasts quivered ever so slightly. She felt a tingling sense of delight as her nipples brushed against her clothes. The sensation was immediately transmitted to the area around her vagina. She unconsciously pressed her hand to her genitals. A powerful sensation went shooting down her legs, like a ball of fire, causing them to shudder with pleasure. Ever so quietly she had awoken to her womanhood. Suddenly she realized that in a short time she would be exposed in public and she hugged her shoulders tightly in fright, her teeth chattering. She could see the sky outside turning gradually from purple-red to the bright blue of morning.

The meditation hall was filled with hundreds of lamas. All the fires had been lit, and the conch-shells, drums, tambourines and cymbals sounded in unison. Sangsang Tashi, dressed in a monk's patched robe with a bright red rosary around her neck, walked to the centre of the cushion, and sat down cross-legged opposite Lobsang Gyamtso, hands on knees and palms turned upward, reciting the dharani of the Five Tantric Bodhisattvas. Her mind was unsettled and her hands trembled; at times she pushed her knees down on her feet out of shame. When the conches sounded up again she realized she had still not entered a trance. In her agitated state she clutched at her mantra and tried immediately to become one with her tutelary deity. But her syntax was back to front. There was not time. She opened her eyes only to see Lobsang Gyamtso parting his robes as he walked towards her. Her eyes looked up at him beseechingly and in terror, while she let herself be pressed down onto the cushions by him. The pain on the inside of her swollen thighs and the weight of the lama on her torso made her dizzy. She felt as though the woman who had been injected into her that morning had, in an instant, been torn to shreds by Lobsang Gyamtso.

The first thing she felt upon regaining consciousness was the perspiration on her back and neck. The lower half of her body no longer felt tender, she was moving in harmony with the motion of the body above her. She seemed to be falling into a black hole. Occasional waves of discomfort welled up from her legs. She was the only one in that hole, she could relax for an instant. Then in a panic she remembered that this was supposed to be a union of the Yab and Yum; she had to use her vital force, her psychic channels and concentration to find the prajna-wisdom in Lobsang Gyamtso's body. Only then could she unite wisdom and its application in herself. But now he pulled her into a standing position and lifted one of her legs around his waist. The jerking movements made her forget the meditational cycle. It was then that she began to feel that her body was withering, Lobsang Gyamtso like a magnet drawing out all of her marrow and vitality. She collapsed, and let Lobsang Gyamtso do with her as he wished. When he sat down cross-legged once more, having positioned her on top of himself, she was like the Wisdom Yidam in the wall paintings, crouching over him and entwining her legs proficiently around him. The breasts that had filled to maturity that very morning seemed withered like an old woman's. The area below her stomach was strained and painful, so much so that her breath became short and the feeling moved from her pubis to her pelvis, from her coccyx, along her vertebrae and up her spine. Her eyes popped open and she saw that the hall was full of bright sunlight, the grey-blue of the incense swirling around her. She saw only the golden smile on the lips of the Sakyamuni Buddha floating on the clouds of incense. She moved her face away from Lobsang Gyamtso's stinking chin and caught sight of Panché's face in the midst of the shiny pates of the assembled lamas. She closed her eyes immediately and buried her face in Lobsang Gyamtso's chest, gritting her teeth.

The ceremony did not end until midday. When she came to her
senses again she was stretched out on the cushions like a dog, her
whole body racked with spasms, her breasts dry and depleted. She was
lying in a pool of sweat. Suddenly she thought of her dying mother.
Two nuns came over to help her up and cleansed the bloody sweat
from her lower body with water from a golden bowl. She couldn't
move, her legs were numb. When she stood the conch-horns sounded,
and the sound of gathas drifted across, mingling with the incense and
the tones of a Turkish flute. The golden bowl containing the intestines
was now offered to the mandala. Lobsang Gyamtso was dressed in his
robes again, and was sitting on a cushion, beaming. She stood there
waiting for the grand ceremony to come to an end, her legs quivering.
That morning, she knew full well, the yoga she had practised all those
years had abandoned her. But the realisation of her womanhood, the
completion of her sexuality, no longer surprised her.

The second night after she was placed in the frozen river,
Sangsang Tashi died. According to the rules governing the ritual she
was to remain in the river in a state of nirvana for three days, after
which time the Womb of All Things would manifest itself. Three lamas
had been taking turns to watch over her, breaking the ice that
solidified around her neck. The spell for fostering fire that she was
most practised in had failed her. As light was about to break, Tsrong
Ripa left the bonfire and trod his way carefully over the snow to see
Sangsang Tashi, just as her head began to sink gradually into the
water. They pulled her onto the ice and discovered that she'd become
as transparent as the ice itself. There was not a hint of blood where the
fish had bitten at her breasts and knees. Her eyes were slightly open as
if in meditation, consuming the light.

The procession that was coming to greet the Tulku arrived at
dawn. They were all dressed in their festival finery and the horses were
decorated with coloured satins. For the monks it was the same if the
Tulku was dead or alive. Nonetheless, they gathered around Sangsang's body for a while in shocked silence. She was lying there frozen
on the ice, the sun shining down on her dispassionately. They could
see every organ of her body, as transparent as ice. A fish that had
somehow got inside her was swimming around her intestines.

I have Sangsang Tashi's skull here with me now. I remember the
man who sold it to me saying that he'd inherited it from his
great-grandfather, who had studied sorcery as a young man at

Manrempa. Her skull had become a holy ritual implement in Dompa Monastery and was placed for obeisance in the main temple. It was only ever used when the anointment ritual was performed. Now the skull cup has turned a yellowish-brown, and there is a crack in it on the left side, as a result of being dropped, heaven knows when. The crack is full of oil and filth. The lines on the outside of the skull look just like the wavy patterns of an encephalogram. According to a friend in medicine, this is a sign that the girl had not reached puberty. The edges of the cup are decorated in engraved brass, and the inside is lined in metal.

The fellow who sold it to me wanted five hundred *yuan* for it, but I beat him down to a hundred. If anyone's got any spare American dollars they don't know what to do with, just get in touch with me. I can use the money to pay for my trip up to the North-East.

from "Stick Out Your Furry Tongue, or Fuck-all"

MA JIAN   Ma Jian

Thus Spake the Tulku

Tashi Dawa

It's rare nowadays to hear that slow-paced, simple Peruvian folk song, "Mountain Eagle". I have it on tape. Whenever I play it I see before me the valleys of the plateau, flocks of sheep wending their way through the gaps left by strewn boulders, the small fields carved into the land in the foothills, the sparse crops, mills beside streams, small peasant dwellings made from piled stones, the mountain people shouldering their loads, bronze bells around cows' necks, lonely little whirlwinds, the dazzling sun.

These are visions not of the plateaus at the foot of the Andes, but of the mountainous areas of Pobunakang in southern Tibet. I can't seem to recall whether I've seen these things in a dream, or if I've really been there. I can't remember. I've been to too many places.

But one day, in the end, I did arrive in Pobunakang, and discovered that the place in my memory was little more than a fine pastoral by Constable.

It is still a serene mountain area, but the people who live there are quietly enjoying a modernized lifestyle. There's a small CAAC airstrip with a scheduled helicopter service into town five times a week, and a solar energy station close by. At an automatic petrol station by the entrance to the village of Dreluk there is a small restaurant where I sat at a table with a bearded fellow who never stopped talking. He was the managing director of the well-known Himalaya Transportation Company, the first in Tibet to have a fleet of container lorries, imported from Germany. I was paying a visit to a local carpet factory, where the technicians use computer technology to design patterns. The satellite relay station transmits five channels, providing local audiences with thirty-eight hours of television a day.

Despite the fact that modern material civilization has liberated people from traditional ideas and attitudes, the locals still retain remnants of their ancient mode of expression. I was talking to a village headman with a PhD in agriculture, and I noticed that he constantly sucked in air and made the self-deprecating "luoluo" sound with his tongue when addressing me. When people asked a favour, they still stuck up their thumb and wiggled it while repeating "guji, guji", a word for supplication. On seeing strangers some of the older people from the city would take off their hats and hold them to their chests, while standing to one side, an expression of sincere respect from the olden times. Although the State had unified weights and measures years ago, people in the area still favoured using an outstretched arm and a slicing movement of the free hand at the wrist, forearm or elbow to indicate a length.

The Tulku Sangjé Dolpo was nearing death. He was the twenty-third reincarnation of the Living Buddha at Djatok Monastery. He was ninety-eight. He would have no successor after he died. This is what made me think of writing a story about him. I'd had something to do with him before. Perhaps after the system of reincarnations has died out and all of their religious leaders great and small have disappeared, Tibetan Lamaism (all of its sects)—one of the weirdest and most mysterious religions in the world—will itself fade away. On one level, I said to him, material reality determines one's consciousness. The Living Buddha shook his head in disagreement. His pupils dilated slowly. "Shambala," his lips trembled. "The war has begun."

According to ancient scriptures, there exists a "Human Pure Land" in the north, a utopia—Shambala. According to legend the Tantric lore originated there. Södchad Nampo, the first king, was instructed by Sakyamuni there, and later he propounded the Tantric teaching of the Kalacakra. According to these records, one day war would erupt in Shambala, a kingdom surrounded by snowy mountains. "You lead the twelve celestial divisions into battle. With your force of celestial soldiers and spirit generals you never look back, galloping forward on your steed. You point your spear at the breast of Halutaimeng, and thrust it at the head of that demon who leads his forces in opposition to Shambala. And then the hosts of demons are exterminated." This is a description of the last king in the *Oath of Shambala*. Sangjé Dolpo had spoken to me of this war before. He said that after centuries of fierce fighting, when the demons were wiped out, Tsongkhapa's tomb at Gandan Monastery would open and the dharma of Sakya would flourish for another thousand years. Following this there would be hurricanes and fires and the world would be submerged in a deluge. At the end of the world there would undoubtedly be a handful of people saved by the gods. Thus, when the world was reborn, religion would also be revived. The Tulku was lying on a couch and entering a trance; he spoke to some invisible presence: "When you have crossed the Gelung Mountains and are standing in

Tashi Dawa is the pen-name of a young Tibetan novelist resident in Lhasa, a leading writer in the Tibetan branch of the Chinese Writers' Association. He was born in Bathang, formerly in the Tibetan province of Kham and now incorporated into Sichuan. Educated in Chinese in Chongqing under the name of Zhang Niansheng, Tashi Dawa has only a limited understanding of spoken Tibetan. He is illiterate in the Tibetan language, and has said that he declines to write in Tibetan because he believes his message too sophisticated for non-Chinese-reading Tibetans. Having worked for some time as a writer in the Song and Dance Ensemble in Lhasa, Zhang became known for a number of short stories that attempt to imitate the magical realist style of Latin American literature which was introduced to China during the early 1980s. The use of local colour in his writing, with liberal smatterings of Tibetan mysticism balanced by an upbeat Marxist-Leninist worldview, parallels the techniques of the "native soil" and "roots" literature of young Hans who often attempt to convert the remnants of traditional culture into a vehicle for their modernist aspirations.

the middle of the lines on the palm of Padmasambhava, seek no further, seek no further. Come to enlightenment in prayer, and from that enlightenment visions will arise. In the web of lines on Padmasambhava's palm, there is only one way to the pure land of humankind and life."

As though in a trance I had a vision of Padmasambhava leaving the earth in a chariot that descended from the heavens. Two celestial maidens accompanied him into the chariot, and they flew off to the distant south.

"Two young folk from Khampa have gone in search of the way to Shambala," the Tulku said.

I looked at him wearily. "Are you saying today—in the year 1984? Two modern-day Khampas? A man and a woman?"

He nodded.

"Did the man have an accident here?"

"You know about it?" the Tulku asked.

He shut his eyes and gave me a disjointed account of the time the two young people came to the area. He said they had told him everything that had happened to them on the way. I realized he was reciting a story I had once made up for myself. I'd never shown it to anyone; it was locked in a chest. He was retelling it virtually word for word. The setting was the track along the road to Pobunakang up to a village called Jia. It was 1984. The characters: a man and a woman. The reason I hadn't shown it to anyone was that not even I knew where they were headed. But now the Tulku had pointed the way. The only difference being that at the conclusion of my story the protagonists got directions from an old man in a wine shop. I hadn't described the directions he gave; not even I knew at the time. Now, here in his cell, the Tulku had pointed out the way for my characters. Another coincidence was that both the old man and the Tulku had spoken of the lines on the palm of Padmasambhava.

In the end people entered the cell and gathered around the Tulku. His eyes were half-closed and he gradually lost consciousness.

Preparations were made for the funeral. The Tulku was to be cremated. I knew people would want to get a sharira, one of his remains, as a keepsake. On the way home, after I'd paid my last respects to Sanjé Dolpo, I ruminated on the whole question of a writer's raison d'être.

Back home I opened the chest on which I had pasted the label "Beloved Foundlings". Inside it lay over a hundred brown paper envelopes, arranged in order: all the works I couldn't or didn't want to have published were there. I took out the envelope numbered 840720.. There was a short story inside about those two young Khampas. It was untitled. It went as follows . . . .

from "Tibet: Soul Tied to a Leather Buckle"

The story that unfolds is of two characters who meet each other in the wilds of Tibet, thereupon joining forces to continue their roaming. Although their destination is unclear they continue on their way together. The man is eventually injured in an accident involving a tractor, the socialist symbol of agricultural modernization, and dies, and the girl, the daughter of a singer of the Tibetan ballad Gesar of Ling, *is picked up by the narrator, who leads her back . . . . to Shambala, mystical land of Tantric learning? No, rather to a China speeding towards the Four Modernizations. Like Ma Jian, the writer makes glib use of one of the most sacred aspects of Tibetan Buddhism, the Tantric teachings of* rgyud. *If Ma aspires to be the Colin Wilson of China, Tashi Dawa sees himself as the Chinese Gabriel Garcia Marquez.*

HAN SHULI: Fading Radiance

A Question

If the situation is as the Chinese claim, that is, that most Tibetans are so happy, why then do they continue to believe me when I tell them the opposite? Most Chinese think Tibet was a poor, backward, dark, cruel and barbaric country. If they have done so much for Tibet, as they claim, how do you explain the way the Tibetans react towards them, and why do they continue to demand their independence so passionately?

The Fourteenth Dalai Lama, October 19, 1987

Appendix:
Chinese Labour Camps
Amnesty International

Rehabilitation through labour

THE CHINESE term *laodong jiaoyang*—more commonly used in its abbreviated form, *laojiao*—can be translated as "rehabilitation through labour", "re-education through labour" or, more briefly, "labour re-education".

Those who are given this "administrative" punishment are sent either to farms holding only labour-rehabilitation offenders or to penal institutions (prison-factories, camps, farms) holding other categories of offenders, in which case they work and live separately from the latter.

Offenders assigned to labour-rehabilitation (or "re-education") generally have a slightly better diet and, at least according to the law, more privileges than convicted prisoners sentenced to reform through labour: in particular, better shopping facilities, the possibility of voicing complaints about their treatment and, if they show "good" behaviour, of being granted brief leave to visit relatives; they also receive a salary. However, in spite of the distinction made by the law between rehabilitation and reform through labour, and although the former is imposed on people who have not been tried and convicted, it is generally reported that the work required of and the discipline imposed on offenders in these two categories are similar. Both categories have to work very hard for an average of eight to ten hours a day and the stigma attached to both punishments is said to be practically the same.

Moreover, there is evidence that many political offenders assigned to labour-rehabilitation after the "anti-rightist" campaign of 1957 were, like convicted offenders, sent to faraway regions to do pioneer work. According to former prisoners, "rightists" from Peking, Shanghai, Canton and other cities were sent mainly to the north-east (formerly Manchuria), the northern part of which is called the "Great Northern Wilderness", *beidahuang*, because of its harsh climate and sparse population. One complex of labour-reform farms in Heilongjiang (the northern-most province on the Soviet border) is known to have held labour-rehabilitation inmates in the 1960s; the complex is known as the *Xingkaihu* and was said to be under the control of Peking's Public Security Bureau. The 850th branch-farm of the *Xingkaihu* complex held labour-rehabilitation offenders. Ding Ling, a well-known woman writer who was branded as a "rightist" in 1957, is reported to have spent a year there before being transferred to another, unknown, place.

Reform through labour

REFORM THROUGH labour in Chinese is *laodong gaizao*, abbreviated to *laogai* (labour-reform).

Labour-reform prisoners serve their sentences in "reform through labour corrective brigades" (abbreviated henceforth to "labour-reform brigades"). These penal brigades may constitute a part or the whole of a prison-factory, farm or camp; they may also constitute a temporary (or mobile) camp set up to build factories, railways, bridges, etc. The labour-reform brigades are known internally by numbers but these are not made public. Prisoners usually refer to their places of detention by the names of the farms, factories or areas where they are established.

Labour-reform prisoners are often transferred from one camp to another according to the state's "economic needs". Those who receive long sentences (generally 10 years or more) are particularly liable to be sent to do pioneer work in sparsely populated areas, often very far from their own homes. There is evidence that even when they remain in their home provinces, labour-reform prisoners are given the hardest work to do for the sake of the country's economy and are used as a mobile, unpaid labour force. It is not uncommon, for instance, for them to have to build their own camp and bring under cultivation previously uncultivated land, and for the camp later to be transformed into a state farm or one managed by mixed labour, while the prisoners are either transferred somewhere else or assigned to the hardest work in the camp. This seems to have been the case with a large camp in the north of Guangdong province called *Yingde*—the name of the county where it is situated.

The *Yingde* camp was established in 1952 for labour-reform prisoners who built their own houses and cleared the land. The camp was then divided into five brigades (*dadui*) each comprising between 500 and 1,000 prisoners, who worked in an agricultural unit and in several mines, including, it is said, a plutonium mine. Over the years, the camp became economically successful. It expanded over a very large area, and a tea plantation producing the "*Yingde* Red Tea" was developed. In 1967, in addition to agricultural brigades and the tea plantation, the camp had a granite and a chalk quarry, a repair plant for agricultural machines, a mechanical plant and a school specializing in the cultivation of tea. It reportedly had then more than 10,000 workers there, including convicted prisoners, labour-rehabilitation offenders, "free-workers" and ordinary workers. According to various sources, in 1969 part of the camp became a May 7th Cadre School, while at the end of 1970 the tea plantation was gradually transformed into a state farm for "educated youths" (urban high school graduates). When these changes occurred, some of the prisoners were transferred to another part of the area covered by the camp, where they again had to do pioneer work.

Location of Places of Detention

THE INFORMATION available to Amnesty International generally confirms that there are a large number of detention centres, prisons and camps spread throughout the country. The Provincial Public Security Departments control the penal institutions established in their respective provinces. In addition, some large labour-reform farms or camps, in sparsely populated border regions, are reported to be under the direct control of the national Ministry of Public Security. . . . The law provides that prisoners may be transferred from their home provinces to other regions, according to the state's economic needs or to the number of prisoners in any one region. There is apparently no restriction on this procedure: prisoners from any part of China may be transferred to a faraway region with a different climate and language from that of their native place, and with practically no prospect of receiving visits from their relatives because of the distance. Prisoners in some pioneer zones are said to have been allowed, before 1960, to request permission for their families to join them as settlers, but after 1960 this privilege was apparently granted only to "free-workers" (ex-prisoners who are retained or placed in the camps after release). The change is attributed to the increased frequency of prisoner transfers from one place to another and to the lack of proper housing accommodation in the camps.

With some exceptions—in particular those provided by law for "major" offenders—criminal and political offenders are mixed in prisons and labour camps.

The north-east of China is one of the pioneer zones where large numbers of prisoners have been sent over the years. According to a former prisoner who was held in the north-east from 1954 to 1972, there are more than a hundred state farms in that region, 60 to 70 per cent of which are penal institutions. Another long-term prisoner who worked from 1953 to 1954 in Jilin province, in Changchun *Jinjianbao* (labour-reform) Brigade No. 1 (a brick factory where there were then about 3,000 prisoners), estimated that there were more than 30 similar brigades in the province.

Although these estimates have not been corroborated by other sources, there are generally reported to be numerous corrective labour settlements in the north-east. In Heilongjiang province, a complex of labour-reform farms was created between 1953 and 1955 in the east of the province, between Mishan and Raohe, near the Oussouri River which runs along the Soviet border up to Lake Xingkai (Xingkaihu). One of these farms, the *Xingkaihu* farm, is named after the nearby lake. In 1960 this farm was divided into nine branch-farms spread among some 60 villages. Part of the farm was closed down in 1964 as a result of the Sino-Soviet dispute and some of the prisoners were transferred to the *Paicheng* camp in Jilin province. (Prisoners near the border in other parts of Heilongjiang were reported to have all been transferred at that time to the "second defence line" and soldiers replaced them in the farms along the border.)

The *Xingkaihu* farm alone is said to have held some 40,000 convicted prisoners, labour-rehabilitation offenders, juvenile delinquents
and "free-workers", plus a large number of their dependants. It was
then a vast complex, having its own tractor-servicing stations, repair
shops, electric power plants, a paper-making factory, a sugar refinery,
a milk-processing plant and a canning factory. The soil in the area is
very rich and fertile, but the climate is extremely hard. As in other
parts of Heilongjiang, the average temperature is about −40°C between
November and March, but work is compulsory for prisoners unless
there is a strong wind. In addition, part of this area consists of marsh-
lands, infested by mosquitoes in the summer and difficult to drain
and cultivate.

Another complex of labour-reform farms exists in the west of
Heilongjiang province. The farms were opened in the mid-1950s near
Zhalaiteqi and Haila'er, in what was then the third district of Inner
Mongolia: Hulunbeier special district (*meng*). This district of Inner
Mongolia has now been integrated into Heilongjiang province.

In Zhalaiteqi, the *Baoanzhao* farm was opened up in 1954 by
prisoners coming from Shanghai and from the provinces of Jiangsu,
Zhejiang, Fujian, etc. (generally from the east coast of China). This
farm is said to cover an area of 600,000 *mou* (about 40,000 ha.) and
to contain about 40,000 prisoners, both criminal and political (it is
not known whether the figure includes "free-workers"). It is divided
into four branch-farms each holding about 10,000 prisoners. During
the four months of the year when there is no frost, the prisoners
work in the fields, growing grain crops, potatoes, sugar beet, etc. For
the rest of the year they work in repair shops, canning and paper-
making factories and a sugar refinery, or at building roads and farms,
digging trenches, and so on.

The existence of labour-reform farms and factories in Inner
Mongolia was mentioned in 1958 in the official newspaper of Inner
Mongolia. The paper criticised waste and bad management in the
penal institutions of the region, mentioning in particular the *Baoanzhao*
farm, three farms in Baotou and a brick- and tile-making factory in
Huhehaote (the capital of Inner Mongolia). According to other reports,
a labour-reform farm called *Zhangyi* was opened in 1960 in Inner
Mongolia to accommodate prisoners working in mines near Baotou
after the mines were turned over to the Ministry of Mines. Prisoners

at this farm worked to transform the arid desert soil into fertile patches of land capable of producing food crops. The Baotou iron and steel factory was built in part by prisoners between 1954 and 1958. It was said still to hold prisoners in the early 1970s, as did the Anshan iron and steel factory in Liaoning province (in the north-east).

Temporary camps are set up also to build railways, roads, dams and other construction projects. The stretch of the Peking-Erlian railway line (at the Mongolian border) which crosses Inner Mongolia was built by prisoners between 1951 and 1954. They were housed in tents and lived and worked in hard conditions. The temperature in this area remains far below zero°C for over five months of the year. It is reported that about 8,000 prisoners from Guangdong province were sent to this area in groups of up to 1,500; other groups were sent from east coast provinces to work on the railway and to do other construction work. Some of them were later assigned to building another major railway line between Baotou (Inner Mongolia) and Lanzhou (Gansu province). Large numbers of prisoners are said to have worked in the 1950s also at building the Chongqing-Chengdu line in Sichuan province and in the 1960s on railway lines between Lanzhou (Gansu province) and the Tsaidam area (Golmo, Ke'ermu in Qinghai province).

There is little precise information on any border region of the PRC except the north-east, although various sources mention the existence of large labour-reform settlements in the Uighur Autonomous Region of Xinjiang (north-west) and in Yunnan province (south). One Xinjiang camp is said to be under direct government control, guarded by soldiers and holding only male offenders, the majority of whom are said to be "historical counter-revolutionaries" (mainly former low-ranking officials of the Guomindang). The *Livre blanc sur le travail forcé dans la République populaire de Chine* (Paris, 1958) reports that towards the end of 1954, prisoners from Shandong province were transferred to the Koko Nor (in Qinghai province), Xinjiang and Tibet. Exiles have reported the existence of labour camps in Tibet near Lakes Nagtsang and Pongong (north-north-west of Lhasa) for mining chromium ore, and of small labour-reform "groups" in the Lhokha administrative area of Tibet, in particular in Tsethang (*Zidang*, south of Lhasa). Prisons of various sizes holding both ordinary criminal and political offenders are also said to exist in the main Tibetan cities, in particular *Dapchi* and *Sangyip* prisons in Lhasa (the first is said to be Prison No. 1 of the Autonomous Region of Tibet), *Karkang* prison in Shigatse and *Sechen Ho* prison (*Shiquanhe*) in Ngari Administrative area. *Sangyip* prison is alleged to have held some 1,800 prisoners in 1972, most of them Tibetan political offenders, whose work was stone-quarrying and brick-making, blacksmithing, building construction and carpentry.

In the east and centre of China, labour camps have, over the years, been located in practically all the provinces, but detailed, up-to-date information is too scanty to give an over-all picture of their present distribution. The examples given below have therefore been limited to a few large cities and regions on which Amnesty International has detailed or cross-checked information. It must be emphasized that all labour-reform farms, prison-factories and camps described by prisoners at one time or another held both criminal and political offenders and that recent reports indicate that a large number of labour-reform establishments exist throughout the country.

Among the earliest accounts, that given in the *Livre blanc* of the organization of camps in Shandong province in 1955 is noteworthy. A reorganization of the administration of the camps is reported to have been carried out in the province in 1954/55, resulting in the creation of six labour-reform "general corps" directly under the jurisdiction of the provincial government. According to this report, the second and fourth "general corps" were located in Jinan (the capital of the province), holding 5,000 and 15,000 offenders respectively, and the first "general corps" was established in Huimin (north of the province) and was said to hold about 40,000 detainees.

The Public Security Bureau of Peking itself directly controls several corrective labour farms, camps and prison-factories, some of which are outside the administrative area under its jurisdiction. The largest ones are the *Xingkaihu* farm in Heilongjiang province (mentioned earlier) and the *Qinghe* farm, east of Tianjin. The *Qinghe* farm was started in 1950 with some 1,200 prisoners from Peking. An official document stated in 1954 that 5,384 people had been released from this farm during the previous four years, which suggests that the prisoner population had rapidly increased since the opening of the farm in 1950. In the 1960s the farm is said to have had some 10,000 convicted prisoners, labour-rehabilitation offenders, "free-workers" and their families; it was divided into three branch-farms and nine agricultural units covering a large area (some 16,000 m wide by 30,000 m long). Branch-farm No. 1 was a maximum discipline camp holding only convicted offenders, mainly troublesome or "dangerous" prisoners. Unlike the *Xingkaihu* farm, however, the *Qinghe* farm held no prisoners serving life sentences. Branch-farm No. 2 held only labour-rehabilitation offenders and branch-farm No. 3 had mixed labour, including juvenile delinquents. The nine agricultural units were established during the Great Leap Forward (1958) and consequently were designated by numbers, starting with 58. One of them, Camp 585, is said to have had the worst living conditions of the whole farm because it held old or sick prisoners, generally unfit to achieve a normal level of production.

In addition to the *Xingkaihu* and *Qinghe* farms, ten smaller labour-reform farms and factories outside Peking were, in the mid 1960s, identified as being under the jurisdiction of the city's Public Security Bureau. Most of them had a mixed labour force of convicted prisoners, labour-rehabilitation offenders and "free-workers". It is not known whether they are still used as penal institutions. In addition, Peking had two prisons. One of them, Peking Prison No. 2, was a prison-factory to the north of the capital. In the early 1960s it held some 2,000 labour-rehabilitation offenders and "free-workers", plus a handful of convicted offenders. Known to outsiders as the "New Capital Engineering Works", it produced mainly radiators and machine parts. Amnesty International has no recent information on this prison.

Another prison in the capital—Peking Prison No. 1—has occasionally been visited by Western journalists. According to various reports, between 1956 and 1957 it held more than 1,200 men and 40 women serving sentences of between 3 and 10 years, plus some serving life imprisonment, and 100 ex-prisoners ("free-workers"); in 1958, it was reported to have 1,500 prisoners, two-thirds of whom were political offenders, including 10 under suspended death sentence; in 1960, the prison had 1,800 prisoners, of whom 40 per cent were political offenders, more than 100 were female offenders and 60 were under suspended death sentence. In 1963-64, the prison population was reported to consist of about 2,000 prisoners (including some 300 women), plus 500 "free-workers", and an unknown number of offenders undergoing labour-rehabilitation. The prison then included five factories (producing stockings, towels and industrial equipment), a translators' brigade, a hospital, and even a theatrical company made up of artist-prisoners and "free-workers" which periodically performed in the camps under the Peking jurisdiction.

Peking Prison No. 1 is situated in the former premises of Peking's Model Prison in the south of the capital. A detention house known as the *nansuo* (southern compound), attached to it, has reportedly held at times as many as 4,000 detainees. It included in the mid-1960s a separate wing for scientists and highly-qualified technicians, most of them serving long sentences.

In 1972, foreigners visited prisons in Shenyang (Liaoning province) and Tianjin. At Shenyang there were 2,000 prisoners (political and criminal offenders) and at Tianjin more than 1,100 prisoners (half of them political offenders), with over 100 female offenders. Shanghai city has one large prison which in 1977 was officially said to have some 2,700 convicted prisoners (including 200 women); about 10 per cent of the 2,700 were said to be political offenders. In the entire administrative area under the jurisdiction of Shanghai Public Security Bureau there are reported to be at least 18 detention centres and three labour-reform farms. In Canton, two prisons are said to be under the city's jurisdiction, and it is reported that the provincial administration of Guangdong controls one prison (Guangdong Province Prison No. 1). Amnesty International has also received information about five labour-reform farms or camps in different counties of Guangdong province and there are said to be many more labour camps in the province. One refugee has alleged that Guangdong province has a prison designated "Prison No. 1 of the PRC", also known as the "Shaoguan Food Processing Factory".

There are numerous detention centres throughout the country, the smaller ones being established in rural counties. In major cities they appear to be distributed in the following way: one small detention centre in each municipal district and one larger one at the city level, which functions as a "head office" for all the others. In addition, some provinces have "receiving centres" (*shourongsuo*) which function as transit centres for detainees and clearing houses for vagrants or people arrested for lack of proper identification papers.

from Political Imprisonment in the People's Republic of China *(1978)*

Authors, Artists and Photographers

Ah Cheng, a self-employed writer, artist, and entrepreneur from Peking, was born in 1949. A fiction writer and close friend of Chen Kaige and Bei Dao, he spent most of 1987 in the United States. He surprised many by his unsympathetic, seemingly callous, comments regarding the fate of Party writers such as Liu Binyan during the 1987 purge. Today (late 1989) he is in America.

Ah Xian, a self-taught artist from Peking, was born in 1960. Unemployed since 1986, he was unsuccessful in his attempts to obtain a passport and therefore was unable to accept invitations to attend exhibitions of his work overseas. An exhibition he and dozens of other artists planned for the first half of 1987 was banned by the Peking authorities. By 1989, however, his fortunes changed. He spent the first part of the year in Australia and returned to China.

Ba Jin, China's most senior literary figure, a novelist and essayist from Shanghai, was born in 1904. He has ceaselessly attacked the Cultural Revolution and extreme leftism over the past eight years, and though he remained silent during the cultural purges of the early 1980s, he supported student demands in May 1989.

Bao Ruowang (Jean Pasqualini) was born in Peking but now lives in Paris. His book *Prisoner of Mao* has been called by Simon Leys "the most fundamental document on the Maoist 'Gulag.' "

Bei Dao, a poet and writer of fiction from Peking, was born in 1949. He was able to leave China in March 1987 just after the campaign against "bourgeois liberalization" began, to take up a position at Durham University in England for a year as a visiting scholar. Previously, after a period in the Esperanto edition of *Beijing Review*, he had a short-lived job with the controversial monthly *China* in 1986 as poetry editor, but has been unemployed since the magazine was forcibly taken over by the commissars of the Chinese Writers' Association later that year. Like other "misty" poets, his work was unpublishable for most of 1987. His wife, the painter Shao Fei, and their child joined him in England. He visited the United States in 1988. Today he remains in exile.

Bo Yang, an essayist and writer of fiction from Taiwan, was born in 1920. After his speech "The Ugly Chinaman" was published and circulated throughout Mainland China during 1986, Bo Yang was denounced by the Mainland press in early 1987. Some of his fiction and historical writing have also been published, however. In late 1987 he produced another controversial work, *Have the Chinese Been Cursed?* He remains critical of the Mainland government and is convinced of the futility of the student movement.

Cai Chunfang, a Han poet working in Tibet, was born in 1964.

Cao Yu is an elderly Chinese playwright who lives in the Muxidi district on West Chang'an Avenue in Peking, reportedly the scene of the most violent slaughter on the night of June 3–4. He congratulated the martial-law troops on a job well done.

Chen Baichen is a Mainland playwright and essayist who was born in 1908.

Chen Kaige, a film director from Peking, was born in 1952. He came under attack from the authorities during the first six months of 1987 and was refused permission to attend Australia's Melbourne Film Festival. However, he completed his third feature film, "King of Children," based on a story by Ah Cheng, later in the year before taking up an invitation to live in New York for a year in October 1987. "King of Children" is set during the Cultural Revolution and is the most startling Mainland Chinese film to appear since Chen's "Yellow Earth." Today (1989) he lives in New York and is planning to direct a new film related to the democracy movement.

Chen Ruoxi, a woman writer from Taiwan, was born in 1938.

Cheng Xiaoyu is a young artist from the Central Academy of Fine Arts.

Cui Jian, a singer and musician from Peking, is of Korean descent. He was born in 1961. He was banned from performing in public on the order of the Peking Municipal Party Committee after he appeared on stage in peasant garb singing "I've Got Nothing to My Name." He was fired from his job with the Peking Philharmonic Orchestra in April 1987, and was only able to perform with his band "A-Do" at foreign embassy functions until later in the year, by which time he was singing in public once more. In 1989, during the protests in Tiananmen Square, Cui Jian wrote a song for the students which he performed himself in the Square.

Dai Houying, a writer from Shanghai, was born in 1938. Attacked a number of times over the years, Dai denounced the 1986 campaign against "bourgeois liberalization" during a trip to Hong Kong. She is a friend of Wang Ruowang, the Shanghai writer expelled from the Party in January 1987. A few weeks after the crushing of the student protests in June 1989, Wang was arrested, according to the *South China Morning Post.*

Daozi, a poet from Shaanxi, was born in 1957.

Deng Pufang, the son of Deng Xiaoping, was crippled during the Cultural Revolution. He heads the Chinese Foundation for the Handicapped and was widely denounced for corruption during the student demonstrations of 1989.

Deng Xiaoping, the paramount leader of China, is a diminutive politician from Sichuan. He "retired" in 1987 at the age of eighty-three, but remains horrifyingly active for a man reported dead on a number of occasions.

Fang Cheng is a Mainland cartoonist in his sixties.

Fang Lizhi, an eminent astrophysicist, was born in Hangzhou in 1937. Hailed by some in the West as China's "Sakharov," Fang was expelled from the Communist Party in January 1988, dismissed from his position as Vice-President of the Chinese University of Science and Technology, and reassigned work at the Peking Observatory. Although he was allowed to travel to Italy following his denunciation in the press, he was subsequently refused permission to take up other such invitations. In early June 1989, he sought asylum in the U.S. Embassy in Peking with his wife, Li Shuxian, and his youngest son.

Gao Xingjian, China's leading avant-garde playwright, is a critic and artist from Peking. He has had so many plays attacked that he was forced to abandon writing for the stage. Gao made this decision in August 1986 when his new play, "The Other Shore," was only allowed to be performed in Peking but without dialogue, on the orders of the directors of the People's Art Theatre, Gao's "work unit." Gao traveled to Germany in mid-1987 and remains in Europe today (1989). He is writing a novel.

Gu Cheng, a leading "misty" poet, was born in Peking in 1956. He was refused permission to leave the country in 1986, but during a period of relaxation in May–June 1987, he was allowed to travel to Europe, whence he made his way to Hong Kong and subsequently to New Zealand, where he is currently teaching Chinese.

Guan Wei, a high school art teacher and artist from Peking, is of Manchurian descent. He was born in 1957 and spent early 1989 in Australia before returning to Peking to teach and paint.

Hah Gong, a satirical columnist from Hong Kong, was born in 1933 and died in June 1987. The journal he began, *Emancipation Monthly*, has been a forum for dissident writing, in particular the powerful essays of Liu Xiaobo.

Han Shuli, an artist from Peking currently working in Lhasa, Tibet, was born in 1948.

Hong Huang, a young poet and critic from Peking, is closely associated with the *Today* poets.

Hu Qiaomu, an elderly ex-Politburo member and chief Party theoretician, was one of the most enthusiastic backers of the "anti-bourgeois liberalization" campaign. He made a number of speeches denouncing Fang, Wang, and Liu. Hu was the man the Party delegated to request Wu Zuguang to resign from the Party in August 1987. At the Thirteenth Party Congress, Hu retired from his Politburo post, although he has taken a position as an ideological watchdog in the Party's Senior Advisory Commission. He is thought to be an enthusiastic architect of the present purge of intellectuals.

Hu Qili, member of the Politburo in charge of ideological and cultural work, was born in 1929.

Hu Yaobang was General Secretary of the Communist Party of China until January 1987. He was born in 1915, and his death on April 15, 1989, was the occasion for the Peking protests, which began in his memory.

Hua Junwu, a Mainland cartoonist, was born in 1915.

Huang Yongyu is an artist, poet, and essayist from Hunan Province. A man in his sixties, Huang continued to paint, travel, and write with impunity during 1987. In early 1989, he suggested that Mao's body be cremated. He fled to Hong Kong in May 1989 and painted satirical caricatures of Chinese Premier Li Peng which were auctioned to support the democracy movement.

Jiang He, a poet from Peking, was born in 1952. He remained in the United States after a poetry tour in 1988 with Bei Dao, Gu Cheng, and others, organized by Allen Ginsberg.

Jin Guantao, a Mainland intellectual and historian, is in his forties. He spent most of 1987 in the United States as a visiting scholar. 1989 found him living in Hong Kong. He has been denounced in the Chinese press as an "instigator of turmoil."

Lan Ma, a poet from Chengdu, was born in 1957.

Lee Yee, a leading intellectual and publisher from Hong Kong, was born in 1936. He was denounced in a government report in June 1989 as an "instigator of turmoil."

Li Ang, a woman writer from Taiwan, was born in 1952.

Li Tuo organized intellectuals to support the students in May 1989. He fled to America in early June.

Li Xianting (pen name, **Li Jiatun**), an editor and art critic from Peking, was born in 1949. He was denounced in 1983 as a "spiritual pollutant" for his support of abstract art. Li is one of the driving forces behind *Fine Arts in China*, the most innovative arts paper in the Mainland (founded in 1985). He has been under considerable pressure from late-1986 onward. Attempts to close the weekly paper down proved unsuccessful, and Li managed to publish a number of controversial articles. He was instrumental in organizing an avant-garde art retrospective in early 1989.

Li Xiaoshan, a controversial art critic, was born in 1957. He published a *History of Modern Chinese Art* with Zhang Shaoxia in December 1986. He left for Canada in 1988.

Ling Bing is a young poet from Peking who has been associated with the Democracy Movement.

Liu Binyan, a Mainland journalist and author of fiction and documentary reportage, was born in 1925. He was expelled from the Communist Party in late January 1988. He was also sacked from his job as a journalist in the *People's Daily*, stripped of his rights as a reporter, and was unable to publish anything. His fall from grace, as in the case of Liu Xinwu, was due to factional politics in the Chinese Politburo. Numerous petitions signed by Overseas writers and sinologists protesting against the treatment of Liu were sent to the Chinese government. He retains his position as Vice-Chairman of the Chinese Writers' Association. He was refused permission to travel overseas in 1987, but by the end of the year he was allowed to travel to the United States. He has lived there ever since and is the author of some of the most naïve analysis of the 1989 crisis. He still appears to place hope in Party "reformers."

Liu Qing, a Democracy Movement activist, is reported to be in a labor camp in Qinghai. His younger brother, Liu Nianchun, was released in 1987 after serving a sentence for "counterrevolutionary activities."

Liu Xiaobo is a young literary critic from Peking and former reporter for the *Shenzhen Youth Daily*. As he is not a Party member, Liu was not named during the "anti-bourgeois liberalization" campaign of 1986–7, but he was attacked throughout 1987 in the press and in scholastic journals for "cultural nihilism." He was not allowed to lecture in public. In April 1989, while visiting the United States, he published an article entitled "Contemporary Chinese Intellectuals and Politics" in which he strongly criticized some of the older Chinese intellectuals. He was a lecturer in Chinese literature at Peking Normal University. Following the declaration of martial law, he and three other activists began a hunger strike on June 2 at the base of the Monument of Revolutionary Heroes in Tiananmen Square. In a proclamation issued at the beginning of the strike, the four stated: "Through our hunger strike, we want also to tell people that what the government media refer to as a small bunch of troublemakers is in fact the whole nation. We may not be students, but we are citizens whose sense of duty makes us support the democracy movement started by the college students." Liu Xiaobo was arrested on June 6 and denounced in the national media as an "instigator of turmoil."

Liu Xinwu, a writer of fiction from Peking, was born in 1942. He was suspended from his post as editor-in-chief of *People's Literature*, the most prestigious literary monthly in China, in February 1987. He was accused of publishing a "story offensive to the Tibetans" by Ma Jian (see below), although the attack on Liu was, in fact, factionally motivated and un-related to questions of editorial policy. He was given permission to visit the United States in October 1987 and was reinstated as editor of *People's Literature* prior to his departure. Although one of the most prominent Party writers, and a literary figure who rose to fame in the late 1970s with the publication of stories on the Cultural Revolution, Liu was unable to publish any work following his denunciation. In 1989 he supported the students and was preparing a study of popular attitudes toward the student movement before falling from sight.

Lu Xun, eminent scholar, essayist, poet, and author of fiction, was born in 1881 and died in 1936.

Ma Desheng, a young artist from Peking, was one of the group known as the Stars. Now studying in Switzerland.

Ma Jian, a writer and photographer from Peking, was born in 1953. He left China for Hong Kong in late 1986, just before his story "Stick Out Your Furry Tongue, or Fuck-all" was published in *People's Literature* in early 1987. Following the denunciation of the story, Ma, riding on a high tide of controversy, published a number of works in the Hong Kong press, including photographs of his Tibetan travels and paintings. He returned to China and was active in Peking during the student demonstrations of 1989. His current whereabouts are unknown.

Ma Long is a cartoonist from Hong Kong.

Mang Ke, a poet from Peking, was born in 1950. He was refused a passport in June 1987, after applying to visit his wife, who was studying in Paris. Mang Ke was, along with Bei Dao, the founding editor of the major unofficial literary journal *Today* of 1978–9. He has been variously per-secuted, and has been unemployed or semi-employed, ever since. He has had only a small number of poems published in the last ten years. Mang was an enthusiastic supporter of the 1989 student demonstrations and hunger strike.

Mi Qiu, an urban planner and photographer from Shanghai, was born in 1960. He left his job at the Chinese Institute for City Planning and Research in August 1987 to travel overseas and arrange exhibitions of his photo-graphs and paintings in Europe. Today he resides in Norway, where he has organized the Solidarity Group for Liu Xiaobo.

Mu Dan, a poet and translator from Tientsin, was born in 1918 and died in 1977.

Niu Han, a Mainland poet and critic, was born in 1923. Editor of the literary journal *China* during 1986, he supported some of the most innovative and outstanding critics and writers to have appeared in China in the 1980s. The journal was taken over by factional enemies in the Writers' Association in late 1986 (causing a scandal), and Niu was removed from his job. He continues to write poetry.

Pei Zhuangxin, a Han artist working in Lhasa, Tibet, was born in 1956.

Shen Qin is a painter from Jiangsu. He is in his twenties.

Shu Ting, a poet from Xiamen, Fujian Province, was born in 1952.

Su Ming is a young writer from Peking who has been associated with the Democracy Movement.

Sun Jingxuan, a Mainland poet, was born around 1930. He has published little of interest since he was denounced for his poem "A Spectre Prowls Our Land" in 1982. In discussing this episode in August 1986, he commented: "I was correct in writing that poem when I did. Again, it was proper of me to write that self-criticism. And although I will not say anything in my defense now, if anyone else chooses to do so, that also, I believe, would be right." He was allowed to travel overseas in late 1987.

Sun Longji (Lung-kee Sun) is a writer and scholar who was born in Shanghai. He currently lives in the United States and works in the Department of History at Memphis State University. Since 1986, he has published scholarly articles on Lu Xun and the Chinese personality. He is currently writing a book on the intellectual history of modern China. He is the author of *The Deep Structure of Chinese Culture*, a book which, despite the fact that it was not officially published in China, had considerable impact in Mainland China.

Tang Qi, a Mainland poet, was born in 1920.

Tao Jun, an amateur playwright from Shanghai, was born in 1959.

Tashi Dawa (Zhang Niansheng), a novelist from Lhasa, Tibet, was born in 1959.

Tenzin Choedrak is personal physician to the Dalai Lama. He was imprisoned for seventeen years in China and Tibet.

Wang Meng, a writer from Peking and Minister of Culture, was born in 1934.

Wang Miao, a young woman photographer from Peking, is a member of the China Modern Photo Salon.

Wang Peigong, a Mainland playwright, is in his forties. He was forced to abandon both the play and the screenplay he was working on at the end of 1986, waiting out the storm by writing politically safe commercial scripts. His earlier play, "WM," about the Cultural Revolution, was banned by a Politburo member in late 1985 and subsequently defended by Wu Zuguang (see below). In 1989, Wang organized a petition of veteran intellectuals in support of the protesting students, and resigned his Party membership on May 20, the day martial law was declared in Peking. He has reportedly been arrested in Guizhou.

Wang Ruoshui, a progressive Mainland journalist and ideologist, was born in 1926. A former editor of the *People's Daily*, he was denounced in the "anti-spiritual pollution" campaign of 1983–4 for his views on socialist humanism and alienation. Wang has had only limited opportunities for publication over the last few years. A volume of his essays and memoirs was to appear in early 1987, but publication was delayed. He was one of five intellectuals named as having been forced out of the Party by a Politburo decision in August 1987 (known popularly as "the five gentlemen"). He refused to resign and his name was subsequently struck off the Party register. While invitations for him to travel overseas were often refused by the authorities, he was nevertheless able to travel to the United States in April 1989. While there, he attended a conference in Bolinas, California, that was openly critical of Deng's government. He returned to China to an uncertain fate.

Wang Ruowang, a novelist from Shanghai, was born in 1917. He was expelled from the Party and denounced during the "anti-bourgeois liberalization" campaign in January 1987. The Public Security Bureau searched his apartment, confiscating many of his notes, letters, and writings. Unrepentant and banned from writing for Mainland publications, Wang started publishing essays highly critical of certain Chinese leaders and Party policy in the Hong Kong press in July 1987. He was arrested in July 1989.

Wang Wenlan, a young photographer from Peking and a member of the China Modern Photo Salon, published photographs of the May 1989 student hunger strike in the *China Daily*.

Wang Xizhe is a young Democracy Movement activist who was imprisoned in the late 1970s. He remains in jail, despite petitions to the government for his release.

Wang Zhiping, a young photographer from Peking, was a member of the China Modern Photo Salon. He now lives in Paris.

Wei Jingsheng, a one-time Red Guard leader, is perhaps the most famous of China's Democracy Movement activists. His manifesto "The Fifth Modernization: Democracy" was posted on the Democracy Wall in Peking in December 1978. It elicited such wide popular support that the authorities decided to suppress the movement and arrest all its leaders. On October 16, 1979, at the end of a parody of a trial, and on the basis of trumped-up charges, Wei was sentenced to fifteen years in prison. In November 1987, Amnesty International announced that it had received unconfirmed reports that Wei had died in a labor camp in Geermu, Qinghai. A Chinese Ministry of Justice spokesman officially denied the report and stated tersely that Wei "is alive," although no details of his whereabouts or state of health were given. Wei is the subject of a play by the sculptor Wang Keping, a former dissident who now lives in Paris, entitled "The Retrial of Wei Jingsheng." Published in early 1989, the play has been performed in Paris, Taipei, and Sydney.

Wu Huan is a young screenwriter and author of fiction from Peking.

Wu Shaoxiang, a sculptor from Peking, was born in 1957. He obtained his master's degree from the Central Academy of Arts and Design in February 1987 and became a teacher in that institution. Although he designed large sculptures for public places in China, Wu was unable to attend exhibitions of his works overseas and had difficulty publishing his theoretical articles on sculpture in Chinese arts journals throughout 1987. The debate resulting from his October 1986 article "The Crisis of Chinese Sculpture" was quashed by the authorities. He was active during the 1989 demonstrations, fled Peking on June 6, and now resides in Austria.

Wu Zuguang, a veteran playwright and critic from Peking, was born in 1917. He was personally "requested" to resign his Party membership in early August 1987 by none other than Mao's one-time secretary and Politburo member Hu Qiaomu. Following this, Wu was allowed to take part in the celebrations of the twentieth anniversary of the Iowa International Writers' Workshop with Zhang Xianliang in October 1987 (Liu Binyan had also been invited to Iowa but was refused permission to go). In 1989, Wu was highly critical of the Chinese government. He continues to live in Peking.

Xia Xiaowan, a lecturer at the Peking Central Drama Academy, was born in 1959.

Xia Yan, a film critic, was publicly critical of Party failures in 1988, and signed a petition in support of the students in 1989.

Xiong Fu, an aged Party ideologue, is editor of *Red Flag*, the Party's main ideological organ. He was virulent in his attacks on "bourgeois liberalization" among Chinese writers and theoreticians in the early months of 1987, going beyond the boundaries set on the movement by then Party General Secretary Zhao Ziyang. At the end of the year, it was announced that *Red Flag* was to be closed down in 1988.

Xu Jingya, a young poet and critic, was fired from his job as literary editor of the *Shenzhen Youth Daily*, which was closed down on orders from Peking early in 1987 for serious ideological deviation. Not a Party member, Xu was persecuted during the "anti-bourgeois liberalization" campaign despite the fact that Zhao Ziyang said it would be "strictly confined to Party ranks." Xu and his writer wife were both unemployed, and although ordered to return to their place of origin in Jilin Province in northeast China, they were told by the local authorities that they would not be given work even if they did go back. Xu may have been unwilling to return, as he was arrested by the Changchun (capital of Jilin Province) police in 1983 for supporting "misty" poetry in a scholarly article.

Xu Wenli, a contemporary of Wei Jingsheng and a young Democracy Movement activist, is now in jail.

Yan Fu, an influential thinker and translator, was born in 1853 and died in 1921.

Yang Jiang, a playwright, author, and translator from Peking, was born in 1911 and is married to the eminent scholar Qian Zhongshu. Yang translated Cervantes into Chinese and wrote a memoir of her experience during the Cultural Revolution, *A Cadre School Life: Six Chapters*. Hu Qiaomu reportedly requested her husband, a writer whom Simon Leys has called "arguably one of the greatest minds of our age," to make an academic denunciation of "wholesale Westernization" in early 1987. Qian is said to have written to Deng Xiaoping asking that "I be permitted to preserve my integrity in my autumn years by remaining silent." Yang published her first novel, *Washing in Public,* in 1988. In 1989, she signed a petition in favor of the students. She continues to live with her husband in Peking.

Yang Li, a poet from Chengdu, was born in 1961.

Yang Lian, a poet and critic from Peking, was born in 1955. He had a number of books banned from publication during the early months of 1987, although he continued to write both poetry and a major work of criticism entitled *The Self-Awareness of Man*. Today (late 1989) he is in exile, temporarily residing in New Zealand.

Yau Ma Tei, a satirical columnist from Hong Kong, was born in 1929.

Yu Luojin, author of *A Chinese Winter's Tale*, was born in 1948. She requested political asylum while visiting West Germany in 1986, having predicted that a new campaign aimed at intellectuals and writers was not far off, and certain that she would be one of its victims. She is currently studying and writing in Germany.

Yu Xiaodong is a young Han artist from northeast China now teaching in Tibet.

Zang Kejia, a Mainland poet, was born in 1905. He was active throughout the "anti-bourgeois liberalization" campaign, taking advantage of the purge to further various personal vendettas.

Zeng Zhuo, a Mainland poet, was born in 1922.

Zhang Qun, a student at the Central Academy of Fine Arts, is in his twenties.

Zhang Xianliang, a middle-aged Mainland writer of fiction, readily joined in the denunciation of "bourgeois liberalization." He declared that the ideological struggle would help Chinese writers become "more perceptive of reality." Having advocated the introduction of capitalism to China in 1986, Zhang, a Party member, avoided becoming a target in the campaign.

Zhang Yimou, a cinematographer from Xi'an, was born in 1951. He played the lead role in *The Old Well*, a film which won four awards at the Tokyo International Film Festival in September 1987. Zhang received the award for best actor. While other members of the Chinese film industry were being attacked for ideological deviation, Zhang was directing his first feature film in the Shandong countryside, a work based on Mo Yan's novel *Red Sorghum*. In mid-July 1989, both films were denounced as "black banners" of "bourgeois liberalization."

Zhang Yu'an is an obscure Mainland poet.

Zhao Ziyang, head of the Chinese Communist Party until mid-June 1989, was born in 1919. Now unemployed and in disgrace for, among other things, splitting the Party leadership; encouraging capitalism, official corruption, and cultural decadence; inciting counterrevolution; and attempting to overthrow the government and establish a "bourgeois republic."

Zhou Lunyou, a poet from Chengdu, was born in 1952.

Zunzi, a political cartoonist from Hong Kong, was born in 1955. Many of his cartoons attacking the Mainland government and supporting the protesters were published in 1989 in the Hong Kong press.

Translators

Unless otherwise stated, translations are by either one of the editors, or both.

Don J. Cohn
  Bo Yang, The Ugly Chinaman
Fan Wen-mei
  Li Ang, Of Hogs and Whores
Fok Shui Che
  Sun Longji, The Deep Structure of Chinese Culture
Seán Golden
  (with David Wakefield & Su Kuichun) poetry of Gu Cheng
  (with JM) poetry of Yang Lian
Hung Ching Tin
  Jin Guantao, Bones of the Buried Dragon
W.J.F. Jenner
  Zhang Yu'an, If Lu Xun were still alive
  Lu Xun, Self-Mockery
Alisa Joyce
  (with JM) Yang Lian, Norlang
Ginger Li
  (with JM) Jiang He, Begin from Here
Rachel May and **Zhu Zhiyu**
  Yu Luojin, Wedding Night
Bonnie S. McDougall
  Bei Dao, 13 Happiness Street, and three poems
Ng Mau-sang
  Xu Jingya, The New Poetry
Tam Kwok-kan and **Terry Yip**
  Su Ming, Lingering Fear
C.C. Wang
  Chen Ruoxi, The Tunnel
Wai-lim Yip
  Jiang He, An Ancient Tale, To the Execution Ground
Zhu Zhiyu
  Dai Houying, The Vagabond; Hong Huang, Misty Manifesto; A Nihilistic Trend; Xu Jingya, Self-criticism

We would also like to thank Myfanwy Eaves, Gong Shifen, Sarah Gorton, Jonathan Hutt and Soh Yung-kian.

Further Reading

GENERAL

Benton, Gregor, ed., *Wild Lilies, Poisonous Weeds: Dissident Voices from People's China*, London: Pluto Press, 1982.

An excellent anthology of dissent from Wang Shiwei down to the present day. Alas, not an easily obtainable book.

Besançon, Alain and George Urban, "Language and Power in Soviet Society", a conversation in two parts, *Encounter*, May and June, 1987.

An important key to understanding the nature of Maospeak and its continued role in Chinese life.

Duke, Michael S., *Blooming and Contending*, Indiana U.P., 1985.

A flawed but interesting study of some of the more controversial writers of the past decade.

Duke, Michael S., ed., *Contemporary Chinese Literature: An Anthology*, New York: M.E. Sharpe, 1985.

Evans, Humphrey, *The Adventures of Li Chi*, New York: Dutton, 1967.

A forgotten masterpiece. The recreation in English of a Chinese anti-hero, pieced together from interviews with refugees in Hong Kong.

Gao Yuan, *Born Red: A Chronicle of the Cultural Revolution*, Stanford U.P., 1987.

The autobiography of a Red Guard.

Kinkley, Jeffrey C., ed., *After Mao: Chinese Literature and Society 1978-81*, Harvard U.P., 1985.

A scholarly but readable collection of essays on aspects of post-Mao literature.

Lee Yee, ed., *The New Realism*, New York: Hippocrene Books, 1982.

Writings from China after the Cultural Revolution.

Leys, Simon, *The Chairman's New Clothes*, London: Allison & Busby, 1977.

Leys, Simon, *Chinese Shadows*, New York: Viking, 1977.

Leys, Simon, *Broken Images*, London: Allison & Busby, 1979.

Leys, Simon, *The Burning Forest*, New York: Holt, Rinehart & Winston, 1986.

All four of Simon Leys' books are required reading for those who wish to familiarize themselves with the reality of contemporary China.

Liang Heng and Judith Shapiro, *Son of the Revolution*, New York: Knopf, 1983.

A very readable account of one young man's experience of the Cultural Revolution.

Liang Heng and Judith Shapiro, *After the Nightmare: A survivor of the Cultural Revolution reports on China today*, New York: Knopf, 1986.
An upbeat and condescending account of Deng's China.

Link, Perry, ed., *Stubborn Weeds: Popular and Controversial Literature after the Cultural Revolution*, Indiana U.P., 1983.
Link, Perry, ed., *Roses and Thorns: The Second Blooming of the Hundred Flowers in Chinese Fiction*, Berkeley: University of California Press, 1984.
Link, Perry, ed., *People or Monsters, and Other Stories and Reportage from China after Mao, by Liu Binyan*, Indiana U.P., 1984.
These three anthologies are uneven but contain some interesting material.
Nien Cheng, *Life and Death in Shanghai*, London: Grafton Books, 1986.
One of the most moving and well-written personal accounts of the Cultural Revolution.
Pang Bingjun and John Minford, with Seán Golden, eds., *100 Modern Chinese Poems*, Hong Kong: Commercial Press, 1987.
This new anthology tries to put the modernists of the 1940s, and the more recent poetic developments on the Mainland, into an historical context.
Siu, Helen and Zelda Stern, eds., *Mao's Harvest: Voices from China's New Generation*, New York: Oxford U.P., 1983.
One of the first anthologies of post-Mao literature, and still useful.
Soong, Stephen, and John Minford, eds., *Trees on the Mountain: An Anthology of New Chinese Writing*, Hong Kong: Chinese University Press, 1984.
The first anthology to represent the revival of interest in modernism in Mainland China, and to put it alongside comparable developments in Hong Kong and Taiwan.
Yue Daiyun and Carolyn Wakeman, *To the Storm: The Odyssey of a Revolutionary Chinese Woman*, Berkeley: University of California Press, 1985.
The frank and disturbing life story of a Chinese "captive mind".
Zhang Xinxin and Sang Ye, *Chinese Lives: An Oral History of Contemporary China*, ed. W.J.F. Jenner and Delia Davin, New York: Pantheon 1987.

WALLS

Bei Dao: fiction—*Waves and other stories*, tr. Cooke & McDougall, Hong Kong: Chinese U.P., 1985. New edition, London: Heinemann, 1987.

Bei Dao: poetry—*Notes from the City of the Sun,* tr. McDougall, revised edition, Cornell University Japan-China Program. 1984.

> A new and more complete anthology is forthcoming from Anvil Press. See also *Renditions* 19/20, 23 and 24.

Chen Ruoxi (Ch'en Jo-hsi): *The Execution of Mayor Yin and other stories from the Cultural Revolution,* Indiana U.P., 1978, also *The Old Man and other stories,* Hong Kong: Renditions Paperback, 1986.

Liu Xinwu: two early stories in *The Wounded,* Hong Kong: Joint Publishing, 1980.

> Another story in *Mao's Harvest.* See also *Black Walls and other stories,* Hong Kong: Renditions Paperback, forthcoming 1988.

PROLEDIC

Amnesty International, *Political Imprisonment in the People's Republic of China,* London 1978.

Amnesty International, *China: Violations of Human Rights,* London 1984.
> Both excellently documented and objective.

Amnesty International, *China: Torture and Ill-Treatment of Prisoners,* London 1987.
> A survey of continued human rights' violations based in the main on official Chinese sources.

Bao Ruo-wang (Jean Pasqualini) and Rudolph Chelminski, *Prisoner of Mao,* Harmondsworth: Penguin Books, 1976.

Chen Baichen, tr. Geremie Barmé, *On Yunmeng Marsh: Memories of the Cultural Revolution,* forthcoming.

Lai Ying, *The Thirty-sixth Way,* New York: Doubleday, 1969.
> Another forgotten classic on the Chinese Gulag, seen through a woman's eyes.

White Book on Forced Labour in the People's Republic of China, compiled by the Commission Internationale contre le Régime Concentrationnaire, Paris 1957.
> An immensely long, harrowing investigation of the subject. This will be suspect to some because of the overtly anti-Communist background of some of the testimony. But most of it is authentic. It should not be forgotten.

Yang Jiang, tr. Barmé & Lee, *A Cadre School Life: Six Chapters,* Hong Kong: Joint Publishing, 1982.

HUMANITY!

Dai Houying, tr. Frances Wood, *Stones of the Wall*, London: Michael Joseph, 1985.
> A flawed, but readable, translation of a fascinating novel about middle-aged intellectuals in Shanghai.

Mu Dan, tr. Pang Bingjun, *Renditions* 21/22.
> More poems by one of the great Chinese poets of this century.

Wang Ruoshui, ed. and tr. Kelly, "Writings on Humanism, Alienation and Philosophy," *Chinese Studies in Philosophy*, Spring 1985.

THORNS

Bo Yang, *Renditions* 23. A complete version of "The Ugly Chinaman." See also *Secrets*, a collection of short stories, Boston: Cheng & Tsui, Hong Kong: Joint Publishing, 1985.

Hah Gong, "More Absurdities", *Renditions* (forthcoming).

Huang Yongyu, tr. Barmé, *The Bestiary of Huang Yongyu*, Hong Kong: Renditions Paperback, forthcoming 1988.

CLOUDS BUT NO RAIN

Li Ang, tr. Howard Goldblatt and Ellen Yeung, *The Butcher's Wife*, San Francisco: North Point Press, 1986.

Li Ang, tr. Fan Wen-mei, *Butcher*, Hong Kong: Renditions Paperback, forthcoming 1988.

Yu Luojin, tr. Rachel May and Zhu Zhiyu, *A Chinese Winter's Tale*, Hong Kong: Renditions Paperback, 1986.
> Translated from the complete text.

Zhang Xianliang, tr. Martha Avery, *Man is Half a Woman*, New York: Viking, 1987.

MISTS

Renditions 19/20, 23.

Tay, William, "Obscure Poetry", in Kinkley, ed., *After Mao*.

FIRE BEHIND BARS

Fraser, John, *The Chinese,* New York: Summit Books, 1980.

Garside, Roger, *Coming Alive: China After Mao,* New York: McGraw Hill, 1981.

Goodman, David, *Beijing Street Voices,* London: Marion Boyars, 1980.
These three books contain useful information on the Democracy Wall period.

Liu Qing, tr. Cohen & Seymour, "Prison Memoirs", in *Chinese Sociology and Anthropology,* Fall-Winter 1982-3.

Nathan, Andrew J., *Chinese Democracy,* London: Tauris, 1986.

Seymour, James, *The Fifth Modernization: China's Human Rights Movement, 1978-9,* New York: Human Rights Publishing Group, 1980.
A comprehensive collection of Democracy Movement writings.

Seymour, James, *China Rights Annals I,* Human Rights in the People's Republic of China from October 1983 to September 1984, New York: M.E. Sharpe, 1985.

SPEARHEAD, Bulletin of the Society for the Protection of East Asians' Human Rights, Nos 1-20, 1979-1984. Address, P.O.B. 1212, Cathedral Station, New York, NY 10025, USA.

THE SHADOW'S FAREWELL

Jenner, W.J.F., "Lu Xun's Last Days and after", *China Quarterly 91,* September 1982.
One of the few really convincing studies of Lu Xun.
See also the four volume selection of his works, translated by Yang Xianyi and Gladys Yang, and published by the Foreign Languages Press, Peking.

BOURGELIB

Ba Jin, tr. Geremie Barmé, *Random Thoughts,* Hong Kong: Joint Publishing, 1984.

Deng Xiaoping, *Fundamental Issues in Present-Day China,* Peking: Foreign Languages Press, 1987.
Although lacking the dialectical flare of Mao Zedong, Deng's speeches are essential reading.

Goldman, Merle, ed., with Timothy Cheek and Carol Lee Hamrin, *China's Intellectuals and the State: In Search of a Relationship,* Cambridge: Harvard U.P., 1987. In particular David A. Kelly's essay, "The Emergence of Humanism: Wang Ruoshui and the Critique of Socialist Alienation."

Kelly, David A., "The Chinese Student Movement of December 1986 and Its Intellectual Antecedents", *Australian Journal of Chinese Affairs*, No. 17, 1988.

McLaren, Anne, "Letter from Shanghai: Smashing the Second Confucius", *Encounter*, April, 1987.

Pepper, Suzanne, "Deng Xiaoping's Political and Economic Reforms and the Chinese Student Protests", *UFSI Reports*, 1986: No. 30, Universities Field Staff International Inc., Indiana.

Tournebise, Jean-Christophe and Lawrence Macdonald, *Le dragon et la souris*, Paris: Christian Bourgois, 1987.
The first book-length account of the December 1986 student demonstrations and their aftermath, by two western journalists.

PRESSURE POINTS

Haraszti, Miklós, *The Velvet Prison: Artists Under State Socialism*, New York: Basic Books, 1987.
A handbook for cultural commissars in post-Mao/Stalinist society.

Konrád, George and Ivan Szelényi, *The Intellectuals on the Road to Class Power*, Brighton: Harvester Press, 1979.
A basic study of a phenomenon widely recognized in Eastern Europe and increasingly familiar to observers of China.

Milosz, Czeslaw, *The Captive Mind*, translated by Jane Zielonko, London: Penguin Books, 1985.
The classic work on the rebirth of intellectuals under Proledic.

BÖD

Avedon, John F., *In Exile from the Land of Snows*, London: Michael Joseph, 1984.

Dalai Lama, the Fourteenth, *My Land and My People*, New York: McGraw-Hill, 1962.

Goodman, Michael Harris, *The Last Dalai Lama: A Biography*, London: Sidgwick and Jackson, 1986.

Han Suyin, *Lhasa, the Open City*, London: Triad Panther Books, 1979 (first published 1977).
The official line on Tibet.

International Commission of Jurists, *Tibet and the Chinese People's Republic*, Geneva, 1960.
A controversial but important work.

Acknowledgements

We are grateful to the following individuals and publishers for permission to reprint copyright material:

1. Simon Leys; Holt, Rinehart & Winston; and Jonathan Cape; for extracts from *The Burning Forest* (1986).

2. *Renditions*, a Chinese-English Translation Magazine, published by the Research Centre for Translation, The Chinese University of Hong Kong, and Renditions Paperbacks, for copyright material by Bei Dao, Bo Yang, Chen Ruoxi, Gu Cheng, Hah Gong, Hong Huang, Huang Yongyu, Jiang He, Li Ang, Liu Xinwu, Mu Dan, Sun Jingxuan, Xu Jingya, Yang Lian, and Yu Luojin.

3. Commercial Press, Hong Kong, for translations of poems by Niu Han, Shu Ting, Tang Qi and Zeng Zhuo, from *100 Modern Chinese Poems*, translated and edited by Pang Bingjun and John Minford, with Seán Golden.

4. Amnesty International, London, for extracts from their 1978 report, *Political Imprisonment in the People's Republic of China.*

5. Jean Pasqualini for extracts from *Prisoner of Mao.*

6. Joint Publishing Co., Hong Kong, for extracts from Yang Jiang, *A Cadre School Life: Six Chapters*, translated by Barmé and Lee.

7. Chen Kaige and Southern Film Distributors (Hong Kong) for the stills from the film "Yellow Earth".

8. W.J.F. Jenner and *The China Quarterly* for the English translation of the poem "If Lu Xun were still alive", which was originally published in *The China Quarterly*, No. 91, September 1982, p. 445.

9. *China News Analysis* for the article on Deng Pufang.

10. Gregor Benton for extracts from Wang Xizhe and Xu Wenli.

11. Tiziano Terzani and *Der Spiegel* for permission to reprint in full Terzani's interview with Fang Lizhi, *Der Spiegel*, July 27, 1987 (translated by Angela Terzani).

12. *New Republic* for extracts from Simon Leys, "China's New Math", *New Republic* magazine, March 2, 1987.

13. John F. Avedon; Alfred A. Knopf; and Michael Joseph; for extracts from *In Exile from the Land of Snows* (1984).

Chinese Sources

The following works are listed according to the order in which they occur in the book. Sources for illustrations are at the end.

p. ii
　“石在，火種是不會絕的”，魯迅，《“題未定”草》(九)，《且介亭雜文》二集。

I

p. 1
　《長城》，魯迅，《華蓋集》。

p. 2
　《幸福大街十三號》，北島，《山西文學》1985.6（評論見於《文藝報》1981.4）。

p. 18
　《牆》，舒婷，《中國近現代詩一百首》(漢英對照)，香港商務印書館，1986（以下簡稱《一百首》）。

p. 19
　《黑牆》，劉心武，《北京文學》1982.10（評論見於《文藝報》1983.4）。

p. 30
　《中國文化的“深層結構”》，孫隆基，香港集賢社，1982（以下簡稱《深層結構》）。

p. 36
　《大雁塔：思想者》，楊煉，《譯叢》1983.19—20。

p. 37
　《從這裡開始》(三)，江河，《譯叢》1985.23。

p. 38
　《魔方．繞道而行》，陶俊，香港《九十年代》1986.5。

p. 46
　《地道》，陳若曦，台北聯經，1978。

p. 62
　《古老的故事》，江河，《譯叢》1983.19—20。(馬德升插圖)

II

p. 63
　《冬天的童話》，遇羅錦（下詳）。

p. 65
　《第二種忠誠》，劉賓雁，《中國新寫實主義文藝作品選》第五編，璧華，楊谷編，香港當代文學研究社，1983。

p. 68

《黎明》，唐祈，《一百首》。

p. 80

《幹校六記：鑿井記勞》，楊絳，香港《廣角鏡》出版社，1981。

p. 88

《雲夢斷憶：甲骨文》，陳白塵，香港三聯書店，1983。

p. 103

《黑夜．森林．優青》，吳歡，《當代》1985.6。

p. 105

《W. M. 冬》，王培公，《九十年代》1985.12。

III

p. 120

《一個幽靈在中國大地游蕩》，孫靜軒，《長安》1981.1（自我檢討見《文藝報》1982.5）。

p. 131

《在歷史表象的背後》，金觀濤，《走向未來叢書》，四川，1983。

p. 135

《大雁塔》，楊煉。

p. 137

《可能發生在2000年的悲劇》，蘇明，《北京之春》1979.5。

IV

p. 150

《爲人道主義辯護》，王若水，《文滙報》1983.1.17。

p. 152

《關於人道主義和異化問題》，胡喬木，《紅旗》1984.1.26。

p. 153

《人啊，人！》，戴厚英，香港香江出版公司，1985。《略談《人啊，人！》的得與失》，《文藝報》1982.5。

p. 163

《深層結構》。

p. 166

"智慧之歌"，穆旦，《譯叢》1984.21—22。

V

p. 168

《醜陋的中國人》，柏楊，台北藝文圖書公司，1985（《賤骨頭的中國人》，王亦令，同上）。

p. 179

《哈公怪論》，哈公，《明報》。（尊子配畫）

p. 189

《大雷雨之夜》，尤瑪蒂，《小劇場》，香港《百姓》1983。（馬龍配畫）

p. 193

《罐齋雜記》（《永玉三記之一》），黃永玉，香港三聯書店，1983。

VI

p. 200

《冬天的童話》，遇羅錦，香港中文大學翻譯中心"翻譯參考資料"，1986（評論文章是關於遇羅錦的《春天的童話》，"評《春》的錯誤傾向"，《羊城晚報》，1982.5.20）。

p. 209

《殺夫》，李昂，台北聯經，1983。

p. 218

《男人的一半是女人》，張賢亮，《收穫》1985.5（《一本暢銷書引起的思考》，韋君宜，《文藝報》1985.12.28）。

p. 226

《深層結構》。

VII

p. 235

《新詩——一個轉折嗎?》，洪荒，《今天》文學研究社 1980.3。

p. 236

《回答》，《一切》，《古寺》，北島，《譯叢》1983.19—20。

p. 238

《簡歷》，《朦朧詩問答》，顧城，《譯叢》1983.19—20。

p. 242

《崛起的詩羣——評中國新詩的現代傾向》，徐敬亞，《當代文藝思潮》1983.1。

p. 243

《時刻牢記社會主義的文藝方向》，徐敬亞，《人民日報》1984.3.5。

p. 244

《從這裡開始》，江河，《譯叢》1983.19—20。

p. 246

《自白. 誕生》，《詩的祭奠》，楊煉，《譯叢》1983.19—20。

p. 247

《火把節》，《諾日朗》，楊煉，《譯叢》1986.23。

p. 249

《對楊煉近作的不同評價》，向川，《文藝通訊》1984.3。

p. 250

《深層結構》。

VIII

p. 253

《"黃土地"給我們帶來了什麼?》, 李陀, 《當代電影》1985.2。

p. 259

《電影參考資料》1984.15; 1985.5。

IX

p. 271

胡喬木, 《新聞戰線》, 1980.6。

p. 272

凌冰, 《北京之春》, 1979.4。

p. 274

《從認識到認同》, 李怡, 香港《七十年代》。

p. 279

《二十世紀的巴士底獄》, 魏京生, 《民主中華》, 香港中文大學學生會編, 1982。

p. 290

《鐵欄與火》, 曾卓, 《一百首》。

p. 291

《華南虎》, 牛漢, 《一百首》。

p. 293

《獄中手記》, 劉青, 百姓半月刊出版社, 1981。

p. 311

《深層結構》。

p. 312

《沒有寫完的詩. 赴刑》, 江河, 《譯叢》1983.19—20。

X

p. 313

《死》, 魯迅, 《且介亭雜文末編》, 1936。

p. 314

《假如魯迅先生還活着》, 《人民日報》1980.10.20。

p. 315

《秋夜》, 尤瑪蒂, 《小劇場》。(馬龍配畫)

p. 322

《影子的告別》, 魯迅, 《野草》。

XI

p. 331

《旗幟鮮明地反對資產階級自由化》，1986.12.30，鄧小平，《建設有中國特色的社會主義》(增訂本)北京人民出版社，1987(以下簡稱《特色》)。

p. 336

《中共安徽省紀委開除方勵之黨籍》，《人民日報》，1987.1.20。

p. 336

《把堅持搞資產階級自由化的頭面人物方勵之堅決清除出黨》，《人民日報》，1987.1.21。

XII

p. 344

《堅持四項基本原則》，1979.3.30，鄧小平，《鄧小平文選(一九七五——一九八二年)》，北京人民出版社，1983。

p. 344

《神州火種》，哈公，《解放月報》，1987.1。

p. 345

《黨在組織戰綫和思想戰綫上的迫功任務》，1983.10.12，鄧小平，《特色》。

p. 346

《旗幟鮮明地反對資產階級自由化》，1986.12.30，同上。

p. 346

《太監治國》，哈公，《解放月報》，1987，2。

p. 347

《我為什麼尋求政治庇護》，遇羅錦，《爭鳴》，1986.5。

p. 348

《鄧小平論述國內形勢》，《瞭望》，1987.17。

p. 350

《在宣傳、理論、新聞、黨校幹部會議上的講話》，1987.5.13，趙紫陽，《人民日報》，1987.7.10。

p. 350

《專訪王若望談黨、國、我》，1987.6.26，韋歌，《百姓半月刊》，1987.7.15。

p. 350

《讓大陸、台灣、香港三家來競爭——李永得、徐璐專訪方勵之》，《自立晚報》，1987.10.11。

p. 351

《沿着有中國特色的社會主義道路前進》，1987.10.25，趙紫陽，《人民日報》，1987.11.4。

p. 353

《趙紫陽總書記答中外記者問》，《人民日報》，1987.11.3。

p. 353

《文藝界暢談十三大稱最光明時代開始》，《大公報》，1987.11.6。

pp. 354-5

《被遺忘的人和被疏遠的文學》，1986.9.13，劉賓雁，《九十年代》，1987.6。

pp. 355-6

《劉賓雁在接受〈深圳青年報〉記者採訪時的講話摘要》，《劉賓雁言論摘編》，北京，1987.1。

p. 356

《劉賓雁在〈改革中社會問題學術討論會〉上的講話摘要》，1986.11.7，《九十年代》，1987.6。

pp. 356-7

《劉賓雁在南開大學的講話摘要》，1986.11.21，《九十年代》，1987.6。

pp. 357-9

《劉賓雁言論摘編》，同上。

p. 358

《中共人民日報社機關紀委決定開除劉賓雁黨籍》，《人民日報》，1987.1.25，《堅持四項基本原則，堅決執行黨的紀律》，《人民日報》，1987.1.25。

pp. 361-2

王若望語錄，《深圳青年報》，1986.9.30。

p. 362

《駁熊復、胡喬木——評「橫比有害論」》，前言，王若望，《百姓半月刊》，1987.7.15。

pp. 362-7

《論中國人的「心防」》，王若望，同上。

p. 363

《中共上海市紀委決定開除王若望黨籍》，《人民日報》，1987.1.15。

p. 365

《旗幟鮮明地反對資產階級自由化》，1986.12.30，鄧小平，同上。

p. 367

《共產黨員要按章辦事——從王若望被開除黨籍談起》，陳沂，《光明日報》，1987.4.19。

pp. 368-9

《實現「雙百」方針有點希望了》，吳祖光，《九十年代》，1987.9。

pp. 370-2

《致中紀委書》，吳祖光，《鏡報》，1987.9。

pp. 373-7

《柏楊談中國與中國人：中華民族是不是受到了詛咒?》，《九十年代》，1987.4。

p. 375

《專訪王若望談黨、國、我》，韋歌，同上。

pp. 378-80

《不要得意忘形》，哈公，《明報》，1987.1.9。

p. 378

《神州火種》，哈公，《解放月報》，1987.1。

p. 379

鄧小平，1986.12.30，同上。

pp. 381-4

《「文革」博物館》，巴金，《新民晚報》，1986.8.26。

p. 384

鄧小平，1986.12.30，同上。

XIII

pp. 388-93

《現代詩人訪問記》，明蕾，《爭鳴》，1987.9。

p. 391

《全國政協六屆五次會議部分委員發言摘要(五)》，臧克家發言，《人民日報》，1987.4.7。

p. 394

《想起你》，諶林，《深圳青年報·中國詩壇1986現代詩羣體大展(第二輯)》，1986.10.21。

pp. 395-7

《中國人的解放在自我覺醒》，白杰明，《九十年代》，1987.3。

pp. 398-9

《房間裏的風景》，楊煉，《知識分子》，1987夏季號。

pp. 400-2

《一無所有》、《不是我不明白》，崔健。

pp. 403-6

《熊復內部講話: 文藝界與外界結合搞「自由化」》，(即《熊復同志的講話》)，《九十年代》，1987.6。

p. 405

《非非主義宣言》，周倫佑、藍馬執筆，《深圳青年報》，同上。

p. 406

《毛澤東，我將永遠記着你》，楊黎，同上。

p. 407

《我為何寫作──「國際寫作計劃」海峽兩岸作家座談紀要》，吳祖光發言，夏雲整理，《爭鳴》，1987.12。

p. 408

《迎接與促進民族精神的新解放》，王蒙，《人民日報》，1987.11.17。

p. 409

《太極詩──獨化: 太極詩派如是觀》，島子，《深圳青年報》，同上。

pp. 410-11

《極地》，組詩八章之八(莊子語錄引自《齊物論》)，島子，同上。

p. 412
　《演出》，穆旦，《譯叢》，1984。

p. 416
　《『後現代』『民族化』和『稻草』(二)》，李家屯(即栗憲庭)，《中國美術報》，1987.2.23。

pp. 433-6
　《甘丹寺隨想(毀滅的頌歌)》，《布達拉宮》，楊煉，《新詩潮詩集》，老木編選，北京
　大學，未名湖叢書，1985。

p. 437
　《瞬間相錯》，蔡椿芳，《深圳青年報》，同上。

pp. 438-47
　《亮出你的舌苔，或空空蕩蕩》，馬健，《人民文學》，1987.1-2合刊。《嚴肅批評〈人
　民文學〉發表醜化污辱藏族同胞小說》，《人民日報》，1987.2.20。

pp. 448-52
　《西藏: 系在皮繩釦上的魂》，扎西達娃，《探索小說集》，程德培、吳亮編，上海文藝
　出版社，1986。

插圖：

p. 2, 15
　《山西文學》，1985.6。

p. 35, 170, 178
　《華君武漫畫(1980年)》，四川人民出版社，1981。
　《華君武漫畫選(1955—1982年)》，英譯本，北京，新世界出版社，1984。

p. 36-7, 68, 134
　《中國現代攝影沙龍 '85》，香港中國攝影出版社，1985。

p. 62, 312
　《譯叢》，1983。

p. 79
　《美術》，1985.10。

p. 120
　《搖籃與墓地》，陳越光，陳小雅編著，四川人民文學出版社，1985。

p. 130, 193-197, 243
　黃永玉，《罐齋雜記》，香港三聯，1983。

p. 151, 235, 239, 249
Tusche Rausch, Bilder 1983-85, Gao Xingjian (高行健), Leibniz-Gesellschaft für
Kulturellen Austausch, 1985.

p. 152
　《方成漫畫選》，方成，上海人民美術出版社，1982。

p. 173, 176
　《諷刺與幽默: 中國漫畫選》，英日譯本，香港三聯，1981。

p. 190, 317
《小劇場》，香港，1983。

p. 224, 228, 230, 240-2
《中國美術報》，1985.6; 1986.1; 1986.12。

p. 254-269
《黃土地》劇照由香港南方影業公司及廣西電影製片廠提供。

p. 323
《中國新興版畫運動五十年》，李樺、李樹聲、馬克編，遼寧美術出版社，1981。

Note on Chinese Texts:
The Chinese texts of works in this book are published together in one volume in the Translation Reference Materials Series produced by the Research Centre for Translation, Chinese University of Hong Kong, Shatin, New Territories, Hong Kong.